IN SEARCH OF A LANGUAGE FOR THE MIND-BRAIN:
Can the Multiple Perspectives be Unified?

THE DOLPHIN

General Editor:
Tabish Khair

33

THE DOLPHIN MIND-BRAIN BOOK

📖

IN SEARCH OF A LANGUAGE FOR THE MIND-BRAIN:
Can the Multiple Perspectives be Unified?

Editors:

Anjum P. Saleemi
Ocke-Schwen Bohn
Albert Gjedde

Aarhus University Press, Denmark

AARHUS UNIVERSITY PRESS
Langelandsgade 177
DK–8200 Aarhus N, Denmark
Fax (+45) 8942 5380
www.unipress.dk

73 Lime Walk
Headington, Oxford OX3 7AD
Fax (+44) 1865 750 079

Box 511
Oakville, Conn. 06779
Fax (+1) 860 945 9468

Editorial address:
THE DOLPHIN
Department of English
University of Aarhus
DK–8000 Aarhus C, Denmark
Fax (+45) 8942 6540

This volume is published with financial support from the Aarhus University Research Foundation and the Danish Research Council for the Humanities.

Note by the General Editor

This number of the Dolphin series differs slightly from its predecessors in being both a collection of new papers written for this publication and a casebook-type reproduction of existing and already published papers/chapters. Those contributions to this issue that were written and published elsewhere as lectures, papers or chapters of books have been retained and reproduced in the form in which they were submitted to Dolphin by the distinguished contributors and the issue editors. As such, the usual Dolphin styleguide has been dispensed with and the papers in this issue sometimes employ different styles of notation and bibliography.

Tabish Khair

Contents

COPYRIGHT ACKNOWLEDGEMENTS

The editors and the Aarhus University Press would like to express their appreciation to the following authors and their publishers (with special additional thanks to Lucia Lobato, Adriana Belletti and Luigi Rizzi) for their generous permission to reprint copyright material.

Martin Atkinson. This paper was written in 1999 and originally appeared in *Essex Research Reports in Linguistics* 34, pp. 1-55. It is published here without modification.

Noam Chomsky. "Language and Mind: Current Thoughts on Ancient Problems (Parts I and II)." *Pesquisa Lingüística* 3.4., 1997.

Also reprinted in: Lyle Jenkins (ed.), *Variation and Universals in Biolinguistics*, Elsevier, and published in: the *Web Journal of Formal, Computational and Cognitive Linguistics*, 1997 (ed.: Dr Valery Solovyev, Kazan University Russia).

Noam Chomsky. "Language and the Brain." From: *Su natura e linguaggio*, Edizioni dell'Universita' di Siena, Siena, 2001.

Also reprinted in: Noam Chomsky, *On Nature and Language* (editors: Adriana Belletti and Luigi Rizzi), pp. 61-91, Cambridge: Cambridge University Press.

Steven Pinker. "Reverse-Engineering the Psyche." From: *How the Mind Works*, New York: W. W.

Preface

This volume has a history of its origins worth telling briefly. About five years ago a number of colleagues from various departments at Aarhus University set up a Mind-Brain Circle, which used to meet regularly to discuss what the mind and the brain were, and how the two were interrelated. Though for a number of reasons these meeting had to come to an end, their one major consequence was the idea of this volume, an idea that continued to grow in spite of the fact that some of us moved away from Aarhus. As a realization of that idea, this book, much like most other ideas, has evolved over the years to its present state in a way that has not been as steady and methodical as one would have liked it to be. However, a point was reached when we came to believe that if this book had to be published, it had to be sooner rather than later, since the collective intellectual momentum that led up to it was becoming rather hard to sustain across huge spans of time and space. We are glad to be able to eventually witness the final outcome of that prolonged endeavour see the light of day. In the course of these years, a lot of people have continued to provide inspiration and encouragement, so the debts owed by now are too numerous to be described exhaustively. As a result, we shall have to be very brief in acknowledging them.

As the previous general editor of the series in which this volume appears, Dominic Rainsford steered the project through much of its early years until Tabish Khair came along to relieve Dominic of one of his many responsibilities, and to add yet another one to his own. Many colleagues and students in various parts of the world have assisted one or more of us in the process of composing a number of graphics, revising and commenting on some manuscripts, or proof-reading. These include Nadeem Siddique and Ajmal Khan in Pakistan; and Loren Billings, Jason Harding, Katherine Hsiao, Nelly Lin, Adam Peng, Daisy Pong, Deborah Teoh and Jose Wang in Taiwan.

Finally, an immense sense of gratitude for Martin Atkinson, Ayesha Aziz, Loren Billings, Peter Cole,Vivian Cook, Martin

Drozda, Glenda Gibbs, Ted Gibson, Jason Harding, Gabriella Hermon, Yumei Hsu, Edith Kaan, Samuel J. Keyser, JoJo and Joe McKinney, Prem Kumar Poddar, Iggy Roca, Margaret Ross, Dora Salaquardova, Annie Saleemi, Teresa Satterfield, Jennifer Show, Maggie Sheng, Rajendra Singh, Karen Willcox, and Ken Wexler for always being somewhere out there so that one could fall back on their (in many cases virtual) support whenever the going got too tough, and to Noam Chomsky, Steven Pinker, and John Searle for reasons too significant to bear anything like a customary recital of them.

The Editors

INTRODUCTION
The Enigma of Unification

Anjum P. Saleemi

1. Preliminary Remarks

A major part of the rationale for this volume arose from an increasingly nagging concern with the apparent disunity of lots of recent research on the study of the mind and the brain, in particular the issue of how to relate these two entities, which on many current interpretations should in principle be relatable in some systematic way. This led to the idea of a volume intended to bring together a variety of viewpoints emerging from various disciplines. Consequently, the present volume covers a wide range of philosophical, linguistic, neurological, psychological, biological, and social issues, all within the wider context of the study of the mind and the brain and how they are causally connected, a major goal being to bring together an array of representative approaches to the problem in hand, in order to figure out to what extent (if at all) they overlap and mesh with each other. It will strive to interweave most of the major concerns, and outline an implicit framework that should enable researchers to place the diversity of human knowledge within a joint ontological perspective. In the programmatic parts of this introduction, I intend to suggest a few ways which could, at the very least, enhance our understanding of the hurdles in the way of a possible unification and how one could go about avoiding them. A related motivation is to show that the variety of perspectives represented is not as discipline-bound as it might appear: there are simply no hard boundaries among the various academic fields. These perspectives and the attendant assumptions, it is far too obvious, transcend traditional

In Search of a Language for the Mind-Brain, ed. Saleemi, Bohn and Gjedde, *The Dolphin* 33 © 2005 by Aarhus University Press, Denmark. ISBN 87 7934 005 9.

boundaries of knowledge and understanding, and compel one to look for the connections between different ways of looking at things, and the nature of things themselves.

Although the issues involved are indeed quite ancient (see Chomsky, 'Language and Mind: Current Thoughts on Ancient Problems,' in this volume), research on the mind-brain has exploded in the course of the last century or so of concerted progress in physical, behavioural, and psychological sciences. At the same time, some major trends have emerged within philosophical and literary traditions, which have a bearing on this progress. In general, there seems to be a sense of euphoria about this topic, an optimistic and welcome development but not necessarily a realistic one, as the work that remains to be done seems enormous, one hopes not insurmountably so. At times, some like Chomsky (for example, see 'Language and the Brain', in this volume) suspect there are sufficient grounds for realistic caution in this regard; as a result, one feels that, if that is indeed the case, then perhaps these grounds should be explored and evaluated alongside the seemingly optimistic view that appears to be prevalent among philosophers, linguists, cognitive scientists and neuroscientists of all stripes.

This proliferation of epistemic viewpoints has obvious consequences for our ontological assumptions. Major questions arise in this context. Is external reality coherent or fragmented? Is mental reality caused by neurological factors in a demonstrably systematic and decisive way? What is the relationship between human language and thought? What sort of object of inquiry is language? Is it biological, social, or both? How best can we characterize human nature in general? To what extent are the social phenomena grounded in the mental and the neuropsychological? What is the significance of the distinction between science and non-science: in other words, between empirical laws, on the one hand, and normative and artistic modes of regulating and capturing our perception of the world, on the other? What are the foundations of rationality, and how valid and sound are they? Further, it appears that some facts would be facts whether or not humankind existed, while others owe their existence to human invention, be they aeroplanes, money and other socio-political constructs, or works of fiction (Searle 1995).

The rest of this paper is organized as follows. After this very brief introduction a rather wide range of somewhat overlapping problems that any current investigation of the mind-brain issues is bedeviled by is set out. Having thus established the necessary background, the second part goes on to offer strategies, ideas and speculations as to how best to effectively tackle the central issue, namely the relationship between the highly abstract mental phenomena and the neurological 'wetware' of the brain. This is done by proposing a sketch of a general theory of causation and locating the mind-brain nexus within it. I then conclude by briefly pointing out how the papers appearing in the present volume fit in with the suggested approach.

2. Why There Is A Unification Problem?

To simply assume that there is a unification problem is clearly question-begging. It must be kept in mind that it is the existence of a variety of epistemic gaps that compels one to consider the unification of knowledge as a major problem. These are discussed in the following pages.

2.1. Epistemic Gaps and the Thesis of Unity of Knowledge

It is uncontentious to say that human knowledge of the world around us, and of ourselves as part of this world, is far from complete. This is evidenced by the large number of gaps that exist in our knowledge, many of which can be readily identified by having a cursory look at the current state of affairs. Here is a brief account of some salient epistemic gaps.

(a) The vast gap between large-scale physics (i.e., the theory of relativity) and small-scale physics (i.e., quantum theory) that still plagues the discipline in question.

(b) The complex and poorly understood relationship between the genome and the corresponding phenome it develops into.

(c) The gap between molecular biology (genetics) and ethology (the study of the behaviour of organisms).

(d) The gap between micro-price-auction economics and macroeconomics (that is, the study of aggregate economic behaviour of a population).

Against the background of the thesis of unity of sciences and its allied assumptions, a good deal of investigation is normally driven by the attempts to discover the missing links, by appeal to either reduction or expansion. As has been mentioned already, there have been, and still are, gaps within each science and between different sciences. The latter are indeed pervasive, and the more worrying in a sense because the researchers in each field normally remain within their respective cubbyholes and are not generally inclined to look across the street to the next department and try to perceive what sort of difficulties they are up against. Recent attempts at bringing together researchers from various disciplines who are working on similar issues, for instance, the non-linear approaches to any systems that go beyond a certain degree of complexity, or human cognition, have of course led to some progress towards integration. In general, though, the fences are not down yet and the distances among the sciences can be expressed as a more general gap expressed in the schema that appears below, where the dotted line indicates a lack of sufficient connections.

$$\text{Science}^X \text{ ------- } \text{Science}^Y$$

With the relative exceptions of physics, chemistry and biology, the dotted lines are all over the place. In fact even between biology and physics reduction does not always seem to work in any simple sense. As Wigner pointed out years ago, an example of this is provided by laws of heredity in biology and physical laws, the biological basis of mental phenomena such as consciousness, and so forth, a situation that, *mutatis mutandis*, remains in essence true even today.

A much more difficult and confusing situation would arise if we could, some day, establish a theory of the phenomena of consciousness, or of biology, which would be as coherent and convincing as our present theories of the inanimate world. Mendel's laws of inheritance and the subsequent work on genes may well form the beginning of such a theory as far as biology is concerned. Furthermore, it is quite possible that an abstract argument can be found which shows that there is a conflict between such a theory and the acceptable principles of physics. The argument could be of such abstract nature that it might not be possible to resolve the conflict, in favor of one or of the other theory, by an experiment. Such a situation would put a heavy strain on our faith in our theories and on our belief in the reality of the concepts which we form. It would give us a deep sense of frustration in our search for what I called the "ultimate truth." The reason that such a situation is conceivable is that, fundamentally, we do not know why our theories work so well. Hence their accuracy may not prove their truth and consistency. Indeed, it is this writer's belief that something rather akin to the situation which was described above exists if the present laws of heredity and of physics are confronted. (Wigner 1960.)

Our main concern, of course, is the causal relationship between the mind and the brain. Like many others, we assume that such a causal relation does exist, and that the Cartesian mind-body dualism is no longer, in fact has not been for a long time, a valid formulation of the problem (e.g., Chomsky 2000; see also Sperry 1980). As has already been implied, on the present view a much better way of probing it is to consider the mind as something that is causally dependent on the brain. This dependence, however, is no simple matter and raises a host of issues, to which we now turn our attention.

2.2. The Array of Mind-Brain Problemss
In the following pages a list of the problems emanating from the causal mind-brain nexus is set out; each problem is identified, briefly described and located within the perspective of the

ongoing discussion. This list is by no means exhaustive, and the choice is determined in part by my own biases and inclinations. Most of these problems involve an epistemic gap between different levels of the same factual realm. For understandable reasons, we start with the overarching issue, namely, *the* mind-brain problem, and then go on to deal with the subparts of the core issue.

(a) The Mind-Brain Problem

Why did Descartes consider animals to be mere, or no more than, biological robots? In part (or largely) because he could not see a way of relating biological bodily mechanisms to mental constructs and phenomena. His flawed vision was necessarily constrained by the incompleteness of the science of his time. With so much scientific water having flowed under the bridge since then, we are in the relatively fortunate position of perceiving that the mystery of the Cartesian soul is likely to be a definable and tractable problem, though admittedly of an enormous magnitude. The prevalent research strategy, shaped partly by functionalism and reasonable up to a point, has been to ignore the existing gap between the mind and the brain, try to investigate both ends of the continuum, until such time that the missing links get established one by one. (In fact, a hard-core, card-carrying functionalist may feel little need to worry about the brain mechanisms at all, now or ever.)

Two related differences between the mind and the brain, though rightly treated as two manifestations of the same entity, need to be pointed out: (i) the mind is the brain viewed at an abstract level; (ii) a brain that has not yet received any acquired information can be a mind only in a minimal sense, whereas the mind is the brain after it has received environmental input, both of the triggering and the non-triggering kind. The triggering input turns it into a functioning system at the level of basic individual psychology; the non-triggering, cultural information makes it sensitive to its immediate environment, enabling it to reap the benefits of historically recorded information. The mind so expanded, one assumes, is still encoded in the neurophysiology of the central nervous system, and thus the expansion is reflected in it by means of synaptic modifications and the like. On this view, some meaningful distinction between the two entities, based on the ontogenetic development, can be made without having to adopt the extremist doctrine of dualism. To clarify matters further, it should be stressed that no sharp distinction between the mind and the brain is being claimed. The two terms are considered, as they often are, as depicting the extreme ends of a continuum. Hence the adoption of the hyphenated term 'mind-brain'. So conceived, the mind is not an insurmountable Cartesian divider, but a bridge between the physical and the abstract, to the extent that 'physical' and 'abstract' are useful concepts. In short, the position adopted is one that is best described as neutral monism, often attributed to Russell (among others).

The core issue of the nexus between the mind and the brain may be conceptualized as shown in Figure 1 below, wherein the lines connecting the mind and the brain stand for a complex relationship, which is probably not unmediated, in the sense that the brain does not project the mind in a way that makes mental phenomena stand in a one-to-one correspondence with their neural correlates. The picture that is slowly beginning to emerge from the innumerable neurophysiological studies is almost certainly compatible with a token physicalist stance, though undoubtedly some parts of the brain appear to be *more* dedicated than others to produce, as if by default, some mental functions and not others. Notably, a consequence of adopting this position is that, by implication, both behaviourist and connectionist viewpoints come perilously close to being dualists, as they assume that most of the mental content of the brain has its origin in environmental input alone. This is particularly remarkable because connectionists and others of their ilk consider themselves to be monists of the type-physicalist variety (e.g., Churchland 1995). This point is worth belabouring further, and is extendible to the neural Darwinism of Edleman (1990, 1993). Even with an ideally completed account of neural mechanisms, which remains a promissory rather than an actualized goal, there would still be no explanatory account of mental information and subjective phenomena (e.g., qualia). Ironically, it seems to me that type physicalism, no matter which specific version of it is adopted, is going to end up as an account that is essentially dualist. Cartesian dualism was at least honest in recognizing that the mind and the body did not appear to be relatable — except through the speculated mediation of the pineal gland! — and were thus ontologically distinct substances. And as has been pointed out time and again by several people, its position was not too inconsistent with the sort of scientific evidence available at the time. The latter-day dualists, on the other hand, hope to be able to eventually explain away the mental; they are virtual dualists without being aware of the contradiction involved in their position, and without realizing that their variety of monism is no less untenable and misguided than, or only as tenable and plausible, as Berkeley's idealistic monism.

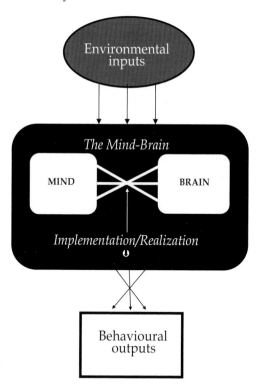

Figure 1: The Core Mind-Brain Issue

Leaving aside the question of the yet undefined limits on plasticity, the current understanding of the brain is confined to its anatomy and physiology — that is, its topography, the massive connectivity of neurons, and the role of electromagnetic and physiological impulses in the overall system. Despite a huge variety of claims about which parts of the brain are activated, and in what manner, when certain cognitive tasks are carried out, the leap from the 'wetware' and the mental phenomena, even of the very simple kind, may be anything but hazardous. It is, for instance, perfectly plausible that there are several more or less abstract intermediate levels that enable the brain to cause the mind. Conceivably, we may not have the least notion of what these levels are and how many of them are there; we probably do not even know where to look to be able to figure out the chain of causation involved in an entity as complex as the mind-brain. It can be claimed that we understand something about the overall brain code and the neural code (at the level of the neuron), but if there are indeed other levels — whether subneural (as in the quantum theories of consciousness) or others lying somewhere between the neuron and the brain — implicated in the process, they remain to be unearthed. This possible state of affairs may be depicted as follows (Figure 2, on the next page).

It is interesting to draw a rather intriguing parallel between Penrose's view of the major gap in physics, namely the one between quantum theory and the theory of relativity, and the gap between the brain and the mind. Penrose (1997) suggests that this difference could well have to do with the fact that in terms of size and time scales as measured by Planck time and Planck length, *homo sapiens'* size and life-span fall roughly in the middle of these universal scales (see Fig. 1.4. in Penrose 1997, p. 5), an implication being that the gap is there due to mankind's epistemic bounds and difficulty of access to relevant constructs that could resolve the conflict. By the same token, it is possible to surmise that the mind-brain continuum also happens to appear discontinuous because the mind represents the large-scale and the brain the small-scale, and that the resulting problem is in some way, at least in part, a product of our epistemic limits, which we may or may not be able to overcome.

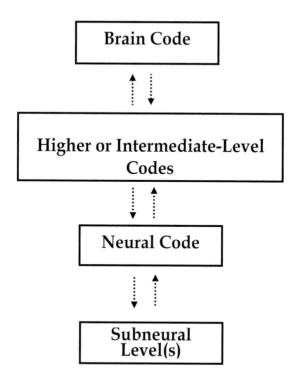

Figure 2: The Possible Mind-Brain Levels

It must be kept in mind that the mind-brain incorporates a host of phenomena of varying complexity: for instance, the more or less dedicated input-output systems (vision, production of speech, hearing, etc.), and the relatively global ones such as rationality, consciousness, etc., most of which are deeply subjective in nature, which is not to say that they are for that reason any less real (see, Searle, in this volume). One of the seemingly great imponderables of brain and cognitive sciences is how real mental phenomena — evidently a far cry from things like atoms, molecules, rocks, and stars, which are supposed to exemplify typical 'objective' stuff — happen to be.

(b) The Hard Problem of Consciousness

Inspired in part by the phenomenal success of the computational and information sciences, the functionalists are traditionally content to focus on those aspects of the mind which seem responsive to a similar treatment. As a result, the intentional and conscious reality of the mind-brain is often put on the back burner. The fact is that it is consciousness that makes it possible for us to develop the lesser forms of intelligence, such as machine intelligence. Machines that can function consciously do not, may perhaps never, exist, as some have claimed, not to mention those who assert, even more controversially and prematurely, that machines can and do indeed think like human beings already. The question therefore remains: Could a non-conscious mechanical entity be worthy of the status of a mind? For example, could a hypothetically complete system of linguistic rules be held to constitute a complete description of language without invoking the intrinsic intentionality of meaning?

(c) The Harder Problem of the Unconscious Mind

Harder still is the problem of the unconscious aspects of the human mind. Long out of circulation in respectable empirical circles, partly due to its psychoanalytic origins and partly due to the familiar premonitions of intractability, the unconscious mind has hardly been at the center of the mind-brain debate. Nonetheless, it is an issue that is neither insignificant nor mystical. Most probably rooted in a combination of consciousness (Edelman's "remembered present") and memory (past experiences), it underpins a whole lot of ordinary and special human endeavours, all the way from the imaginative and the literary to the rigorously scientific. A major question is: Why are unconscious phenomena so hard to access, if at all? There is of course another variety of 'unconscious' laws, so called because they are merely descriptions or models of the underlying brute physical facts. These, Searle (1992) argues, are distinct and require different treatments, as they are abstract, intentional constructs. On the other hand, the unconscious mental states are ontologically real in their own right.

One way to look at the complexity of the mind is to try to consider those aspects of it which are not accessible to consciousness. These include (i) information which at some point has to pass through the conscious mind, or penetrate around its edges into the deeper layers of stored information or memory, and is regarded as accessible in principle by some (e.g., Searle 1992), and (ii) patterns too deeply embedded (more or less 'hard-wired', as it were) in the mind-brain to be brought to the surface, such as those exemplified by rules of language and vision. Insofar as these latter are biologically predetermined, any laws describing them will be epistemic abstractions over the neurological phenomena underlying them. The notion of the accessible unconscious assumed here is Freudian only in spirit, and should not conjure up the idea, for example, of the Oedipus Complex! The unconscious information, on our interpretation, is information that gets buried in a memory that operates in the manner of a top-down stack. Of course some information, maybe a lot of it, can get buried for emotive reasons (e.g., of the sort suggested by Freud) or pathological factors. At any rate, the mind, it appears, cannot afford to be afflicted with total recall if it is to retain the spotlight of consciousness, to exploit a metaphor made popular by Baars (1997). Most probably, one secret of the spectacular effectiveness of consciousness is that it is able to focus on a small number of facts at a time, a task in which it is crucially aided by the working memory and the short-term memory. Perhaps if consciousness were not so limited, it would cease to have the properties that it does have (see Searle, this volume, on these properties). Note that in Figure 3, which is a schematic representation of the foregoing view, the conscious (the white cone) and unconscious (the grey cone) parts of the mind-brain are represented as blending gradually into each other.

It is pertinent to make some remarks about intentionality at this point, which is either conceptualized in weaker terms of 'aboutness' or 'extrinsic intentionality' or the stronger ones of 'intrinsic intentionality' (Searle 1992, 1999, etc.). Whichever usage is preferred, there is nothing in the view of conscious-unconscious represented in our view (embodied in Figure 3) that rules out intentional acts that are driven by motives and factors not explicitly known to the acting agent. True, many acts that humans perform are intentional in the sense that people who perform them are doing so deliberately. But it is also true that many other behaviours are caused by factors which do not pass through the window of consciousness. Such is the daunting complexity of the architecture of the mind! The conscious mind, in other words, could well be just the tip of the iceberg, albeit a crucial one: intentionality without consciousness would not be great fun, since (among other things) it would not make it possible for most unconscious information to come into being in the first instance. To take an example, would an intentional being without consciousness be able to have dreams, which are very often related to the dreamer's (in large part suppressed) autobiographical memory? The absurdity of the foregoing question becomes apparent the moment it is posed: such a hypothetical dreamer would not be able to know if he/she experienced any dreams in the sleeping state, or indeed that there was such a thing as the sleeping state!

The memory is a great maze of innumerable interconnected lanes and obscure, hidden caves. There is probably no way to remain fully conscious, AND to have access to hidden or suppressed memories at the same time. That is why I do not think dreams are mere illusions, though they do appear to be very distorted versions of real-life memories, reactions, and expectations, not to be taken literally, but equally recalcitrant to any pre-conceived system of interpretation, such as Freud's. In its present state, science simply stops in its tracks when it comes to explaining subjective facts like dreams, in spite of the fact that a lot is understood about their neurophysiology (see, e.g., Hobson 1994, Hobson et al. 2000).

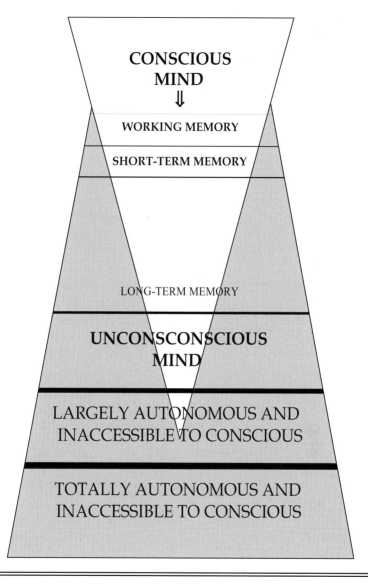

The white inverted cone is the one representing decreasingly conscious phenomena, whereas the gray cone stands for increasingly unconscious ones. Also note the way the lines dividing the memory cones grow progressively thicker as we move from top to bottom, indicating successive decrease in the degree of conscious access.

Figure 3: Mind Cones

(d) The Reason-Emotion Problem

Just as the unconscious has in general been ignored by cognitive science and analytic philosophy, the emotional part of the mind and the emotional underpinnings of reasoning have been kept out of the core of the discussion. Now, however, researchers like Damasio (1994, 1999, 2001) have brought this issue to the forefront of the battle for the mind. His assertion is that emotions (and, for that matter, the body as a whole) are not peripheral to rational operations. In fact it could well be that what we are looking at is two facets of the same problem, or, as it were, two sides of the same coin. The interrelationships between the two are apparently intricate, but nevertheless vital to a full understanding of each. I would like to add here that the intellectual and the emotional are asymmetrically connected; that is to say, ratiocination can, at least in principle, occur without the involvement of emotions (perhaps in an almost zombie-like fashion), but the latter have to engage the rational and representational capacities, as emotions in general are about something or the other, and most things have structure that is best understood by the exercise of rationality. All the same, their mutual dependence in real life is undeniable, and their exact relationships pose a major challenge to the psychological sciences.

(e) The Problem of First- and Third-Person Ontology

This is an epistemic problem, as it questions why there is such an enormous discontinuity between first-person and third-person ontology, the so-called problem of our knowledge of the Other Minds. What is it to be somebody else? How do we know that there are other people around who are like us? In this connection, there are at least three sets of criteria that can be applied to ascertain that this is in fact the case: behavioural similarities, 'folk scientific' similarities, and, finally, empirically verified or verifiable likenesses, as shown in Figure 4.

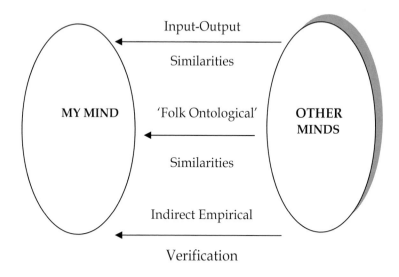

Figure 4: First-person Consciousness and Other Minds

In Searle's view, the verification of behavioural similarities is the weakest of these conditions, since behaviour by itself is neither necessary nor sufficient to determine that its mental causes exist and are similar across individuals. According to him, our common-sense ('folk') background knowledge of anatomical and physiological features is another major factor in such a decision. In addition, such 'folk' science can (given a lot of luck) be buttressed by (usually indirect) scientific empirical evidence. (Searle 1999.)

The problem under consideration is a subset of the larger problem of the relationships between the mind and the world at large, which is delineated next.

(f) The Mind-World Problem
Whatever our preferred picture of the mind-brain, it so happens that some phenomena are intrinsically mental, whereas others are mental only in a derivative or secondary sense, such as the social and environmental ones. In the increasingly widening circles of a

holistic ontological map, the mind-world and the mind-society relationships must have a place. By the same token, the mind-brain and the rest of the world surrounding it have to be causally connected, inclusive of the countless other minds seemingly floating around us. There have been varieties of idealism, radical relativism (e.g., post-modernist thinking) that deny the existence of an objectively unified reality. (See Searle 1995, Nagel 1997, and Saleemi, this volume, for a cogent refutation of such misguided views.)

Many of the problems discussed above have one property in common, that they signify huge gaps in our understanding of the overarching mind-brain problem: between mental phenomena in their totality and the computational modules of the mind, between the conscious and the unconscious brain, between the emotional and the rational aspects of cognition, between the mind and the world, and so forth. The situation is not at all unfamiliar; as we know, it has marked the historical progress of science in many other domains of inquiry.

2.3. The Epistemological Problems

The problems touched upon here pertain to our natural and acquired knowledge of facts, which is transformed through experience in at least two distinct ways. To illustrate, the child learner of a body of knowledge (let us say a natural language) appears to have the ability to use the knowledge in question with little awareness of its rather complex mechanisms, as Chomsky has pointed out time and time again (e.g., Chomsky 1986); on the other hand, an 'expert', in this case a linguist, has to make protracted deliberate efforts, over a considerably longer span of time than it takes the child to acquire the object of learning, to discover only some of the set of rules 'known' to any child who is exposed to any natural language whatsoever. My intention in this paper is to focus largely on the ontological issues, without of course implying that the epistemological dimension is in the least trivial.

The problems described in the foregoing pages were essentially empirical, most of them ontological with the exception of the last one. Those that appear below, however, are largely methodological, directly bearing on the nature of science and inevitably indirectly on the nature of facts and our knowledge of them — not quite out of place, I gather, in the present discussion. The recent history of human knowledge persistently shows twin philosophical mistakes. It conflates epistemology and ontology, failing to distinguish epistemic objects from ontological ones, and it considers scientific laws to be identical to natural laws. It is important to stress that scientific theories are essentially epistemic objects, and whatever they have to say regarding the patterns exhibited by reality is not a substitute for these patterns. I believe a consideration of the following two issues is significant in this context, as they shed some light on the relationships between facts and our theories of them.

(a) The Reduction-Expansion Problem

Since Fodor's classic arguments against the feasibility of reductionism (Fodor 1974), it has been pointed out, in particular by Chomsky (see, for instance, Chomsky 1995a, 2000), that the progress of science exemplifies expansion as well as a certain amount of successful reduction. Thus although chemistry and ultimately biology are reducible to the laws of physics in essential respects, paradoxically the concept of matter within physics had to expand to include various forms of energy, space, and so forth, in order to make the reduction possible. It appears in general that things can evolve in either direction, and the more complex the phenomena under consideration, the greater will be the likelihood that expansion rather than reduction is going to happen. At present, we do not know how to fit mental states (e.g., consciousness) into a physical universe; even neurobiological correlates of these that have been discovered are just that: correlates. They do not explain the intrinsic subjectivity of the mind. It is not unlikely that eventually there will be a broader picture in which fundamental, first-order mental events will figure as part of the substance our world is composed of.

(b) The Problem of the (Dis)unity of Science

This problem is clearly a superset of the former, but both deserve independent treatment for obvious reasons. Whether we follow

Fodor (1974) or Searle (1995), the unity of science appears to be the default and desirable position, to the extent of forming the cornerstone of all scientific endeavour. Undoubtedly commonsensical and sound, one should point out that this viewpoint is essentially a wishful article of faith. It could turn out that the world, contrary to our general expectations, is in fact hopelessly disunited. If it so happened, one would obviously be forced to retrace one's steps to square one in our understanding of certain phenomena, and the scientific buck (at least as it is currently valued) might have to stop there and then in some cases, as some of the facts that belong to a part of the world we do not belong to might be out of our reach altogether. Needless to say, no one, to my mind, would be happy at this prospect except post-modernists, anti-rationalists, and their other relativistic colleagues for whom even the way the world is presently understood appears to be based on a view unjustifiably biased in favour of unity. In addition, those adhering to a Platonic view of certain ideational objects, such as mathematical concepts, may prove to be correct, though this latter possibility would not by any means usher in an era of absolute relativism. To summarize certain points raised above:

- The thesis of the unifiability of reality, in spite of the fallibility of our knowledge (= science), is admittedly fraught with many difficulties. Is apparent order in the universe an illusion? Is the possibility of unification realistic? Is the reality fragmented, or is it the case that merely our knowledge of it is? However, it appears reasonable to assume that the latter is the more reasonable possibility.

- It seems we can understand ontology without understanding epistemology. It is relatively easier to understand the reality around us than to understand how we come to understand it.

This brings us to the crux of the debate: What kind of possible causal links unite this universe of ours?

3. Causation as Explanation

The very first step towards a possible integration of science, in my view, is to develop a coherent framework, within which the interaction of all kinds of causation can be located. In regard to the study of the mind-brain, arguably the most complex known entity in the universe, it is crucial that a unified strategy is devised that enables researchers from various disciplines to communicate and work with each other, and which, more importantly, is plausible enough to yield the right results. In the following pages, an attempt will be made to outline exactly such a strategy that is general enough to have the broad coverage required but at the same time is sufficiently constrained to be effective.

Let me first address an obvious question: Why should we consider unifiability to be more plausible and desirable? One argument in support of the unification hypothesis is that it is compatible with Occam's Razor, as the thesis that the ontology is unifiable is much more economical than that it is not. In addition to this methodological point, there are some empirical grounds for taking this hypothesis seriously. Let us consider, for the sake of argument, the ontological status of Platonic entities as opposed to the mental ones. I take it that one may safely assume that (i) and (ii) are true:

(i) We all are aware of the existence of mental entities.
(ii) We can also be made aware of the so-called Platonic abstractions.

If indeed any two worlds, let us say W^X and W^Y, were disjoint from each other, i.e., $W^X \not\subset W^Y$ and $W^Y \not\subset W^X$, then there would be no epistemic pathway from one to the other. The fact that (i) and (ii) are true demonstrates that the entities in question are all of them mental, and that there is no need to postulate that the two are distinct. The same kind of argument can be extended to the chasm between the first-person and the third-person ontologies. It could run as follows. Consider a first-person account FP^i of an event E attributed to a person *i* and a TPj account by person *j* of the same event. FPi and TPj could not be the same or even overlapping if there were an insurmountable gap between the two. The fact of the matter is that if FPi $\cap$ TPj, then it must be that $i \wedge j \, \varepsilon \, \{W\}$, where $\{W\}$ is the set of objects constituting the world W. Finally, it does not seem unreasonable to believe that if we are able to perceive the gaps, there should be hope that these can be bridged. Clearly, in the event of a total lack of awareness of their existence, the possibility of bridging must be very remote, if not a downright impossibility, for the following simple reason: How can we hope to know something if we do not know that we do not know it? (Cf. Bromberger 1992.)

To return to the problem of causation, there are two aspects of it which are fundamental to the framework that is suggested in the following pages: an all-encompassing ontological view, and a corresponding causal framework. This framework, in part due to Searle (1995), rests upon the following crucial assumptions:

(a) There are various levels of reality, roughly differing in terms of their order of complexity. The degrees of complexity result from the interaction of various forms of causation operating on facts at different levels. Facts can be *brute* or *emergent*: brute facts are those 'physical' facts that would be there even if there was no observer in existence to perceive them. *Emergent facts*, on the other hand, are irreducible to their constitive brute facts, and can therefore be terms in the laws of complex causation in their own right. A subtype of emergent facts, of particular importance in the present discussion, are *intentional, mental facts*, which in turn may be individual or institutional (i.e., those brought into being by an exercise of collective or social will), conscious or unconscious.

(b) There are, accordingly different sorts of causation. These are discussed below in due course.

The various levels of reality and the causal relationships operating between them, not surprisingly, represent a paradoxical picture: construed as brute, physical facts, all facts fall into a hierarchy wherein, to begin with, everything is physical, with progressively decreasing levels of containment pertaining to chemical, biological, intentional and social facts emerging as one proceeds from simple to complex facts. Looked upon from the angle of increasing complexity, however, the hierarchy can be viewed in the reverse order. This paradox is captured in Figure 5.

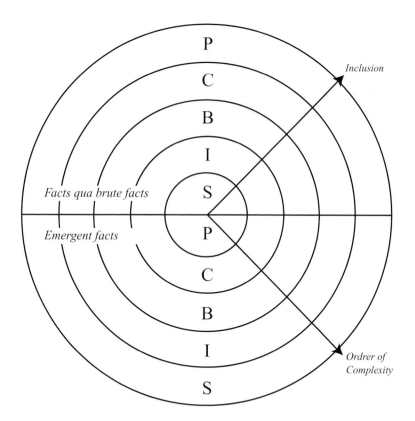

Figure 5: Paradox of Complexity - Brute and Emergent Facts
[S= Social; I= Intentional; B = Biological; C = Chemical; P = Physical]

Clearly, what is equally central to this framework is a related multiple view of causation. In particular, the following types need to be identified in respect of the mind-brain issues.

(i)   Primary Causation:
       (a)   Brute Causation.
       (b)   Intentional Causation.

(ii) Secondary Causation:
       (a)   Ontogenetic Causation.
       (b)   Phylogenetic Causation.
       (c)   Historical Causation.

In (i) time is important only to the extent that it is required in the execution of various natural processes. In (ii), on the other hand, the arrow of time is the primary factor, as the time involved must go well beyond that required as a matter of natural necessity. Further, (c) is apparently about individual development into adulthood, (d) refers to time as relevant to biological evolution (and, by implication, to evolutionary psychology), and (e) to non-biological changes whose time scale is typically beyond early development but considerably shorter than geological time; moreover, whereas both (c) and (d) may involve contingent factors, (e) is intentional as well as contingent. Needless to say, 'intentional' here is presumed to encompass both the individual and the collective phenomena. A few more expository words about intentionality should be in order here. I have in mind both intrinsic (first-person, subjective) and extrinsic or derived intentionality. (The latter is meaningful in the sense in which the sentences of a language, ultimately dependent upon speaker intentionality, are often said to be intentional.) Further, I take it that to the extent that intentional processes are computational, they belong to the category of brute facts. (See Searle 1992 and Fodor 2000 for an extensive discussion of this and related issues.)

Considering the presence of intrinsic intentionality, downward causation, namely the mental-intentional causation of brute facts, has to be considered part and parcel of nature. A distinction between upward and downward causation (Andersen et al. 2000), such that the former implies brute-to-emergent directionality and the latter emergent-to-brute directionality, is both useful and necessary. In the words of Roger Sperry:

> ... the conscious subjective properties in our present view are interpreted to have causal potency in regulating the course of brain events; that is, the mental forces or properties exert regulative control influence in brain physiology. (Sperry 1976.)

To give a trivial example, I can formulate an intention for a chair to be removed from my office that causes the relevant neurological and other bodily mechanisms to act accordingly. (Likewise, social events can 'downwardly' cause mental events.) However, it is important to keep in mind that minds cannot ever alter primary, brute laws; thus no degree of strength of free will can modify or bypass, let us say, the laws of gravity. This calls for a recognition of the limits on the reach of downward causation. I propose the following principle to capture this obvious but useful observation.

The Principle of Bounded Downward Causation
Upward causation is primary and universal, whereas downward causation is secondary and contingent. It is secondary because it would not exist without the laws of brute causation, and it is contingent in that it is subject to the exercise of free will and the laws of probability. Intentional causation can never alter the primary laws of brute causation, but can influence complex brute phenomena to the extent that it can alter their initial triggering conditions.

I think by now we have the sketch of an approach that can be employed to incorporate apparently disjointed perspectives into an ontological, epistemic and causal framework that (hopefully!) can be made to hang together. If the very sketchy framework that has been described is indeed along the right lines, the following outline shows how the papers that appear in this volume can be contextualized within this broad perspective.

4. An Outline

The two papers by Chomsky (chapters 2 and 5) span the whole spectrum of issues pertaining to the nature of the mind through its possible links with the brain. This is done largely by discussing natural language, a system that is presumably grounded in the mental but that also functions as the bridge that connects various individual minds out there. Atkinson (chapter 6) investigates some more specific linguistic patterns in terms of one of the latest versions of contemporary linguistic theory, namely Chomsky's Minimalist Program (Chomsky 1995b), thereby exemplifying mental constructs conceived at a fairly high level of abstraction. Searle (chapter 3) explores consciousness, an area of cognition that hardly ever figures in linguistic theory, which is typically concerned with the formal, linguistic aspects of the mind rather than its intrinsic, intentional content. This broadens the concept of the mental well beyond the scope of functionalist philosophy and computational psychology that was prevalent until recently in the cognitive sciences. Whereas Searle's concerns are primarily philosophical, Gjedde (chapter 7) focuses specifically on the neurobiology of consciousness. Pinker (chapter 4) contains a very lucid statement of evolutionary psychology, introducing the arrow of time into the computational approach to the mind. Sinha (chapter 8) advocates an emergent view that focuses on the contribution of culture to human cognition. Contrary to the general perception, such a view is not committed to denying the existence of the mental; it is just that it adopts a different conception of mental development, and chooses to emphasize certain aspects of reality rather than others. Shorish (chapter 9) considers certain intricacies of the economic part of social complexity, a very pertinent example of man-made, institutionalized social reality which, once in place, is no less objective than physical entities. Rainsford (chapter 10) makes an attempt to weave together the scientific analysis of consciousness and how this phenomenon is manifested in literary expression; after all, artistic reality also has to be accounted for in this universe, which, according to the current physical sciences should consist "entirely of physical particles in fields of force" (Searle 1995: xi). Finally, Saleemi (chapter 11) attempts to marshal arguments against radical relativistic viewpoints of the sort that by definition are committed to denying the validity of unification across the multiple levels of reality.

5. Conclusion

The brain was 'designed' by the invisible hand of biological evolution, although "designed" is not exactly the accurate expression in this context (except in a metaphorical or 'as-if' sense), as it attributes intentionality to biological evolution. Presumably, it came into being initially, very gradually and slowly, to cater to the needs of the body as a whole. However, eventually the *human* brain appears to have grown into a formidable organ that is capable of accomplishing much more than that, of course with considerable help from other human brains and from the mediation of time and culture. In fact, by now it has acquired such rich dimensions that there is a possibility it might ultimately be able to alter ("rewire") itself, at least to a certain extent. It has got to do something more than merely regulate and look after the body, as by successive evolutionary accidents it has turned into a Frankenstein for its 'creator', and a virtual white-elephant for the body designed to consume a disproportionate amount of its nutritional resources.

Further, what the evolution has brought into being has another curious property: the brain is locked onto the physical universe without. The first-person, subjective events and states are the norm within it, *in spite of the fact* that the brute physical laws underpinning it are, to the best of our knowledge, the same as those that govern the outside world. It would not be unreasonable to state that the real brain is not too unlike the philosopher's 'brain in a vat', though in this case the vat is the cranium, a semi-spherical casket of various jagged pieces of bone that fit with each other like a rather complicated jigsaw puzzle. It is earnestly hoped by the editors of the present collection that reading the papers contained herein will bring our readers a step closer to a better understanding what goes inside this organic vat.

References

Andersen, P. B., P. V. Christiansen, C. Emmeche and N. O. Finnemann (eds.). 2000. *Downward Causation: Minds, Bodies and Matter*. Aarhus: Aarhus University Press.

Baars, Bernard. 1997. *In the Theatre of Consciousness: The Workplace of the Mind*. New York/Oxford: Oxford University Press.

Bromberger, Sylvain. 1992. *On What We Know We Don't Know*. Chicago: University of Chicago Press.

Chomsky, Noam. 1986. *Knowledge of Language: Its Nature, Origin and Use*. New York: Praeger.

Chomsky, Noam. 1995a. Language and nature. *Mind* 104: 1-61.

Chomsky, Noam. 1995b. *The Minimalist Program*. Cambridge, MA: MIT Press.

Chomsky, Noam. 1997. *Language and mind: Current thoughts on ancient problems* (Parts I and II: Brazil lectures). (*Pesquisa Linguistica* 3.4.) Also this volume.

Chomsky, Noam. 2000. *New Horizons in the Study of Language and Mind*. Cambridge: Cambridge University Press.

Churchland, Paul. 1995. *The Engine of Reason, The Seat of the Soul*. Cambridge, MA: MIT Press.

Damasio, Antonio R. 1994. *Descartes' Error: Emotion, Reason and the Human Brain*. New York: Avon Books.

Damasio, Antonio. 1999. *The Feeling of What Happens: Body and Emotion in the Making of Consciousness*. New York: Harcourt Brace.

Damasio, Antonio. 2001. Reflections on the neurobiology of emotion and feeling. In Branquinho, J. (ed.), *The Foundations of Cognitive Science*, Oxford: Oxford University Press (Clarendon Press): 99-108.

Edelman, Gerald. 1990. *Remembered Present: A Biological Theory of Consciousness*. New York: Basic Books.

Edelman, Gerald (1993). *Brilliant Air, Brilliant Fire: On the Matter of the Mind*. New York: Basic Books.

Fodor, Jerry. 1974. Special sciences. *Synthese* 2: 97-115.

Fodor, Jerry. 2000. *The Mind Doesn't Work That Way*. Canbridge, MA: MIT Press.

Hobson, J. Allan. 1994. *The Chemistry of Conscious States: How the Brain Changes Its Mind*. Boston: Little Brown.

Hobson, J. Allan, Edward Pace-Schott, and Robert Stockgold. 2000. Dreaming and the brain: Toward a cognitive neuroscience of conscious states. *Behaviral and Brain Sciences* 23.6.

Nagel, Thomas. 1997. *The Last Word*. New York: Oxford University Press.

Penrose, Roger. 1997. *The Large, the Small and the Human Mind*. Cambridge: Cambridge University Press.

Saleemi, Anjum P. 2000. Linguistic, mental and biological laws. In I. Johansen (ed.), *Fins de Siècle/New Beginnings*. Aarhus: Aarhus University Press.

Searle, John. 1992. *The Rediscovery of the Mind*. Cambridge, Mass: MIT Press.

Searle, John. 1995. *The Construction of Social Reality*. New York: The Free Press.

Searle, John. 1999. *Mind, Language and Philosophy: Doing Philosophy in the Real World*. London: Weidenfeld and Nicolson.

Sperry, Roger. 1976. Mental Phenomenon as Causal Determinants in Brain Function. In G. Globus, G. Maxwell, and I. Savidnik, eds., *Consciousness and the Brain: A Scientific and Philosophical Inquiry*, New York: Plenum Press.

Sperry, Roger. 1980. Mind-Brain Interaction: Mentalism, Yes; Dualism, No. *Neuroscience* 5: 195-206.

Wigner, Eugene. 1960. The Unreasonable Effectiveness of Mathematics in the Natural Sciences. *Communications in Pure and Applied Mathematics*, New York: John Wiley.

Language and Mind:
Current Thoughts on Ancient Problems

Noam Chomsky

Part 1

The study of language is one of the oldest branches of systematic inquiry, tracing back to classical India and Greece, with a rich and fruitful history of achievement. From a different point of view, it is quite young.

The major research enterprises of today took shape only about 40 years ago, when some of the leading ideas of the tradition were revived and reconstructed, opening the way to what has proven to be very productive inquiry.

That language should have exercised such fascination over the years is not surprising. The human faculty of language seems to be a true "species property", varying little among humans and without significant analogue elsewhere. Probably the closest analogues are found in insects, at an evolutionary distance of a billion years. The communication system of bees, for example, shares with human language the property of "displaced reference", our ability to talk about something that is remote from us in space or time; bees use an intricate "dance" to communicate the direction, distance, and desirability of a remote source of honey. Nothing similar is known elsewhere in nature. Even in this case, the analogy is very weak.

Vocal learning has evolved in birds, but in three unrelated groups, independently it is assumed; here the analogies to human language are even more superficial.

Human language appears to be biologically isolated in its essential properties, and a rather recent development from an

In Search of a Language for the Mind-Brain, ed. Saleemi, Bohn and Gjedde, *The Dolphin* 33 © 2005 by Aarhus University Press, Denmark. ISBN 87 7934 005 9.

evolutionary perspective. There is no serious reason today to challenge the Cartesian view that the ability to use linguistic signs to express freely-formed thoughts marks "the true distinction between man and animal" or machine, whether by "machine" we mean the automata that captured the imagination of the 17th and 18th century, or those that are providing a stimulus to thought and imagination today.

Furthermore, the faculty of language enters crucially into every aspect of human life, thought, and interaction. It is largely responsible for the fact that alone in the biological world, humans have a history, cultural evolution and diversity of any complexity and richness, even biological success in the technical sense that their numbers are huge. A Marsian scientist observing the strange doings on Earth could hardly fail to be struck by the emergence and significance of this apparently unique form of intellectual organization. It is even more natural that the topic, with its many mysteries, should have stimulated the curiosity of those who seek to understand their own nature and their place within the wider world.

Human language is based on an elementary property that also seems to be biologically isolated: the property of discrete infinity, which is exhibited in its purest form by the natural numbers 1, 2, 3,... Children do not learn this property of the number system. Unless the mind already possesses the basic principles, no amount of evidence could provide them; and they are completely beyond the intellectual range of other organisms.

Similarly, no child has to learn that there are three word sentences and four word sentences, but no three-and-a-half word sentences, and that it is always possible to construct a more complex one, with a definite form and meaning. Such knowledge must come to us from "the original hand of nature", in David Hume's phrase, as part of our biological endowment.

This property intrigued Galileo, who regarded the discovery of a means to communicate our "most secret thoughts to any other person with 24 little characters" as the greatest of all human inventions. The invention succeeds because it reflects the discrete infinity of the language that these characters are used to represent. Shortly after, the authors of the Port Royal Grammar.

were struck by the "marvellous invention" of a means to construct from a few dozen sounds an infinity of expressions that enable us to reveal to others what we think and imagine and feel - from a contemporary standpoint, not an "invention" but no less "marvellous" as a product of biological evolution, about which virtually nothing is known, in this case.

The faculty of language can reasonably be regarded as a "language organ" in the sense in which scientists speak of the visual system, or immune system, or circulatory system, as organs of the body. Understood in this way, an organ is not something that can be removed from the body, leaving the rest intact. It is a subsystem of a more complex structure. We hope to understand the full complexity by investigating parts that have distinctive characteristics, and their interactions. Study of the faculty of language proceeds in the same way.

We assume further that the language organ is like others in that its basic character is an expression of the genes. How that happens remains a distant prospect for inquiry, but we can investigate the genetically determined "initial state" of the language faculty in other ways. Evidently, each language is the result of the interplay of two factors: the initial state and the course of experience. We can think of the initial state as a "language acquisition device" that takes experience as "input" and gives the language as an "output", an "output" that is internally represented in the mind/brain. The input and the output are both open to examination: we can study the course of experience and the properties of the languages that are acquired.

What is learned in this way can tell us quite a lot about the initial state that mediates between them. Furthermore, there is strong reason to believe that the initial state is common to the species: if my children had grown up in Tokyo, they would speak Japanese. That means that evidence about Japanese bears directly on the assumptions concerning the initial state for English. The shared initial state must be rich enough to yield each language, given appropriate experience; but not so rich as to exclude any language that humans can attain. We can establish strong empirical conditions that the theory of the initial state must satisfy, and pose several problems for the biology of language:

How do the genes determine the initial state, and what are the brain mechanisms involved in the states that the language organ assumes? These are hard problems, even for much simpler systems where direct experiment is possible, but some may be at the horizons of inquiry.

To proceed, we should be more clear about what we mean by "a language".

There has been much impassioned controversy about the right answer to this question, and more generally, to the question of how languages should be studied. The controversy is pointless, because there is no right answer. If we are interested in how bees communicate, we will try to learn something about their internal nature, social arrangements, and physical environment.

These approaches are not in conflict; they are mutually supportive. The same is true of the study of human language: it can be investigated from the biological point of view, and from numerous others. Each approach defines the object of its inquiry in the light of its special concerns; and each should try to learn what it can from other approaches. Why such matters arouse great emotion in the study of humans is perhaps an interesting question, but I will put it aside for now.

The purely internalist approach I have been outlining is concerned with the faculty of language: its initial state, and the states it assumes. Suppose that Peter's language organ is in state L. We can think of L as Peter's language; when I speak of a language here, that is what I mean. So understood, a language is something like "the way we speak and understand", one traditional conception of language. The theory of Peter's language is often called the "grammar" of his language, and the theory of the initial state of the faculty of language is called "universal grammar", adapting traditional terms to a different framework. Peter's language determines an infinite array of expressions, each with its sound and meaning. In technical terms, his language "generates" the expressions of his language.

The theory of his language is therefore called a generative grammar. Each expression is a complex of properties, which provide "instructions" for Peter's performance systems: his articulatory apparatus, his modes of organizing his thoughts, and so on. With his language and the associated performance systems in place, Peter has a vast amount of knowledge about the sound and meaning of expressions, and a corresponding capacity to interpret what he hears, to express his thoughts, and to use his language in a variety of other ways.

Generative grammar arose in the context of what is often called "the cognitive revolution" of the 1950s, and was an important factor in its development. Whether the term "revolution" is appropriate or not can be questioned, but there was an important change of perspective: from the study of behavior and its products (such as texts), to the inner mechanisms that enter into human thought and action. The cognitive perspective regards behavior and its products not as the object of inquiry, but as data that may provide evidence about the inner mechanisms of mind and the ways these mechanisms operate in executing actions and interpreting experience. The properties and patterns that were the focus of attention in structural linguistics find their place, but as phenomena to be explained along with innumerable others, in terms of the inner mechanisms that generate expressions.

The "cognitive revolution" renewed and reshaped many of the insights, achievements, and quandaries of what we might call "the first cognitive revolution" of the 17th and 18th century, which was part of the scientific revolution that so radically modified our understanding of the world. It was recognized at the time that language involves "the infinite use of finite means", in von Humboldt's phrase; but the insight could be developed only in limited ways, because the basic ideas remained vague and obscure.

By mid-20th century, advances in the formal sciences had provided appropriate concepts in a very sharp and clear form, making it possible to give a precise account of the computational principles that generate the expressions of a language. Other advances also opened the way to investigation of traditional questions with greater hope of success. The study of language change had registered major achievements. Anthropological linguistics provided a far richer understanding of the nature and variety of languages, also undermining many stereotypes. And certain topics, notably the study of sound systems, had been much advanced by the structural linguistics of the 20th century.

The last prominent inheritor of the tradition, before it was swept aside by structuralist and behaviorist currents, was the Danish linguist Otto Jespersen. He argued 75 years ago that the fundamental goal of linguistics is to discover the "notion of structure" that is in the mind of the speaker, enabling him to produce and understand "free expressions" that are new to speaker and hearer or even the history of the language, a regular occurrence of everyday life. Jespersen's "notion of structure" is similar in spirit to what I have called "a language". The goal of a theory of the language is to unearth some of the factors that enter into the ability to produce and understand "free expressions". Only SOME of the factors, however, just as the study of computational mechanisms falls considerably short of capturing the idea of "infinite use of finite means", or addressing the issues that were fundamental to the first cognitive revolution, a matter to which I will return.

The earliest attempts to carry out the program of generative grammar, about 40 years ago, quickly revealed that even in the best studied languages, elementary properties had passed unrecognized, and that the most comprehensive traditional grammars and dictionaries only skim the surface.

The basic properties of particular languages and of the general faculty of language are unconsciously presupposed throughout, unrecognized and unexpressed. That is quite appropriate if the goal is to help people to learn a second language, to find the conventional meaning and pronunciation of words, or to have some general idea of how languages differ. But if our goal is to understand the language faculty and the states it can assume, we cannot tacitly presuppose "the intelligence of the reader". Rather, this is the object of inquiry.

The study of language acquisition leads to the same conclusion. A careful look at the interpretation of expressions reveals very quickly that from the earliest stages, the child knows vastly more than experience has provided. That is true even of simple words. Young children acquire words at a rate of about one every waking hour, with extremely limited exposure under highly ambiguous conditions. The words are understood in delicate and intricate ways that are far beyond the reach of any dictionary, and are only beginning to be investigated. When we move beyond single words, the conclusion becomes even more dramatic. Language acquisition seems much like the growth of organs generally; it is something that happens to a child, not that the child does. And while the environment plainly matters, the general course of development and the basic features of what emerges are predetermined by the initial state. But the initial state is a common human possession. It must be, then, that in their essential properties, languages are cast to the same mold. The Martian scientist might reasonably conclude that there is a single human language, with differences only at the margins.

For our lives, the slight differences are what matter, not the overwhelming similarities, which we unconsciously take for granted. No doubt frogs look at other frogs the same way. But if we want to understand what kind of creature we are, we have to adopt a very different point of view, basically that of the Martian studying humans.

That is, in fact, the point of view we adopt when we study other organisms, or even humans apart from their mental aspects - humans "below the neck", metaphorically speaking. There is every reason to study what is above the neck in the same manner.

As languages were more carefully investigated from the point of view of generative grammar, it became clear that their diversity had been underestimated as radically as their complexity. At the same time, we know that the diversity and complexity can be no more than superficial appearance.

The conclusions are paradoxical, but undeniable. They pose in a stark form what has become the central problem of the modern study of language: How can we show that all languages are variations on a single theme, while at the same time recording faithfully their intricate properties of sound and meaning, superficially diverse? A genuine theory of human language has to satisfy two conditions: "descriptive adequacy" and "explanatory adequacy".

The condition of descriptive adequacy holds for a grammar of a particular language. The grammar satisfies the condition insofar as it gives a full and accurate account of the properties of the language, of what the speaker of the language knows. The condition of explanatory adequacy holds for the general theory of language, universal grammar. To satisfy the condition, universal grammar must show that each particular language is a specific instantiation of the uniform initial state, derived from it under the "boundary conditions" set by experience. We would then have an explanation of the properties of languages at a deeper level. To the extent that universal grammar satisfies the condition of explanatory adequacy, it offers a solution to what is sometimes called "the logical problem of language acquisition". It shows how that problem can be solved in principle, and thus provides a framework for the study of how the process actually takes place.

There is a serious tension between these two research tasks. The search for descriptive adequacy seems to lead to ever-greater complexity and variety of rule systems, while the search for explanatory adequacy requires that language structure must be largely invariant. It is this tension that has largely set the guidelines for research. The natural way to resolve the tension is to challenge the traditional assumption, carried over to early generative grammar, that a language is a complex system of rules, each specific to particular languages and particular grammatical constructions: rules for forming relative clauses in Hindi, verb phrases in Bantu, passives in Japanese, and so on. Considerations of explanatory adequacy indicate that this cannot be correct.

The problem was faced by attempts to find general properties of rule systems that can be attributed to the faculty of language itself, in the hope that the residue will prove to be more simple and uniform.

About 15 years ago, these efforts crystallized in an approach to language that was a much more radical departure from the tradition than earlier generative grammar had been. This "Principles and Parameters" approach, as it has been called, rejected the concept of rule and grammatical construction entirely; there are no rules for forming relative clauses in Hindi, verb phrases in Bantu, passives in Japanese, and so on. The familiar grammatical constructions are taken to be taxonomic artifacts, useful for informal description perhaps but with no theoretical standing. They have something like the status of "terrestial mammal" or "household pet". And the rules are decomposed into general principles of the faculty of language, which interact to yield the properties of expressions. We can think of the initial state of the faculty of language as a fixed network connected to a switch box; the network is constituted of the principles of language, while the switches are the options to be determined by experience. When the switches are set one way, we have Bantu; when they are set another way, we have Japanese. Each possible human language is identified as a particular setting of the switches - a setting of parameters, in technical terminology. If the research program succeeds, we should be able literally to deduce Bantu from one choice of settings, Japanese from another, and so on through the languages that humans can acquire. The empirical conditions of language acquisition require that the switches can be set on the basis of the very limited information that is available to the child. Notice that small changes in switch settings can lead to great apparent variety in output, as the effects proliferate through the system. These are the general properties of language that any genuine theory must capture somehow.

This is, of course, a program, far from a finished product. The conclusions tentatively reached are unlikely to stand in their present form; and, needless to say, one can have no certainty that the whole approach is on the right track. As a research program, however, it has been highly successful, leading to a real explosion of empirical inquiry into languages of a very broad typological range, to new questions that could never even have been formulated before, and to many intriguing answers. Questions of acquisition, processing, pathology, and others also took new forms, which have proven very productive as well. Furthermore, whatever its fate, the program suggests how the theory of language might satisfy the conflicting conditions of descriptive and explanatory adequacy. It gives at least an outline of a genuine theory of language, really for the first time.

Within this research program, the main task is to discover the principles and parameters. While a great deal remains obscure, there has been enough progress to consider some new and more far-reaching questions about the design of language. In particular, we can ask how good is the design. How close does language come to what some super-engineer would construct, given the conditions that the language faculty must satisfy? How "perfect" is language, to put it picturesquely?

This question carries us right to the borders of current inquiry, which has given some reason to believe that the answer is: "surprisingly perfect" - surprising, for several reasons to which I'll return. At this point it is hard to proceed without more technical apparatus. I will put that off until tomorrow, and turn now to some other topics of a more general nature, having to do with the ways the internalist study of language relates to the external world.

These questions fall into two categories: First, relations of mind and brain; second, questions of language use. Let's begin with the first.

The internalist study of language tries to discover the properties of the initial state of the faculty of language, and the states it assumes under the influence of experience. The initial and attained states are states of the brain primarily, but described abstractly, not in terms of cells but in terms of properties that the brain mechanisms must somehow satisfy.

It is commonly held that this picture is misguided in principle. The basic criticism has been presented most clearly by philosopher John Searle: The faculty of language is indeed "innate in human brains", he writes, but the evidence that has been used to attribute properties and principles to this innate faculty "is much more simply accounted for by the... hypothesis" that there is "a hardware level of explanation in terms of the structure of the device".

Exactly what is at stake?

The existence of the hardware level is not in question, if by that we mean that cells are involved in "the structure of the device" that is "innate in human brains". But it remains to discover the structure of the device, its properties and principles. The only question has to do with the status of the theory that expresses these properties. Searle says there would be "no further predictive or explanatory power by saying that there is a level of deep unconscious" principles of the faculty of language. That is quite true. Similarly chemistry is uninteresting if it says only that there are deep structural properties of matter. But chemistry is not uninteresting at all if puts forth theories about these properties, and the same is true of the study of language. And in both cases, one takes the entities and principles postulated to be real, because we have no other concept of reality. There is no issue, simply a serious confusion that is pervasive in discussion of mental aspects of the world.

An analogy to chemistry is instructive. Throughout its modern history, chemistry has tried to discover properties of complex objects in the world, offering an account in terms of chemical elements of the kind postulated by Lavoisier, atoms and molecules, valence, structural formulas for organic compounds, laws governing the combination of these objects, and so on. The entities and principles postulated were abstract, in the sense that there was no way to account for them in terms of known physical mechanisms. There was much debate over the centuries about the status of these hypothetical constructs; Are they real? Are they just calculating devices? Can they be reduced to physics? The debate continued until early in this century. It is now understood to have been completely senseless. It turned out that in fact, chemistry was not reducible to physics, because the assumptions of basic physics were wrong. With the quantum revolution, it was possible to proceed to unification of chemistry and physics, about 60 years ago. Now chemistry is considered to be part of physics, though it was not reduced to physics.

It would have been irrational to have claimed for centuries that chemistry is mistaken because its principles are "much more simply accounted for by a hardware level of explanation in terms of the entities and principles postulated by physicists"; and as we now know, the claim was not only irrational but false. For the same reason, it would be irrational to hold that a theory of language can be dispensed with in favor of an account in terms of atoms or neurons, even if there were much to say at this level. In fact, there is not, which should come as no surprise.

For the brain sciences, the abstract study of states of the brain provides guidelines for inquiry: they seek to discover what kinds of mechanisms might have these properties. The mechanisms might turn out to be quite different from anything contemplated today, as has been the case throughout the history of science. We do not advance the brain sciences by a proposal to stop trying to find the properties of states of the brain, or by assuming, dogmatically, that the little bit that is now known about the brain must provide the answers, or by saying that we can look for the properties, but we should not go on to attribute them to the brain and its states - "deep unconscious rules", if that is what the best theory concludes.

In the background lies what seems to be a deeper problem: the problem of dualism, of mind and body. The abstract study of language seems to fall on the mental side of the divide, hence to be highly problematic. It calls into question the "basic materialist premise" that "All reality is physical", to quote a recent study of "mental reality" by Galen Strawson, the most sophisticated and valuable account I know of the problem of materialism, which is widely held to be fundamental to contemporary thought.

Strawson points out that the problem "came to seem acute" in the 16th-17th centuries with the rise of "a scientific conception of the physical as nothing more than particles in motion". That is true, but the way this conception was formed raises some questions about the materialist premise and the quest for a "clear line between the mental and the nonmental" that Strawson and others consider critical for the philosophy of mind.

The "scientific conception" took shape as "the mechanical philosophy", based on the principle that matter is inert and interactions are through contact, with no "occult qualities" of the kind postulated by Scholastic doctrine. These were dismissed as "so great an Absurdity that I believe no Man who has in philosophical matters a competent Faculty of thinking, can ever fall into it". The words are Newton's, but they refer not to the occult qualities of Scholasticism that were in such disrepute, but to his own startling conclusion that gravity, though no less mystical, "does really exist". Historians of science point out that "Newton had no physical explanation of gravity at all", a deep problem for him and eminent contemporaries who correctly "accused him of reintroducing occult qualities", with no "physical, material substrate" that "human beings can understand". To the end of his life, Newton sought to escape the absurdity, as did Euler, D'Alembert, and many since, but in vain. Nothing has weakened the force of David Hume's judgment that by refuting the self-evident mechanical philosophy, Newton "restored (Nature's) ultimate secrets to that obscurity in which they ever did and ever will remain".

It is true that the "scientific conception of the physical" has incorporated "particles in motion," but without "human understanding" in the sense of the earlier enterprise; rather, with resort to Newtonian "absurdities" and worse, leaving us "ignorant of the nature of the physical in some fundamental way". I am quoting Strawson's reference to the core problems of mind, but they are not alone in this regard. The properties of particles in motion also surpass human understanding, although we "accustomed ourselves to the abstract notion of forces, or rather to a notion hovering in a mystic obscurity between abstraction and concrete comprehension", Friedrich Lange points out in his classic scholarly study of materialism, discussing this "turning point" in its history, which deprives the doctrine of much significance. The sciences came to accept the conclusion that "a purely materialistic or mechanistic physics" is "impossible" (Alexander Koyré). From hard science to soft, inquiry can do no more than to seek the best theoretical account, hoping for unification if possible, though how, no one can tell in advance.

In terms of the mechanical philosophy, Descartes had been able to pose a fairly intelligible version of the mind-body problem, the problem of "the ghost in the machine", as it is sometimes called. But Newton showed that the machine does not exist, though he left the ghost intact. With Newton's demonstration that there are no bodies in anything like the sense assumed, the existing version of the mind-body problem collapses; or any other, until some new notion of body is proposed. But the sciences offer none: there is a world, with whatever strange properties it has, including its optical, chemical, organic, mental, and other aspects, which we try to discover. All are part of nature.

That seems to have been Newton's view. To his last days, he sought some "subtle spirit" that would account for a broad range of phenomena that appeared to be beyond explanation in terms truly comprehensible to humans, including interaction of bodies, electrical attraction and repulsion, light, sensation, and the way "members of animal bodies move at the command of the will". Chemist Joseph Black recommended that "chemical affinity be received as a first principle, which we cannot explain any more than Newton could explain gravitation, and let us defer accounting for the laws of affinity, till we have established such a body of doctrine as Newton has established concerning the laws of gravitation". Chemistry proceeded to establish a rich body of doctrine, achieving its "triumphs... in isolation from the newly emerging science of physics", a leading historian of chemistry points out. As I mentioned, unification was finally achieved, quite recently, though not by reduction.

Apart from its theological framework, there has been, since Newton, no reasonable alternative to John Locke's suggestion that God might have chosen to "superadd to matter a faculty of thinking" just as he "annexed effects to motion, which we can in no way conceive motion able to produce".

As the 18th chemist Joseph Priestley later elaborated, we must regard the properties "termed mental" as the result of "such an organical structure as that of the brain", superadded to others, none of which need be comprehensible in the sense sought by earlier science. That includes the study of language, which tries to develop bodies of doctrine with constructs and principles that can properly be "termed mental", and assumed to be "the result of organical structure" – how, it remains to discover.

The approach is "mentalistic", but in what should be an uncontroversial sense. It undertakes to study a real object in the natural world - the brain, its states and functions - and thus to move the study of the mind towards eventual integration with the biological sciences.

It might be mentioned that such problems are mostly unsolved even for much simpler systems where direct experiment is possible. One of the best-studied cases is the neroatode, little worms with a three-day maturation period, with a wiring diagram that is completely analyzed.

It is only very recently that some understanding has been gained of the neural basis of their behavior, and that remains limited and controversial.

Another question of the same category has to do with the way the genes express the properties of the initial state. That too is a very hard problem, barely understood even in far simpler cases. The "epigenetic laws" that transform genes to developed organisms are mostly unknown, a large gap in evolutionary theory as scientists have often pointed out, because the theory requires an understanding of genotype-phenotype correspondence, of the range of organisms that can develop from some complex of genes. I mention these facts only as a word of caution about strange conclusions that have been expressed, often with great passion again, about observations on the biological isolation of language and the richness of the initial state. There is much more to say about this topic, a very lively one today, but I will put it aside and turn to the second category of questions about how language engages the world: questions of language use.

For simplicity, let's keep to simple words. Suppose that "book" is a word in Peter's lexicon. The word is a complex of properties: in technical usage, phonetic and semantic features. The sensorimotor systems use the phonetic properties for articulation and perception, relating them to external events: motions of molecules, for example. Other systems of mind use the semantic properties of the word when Peter talks about the world and interprets what others say about it.

There is no far-reaching controversy about how to proceed on the sound side, but on the meaning side there are profound disagreements.

Empirically oriented studies seem to me to approach problems of meaning rather in the way they study sound. They try to find the phonetic properties of the word "book" that are used by articulatory and perceptual systems. And similarly, they try to find the semantic properties of the word "book" that are used by other systems of the mind/brain: that it is nominal not verbal, used to refer to an artifact not a substance like water or an abstraction like health, and so on. One might ask whether these properties are part of the meaning of the word "book" or of the concept associated with the wordy it is not clear how to distinguish these proposals, but perhaps an empirical issue can be unearthed. Either way, some features of the lexical item "book" that are internal to it determine modes of interpretation of the kind just mentioned.

Investigating language use, we find that words are interpreted in terms of such factors as material constitution, design, intended and characteristic use, institutional role, and so on. The notions can be traced to Aristotelian origin, philosopher Julius Moravcsik has pointed out in very interesting work. Things are identified and assigned to categories in terms of such properties, which I am taking to be semantic features, on a par with phonetic features that determine its sound. The use of language can attend in various ways to these semantic features.

Suppose the library has two copies of Tolstoy's *War and Peace*, Peter takes out one, and John the other. Did Peter and John take out the same book, or different books? If we attend to the material factor of the lexical item, they took out different books; if we focus on its abstract component, they took out the same book. We can attend to both material and abstract factors simultaneously, as when we say that his book is in every store in the country, or that the book he is planning will weigh at least five pounds if he ever writes it. Similarly, we can paint the door white and walk through it, using the pronoun "it" to refer ambiguously to figure and ground. We can report that the bank was blown up after it raised the interest rate, or that it raised the rate to keep from being blown up. Here the pronoun "it", and the "empty category" that is the subject of "being blown up", simultaneously adopt both the material and institutional factors.

The same is true if my house is destroyed and I re-build it, perhaps somewhere else; it is not the same house, even if I use the same materials, though I re-built it. The referential terms "re" and "it" cross the boundary. Cities are still different. London could be destroyed by fire and IT could be rebuilt somewhere else, from completely different materials and looking quite different, but still London. Carthage could be rebuilt today, and still be Carthage.

Consider the city that is regarded as holy by the faiths that trace to the Old Testament. The Islamic world calls it "AI-Quds", Israel uses a different name, as does the Christian world: in English, it is pronounced "Jerusalem". There is a good deal of conflict over this city. The *New York Times* has just offered what it calls a "promising solution". Israel should keep all of Jerusalem, but "AI-Quds" should be rebuilt outside the current boundaries of Jerusalem. The proposal is perfectly intelligible - which is why it arouses considerable outrage outside circles in which the doctrine of the powerful reigns unchallenged. And the plan could be implemented.

What is the city to which we will then refer when we say that IT was left where it was while moved somewhere else?

The meanings of words have other curious properties. Thus if I tell you that I painted my house brown, I mean you to understand that I placed the paint on the exterior surface, not the interior surface. If I want you to know that it was the interior surface, I have to say that I painted my house brown on the inside. In technical terminology, there is a marked and unmarked usage; without specific indications, we give the words their unmarked interpretation. These are properties of houses, not just of the word "paint". Thus if I see the house, I see its exterior surface, though if I am sitting inside I can see the interior walls. Although the unmarked interpretation selects the exterior surface, I surely do not regard the house as just a surface. If you and I are outside the house, you can be nearer to it than I am; but if we are both in the house, that cannot be the case, even if you are closer to the surface. Neither of us is near the house. So we regard the house as an exterior surface, but with an interior as well. If I decide to use my house to store my car, living somewhere else, it is no longer a house at all, rather a garage, though the material constitution hasn't changed. Such properties hold quite generally, even for invented objects, even impossible ones. If I paint my spherical cube brown, I painted the exterior surface brown.

Such properties are not limited to artifacts. We call England an island, but if the sea level dropped enough, it would be a mountain, by virtue of the faculties of the mind. The prototypical simple substance is water. But even here, immaterial factors enter into individuation. Suppose a cup is filled with pure H20 and I dip a tea bag into it. It is then tea, not water. Suppose a second cup is filled from a river.

It could be chemically identical with the contents of the first cup - perhaps a ship dumped tea bags in the river. But it is water, not tea, and that is what I would call it even if I knew all the facts. What people call "water" is correlated with H20 content, but only weakly, experimental studies have shown. Doubtless in this extreme case, constitution is a major factor in deciding whether something is water, but even here, not the only one. As I mentioned, the observations extend to the simplest referential and referentially dependent elements; and to proper names, which have rich semantic-conceptual properties. Something is named as a person, a river, a city, with the complexity of understanding that goes along with these categories. Language has no logically proper names, stripped of such properties, as Oxford philosopher Peter Strawson pointed out many years ago.

The facts about such matters are often clear, but not trivial. Such properties can be investigated in many ways: language acquisition, generality among languages, invented forms, etc. What we discover is surprisingly intricate; and not surprisingly, largely known in advance of any evidence, hence shared among languages. There is no a priori reason to expect that human language will have such properties; Martian could be different. The symbolic systems of science and mathematics surely are.

It is sometimes suggested that these are just things we know from experience with books, cities, houses, people, and so on. That is in part correct, but begs the question. We know all of this about parts of our experience that we construe as books, or cities, and so on, by virtue of the design of our languages and mental organization. To borrow the terminology of the cognitive revolution of the 17th century, what the senses convey gives the mind "an occasion to exercise its own activity" to construct "intelligible ideas and conceptions of things from within itself" as "rules", "patterns", exemplars" and "anticipations" that yield Gestalt properties and others, and "one comprehensive idea of the whole". There is good reason to adopt Hume's principle that the "identity which we ascribe" to things is "only a fictitious one", established by the human understanding, a picture developed further by Kant, Schopenhauer, and others. People think and talk about the world in terms of the perspectives made available by the resources of the mind, including the meanings of the terms in which their thoughts are expressed. The comparison to phonetic interpretation is not unreasonable.

Much of contemporary philosophy of language and mind follows a different course. It asks to what a word refers, giving various answers. But the question has no clear meaning. It makes little sense to ask to what thing the expression "Tolstoy's *War and Peace*" refers. The answer depends on how the semantic features are used when we think and talk, one way or another.

In general, a word, even of the simplest kind, does not pick out an entity of the world, or of our "belief space" - which is not to deny, of course, that there are books and banks, or that we are talking about something if we discuss the fate of the earth and conclude that IT is grim. But we should follow the good advice of the 18th century philosopher Thomas Reid and his modern successors Wittgenstein and others, and not draw unwarranted conclusions from common usage.

We can, if we like, say that the word "book" refers to books, "sky" to the sky, "health" to health, and so on. Such conventions basically express lack of interest in the semantic properties of words and how they are used to talk about things. We could avoid the issues of acoustic and articulatory phonetics the same way. To say this is not to criticize the decision; any inquiry focuses on certain questions and ignores others. There has been a great deal of exciting work on the aspects of language that relate to phonetic interpretation and to semantic interpretation, but it should properly be called syntax, in my opinion, a study of the operations of the faculty of language, part of the mind. The ways language is used to engage the world lie beyond.

In this connection, let us return to my comment that generative grammar has sought to address concerns that animated the tradition, in particular, the Cartesian idea that "the true distinction" between humans and other creatures or machines is the ability to act in the manner they took to be roost clearly illustrated in the ordinary use of language: without finite limits, influenced but not determined by internal state, appropriate to situations but not caused by them, coherent and evoking thoughts that the hearer might have expressed, and so on. That is only partly correct. The goal of the work I have been discussing is to unearth some of the factors that enter into such normal practice. Only SOME of these, however.

Generative grammar seeks to discover the mechanisms that are used, thus contributing to the study of HOW they are used in the creative fashion of normal life. How they are used is the problem that intrigued the Cartesians, and it remains as mysterious to us as it was to them, even though far more is understood today about the mechanisms that are involved.

In this respect, the study of language is again much like that of other organs. Study of the visual and motor systems has uncovered mechanisms by which the brain interprets scattered stimuli as a cube and by which the arm reaches for a book on the table. But these branches of science do not raise the question of how people decide to do such things, and speculations about the use of the visual or motor systems, or others, amount to very little.

It is these capacities, manifested most strikingly in language use, that are at the heart of traditional concerns: for Descartes, they are "the noblest thing we can have" and all that "truly belongs" to us. Half a century before Descartes, the Spanish philosopher-physician Juan Huarte observed that this "generative faculty" of ordinary human understanding and action, though foreign to "beasts and plants", is only a lower form of understanding. It falls short of true exercise of the creative imagination.

Even the lower form lies beyond our theoretical reach, apart from the study of mechanisms that enter into it.

In a number of areas, language included, a lot has been learned in recent years about these mechanisms. The problems that can now be faced are hard and challenging, but many mysteries still lie beyond the reach of the form of human inquiry we call "science", a conclusion that we should not find surprising if we consider humans to be part of the organic world, and perhaps one we should not find distressing either.

Part 2

Yesterday, I discussed two basic questions about language, one internalist and the other externalist. The internalist question asks what kind of a system language is. The externalist question asks how language relates to other parts of the mind and to the external world, including problems of unification and of language use. The discussion kept to a very general level, trying to sort out the kinds of problems that arise and the ways it seems to make sense to deal with them. I would now like to look a little more closely at some current thinking about the internalist question.

To review the context, the study of language took a somewhat different path about 40 years ago as part of the so-called "cognitive revolution" of the 1950s, which revived and reshaped traditional questions and concerns about many topics, including language and its use and the significance of these matters for the study of the human mind. Earlier attempts to explore these questions had run up against conceptual barriers and limits of understanding. By mid-century, these had to some extent been overcome, making it possible to proceed in a more fruitful way. The basic problem was to find some way to resolve the tension between the conflicting demands of descriptive and explanatory adequacy. The research program that developed led finally to a picture of language that was a considerable departure from the long and rich tradition; the Principles-and-Parameters approach, which is based on the idea that the initial state of the language faculty consists of invariant principles and a finite array of choices as to how the whole system can function. A particular language is determined by making these choices in a specific way. We have at least the outlines of a genuine theory of language, which might be able to satisfy the conditions of descriptive and explanatory adequacy, and approach the logical problem of language acquisition in a constructive way.

Since this picture took form about 15 years ago, the major research effort has been directed to trying to discover and make explicit the principles and the parameters. Inquiry has extended very rapidly both in depth, in individual languages, and in scope, as similar ideas were applied to languages of a very broad typological range. The problems that remain are considerable, to put it mildly. The human mind/brain is perhaps the most complex object in the universe, and we barely begin to comprehend the ways it is constituted and functions. Within it, language seems to occupy a central place, and at least on the surface, the variety and complexity are daunting. Nevertheless, there has been a good deal of progress, enough so that it seems reasonable to consider some more far-reaching questions about the design of language, in particular, questions about optimality of design. I dropped the matter at this point yesterday, turning to other topics. Let us now return to it, and see where inquiry into these questions might lead.

We are now asking how well language is designed. How closely does language resemble what a superbly competent engineer might have constructed, given certain design specifications. To study the question, we have to say more about these specifications. Some are internal and general, having to do with conceptual naturalness and simplicity, notions that are hardly crystal clear but can be sharpened in many ways. Others are external and specific, having to do with the conditions imposed by the systems of the mind/brain with which the faculty of language interacts. I suggested that the answer to the question might turn out to be that language is very well designed, perhaps close to "perfect" in satisfying external conditions.

If there is any truth to this conclusion, it is rather surprising, for several reasons. First, languages have often been assumed to be such complex and defective objects as to be hardly worth studying from a stern theoretical perspective. They require reform or regimentation, or replacement by something quite different, if they are to serve some purpose other than the confused and intricate affairs of daily life. That is the leading idea that inspired traditional attempts to devise a universal perfect language, or on theological assumptions, to recover the original Adamic language; and something similar has been taken for granted in much modern work from Frege to the present. Second, one might not expect to find such design properties in biological systems, which evolve over long periods through incremental changes under complicated and accidental circumstances, making the best of difficult and murky contingencies.

Suppose nonetheless that we turn aside initial skepticism and try to formulate some reasonably clear questions about optimality of language design. The "minimalist program", as it has come to be called, is an effort to examine such questions. It is too soon to offer a judgment about the project with any confidence. My own judgment is that early results are promising, but only time will tell.

Note that the minimalist program is a PROGRAM, not a theory, even less so than the Principles-and-Parameters approach. There are minimalist questions, but no specific minimalist answers. The answers are whatever is found by carrying out the program: perhaps that some of the questions have no interesting answers, while others are premature. There might be no interesting answers because human language is a case of what Nobel laureate Francois Jacob once called "bricolage"; evolution is an opportunist, an inventor that takes whatever materials are at hand and tinkers with them, introducing slight changes so that they might work a bit better than before.

This is, of course, intended only as a picturesque image. There are other factors to consider. Uncontroversially, evolution proceeds within a framework established by the laws of physics and chemistry and the properties of complex systems, about which very little is known. Within this physical channel, natural selection plays a role that may range from zero to quite substantial.

From the Big Bang to large molecules, design results from the operation of physical law, the properties of Helium or snowflakes, for example. The effects of selection begin to appear with more complex organic forms, though understanding declines as complexity increases, and one must be wary of what evolutionary biologists Richard Lewontin, Stuart Kauffman, and others, have called "Just So Stories" - stories about how things might have happened, or maybe not. Kauffman, for example, has argued that many of the properties of "the genomic regulatory system that constrains into useful behavior the patterns of gene activity" during the growth of organisms "are spontaneous, self-organized features of complex control systems which required almost no selection at all", suggesting that "we must rethink evolutionary biology" and look for "sources of order outside selection." It is a rare evolutionary biologist who dismisses such ideas as unworthy of attention. Looking beyond, it is generally assumed that such phenomena as the polyhedral shells of viruses, or the appearance in organic forms of properties of a well-known arithmetical series called the Fibonacci series ("phyllotaxis"), probably fall together with snowf lakes rather than the distribution of dark and light moths or the neck of a giraffe.

Uncontroversially, for any case one studies it has to be determined how the physical channel constrains outcomes and what options it allows. Furthermore, there are independent issues that have to be disentangled.

What looks like wonderful design may well be a paradigm example of gradualism that is independent of the function in question. The ordinary use of language, for example, relies on bones of the inner ear that migrated from the jaws of reptiles. The process is currently believed to be the consequence of growth of the neocortex in mammals, and "sets true mammals apart from every other vertebrate" (*Science,* Dec. 1 1995). An engineer would find that this "delicate sound-amplifying system" is superbly designed for language function, but Mother Nature did not have that in mind when the process began 160 million years ago, nor is there any known selectional effect of the takeover of the system for language use.

Human language lies well beyond the limits of serious understanding of evolutionary processes, though there are suggestive speculations. Let us add another. Suppose we make up a "Just So Story" with imagery derived from snowflakes rather than colors of moths and necks of giraffes, with design determined by natural law rather than bricolage through selection. Suppose that there was an ancient primate with the whole human mental architecture in place, but no language faculty. The creature shared our modes of perceptual organization, our beliefs and desires, our hopes and fears, insofar as these are not formed and mediated by language. Perhaps it had a "language of thought" in the sense of Jerry Fodor and others, but no way to form linguistic expressions associated with the thoughts that this *lingua mentis* makes available.

Suppose a mutation took place in the genetic instructions for the brain, which was then reorganized in accord with the laws of physics and chemistry to install a faculty of language. Suppose the new system was, furthermore, beautifully designed, a near-perfect solution to the conditions imposed by the general architecture of the mind-brain in which it is inserted, another illustration of how natural laws work out in wondrous ways; or if one prefers, an illustration of how the evolutionary tinkerer could satisfy complex design conditions with very simple tools.

To be clear, these are fables. Their only redeeming value is that they may not be more implausible than others, and might even turn out to have some elements of validity. The imagery serves its function if it helps us pose a problem that could turn out to be meaningful and even significant: basically, the problem that motivates the minimalist program, which explores the intuition that the outcome of the fable might be accurate in interesting ways.

Notice a certain resemblance to the logical problem of language acquisition, a reformulation of the condition of explanatory adequacy as a device that converts experience to a language, taken to be a state of a component of the brain. The operation is instantaneous, though the process plainly is not. The serious empirical question is how much distortion is introduced by the abstraction. Rather surprisingly, perhaps, it seems that little if any distortion is introduced: it is AS IF the language appears instantaneously, by selection of the options available in the initial state. Despite great variation in experience, outcomes seem to be remarkably similar, with shared interpretations, often of extreme delicacy, for linguistic expressions of kinds that have little resemblance to anything experienced. That is not what we would expect if the abstraction to instantaneous acquisition introduced severe distortions. Perhaps the conclusion reflects our ignorance, but the empirical evidence seems to support it. Independently of that, insofar as it has been possible to account for properties of individual languages in terms of the abstraction, we have further evidence that the abstraction does capture real properties of a complex reality.

The issues posed by the minimalist program are somewhat similar. Plainly, the faculty of language was not instantaneously inserted into a mind/brain with the rest of its architecture fully intact. But we are now asking how well it is designed on that counterfactual assumption. How much does the abstraction distort a vastly more complex reality? We can try to answer the question much as we do the analogous one about the logical problem of language acquisition.

To pursue the program we have to have to sharpen ideas considerably, and there are ways to proceed. The faculty of language is embedded within the broader architecture of the mind/brain. It interacts with other systems, which impose conditions that language must satisfy if it is to be usable at all. We might think of these as "legibility conditions", called "bare output conditions" in the technical literature. The systems within which the language faculty is embedded must be able to "read" the expressions of the language and use them as "instructions" for thought and action. The sensorimotor systems, for example, have to be able to read the instructions having to do with sound. The articulatory and perceptual apparatus have specific design that enables them to interpret certain properties, not others. These systems thus impose legibility conditions on the generative processes of the faculty of language, which must provide expressions with the proper "phonetic representation."

The same is true of conceptual and other systems that make use of the resources of the faculty of language. They have their intrinsic properties, which require that the expressions generated by the language have certain kinds of "semantic representations", not others.

We can therefore rephrase the initial question in a somewhat more explicit form. We now ask to what extent language is a "good solution" to the legibility conditions imposed by the external systems with which it interacts. If the external systems were perfectly understood, so that we knew exactly what the legibility conditions were, the problem we are raising would still require clarification; we would have to explain more clearly what we mean by "optimal design", not a trivial matter, though not hopeless either. But life is never that easy. The external systems are not very well understood, and in fact, progress in understanding them goes hand-in-hand with progress in understanding the language system that interacts with them. So we face the daunting task of simultaneously setting the conditions of the problem and trying to satisfy them, with the conditions changing as we learn more about how to satisfy them. But that is what one expects in trying to understand the nature of a complex system. We therefore tentatively establish whatever ground seems reasonably firm, and try to proceed from there, knowing well that the ground is likely to shift.

The minimalist program requires that we subject conventional assumptions to careful scrutiny. The most venerable of these is that language has sound and meaning. In current terms, that translates to the thesis that the faculty of language engages other systems of the mind/brain at two "interface levels", one related to sound, the other to meaning. A particular expression generated by the language contains a phonetic representation that is legible to the sensorimotor systems, and a semantic representation that is legible to conceptual and other systems of thought and action, and may consist just of these paired objects.

If this much is correct, we next have to ask just where the interface is located. On the sound side, it has to be determined to what extent, if any, sensorimotor systems are language-specific, hence within the faculty of language; there is considerable disagreement about the matter. On the meaning side, the questions have to do with the relations between the faculty of language and other cognitive systems - the relations between language and thought. On the sound side, the questions have been studied intensively with sophisticated technology for half a century, but the problems are hard, and understanding remains limited. On the meaning side, the questions are much more obscure. Far less is known about the language-external systems; much of the evidence about them is so closely linked to language that it is notoriously difficult to determine when it bears on language, when on other systems (insofar as they are distinct).

And direct investigation of the kind possible for sensorimotor systems is in its infancy. Nonetheless, there is a huge amount of data about how expressions are used and understood in particular circumstances, enough so that natural language semantics is one of the liveliest areas of study of language, and we can make at least some plausible guesses about the nature of the interface level and the legibility conditions it must meet.

With some tentative assumptions about the interface, we can proceed to further questions. We ask how much of what we are attributing to the faculty of language is really motivated by empirical evidence, and how much is a kind of technology, adopted in order to present data in a convenient form while covering up gaps of understanding. Not infrequently, accounts that are offered in technical work turn out on investigation to be of roughly the order of complexity of what is to be explained, and involve assumptions that are not independently very well-grounded. That is not problematic as long as we do not mislead ourselves into thinking that useful and informative descriptions, which may provide stepping stones for further inquiry, are something more than that.

Such questions are always appropriate in principle, but often not worth posing in practice; they may be premature, because understanding is just too limited. Even in the hard sciences, in fact even mathematics, questions of this kind have commonly been put to the side. But the questions are nevertheless real, and with a more plausible concept of the general character of language at hand, perhaps worth exploring.

Let us turn to the question of optimality of language design: How good a solution is language to the general conditions imposed by the architecture of the mind/brain? This question too might be premature, but unlike the problem of distinguishing between principled assumptions and descriptive technology, it might have no answer at all: as I mentioned, there is no good reason to expect that biological systems will be well-designed in anything like this sense.

Let us tentatively assume that both of these questions are appropriate ones, in practice as well as principle. We now proceed to subject postulated principles of language to close scrutiny to see if they are empirically justified in terms of legibility conditions. I will mention a few examples, apologizing in advance for the use of some technical terminology, which I'll try to keep to a minimum, but have no time here to explain in any satisfactory way.

One question is whether there are levels other than the interface levels: Are there levels "internal" to the language, in particular, the levels of deep and surface structure that have played a substantial role in modern work? The minimalist program seeks to show that everything that has been accounted for in terms of these levels has been misdescribed, and is as well or better understood in terms of legibility conditions at the interface: for those of you who know the technical literature, that means the projection principle, binding theory, Case theory, the chain condition, and so on.

We also try to show that the only computational operations are those that are unavoidable on the weakest assumptions about interface properties. One such assumption is that there are word-like units: the external systems have to be able to interpret such items as "man" and "tall." Another is that these items are organized into larger expressions, such as "tall man." A third is that the items have properties of sound and meaning: the word "man" in English begins with closure of the lips and is used to refer to persons, a subtle notion. The language therefore involves three kinds of elements: the properties of sound and meaning, called "features"; the items that are assembled from these properties, called "lexical items"; and the complex expressions constructed from these "atomic" units. It follows that the computational system that generates expressions has two basic operations: one assembles features into lexical items, the second forms larger syntactic objects out of those already constructed, beginning with lexical items.

We can think of the first operation as essentially a list of lexical items. In traditional terms, this list, called the lexicon, is the list of "exceptions", arbitrary associations of sound and meaning and particular choices among the morphological properties made available by the faculty of language. I will keep here to what are traditionally called "inflectional features", which indicate that nouns and verbs are plural or singular, that nouns have nominative or accusative case while verbs have tense and aspect, and so on. These inflectional features turn out to play a central role in computation.

Optimal design would introduce no new features in the course of computation. There should be no phrasal units or bar levels, hence no phrase structure rules or X-bar theory; and no indices, hence no binding theory using indices. We also try to show that no structural relations are invoked other than those forced by legibility conditions or induced in some natural way by the computation itself. In the first category we have such properties as adjacency at the phonetic level, and at the semantic level, argument structure and quantifier-variable relations. In the second category, we have elementary relations between two syntactic objects joined together in the course of computation; the relation holding between one of these and the parts of the other is a fair candidate; it is, in essence, the relation of c-command, as Samuel Epstein has pointed out, a notion that plays a central role throughout language design and has been regarded as highly unnatural, though it falls into place in a natural way from this perspective. Similarly, we can use very local relations between features; the most local, hence the best, are those that are internal to word-like units constructed from lexical items. But we exclude government and proper government, binding relations internal to the derivation of expressions, and a variety of other relations and interactions.

As anyone familiar with recent work will be aware, there is ample empirical evidence to support the opposite conclusion throughout. Worse yet, a core assumption of the work within the Principles-and-Parameters framework, and its fairly impressive achievements, is that everything I have just proposed is false - that language is highly "imperfect" in these respects, as might well be expected. So it is no small task to show that such apparatus is eliminable as unwanted descriptive technology; or even better, that descriptive and explanatory force are extended if such "excess baggage" is shed. Nevertheless, I think that work of the past few years suggests that these conclusions, which seemed out of the question a few years ago, are at least plausible, quite possibly correct.

Languages plainly differ, and we want to know how. One respect is in choice of sounds, which vary within a certain range. Another is in the association of sound and meaning, essentially arbitrary. These are straightforward and need not detain us. More interesting is the fact that languages differ in inflectional systems: case systems, for example. We find that these are fairly rich in Latin, even more so in Sanskrit or Finnish, but minimal in English and invisible in Chinese. Or so it appears; considerations of explanatory adequacy suggest that here too appearance may be misleading; and in fact, recent work indicates that these systems vary much less than the surface forms suggest. Chinese and English, for example, may have the same case system as Latin, but a different phonetic realization, though the effects show up in other ways. Furthermore, it seems that much of the variety of language can be reduced to properties of inflectional systems.

If this is correct, then language variation is located in a narrow part of the lexicon.

Inflectional features differ from those that constitute lexical items. Consider any word, say the verb "see." Its phonetic and semantic properties are intrinsic to it, as is its lexical category as a verb.

But it may appear with either singular or plural inflection. Typically a verb has one value along this inflectional dimension, but it is not part of its intrinsic nature. The same is true fairly generally of the substantive categories noun, verb, adjective, sometimes called "open classes" because new elements can be added to them rather freely, in contrast to inflectional systems, which are fixed early in language acquisition. There are second-order complexities and refinements, but the basic distinction between the substantive categories and the inflectional devices is reasonably clear not only in language structure, but also in acquisition and pathology, and recently there is even some suggestive work on brain imaging. We can put the complications to the side, and adopt an idealization that distinguishes sharply between substantive lexical items like "see" and "house", and the inflectional features that are associated with them but are not part of their intrinsic nature.

Legibility conditions impose a three-way division among the features assembled into lexical items:

(1) semantic features, interpreted at the semantic interface
(2) phonetic features, interpreted at the phonetic interface
(3) features that are not interpreted at either interface

We assume that phonetic and semantic features are interpretable uniformly in all languages: the external systems at the interface are invariant; again, a standard assumption, though by no means an obvious one.

Independently, features are subdivided into the "formal features" that are used by the computatational operations that construct the derivation of an expression, and others that are not accessed directly, but just "carried along." A natural principle that would sharply restrict language variation is that only inflectional properties are formal features: only these are accessed by the computational processes. That may well be correct, an important matter that I will only be able to touch on briefly and inadequately. A still stronger condition would be that all inflectional features are formal, accessible in principle by the computational processes, and still stronger conditions can be imposed, topics that are now under active investigation, often pursuing sharply different intuitions.

One standard and shared assumption, which seems correct and principled, is that phonetic features are neither semantic nor formal: they receive no interpretation at the semantic interface and are not accessed by computational operations. Again, there are second-order complexities, but we may put them aside. We can think of phonetic features as being "stripped away" from the derivation by an operation that applies to the syntactic object already formed. This operation activates the phonological component of the grammar, which converts the syntactic object to a phonetic form.

With the phonetic features stripped away, the derivation continues, but using the stripped-down residue lacking phonetic features, which is converted to the semantic representation. One natural principle of optimal design is that operations can apply anywhere, including this one. Assuming so, we can make a distinction between the OVERT operations that apply before the phonetic features are stripped away, and COVERT operations that carry the residue on to semantic representation. Covert operations have no effect on the sound of an expression, only on what it means.

Another property of optimal design is that the computation from lexical items to semantic representation is uniform: the same operations should apply throughout, whether covert or overt. There seems to be an important sense in which that is true. Although covert and overt operations have different properties, with interesting empirical consequences, these distinctions may be reducible to legibility conditions at the sensorimotor interface. If so, they are "extrinsic" to core language design in a fundamental way. I'll try to explain what I mean by that later on.

We assume, then, that in a particular language, features are assembled into lexical items, and then the fixed and invariant computational operations construct semantic representations from these in a uniform manner. At some point in the derivation, the phonological component accesses the derivation, stripping away the phonetic features and converting the syntactic object to phonetic form, while the residue proceeds to semantic representation by covert operations. We also assume that the formal features are inflectional, not substantive, so not only the phonetic features but also the substantive semantic features are inaccessible to the computation. The computational operations are therefore very restricted and elementary in character, and the apparent complexity and variety of languages should reduce essentially to inflectional properties.

Though the substantive semantic features are not formal, formal features may be semantic, with an intrinsic meaning. Take the inflectional property of number. A noun or a verb may be singular or plural, an inflectional property, not part of its intrinsic nature. For nouns, the number assigned has a semantic interpretion: the sentences "He sees the book" and "He sees the books" have different meanings. For the verb, however, the number has no semantic interpretation; it adds nothing that is not already determined by the expression in which it appears, in this case, its grammatical subject "He." On the surface, what I just said seems untrue, for example, in sentences that seem to lack a subject, a common phenomenon in the Romance languages and many others. But a closer look gives strong reason to believe that subject is actually there, heard by the mind though not by the ear.

The importance of the distinction between interpretable and uninterpretable formal features was not recognized until very recently, in the course of pursuit of the minimalist program. It seems to be central to language design.

In a perfectly designed language, each feature would be semantic or phonetic, not merely a device to create a position or to facilitate computation. If so, there would be no uninterpretable features. But as we have just seen, that that is too strong a requirement. Nominative and accusative case features violate the condition, for example. These have no interpretation at the semantic interface, and need not be expressed at the phonetic level. The same is true of inflectional properties of verbs and adjectives, and there are others as well, which are not so obvious on the surface. We can therefore consider a weaker though still quite strong requirement approaching optimal design: each feature is either semantic or is accessible to the phonological component, which may (and sometimes does) use the feature in question to determine the phonetic representation. In particular, formal features are either interpretable or accessible to the phonological component. Case features are uninterpretable but may have phonetic effects, though they need not, as in Chinese and generally English, or even sometimes in languages with more visible inflection, like Latin. The same is true of other uninterpretable formal features. Let us assume (controversially) that this weaker condition holds. We are left with one imperfection of language design: the existence of uninterpretable formal features, which we now assume to be inflectional features only.

There seems to be a second and more dramatic imperfection in language design: the "displacement property" that is a pervasive aspect of language: phrases are interpreted as if they were in a different position in the expression, where similar items sometimes do appear and are interpreted in terms of natural local relations. Take the sentence "Clinton seems to have been elected." We understand the relation of "elect" and "Clinton" as we do when they are locally related in the sentence "It seems that they elected Clinton": "Clinton" is the direct object of "elect", in traditional terms, though "displaced" to the position of subject of "seems." The subject "Clinton" and the verb "seems" agree in inflectional features in this case, but have no semantic relation; the semantic relation of the subject is to the remote verb "elect."

We now have two "imperfections": uninterpretable formal features, and the displacement property. On the assumption of optimal design, we would expect them to reduce to the same cause, and that seems to be the case: uninterpretable formal features provide the mechanism that implements the displacement property.

The displacement property is never built into the symbolic systems that are designed for special purposes, called "languages" or "formal languages" in a metaphoric usage that has been highly misleading, I think: "the language of arithmetic", or "computer languages", or "the languages of science." These systems also have no inflectional systems, hence no uninterpreted formal features. Displacement and inflection are special properties of human language, among the many that are ignored when symbolic systems are designed for other purposes, free to disregard the legibility conditions imposed on human language by the architecture of the mind/brain.

Why language should have the displacement property is an interesting question, which has been discussed for many years without resolution. One early proposal is that the property reflects processing conditions. If so, it may in part be reducible to properties of the articulatory and perceptual apparatus, hence forced by legibility conditions at the phonetic interface. I suspect that another part of the reason may have to do with phenomena that have been described in terms of surface structure interpretation: topic-comment, specif icily, new and old information, the agentive force that we find even in displaced position, and so on. These seem to require particular positions in temporal linear order, typically at the edge of some construction. If so, then the displacement property also reflects legibility conditions at the semantic interface; it is motivated by interpretive requirements that are externally imposed by our systems of thought, which have these special properties, so it appears. These questions are currently being investigated in interesting ways, which I cannot go into here.

From the origins of generative grammar, the computational operations were assumed to be of two kinds; phrase structure rules that form larger syntactic objects from lexical items, and transformational rules that express the displacement property. Both have traditional roots; their first moderately clear formulation was in the influential Port Royal grammar of 1660. But it was quickly found that the operations differ substantially from what had been supposed, with unsuspected variety and complexity - conclusions that had to be false for the reasons I discussed yesterday. The research program sought to show that the complexity and variety are only apparent, and that the two kinds of rules can be reduced to simpler form. A "perfect" solution to the problem of phrase structure rules would be to eliminate them entirely in favor of the irreducible operation that takes two objects already formed and attaches one to the other, forming a larger object with just the properties of the target of attachment: the operation we can call Merge. That goal may be attainable, recent work indicates, in a system called "bare phrase structure."

Assuming so, the optimal computational procedure consists of the operation Merge and operations to express the displacement property: transformational operations or some counterpart. The second of the two parallel endeavors sought to reduce these to the simplest form, though unlike phrase structure rules, they seem to be ineliminable. The end result was the thesis that for a core set of phenomena, there is just a single operation Move - basically, move anything anywhere, with no properties specific to languages or particular constructions. How the operation Move applies is determined by general principles of language interacting with the specific parameter choices that determine a particular language.

The operation Merge takes two distinct objects X and Y and attaches Y to X.

The operation Move takes a single object X and an object Y that is part of X, and merges Y to X. In both cases, the new unit has the properties of the target, X. The object formed by the operation Move includes two occurrences of the moved element Y: in technical terms, the CHAIN consisting of these two occurrences of Y. The occurrence in the original position is called THE TRACE. There is strong evidence that both positions enter into semantic interpretation in many ways. Both, for example, enter into scopal relations and binding relations with anaphoric elements, reflexives and pronouns.

When longer chains are constructed by successive steps of movement, the intermediate positions also enter into such relations. To determine just how this works is a very live research topic, which, on minimalist assumptions, should be restricted to interpretive operations at the semantic interface; again, a highly controversial thesis.

The next problem is to show that uninterpretable formal features are indeed the mechanism that implements the displacement property, so that the two basic imperfections of the computational system reduce to one. If it turns out further that the displacement property is motivated by legibility conditions imposed by external systems, as I just suggested, then the two imperfections are eliminated completely and language design turns out to be optimal after all: uninterpreted formal features are required as a mechanism to satisfy legibility conditions imposed by the general architecture of the mind/brain, properties of the processing apparatus and the systems of thought.

The unification of uninterpretable formal features and the displacement property is based on quite simple ideas, but to explain them coherently would go beyond the scope of these remarks. The basic intuition rests on an empirical fact coupled with a design principle.

The fact is that: uninterprefcable formal features have to be erased for the expression to be legible at the semantic Interface; the design principle Is that erasure requires a local relation between the offending feature and a matching feature. Typically these two features are remote from one another, for reasons having to do with semantic interpretation.

For example, in the sentence "Clinton seems to have been elected", semantic interpretation requires that "elect" and "Clinton" be locally related in the phrase "elect Clinton" for the construction to be properly interpreted, as if the sentence were actually "seems to have been elected Clinton". The main verb of the sentence, "seems", has inflectional features that are uninterpretable, as we have seen: its number and person, for example. These offending features of "seems" therefore have to be erased in a local relation with the matching features of the phrase "Clinton." The matching features are attracted by the offending features of the main verb "seems", which are then erased under local matching. The traditional descriptive term for the phenomenon we are looking at is "agreement", but we have to give it explicit content, and as usual, unexpected properties come to the fore when we do so.

If this can be worked out properly, we conclude that a particular language consists of a lexicon, a phonological system, and two computational operations: Merge and Attract. Attract is driven by the principle that uninterpretable formal features must be erased in a local relation, and something similar extends to Merge.

Note that only the FEATURES of "Clinton" are attracted; we still have not dealt with the overtly visible displacement property, the fact that the full phrase in which the features appear, the word "Clinton" in this case, is carried along with the formal inflectional features that erase the target features. Why does the full phrase move, not just the features? The natural idea is that the reasons have to do with the poverty of the sensorimotor system, which is unable to "pronounce" or "hear" isolated features separated from the words of which they are a part. Hence in such sentences as "Clinton seems to have been elected", the full phrase "Clinton" moves along as a reflex of the attraction of the formal features of "Clinton." In the sentence "an unpopular candidate seems to have been elected", the full phrase "an unpopular candidate" is carried along as a reflex of the attraction of the formal features of "candidate." There are much more complex examples.

Suppose that the phonological component is inactivated. Then the features alone raise, and alongside of the sentence "an unpopular candidate seems to have been elected", with overt displacement, we have the corresponding expression "seems to have been elected an unpopular candidate"; here the remote phrase "an unpopular candidate" agrees with the verb "seems", which means that its features have been attracted to a local relation with "seem" while leaving the rest of the phrase behind.

Such inactivation of the phonological component in fact takes place. For other reasons, we do not see exactly this pattern with definite noun phrases like "Clinton", but it is standard with indefinite ones such as "an unpopular candidate." Thus we have, side by side, the two sentences "an unpopular candidate seems to have been elected" and "seems to have been elected an unpopular candidate." The latter expression is normal in many languages, including most of the Romance languages.

English, French, and other languages have them them too, though it is necessary for other reasons to introduce a semantically empty element as apparent subject; In English, the word "there", so that we have the sentence "there seems to have been elected an unpopular candidate." It is also necessary in English, though not in closely related languages, to carry out an inversion of order, for quite interesting reasons that hold much more generally for the language; hence what we actually say in English is the sentence "there seems to have been an unpopular candidate elected."

Taking a slightly closer look, suppose that X is a feature that is uninterpretable and therefore must erase. It therefore attracts the closest feature Y that matches it. Y attaches to X, and the attractor X erases. Y will also erase if uninterpretable, and will remain if it is interpretable. This is the source of successive-cyclic movement, among other properties.

Note that we have to explain what we mean by "closest", another question with interesting ramifications. For covert movement, that is all there is to say: features attract, and erase when they must. Covert operations should be pure feature attraction, with no visible movement of phrases, though with effects on such matters as agreement, control and binding, again a topic that been studied in the past few years, with some interesting results. If the sound system has not been inactivated, we have the reflex that raises a full phrase, placing it as close as possible to the attracted feature Y; in technical terms, this translates to movement of the phrase to the specifier of the head to which Y has attached. The operation is a generalized version of what has been called "pied-piping" in the technical literature. The proposal opens very substantial and quite difficult empirical problems, which have only been very partially examined. The basic problem is to show that the choice of the phrase that is moved is determined by other properties of the language, within minimalist assumptions. Insofar as these problems are solved, we have a mechanism that implements core aspects of the displacement property in a natural way.

In a large range of cases, the apparent variety and complexity is superficial, reducing to minor parametric differences and a straightforward legibility condition: uninterpretable formal features must be erased, and on assumptions of optimal design, erased in a local relation with a matching feature. The displacement property that is required for semantic interpretation at the interface follows as a reflex, induced by the primitive character of modes of sensory interpretation.

Combining these various ideas, some still highly speculative, we can envisage both a motivation and a trigger for the displacement property.

Note that these have to be distinguished. An embryologist studying the development of the eye may take note of the fact that for an organism to survive, it would be helpful for the lens to contain something that protects it from damage and something that refracts light; and looking further, would discover that crystallin proteins have both these properties and also seem to be ubiquitous components of the lens of the eye, showing up on independent evolutionary paths. The first property has to do with "motivation" or "functional design", the second with the trigger that yields the right functional design. There is an indirect and important relation between them, but it would be an error to confound them. Thus a biologist accepting all of this would not offer the functional design property as the mechanism of embryological development of the eye.

Similarly, we do not want to confound functional motivations for properties of language with the specific mechanisms that implement them. We do not want to confound the fact that the displacement property is required by external systems with the mechanisms of the operations Attract and its reflex.

The phonological component is responsible for other respects in which the design of language is "imperfect." It includes operations beyond those that are required for any language-like system, and these introduce new features and elements that are not in lexical items: intonational features, narrow phonetics, perhaps even temporal order, in a version of ideas developed by Richard Kayne. "Imperfections" in this component of language would not be very surprising: for one reason, because direct evidence is available to the language learner; for another, because of special properties of sensorimotor systems. If the overt manifestation of the displacement property also reduces to special features of the sensorimotor system, as I just suggested, then a large range of imperfections may have to do with the need to "externalize" language. If we could communicate by telepathy, they would not arise. The phonological component is in a certain sense "extrinsic" to language, and the locus of a good part of its imperfection, so one might speculate.

At this point, we are moving to questions that go far beyond anything I can try to discuss here. To the extent that the many problems fall into place, it will follow that language is a good - maybe very good - solution to the conditions imposed by the general architecture of the mind/brain, an unexpected conclusion if true, hence an intriguing one. And like the Principles-and-Parameters approach more generally, whether it turns out to be on the right track or not, it is currently serving to stimulate a good deal of empirical research with sometimes surprising results, and a host of new and challenging problems, which is all that one can ask.

Consciousness

John R. Searle

Abstract
Until very recently, most neurobiologists did not regard consciousness as a suitable topic for scientific investigation. This reluctance was based on certain philosophical mistakes, primarily the mistake of supposing that the subjectivity of consciousness made it beyond the reach of an objective science. Once we see that science is a biological phenomenon like any other, then it can be investigated neurobiologically. Consciousness is entirely caused by neurobiological processes and is realized in brain structures. The essential trait of consciousness that we need to explain is unified qualitative subjectivity. Consciousness thus differs from other biological phenomena in that it has a subjective or first-person ontology, but this subjective ontology does not prevent us from having an epistemically objective science of consciousness. We need to overcome the philosophical tradition that treats the mental and the physical as two distinct metaphysical realms. Two common approaches to consciousness are those that adopt the building block model, according to which any conscious field is made of its various parts, and the unified field model, according to which we should try to explain the unified character of subjective states of consciousness. These two approaches are discussed and reasons are given for preferring the unified field theory to the building block model. Some relevant research on consciousness involves the subjects of blindsight, the split-brain experiments, binocular rivalry, and gestalt switching.

Resistance to the Problem

As recently as two decades ago there was little interest among neuroscientists, philosophers, psychologists and cognitive

In Search of a Language for the Mind-Brain, ed. Saleemi, Bohn and Gjedde, *The Dolphin* 33 © 2005 by Aarhus University Press, Denmark. ISBN 87 7934 005 9.

scientists generally in the problem of consciousness. Reasons for the resistance to the problem varied from discipline to discipline. Philosophers had turned to the analysis of language, psychologists had become convinced that a scientific psychology must be a science of behavior, and cognitive scientists took their research program to be the discovery of the computer programs in the brain that, they thought, would explain cognition. It seemed especially puzzling that neuroscientists should be reluctant to deal with the problem of consciousness, because one of the chief functions of the brain is to cause and sustain conscious states. Studying the brain without studying consciousness would be like studying the stomach without studying digestion, or studying genetics without studying the inheritance of traits. When I first got interested in this problem seriously and tried to discuss it with brain scientists, I found that most of them were not interested in the question.

The reasons for this resistance were various but they mostly boiled down to two. First, many neuroscientists felt—and some still do — that consciousness is not a suitable subject for neuroscientific investigation at all. A legitimate brain science can study the microanatomy of the Purkinje cell, or attempt to discover new neurotransmitters, but consciousness seems too airy-fairy and touchy-feely to be a real scientific subject. Others did not exclude consciousness from scientific investigation, but they had a second reason: "We are not ready" to tackle the problem of consciousness. They may be right about that, but my guess is that a lot of people in the early 1950s thought we were not ready to tackle the problem of the molecular basis of life and heredity. They were wrong; and I suggest for the current question, the best way to get ready to deal with a research problem may be to try to solve it.

There were, of course, famous earlier twentieth century exceptions to the general reluctance to deal with consciousness, and their work has been valuable. I am thinking in particular of the work of Sir Arthur Sherrington, Roger Sperry, and Sir John Eccles.

Whatever was the case 20 years ago, today many serious researchers are attempting to tackle the problem. Among neuroscientists who have written recent books about consciousness are Cotterill (1998), Crick (1994), Damasio (1999), Edelman (1989, 1992), Freeman (1995), Gazzaniga (1988), Greenfield (1995), Hobson (1999), Libet (1993, and Weiskrantz (1997). As far as I can tell, the race to solve the problem of consciousness is already on. My aim here is not to try to survey this literature but to characterize some of the neurobiological problems of consciousness from a philosophical point of view.

Consciousness as a Biological Problem
What exactly is the neurobiological problem of consciousness? The problem, in its crudest terms, is this: How exactly do brain processes cause conscious states and how exactly are those states realized in brain structures? So stated, this problem naturally breaks down into a number of smaller but still large problems: What exactly are the neurobiological correlates of conscious states (NCC), and which of those correlates are actually causally responsible for the production of consciousness? What are the principles according to which biological phenomena such as neuron firings can bring about subjective states of sentience or awareness? How do those principles relate to the already well-understood principles of biology? Can we explain consciousness with the existing theoretical apparatus or do we need some revolutionary new theoretical concepts to explain it? Is consciousness localized in certain regions of the brain or is it a global phenomenon? If it is confined to certain regions, which ones? Is it correlated with specific anatomical features, such as specific types of neurons, or is it to be explained functionally with a variety of anatomical correlates? What is the right level for explaining consciousness? Is it the level of neurons and synapses, as most researchers seem to think, or do we have to go to higher functional levels such as neuronal maps (Edelman 1989, 1992), or whole clouds of neurons (Freeman 1995), or are all of these levels much too high and we have to go below the level of neurons and synapses to the level of the microtubules (Penrose 1994 and Hameroff 1998a, 1998b)? Or do we have to think much more globally in terms of Fourier transforms and holography (Pribram 1976, 1991, 1999)?

As stated, this cluster of problems sounds similar to any other such set of problems in biology or in the sciences in general. It sounds like the problem concerning microorganisms: How, exactly, do they cause disease symptoms and how are those symptoms manifested in patients? Or the problem in genetics: By what mechanisms exactly does the genetic structure of the zygote produce the phenotypical traits of the mature organism? In the end I think that is the right way to think of the problem of consciousness—it is a biological problem like any other, because consciousness is a biological phenomenon in exactly the same sense as digestion, growth, or photosynthesis. But unlike other problems in biology, there is a persistent series of philosophical problems that surround the problem of consciousness and before addressing some current research I would like to address some of these problems.

Identifying the Target: The Definition of Consciousness

One often hears it said that "consciousness" is frightfully hard to define. But if we are talking about a definition in common sense terms, sufficient to identify the target of the investigation, as opposed to a precise scientific definition of the sort that typically comes at the end of a scientific investigation, then the word does not seem to me hard to define. Here is the definition: Consciousness consists of inner, qualitative, subjective states and processes of sentience or awareness. Consciousness, so defined, begins when we wake in the morning from a dreamless sleep - and continues until we fall asleep again, die, go into a coma or otherwise become "unconscious." It includes all of the enormous variety of the awareness that we think of as characteristic of our waking life. It includes everything from feeling a pain, to perceiving objects visually, to states of anxiety and depression, to working out cross word puzzles, playing chess, trying to remember your aunt's phone number, arguing about politics, or to just wishing you were somewhere else. Dreams on this definition are a form of consciousness, though of course they are in many respects quite different from waking consciousness.

This definition is not universally accepted and the word consciousness is used in a variety of other ways. Some authors use the word only to refer to states of selfconsciousness, i.e. the consciousness that humans and some primates have of themselves as agents. Some use it to refer to the second-order mental *states about other mental states;* so according to this definition, a pain would not be a conscious state, but worrying about a pain would be a conscious state. Some use "consciousness" behavioristically to refer to any form of complex intelligent behavior. It is, of course, open to anyone to use any word anyway he likes, and we can always redefine consciousness as a technical term. Nonetheless, there is a genuine phenomenon of consciousness in the ordinary sense, however we choose to name it; and it is that phenomenon that I am trying to identify now, because I believe it is the proper target of the investigation.

Consciousness has distinctive features that we need to explain. Because I believe that some, not all, of the problems of consciousness are going to have a neurobiological solution, what follows is a shopping list of what a neurobiological account of consciousness should explain.

The Essential Feature of Consciousness: The Combination of Qualitativeness, Subjectivity and Unity

Consciousness has three aspects that make it different from other biological phenomena, and indeed different from other phenomena in the natural world. These three aspects are qualitativeness, subjectivity, and unity. I used to think that for investigative purposes we could treat them as three distinct features, but because they are logically interrelated, I now think it best to treat them together, as different aspects of the same feature. They are not separate because the first implies the second, and the second implies the third. I discuss them in order.

Qualitativeness

Every conscious state has a certain qualitative feel to it, and you can see this clearly if you consider examples. The experience of tasting beer is very different from hearing Beethoven's Ninth Symphony, and both of those have a different qualitative character from smelling a rose or seeing a sunset. These examples illustrate the different qualitative features of conscious experiences. One way to put this point is to say that for every conscious experience there is something that it feels like, or something that it is like to have that conscious experience. Nagel (1974) made this point over two decades ago when he pointed out that if bats are conscious, then there is something that "it is like" to be a bat. This distinguishes consciousness from other features of the world, because in this sense, for a nonconscious entity such as a car or a brick there is nothing that "it is like" to be that entity. Some philosophers describe this feature of consciousness with the word qualia, and they say there is a special problem of qualia. I am reluctant to adopt this usage, because it seems to imply that there are two separate problems, the problem of consciousness and the problem of qualia. But as I understand these terms, "qualia" is just a plural name for conscious states. Because "consciousness" and "qualia" are coextensive, there seems no point in introducing a special term. Some people think that qualia are characteristic only of perceptual experiences, such as seeing colors and having sensations such as pains, but that there is no qualitative character to thinking. As I understand these terms, that is wrong. Even conscious thinking has a qualitative feel to it. There is something it is like to think that two plus two equals four. There is no way to describe it except by saying that it is the character of thinking consciously "two plus two equals four". But if you believe there is no qualitative character to thinking that, then try to think the same thought in a language you do not know well. If I think in French "deux et deux fait quatre," I find that it feels quite different. Or try thinking, more painfully, "two plus two equals one hundred eighty-seven." Once again I think you will agree that these conscious thoughts have different characters. However, the point must be trivial; that is, whether or not conscious thoughts are qualia must follow from our definition of qualia. As I am using the term, thoughts definitely are qualia.

Subjectivity
Conscious states only exist when they are experienced by some human or animal subject. In that sense, they are essentially subjective. I used to treat subjectivity and qualitativeness as distinct features, but it now seems to me that properly

understood, qualitativeness implies subjectivity, because in order for there to be a qualitative feel to some event, there must be some subject that experiences the event. No subjectivity, no experience. Even if more than one subject experiences a similar phenomenon, say two people listening to the same concert, all the same, the qualitative experience can only exist as experienced by some subject or subjects. And even if the different token experiences are qualitatively identical, that is they all exemplify the same type, nonetheless each token experience can only exist if the subject of that experience has it. Because conscious states are subjective in this sense, they have what I will call a first-person ontology, as opposed to the third-person ontology of mountains and molecules, which can exist even if no living creatures exist. Subjective conscious states have a first-person ontology ("ontology" here means mode of existence) because they only exist when they are experienced by some human or animal agent. They are experienced by some "I" that has the experience, and it is in that sense that they have a first-person ontology.

Unity

All conscious experiences at any given point in an agent's life come as part of one unified conscious field. If I am sitting at my desk looking out the window, I do not just see the sky above and the brook below shrouded by the trees, and at the same time feel the pressure of my body against the chair, the shirt against my back, and the aftertaste of coffee in my mouth, rather I experience all of these as part of a single unified conscious field. This unity of any state of qualitative subjectivity has important consequences for a scientific study of consciousness. I say more about them later on. At present I just want to call attention to the fact that the unity is already implicit in subjectivity and qualitativeness for the following reason: If you try to imagine that my conscious state is broken into 17 parts, what you imagine is not a single conscious subject with 17 different conscious states but rather 17 different centers of consciousness. A conscious state, in short, is by definition unified, and the unity will follow from the subjectivity and the qualitativeness, because there is no way you could have subjectivity and qualitativeness except with that particular form of unity.

There are two areas of current research where the aspect of unity is especially important. These are first, the study of the split-brain patients by Gazzaniga, (1998) and others (Gazzaniga, Bogen, and Sperry 1962, 1963), and second, the study of the binding problem by a number of contemporary researchers. The interest of the split-brain patients is that both the anatomical and the behavioral evidence suggest that in these patients there are two centers of consciousness that after commissurotomy are communicating with each other imperfectly. They seem to have, so to speak, two conscious minds inside one skull.

The interest of the binding problem is that it looks like this problem might give us in microcosm a way of studying the nature of consciousness, because just as the visual system binds all of the different stimulus inputs into a single unified visual percept, so the entire brain somehow unites all of the variety of our different stimulus inputs into a single unified conscious experience. Several researchers have explored the role of synchronized neuron firings in the range of 40hz to account for the capacity of different perceptual systems to bind the diverse stimuli of anatomically distinct neurons into a single perceptual experience. (Llinas 1990, Llinas and Pare 1991, Llinas and Ribary 1993, Llinas and Ribary, 1992, Singer 1993, 1995, Singer and Gray, 1995,) For example in the case of vision, anatomically separate neurons specialized for such things as line, angle and color all contribute to a single, unified, conscious visual experience of an object. Crick (1994) extended the proposal for the binding problem to a general hypothesis about the NCC. He put forward a tentative hypothesis that the NCC consists of synchronized neuron firings in the general range of 40 Hz in various networks in the thalamocortical system, specifically in connections between the thalamus and layers four and six of the cortex.

This kind of instantaneous unity has to be distinguished from the organized unification of conscious sequences that we get from short term or iconic memory. For nonpathological forms of consciousness at least some memory is essential in order that the conscious sequence across time can come in an organized fashion.

For example, when I speak a sentence I have to be able to remember the beginning of the sentence at the time I get to the end if I am to produce coherent speech. Whereas instantaneous unity is essential to, and is part of, the definition of consciousness, organized unity across time is essential to the healthy functioning of the conscious organism, but it is not necessary for the very existence of conscious subjectivity.

This combined feature of qualitative, unified subjectivity is the essence of consciousness and it, more than anything else, is what makes consciousness different from other phenomena studied by the natural sciences. The problem is to explain how brain processes, which are objective third person biological, chemical and electrical processes, produce subjective states of feeling and thinking. How does the brain get us over the hump, so to speak, from events in the synaptic cleft and the ion channels to conscious thoughts and feelings? If you take seriously this combined feature as the target of explanation, I believe you get a different sort of research project from what is currently the most influential. Most neurobiologists take what I will call the building block approach: Find the NCC for specific elements in the conscious field such as the experience of color, and then construct the whole field out of such building blocks. Another approach, which I will call the unified field approach, would take the research problem to be one of explaining how the brain produces a unified field of subjectivity to start with. On the unified field approach, there are no building blocks, rather there are just modifications of the already existing field of qualitative subjectivity. I say more about this later.

Some philosophers and neuroscientists think we can never have an explanation of subjectivity: We can never explain why warm things feel warm and red things look red. To these skeptics there is a simple answer: We know it happens. We know that brain processes cause all of our inner qualitative, subjective thoughts and feelings. Because we know that it happens we ought to try to figure out how it happens. Perhaps in the end we will fail but we cannot assume the impossibility of success before we try.

Many philosophers and scientists also think that the subjectivity of conscious states makes it impossible to have a strict science of consciousness. For, they argue, if science is by definition objective, and consciousness is by definition subjective, it follows that there cannot be a science of consciousness. This argument is fallacious. It commits the fallacy of ambiguity over the terms objective and subjective. Here is the ambiguity: We need to distinguish two different senses of the objective-subjective distinction. In one sense, the epistemic sense ("epistemic" here means having to do with knowledge), science is indeed objective. Scientists seek truths that are equally accessible to any competent observer and that are independent of the feelings and attitudes of the experimenters in question. An example of an epistemically objective claim would be "Bill Clinton weighs 210 pounds". An example of an epistemically subjective claim would be "Bill Clinton is a good president". The first is objective because its truth or falsity is settleable in a way that is independent of the feelings and attitudes of the investigators. The second is subjective because it is not so settleable. But there is another sense of the objective-subjective distinction, and that is the ontological sense ("ontological" here means having to do with existence). Some entities, such as pains, tickles, and itches, have a subjective mode of existence, in the sense that they exist only as experienced by a conscious subject. Others, such as mountains, molecules and tectonic plates have an objective mode of existence, in the sense that their existence does not depend on any consciousness. The point of making this distinction is to call attention to the fact that the scientific requirement of epistemic objectivity does not preclude ontological subjectivity as a domain of investigation. There is no reason whatever why we cannot have an objective science of pain, even though pains only exist when they are felt by conscious agents. The ontological subjectivity of the feeling of pain does not preclude an epistemically objective science of pain. Though many philosophers and neuroscientists are reluctant to think of subjectivity as a proper domain of scientific investigation, in actual practice, we work on it all the time. Any neurology textbook will contain extensive discussions of the etiology and treatment of such ontologically subjective states as pains and anxieties.

Some Other Features
To keep this list short, I mention some other features of consciousness only briefly.

Feature 2: Intentionality
Most important, conscious states typically have "intentionality," that property of mental states by which they are directed at or about objects and states of affairs in the world. Philosophers use the word intentionality- not just for "intending" in the ordinary sense but for any mental phenomena at all that have referential content. According to this usage, beliefs, hopes, intentions, fears, desires and perceptions all are intentional. So if I have a belief I must have a belief about something. If I have a normal visual experience, it must seem to me that I am actually seeing something, etc. Not all conscious states are intentional and not all intentionality is conscious; for example, undirected anxiety lacks intentionality, and the beliefs a man has even when he is asleep lack consciousness then and there. But I think it is obvious that many of the important evolutionary functions of consciousness are intentional: For example, an animal has conscious feelings of hunger and thirst, engages in conscious perceptual discriminations, embarks on conscious intentional actions, and consciously recognizes both friend and foe. All of these are conscious intentional phenomena and all are essential for biological survival. A general neurobiological account of consciousness will explain the intentionality of conscious states. For example, an account of color vision will naturally explain the capacity of agents to make color discriminations.

Feature 3: The Distinction between Center and Periphery of Attention
It is a remarkable fact that within my conscious field at any given time I can shift my *attention* at will from one aspect to another. So for example, right now I am not paying any attention to the pressure of the shoes on my feet or the feeling of the shirt on my

neck. But I can shift my attention to them any time I want. There
is already a fair amount of useful work done on attention.

Feature 4: All Human Conscious Experiences are in Some Mood or Other

There is always a certain flavor to one's conscious states, always
an answer to the question "How are you feeling?". The moods do
not necessarily have names. Right now I am not especially elated
or annoyed, not ecstatic or depressed, not even just blah. But all
the same I will become acutely aware of my mood if there is a
dramatic change, if I receive some extremely good or bad news,
for example. Moods are not the same as emotions, though the
mood we are in will predispose us to having certain emotions.

We are, by the way, closer to having pharmacological control
of moods with such drugs as Prozac than we are to having control
of other internal features of consciousness.

Feature 5: All Conscious States Come to Us in the Pleasure/Unpleasure Dimension

For any total conscious experience there is always an answer to
the question of whether it was pleasant, painful, unpleasant,
neutral, etc. The pleasure/unpleasure feature is not the same as
mood, though of course some moods are more pleasant than
others.

Feature 6: Gestalt Structure

The brain has a remarkable capacity to organize very degenerate
perceptual stimuli into coherent conscious perceptual forms. I
can, for example, recognize a face, or a car, on the basis of very
limited stimuli. The best-known examples of Gestalt structures
come from the researches of the Gestalt psychologists.

Feature 7: Familiarity

There is in varying degrees a sense of familiarity that pervades
our conscious experiences. Even if I see a house I have never seen
before, I still recognize it as a house; it is of a form and structure
that is familiar to me. Surrealist painters try to break this sense of
the familiarity and ordinariness of our experiences, but even in

surrealist paintings the drooping watch still looks like a watch, and the three-headed dog still looks like a dog.

One could continue this list, and I have done so in other writings (Searle 1992). The point now is to get a minimal shopping list of the features that we want a neurobiology of consciousness to explain. In order to look for a causal explanation we need to know what the effects are that need explanation. Before examining some current research projects, we need to clear more of the ground.

The Traditional Mind-Body Problem and How to Avoid it

The confusion about objectivity and subjectivity I mentioned earlier is just the tip of the iceberg of the traditional mind-body problem. Though ideally I think scientists would be better off if they just ignored this problem, the fact is that they are as much victims of the philosophical traditions as anyone else, and many scientists, like many philosophers, are still in the grip of the traditional categories of mind and body, mental and physical, dualism and materialism, etc. This is not the place for a detailed discussion of the mind-body problem, but I need to say a few words about it so that, in the discussion that follows, we can avoid the confusions that it has engendered.

The simplest form of the mind body problem is this: What exactly is the relation of consciousness to the brain? There are two parts to this problem, a philosophical part and a scientific part. I have already been assuming a simple solution to the philosophical part. The solution, I believe, is consistent with everything we know about biology and about how the world works. It is this: Consciousness and other sorts of mental phenomena are caused by neurobiological processes in the brain, and they are realized in the structure of the brain. In a word, the conscious mind is caused by brain processes and is itself a higher-level feature of the brain.

The philosophical part is relatively easy but the scientific part is much harder. How, exactly, do brain processes cause consciousness and how, exactly, is consciousness realized in the brain? I want to be very clear about the philosophical part, because it is not possible to approach the scientific question intelligently if the philosophical issues are unclear. Notice two features of the philosophical solution. First, the relationship of brain mechanisms to consciousness is one of causation. Processes in the brain cause our conscious experiences. Second, this does not force us to any kind of dualism because the form of causation is bottom-up, and the resulting effect is simply a higherlevel feature of the brain itself, not a separate substance. Consciousness is not like some fluid squirted out by the brain. A conscious state is rather a state that the brain is in. Just as water can be in a liquid or solid state without liquidity and solidity being separate substances, so consciousness is a state that the brain is in without consciousness being a separate substance.

Notice that I stated the philosophical solution without using any of the traditional categories of "dualism," "monism," "materialism," and all the rest of it. Frankly, I think those categories are obsolete. But if we accept those categories at face value, then we get the following picture: You have a choice between dualism and materialism. According to dualism, consciousness and other mental phenomena exist in a different ontological realm altogether from the ordinary physical world of physics, chemistry, and biology. According to materialism consciousness as I have described it does not exist. Neither dualism nor materialism as traditionally construed, allows us to get an answer to our question. Dualism says that there are two kinds of phenomena in the world, the mental and the physical; materialism says that there is only one, the material. Dualism ends up with an impossible bifurcation of reality into two separate categories and thus makes it impossible to explain the relation between the mental and the physical. But materialism ends up denying the existence of any irreducible subjective qualitative states of sentience or awareness. In short, dualism makes the problem insoluble; materialism denies the existence of any phenomenon to study, and hence of any problem.

On the view that I am proposing, we should reject those categories altogether. We know enough about how the world works to know that consciousness is a biological phenomenon caused by brain processes and realized in the structure of the brain. It is irreducible not because it is ineffable or mysterious, but because it has a first person ontology, and therefore cannot be reduced to phenomena with a third person ontology. The traditional mistake that people have made in both science and philosophy has been to suppose that if we reject dualism, as I believe we must, then we have to embrace materialism. But on the view that I am putting forward, materialism is just as confused as dualism because it denies the existence of ontologically subjective consciousness in the first place. Just to give it a name, the resulting view that denies both dualism and materialism, I call biological naturalism.

How did we get into this Mess?: A Historical Digression

For a long time I thought scientists would be better off if they ignored the history of the mind-body problem, but I now think that unless you understand something about the history, you will always be in the grip of historical categories. I discovered this when I was debating people in artificial intelligence and found that many of them were in the grip of Descartes, a philosopher many of them had not even read.

What we now think of as the natural sciences did not really begin with Ancient Greece. The Greeks had almost everything, and in particular they had the wonderful idea of a "theory". The invention of the idea of a theory—a systematic set of logically related propositions that attempt to explain the phenomena of some domain -- was perhaps the greatest single achievement of Greek civilization. However, they did not have the institutionalized practice of systematic observation and experiment. That only came after the Renaissance, especially in the 17th century. When you combine systematic experiment and testability with the idea of a theory, you get the possibility of science as we think of it today. But there was a feature of the seventeenth century, which was a local accident and which is still blocking our path. It is that in the seventeenth century there was a very serious conflict between science and religion, and it seemed that science was a threat to religion. Part of the way that the apparent threat posed by science to orthodox Christianity was deflected was due to Descartes and Galileo. Descartes, in particular, argued that reality divides into two kinds, the mental and the physical, *res cogitans* and *res extensa*. Descartes made a useful division of the territory: Religion had the territory of the soul, and science could have material reality. But this gave people the mistaken conception that science could only deal with objective third person phenomena, it could not deal with the inner qualitative subjective experiences that make up our conscious life. This was a perfectly harmless move in the 17th century because it kept the church authorities off the backs of the scientists. (It was only partly successful. Descartes, after all, had to leave Paris and go live in Holland where there was more tolerance, and Galileo had to make his famous recantation to the church authorities of his heliocentric theory of the planetary system.) However, this history has left us with a tradition and a tendency not to think of consciousness as an appropriate subject for the natural sciences, in the way that we think of disease, digestion, or tectonic plates as subjects of the natural sciences. I urge us to overcome this reluctance, and in order to overcome it we need to overcome the historical tradition that made it seem perfectly natural to avoid the topic of consciousness altogether in scientific investigation.

Summary of the Argument to this Point
I am assuming that we have established the following: Consciousness is a biological phenomenon like any other. It consists of inner qualitative subjective states of perceiving, feeling and thinking. Its essential feature is unified, qualitative subjectivity. Conscious states are caused by neurobiological processes in the brain, and they are realized in the structure of the brain. To say this is exactly analogous to saying that digestive processes are caused by chemical processes in the stomach and the rest of the digestive tract, and that these processes are realized in the stomach and the digestive tract. Consciousness differs from other biological phenomena in that it has a subjective or first person ontology. But ontological subjectivity does not prevent us from having epistemic objectivity. We can still have an objective science of consciousness. We abandon the traditional categories of dualism and materialism, for the same reason we abandon the categories of phlogiston and vital spirits: They have no application to the real world.

The Scientific Study of Consciousness

How, then, should we proceed in a scientific investigation of the phenomena involved? Seen from the outside it looks deceptively simple. There are three steps. First, one finds the neurobiological events that are correlated with consciousness (the NCC). Second, one tests to see that the correlation is a genuine causal relation. And third, one tries to develop a theory, ideally in the form of a set of laws, that would formalize the causal relationships.

These three steps are typical of the history of science. Think, for example, of the development of the germ theory of disease. First we find correlations between brute empirical phenomena. Then we test the correlations for causality by manipulating one variable and seeing how it affects the others. Then we develop a theory of the mechanisms involved and test the theory by further experiment. For example, Semmelweis in Vienna in the 1840s found that women obstetric patients in hospitals died more often from puerperal fever than did those who stayed at home. So he looked more closely and found that women examined by medical students who had just come from the autopsy room without washing their hands had an exceptionally high rate of puerperal fever. Here was an empirical correlation. When he made these young doctors wash their hands in chlorinated lime, the mortality rate went way down. He did not yet have the germ theory of disease, but he was moving in that direction. In the study of consciousness we appear to be in the early Semmelweis phase.

At the time of this writing we are still looking for the NCC. Suppose, for example, that we found, as Francis Crick once put forward as a tentative hypothesis, that the neurobiological correlate of consciousness was a set of neuron firings between the thalamus and the cortex layers 4 and 6, in the range of 40 Hz. That would be step one. And step two would be to manipulate the phenomena in question to see if you could show a causal relation. Ideally, we need to test for whether the NCC in question is both necessary and sufficient for the existence of consciousness. To establish necessity, we find out whether a subject who has the putative NCC removed thereby loses consciousness; and to establish sufficiency, we find out whether an otherwise unconscious subject can be brought to consciousness by inducing the putative NCC. Pure cases of causal sufficiency are rare in biology, and we usually have to understand the notion of sufficient conditions against a set of background presuppositions, that is, within a specific biological context. Thus our sufficient conditions for consciousness would presumably only operate in a subject who was alive, had his brain functioning at a certain level of activity, at a certain appropriate temperature, etc. But what we are trying to establish ideally is a proof that the element is not just correlated with consciousness, but that it is both causally necessary and sufficient, other things being equal, for the presence of consciousness. Seen from the outsider's point of view, that looks like the ideal way to proceed. Why has it not yet been done? I do not know. It turns out, for example, that it is very hard to find an exact NCC, and the current investigative tools, most notably in the form of positron emission tomagraphy scans, CAT scans, and functional magnetic resonance imaging techniques, have not yet identified the NCC. There are interesting differences between the scans of conscious subjects and sleeping subjects with REM sleep, on the one hand, and slow wave sleeping subjects on the other. But it is not easy to tell how much of the differences are related to consciousness. Lots of things are going on in both the conscious and the unconscious subjects' brains that have nothing to do with the production of consciousness. Given that a subject is already conscious, you can get parts of his or her brain to light up by getting him or her to perform various cognitive tasks such as perception or memory. But that does not give you the difference between being conscious in general, and being totally unconscious. So, to establish this first step, we still appear to be in an early a state of the technology of brain research. In spite of all of the hype surrounding the development of imaging techniques, we still, as far as I know, have not found a way to image the NCC.

With all this in mind, let us turn to some actual efforts at solving the problem of consciousness.

The Standard Approach to Consciousness: The Building Block Model

Most theorists tacitly adopt the building block theory of consciousness. The idea is that any conscious field is made of its various parts: the visual experience of red, the taste of coffee, the feeling of the wind coming in through the window. It seems that if we could figure out what makes even one building block conscious we would have the key to the whole structure. If we could, for example, crack visual consciousness that would give us the key to all the other modalities. This view is explicit in the work of Crick & Koch (1998). Their idea is that if we could find the NCC for vision, then we could explain visual consciousness, and we would then know what to look for to find the NCC for hearing, and for the other modalities, and if we put all those together, we would have the whole conscious field.

The strongest and most original statement I know of the building block theory is by Bartels & Zeki (1998, Zeki & Bartels, 1998). They see the binding activity of the brain not as one that generates a conscious experience that is unified, is not a unitary faculty, but.. it consists of many micro- but rather one that brings together a whole lot of already conscious experiences. As they put it (Bartels & Zeki 1998: 2327), "[C]onsciousness consciousnesses." Our field of consciousness is thus made up of a lot of building blocks of microconsciousnesses. "Activity at each stage or node of a processing-perceptual system has a conscious correlate. Binding cellular activity at different nodes is therefore not a process preceding or even facilitating conscious experience, but rather bringing different conscious experiences together" (Bartels & Zeki 1998: 2330).

There are at least three lines of research that are consistent with, and often used to support, the building block theory.

Blindsight

Blindsight is the name given by the psychologist Lawrence Weiskrantz to the phenomenon whereby certain patients with damage to V1 can report incidents occurring in their visual field even though they report no visual awareness of the stimulus. For example, in the case of DB, the earliest patient studied, if an X or an O were shown on a screen in that portion of DB's visual field where he was blind, the patient when asked what he saw, would deny that he saw anything. But if asked to guess, he would guess correctly that it was an X or an O. His guesses were right nearly all the time. Furthermore, the subjects in these experiments are usually surprised at their results. When the experimenter asked DB in an interview after one experiment, "Did you know how well you had done?", DB answered, "No, I didn't, because I couldn't see anything. I couldn't see a darn thing." (Weiskrantz 1986: 24). This research has subsequently been carried on with a number of other patients, and blindsight is now also experimentally induced in monkeys (Stoerig and Cowey, 1997).

Some researchers suppose that we might use blindsight as the key to understanding consciousness. The argument is the following: In the case of blindsight, we have a clear difference between conscious vision and unconscious information processing. It seems that if we could discover the physiological and anatomical difference between regular sight and blindsight, we might have the key to analyzing consciousness, because we would have a clear neurological distinction between the conscious and the unconscious cases.

Binocular Rivalry and Gestalt Switching
One exciting proposal for finding the NCC for vision is to study cases where the external stimulus is constant but where the internal subjective experience varies. Two examples of this are the gestalt switch, where the same figure, such as the Neckar cube, is perceived in two different ways, and binocular rivalry, where different stimuli are presented to each eye but the visual experience at any instant is of one or the other stimulus, not both. In such cases the experimenter has a chance to isolate a specific NCC for the visual experience, independently of the neurological correlates of the retinal stimulus (Logothetis, 1998, Logothetis & Schall, 1989). The beauty of this research is that it seems to isolate a precise NCC for a precise conscious experience. Because the external stimulus is constant and there are (at least) two different conscious experiences A and B, it seems there must be some point in the neural pathways where one sequence of neural events causes experience A and another point where a second sequence causes experience B. Find those two points and you have found the precise NCCs for two different building blocks of the whole conscious field.

The Neural Correlates of Vision

Perhaps the most obvious way to look for the NCC is to track the neurobiological causes of a specific perceptual modality such as vision. The best known such efforts to me are those of Francis Crick and Christof Koch. In a recent article, Crick & Koch (1998) assume as a working hypothesis that only some specific types of neurons will manifest the NCC. They do not think that any of the NCC of vision are in V1 (1995). The reason for thinking that V1 does not contain the NCC is that V1 does not connect to the frontal lobes in such a way that would make V1 contribute directly to the essential information processing aspect of visual perception. Their idea is that the function of visual consciousness is to provide visual information directly to the parts of the brain that organize voluntary motor output, including speech. Thus, because the information in V1 is recoded in subsequent visual areas and does not transmit directly to the frontal cortex, they believe that V1 does not correlate directly with visual consciousness.

Doubts about the Building Block Theory

The building block theory may be right but it has some worrisome features. Most important, all the research done to identify the NCCs has been carried out with subjects who are already conscious, independently of the NCC in question. Going through the cases in order, the problem with the blindsight research as a method of discovering the NCC is that the patients in question only exhibit blindsight if they are already conscious. That is, it is only in the case of fully conscious patients that we can elicit the evidence of information processing that we get in the blindsight examples. So we cannot investigate consciousness in general by studying the difference between the blindsight patient and the normally sighted patient, because both patients are fully conscious. It might turn out that what we need in our theory of consciousness is an explanation of the conscious field that is essential to both blindsight and normal vision or, for that matter, to any other sensory modality.

Similar remarks apply to the binocular rivalry experiments. All this research is immensely valuable but it is not clear how it will give us an understanding of the exact differences between the conscious brain and the unconscious brain, because for both experiences in binocular rivalry the brain is fully conscious.

Similarly, Crick (1996) and Crick & Koch (1998) only investigated subjects who are already conscious. What one wants to know is, how is it possible for the subject to be conscious at all? Given that a subject is conscious, his consciousness will be modified by having a visual experience, but it does not follow that the consciousness is made up of various building blocks of which the visual experience is just one.

I wish to state my doubts precisely. There are (at least) two possible hypotheses.

1. The building block theory: The conscious field is made up of small components that combine to form the field. To find the causal NCC for any component is to find an element that is causally necessary and sufficient for that conscious experience. Hence to find even one is, in an important sense, to crack the problem of consciousness.

2. The unified field theory (explained in more detail below): Conscious experiences come in unified fields. In order to have a visual experience, a subject has to be conscious already and the experience is a modification of the field. Neither blindsight, binocular rivalry nor normal vision can give us a genuine causal NCC because only already conscious subjects can have these experiences.

It is important to emphasize that both hypotheses are rival empirical hypotheses to be settled by scientific research and not by philosophical argument. Why then do I prefer hypothesis 2 to hypothesis 1? The building block theory predicts that in a totally unconscious patient, if the patient meets certain minimal physiological conditions (he is alive, the brainis functioning normally, he has the right temperature, etc.), and if you could trigger the NCC for say the experience of red, then the unconscious subject would suddenly have a conscious experience of red and nothing else. One building block is as good as another. Research may prove me wrong, but on the basis of what little I know about the brain, I do not believe that is possible. Only a brain that is already over the threshold of consciousness, that already has a conscious field, can have a visual experience of red.

Furthermore on the multistage theory of Bartels & Zeki (1998, Zeki & Bartels 1998), the microconsciousnesses are all capable of a separate and independent existence. It is not clear to me what this means. I know what it is like for me to experience my current conscious field, but who experiences all the tiny microconsciousnesses? And what would it be like for each of them to exist separately?

Basal Consciousness and a Unified Field Theory

There is another way to look at matters that implies another research approach. Imagine that you wake from a dreamless sleep in a completely dark room. So far you have no coherent stream of thought and almost no perceptual stimulus. Save for the pressure of your body on the bed and the sense of the covers on top of your body, you are receiving no outside sensory stimuli. All the same there must be a difference in your brain between the state of minimal wakefulness you are now in and the state of unconsciousness you were in before. That difference is the NCC I believe we should be looking for. This state of wakefulness is basal or background consciousness.

Now you turn on the light, get up, move about, etc. What happens? Do you create new conscious states? Well, in one sense you obviously do, because previously you were not consciously aware of visual stimuli and now you are. But do the visual experiences stand to the whole field of consciousness in the part whole relation? Well, that is what nearly everybody thinks and what I used to think, but here is another way of looking at it. Think of the visual experience of the table not as an object in the conscious field the way the table is an object in the room, but think of the experience as a modification of the conscious field, as a new form that the unified field takes. As Llinas and his colleagues put it, consciousness is "modulated rather than generated by the senses" (1998:1841).

I want to avoid the part whole metaphor but I also want to avoid the proscenium metaphor. We should not think of my new experiences as new actors on the stage of consciousness but as new bumps or forms or features in the unified field of consciousness. What is the difference? The proscenium metaphor gives us a constant background stage with various actors on it. I think that is wrong. There is just the unified conscious field, nothing else, and it takes different forms.

If this is the right way to look at things (and again this is a hypothesis on my part, nothing more) then we get a different sort of research project. There is no such thing as a separate visual consciousness, so looking for the NCC for vision is barking up the wrong tree. Only the already conscious subject can have visual experiences, so the introduction of visual experiences is not an introduction of consciousness but a modification of a preexisting consciousness.

The research program that is implicit in the hypothesis of unified field consciousness is that at some point we need to investigate the general condition of the conscious brain as opposed to the condition of the unconscious brain. We will not explain the general phenomenon of unified qualitative subjectivity by looking for specific local NCCs. The important question is not what the NCC for visual consciousness is, but how does the visual system introduce visual experiences into an already unified conscious field, and how does the brain create that unified conscious field in the first place. The problem becomes more specific. What we are trying to find is which features of a system that is made up of a hundred billion discreet elements, neurons, connected by synapses can produce a conscious field of the sort that I have described. There is a perfectly ordinary sense in which consciousness is unified and holistic, but the brain is not in that way unified and holistic. So what we have to look for is some massive activity of the brain capable of producing a unified holistic conscious experience. For reasons that we now know from lesion studies, we are unlikely to find this as a global property of the brain, and we have very good reason to believe that activity in the thalamocortical system is probably the place to look for unified field consciousness. The working hypothesis would be that consciousness is in large part localized in the thalamocortical system, and that the various other systems feed information to the thalamocortical system that produces modifications corresponding to the various sensory modalities. To put it simply, I do not believe we will find visual consciousness in the visual system and auditory consciousness in the auditory system. We will find a single, unified, conscious field containing visual, auditory, and other aspects.

Notice that if this hypothesis is right, it will solve the binding problem for consciousness automatically. The production of any state of consciousness at all by the brain is the production of a unified consciousness.

We are tempted to think of our conscious field as made up of the various components - visual, tactile, auditory, the stream of thought, etc. The approach whereby we think of big things as being made up of little things has proved so spectacularly successful in the rest of science that it is almost irresistible to us. Atomic theory, the cellular theory in biology, and the germ theory of disease are all examples. The urge to think of consciousness as likewise made of smaller building blocks is overwhelming. But I think it may be wrong for consciousness. Maybe we should think of consciousness holistically, and perhaps for consciousness we can make sense of the claim that "the whole is greater than the sum of the parts." Indeed, maybe it is wrong to think of consciousness as made up parts at all. I want to suggest that if we think of consciousness holistically then the aspects I have mentioned so far, especially our original combination of subjectivity, qualitativeness and unity all into one feature, will seem less mysterious. Instead of thinking of my current state of consciousness as made up of the various bits, the perception of the computer screen, the sound of the brook outside, the shadows cast by the evening sun falling on the wall -- we should think of all of these as modifications, forms that the underlying basal conscious field takes after my peripheral nerve endings have been assaulted by the various external stimuli. The research implication of this is that we should look for activities of large masses of neurons, and which cannot be explained by the activities of individual neurons. I am, in sum, urging that we take the unified field approach seriously as an alternative to the more common building block approach.

Variations on the Unified Field Theory

The idea that one should investigate consciousness as a unified field is not new and it goes back at at least as far as Kant's doctrine of the transcendental unity of apperception (Kant, 1787). In neurobiology I have not found any contemporary authors who state a clear distinction between what I have been calling the building block thery and the unified field theory but at least two lines of contemporary research are consistent with the approach urged here, the work of Llinas and his colleagues (Llinas, 1990, Llinas et al, 1998) and Tononi, Edelman and Sporns (Tononi & Edelman, 1998, Tononi, Edelman & Sporns 1998, Tononi, Sporns & Edelman, 1992). On the view of Llinas and his colleagues (1998) we should not think of consciousness as produced by sensory inputs but rather as a functional state of large portions of the brain, primarily the thalamocortical system, and we should think of sensory inputs serving to modulate a preexisting consciousness rather than creating consciousness anew. On their view consciousness is an "intrinsic" state of the brain, not a response to sensory stimulus inputs. Dreams are of special interest to them, because in a dream the brain is conscious but unable to perceive the external world through sensory inputs. They believe the NCC is synchronized oscillatory activity in the thalamocartical system (1998: 1845)

Tononi and Edelman have advanced what they call the dynamic core hypothesis (1998). They are struck by the fact that consciousness has two remarkable properties, the unity mentioned earlier and the extreme differentiation or complexity within any conscious field. This suggests to them that we should not look for consciousness in a specific sort of neuronal type, but rather in the activities of large neuronal populations. They seek the NCC for the unity of consciousness in the rapid integration that is achieved through the reentry mechanisms of the thalamocortical system. The idea they have is that in order to account for the combination of integration and differentiation in any conscious field, they have to identify large clusters of neurons that function together, that fire in a synchronized fashion. Furthermore this cluster, which they call a functional cluster, should also show a great deal of differentiation within its

component elements in order to account for the different elements of consciousness. They think that synchronous firing among cortical regions between the cortex and the thalamus is an indirect indicator of this functional clustering. Then once such a functional cluster has been identified, they wish to investigate whether or not it contains different activity patterns of neuronal states within it. The combination of functional clustering together with differentiation they submit as the dynamic core hypothesis of consciousness. They believe a unified neural process of high complexity constitutes a dynamic core. They also believe the dynamic core is not spread over the brain but is primarily in the thalamocortical regions, especially those involved in perceptual categorization and containing reentry mechanisms of the sort that Edelman discussed in his earlier books (1989, 1992). In a new study, they and their colleagues (Srinivasan et al 1999) claim to find direct evidence of the role of reentry mapping in the NCC. Like the adherents of the building block theory, they seek such NCCs of consciousness as one can find in the studies of binocular rivalry. As I understand this view, it seems to combine features of both the building block and the unified field approach.

Conclusion

In my view the most important problem in the biological sciences today is the problem of consciousness. I believe we are now at a point where we can address this problem as a biological problem like any other. For decades research has been impeded by two mistaken views: first, that consciousness is just a special sort of computer program, a special software in the hardware of the brain; and second that consciousness was just a matter of information processing. The right sort of information processing — or on some views any sort of information processing -- would be sufficient to guarantee consciousness. I have criticized these views at length elsewhere (Searle 1980, 1992, 1997) and do not repeat these criticisms here. But it is important to remind ourselves how profoundly anti-biological these views are. On these views brains do not really matter. We just happen to be implemented in brains, but any hardware that could carry the program or process the information would do just as well. I believe, on the contrary, that understanding the nature of consciousness crucially requires understanding how brain processes cause and realize consciousness. Perhaps when we understand how brains do that, we can build conscious artifacts using some nonbiological materials that duplicate, and not merely simulate, the causal powers that brains have. But first we need to understand how brains do it.

Acknowledgements

I am indebted to many people for discussion of these issues. None of them is responsible for any mistakes. I especially wish to thank Samuel Barondes, Dale Berger, Francis Crick, Gerald Edelman, Susan Greenfield, Jennifer Hudin, John Kihlstrom, Jessica Samuels, Dagmar Searle, Wolf Singer, Barry Smith, and Gunther Stent.

References

Bartels A, Zeki S. 1998. The theory of multistage integration in the visual brain. *Proc. R. Soc. London B*. 265:2327-32

Cotterill R. 1998. Enchanted Looms: Consciousness Networks in Brains and Computers. Cambridge, UK: NY, Cambridge University Press

Crick F. 1994. *The Astonishing Hypothesis: The Scientific Search for the Soul*. New York: Scribner

Crick F. 1996. Visual perception: rivalry and consciousness. *Nature* 379:485-86

Crick F, Koch C. 1995. Are we aware of neural activity in primary visual cortex? *Nature* 374:121-23

Crick F, Koch C. 1998. Consciousness and Neuroscience. *Cerebral Cortex* 8:97-107

Damasio A. 1999. *The Feeling of What Happens, Body and Emotion in the Making of Consciousness*. New York: Harcourt, Brace, & Company

Edelman G. 1989. *The Remembered Present: A Biological Theory of Consciousness*. New York: Basic Books

Edelman G. 1992. *Bright Air, Brilliant Fire: On the Matter of the Mind*. New York: Basic Books

Freeman W. 1995. *Societies of Brains, A Study in the Neuroscience of Love and Hate*. Hillsdale, New Jersey: Lawrence Erlbaum Associates, Inc.

Gazzaniga M. 1988. *How Mind and Brain Interact to Create Our Conscious Lives*. Boston: Houghton Mifflin; Cambridge, Massachussetts, in association with MIT Press

Gazzaniga M. 1998. The split brain revisited. *Scientific American*. 279:35-39

Gazzaniga M, Bogen J, Sperry R. 1962. Some functional effects of sectioning the cerebral commissures in man. *Proc. Natl Ac. of Sci.*, 48:1765-69

Gazzaniga M, Bogen J, Sperry R. 1963. Laterality effects in somesthesis following cerebral commissurotomy in man. *Neuropsychologia* 1:209-15

Greenfield S. 1995. *Journeys to the Centers of the Mind: Toward a Science of Consciousness*. New York: WH Freeman

Hameroff S. 1998a. Funda-Mentality: Is the conscious mind subtly linked to a basic level of the universe? *Trends in Cognitive Sciences* 2(4):119-127

Hameroff S. 1998b. Quantum computation in brain microtubules? The Penrose-Hameroff "Orch OR" model of consciousness. *Phil. Trans. R. Soc. Lond. A*, 356:1869-96

Hobson J. 1999. *Consciousness*. New York: Scientific American Library, Distributed by W.H. Freeman

Kant I. 1787. *The Critique of Pure Reason*. Riga: Johann Friedrich Hartknoch

Libet B. 1993. *Neurophysiology of Consciousness: Selected Papers and New Essays by Benjamin Libet*. Boston: Birkhauser

Llinas R. 1990. Intrinsic Electrical Properties of Mammalian Neurons and CNS Function. *Fidia Research Foundation Neuroscience Award Lectures* 4:1-10, New York: Raven Press Ltd.

Llinas R, Pare D. 1991. Of Dreaming and Wakefulness. *Neuroscience* 44: 521-535

Llinas R, Ribary U. 1992. Rostrocaudal Scan in Human Brain: A Global Characteristic of the 40-Hz Response During Sensory Input, *Induced Rhythms in the Brain*, ed. Basar & Bullock, pp.147-54, Boston, MA: Birkhauser

Llinas R, Ribary U. 1993. Coherent 40-Hz Oscillation Characterizes Dream State in Humans. *Proc. Natl. Acad. Sci. USA* 90:2078-81

Llinas R, Ribary U, Contreras D, Pedroarena C. 1998. The Neuronal Basis for Consciousness. *Phil. Trans. R. Soc. Lond. B* 353: 1841-49

Logothetis N, Schall J. 1989. Neuronal correlates of subjective visual perception. *Science* 245:761-63

Logothetis N. 1998 Single Units and Conscious Vision. *Phil. Trans. R. Soci. Lond. B* 353:1801-18

Nagel T. 1974. What is it like to be a bat? *Philosophical Review* 83:435-50

Penrose R. 1994. *Shadows of the Mind: A Search for the Missing Science of Consciousness*. New York: Oxford University Press

Pollen D. 1999. On the neural correlates of visual perception. *Cerebral Cortex* 9:4-19

Pribram K. 1976. Problems Concerning the Structure of Consciousness. In *Consciousness and Brain: A Scientific and Philosophical Inquiry*, ed. G Globus, G Maxwell, I Savodnik, pp.297-313. New York: Plenum

Pribram K. 1991. *Brain and Perception: Holonomy and Structure in Figural Processing*. New Jersey: Lawrence Erlbaum Associates

Pribram K. 1999 Brain and the Composition of Conscious Experience. *Journal of Consciousness Studies* 6:5: 19-42

Searle JR. 1980. Minds, brains and programs. *Behavioral and Brain Sciences* 3:417-57

Searle, JR. 1992. *The Rediscovery of the Mind*. Cambridge: MIT Press

Searle JR. 1997. *The Mystery of Consciousness*. New York: A New York Review Book

Singer W. 1993. Synchronization of Cortical Activity and its Putative Role in Information Processing and Learning. *Annual Review of Physiology* 55:349-75

Singer W, Gray C. 1995. Visual Feature Integration and the Temporal Correlation Hypothesis. *Annual Review of Neuroscience* 18:555-86

Singer W. 1995. Development and Plasticity of Cortical Processing Architectures. *Science* 270:758-64

Srinivasan R, Russell D, Edelman G, Tononi G. 1999. Frequency tagging competing stimuli in binocular rivalry reveals increased synchronization of neuromagnetic responses during conscious perception. Journal of Neuroscience. In press.

Stoerig P, Cowey A. 1997. Blindsight in Man and Monkey. *Brain* 12:535-59

Tononi G, Edelman G, Sporns O. 1998. Complexity and coherency: integrating information in the brain. *Trends in Cognitive Science* 2:12:474-84

Tononi G, Edelman G. 1998. Consciousness and complexity. *Science* 282:1846-51

Tononi G, Sporns O, Edelman G. 1992. Reentry and the problem of integrating multiple cortical areas: simulation of dynamic integration in the visual system. *Cerebral Cortex* 2:310-35

Tononi G, Srinivasan R, Russell D, Edelman G. 1998. Investigating neural correlates of conscious perception by frequency-tagged neuromagnetic responses. *Proc. Natl. Acad. Sci. USA* 95:3198-203

Weiskrantz L. 1986. *Blindsight: A Case Study and Implications*. New York: Oxford University Press

Weiskrantz L. 1997. *Consciousness Lost and Found: A Neuropsychological Exploration*. Oxford, NY: Oxford University Press

Zeki S, Bartels A. 1998. The Autonomy of the Visual Systems and the Modularity of Conscious Vision. *Phil. Trans. R. Soc. Lond. B* 353: 1911-14

Reverse-Engineering the Psyche

Steven Pinker

The complex structure of the mind is the subject of this book.[1] Its key idea can be captured in a sentence: The mind is a system of organs of computation, designed by natural selection to solve the kinds of problems our ancestors faced in their foraging way of life, in particular, understanding and outmaneuvering objects, animals, plants, and other people. The summary can be unpacked into several claims. The mind is what the brain does; specifically, the brain processes information, and thinking is a kind of computation. The mind is organized into modules or mental organs, each with a specialized design that makes it an expert in one arena of interaction with the world. The modules' basic logic is specified by our genetic program. Their operation was shaped by natural selection to solve the problems of the hunting and gathering life led by our ancestors in most of our evolutionary history. The various problems for our ancestors were subtasks of one big problem for their genes, maximizing the number of copies that made it into the next generation.

On this view, psychology is engineering in reverse. In forward-engineering, one designs a machine to do something; in reverse-engineering, one figures out what a machine was designed to do. Reverse-engineering is what the boffins at Sony do when a new product is announced by Panasonic, or vice versa. They buy one, bring it back to the lab, take a screwdriver to it, and try to figure out what all the parts are for and how they combine to make the device work. We all engage in reverse-engineering when we face an interesting new gadget. In rummaging through an antique store, we may find a contraption that is inscrutable until we figure out what it was designed to do. When we realize that it is an olive-pitter, we suddenly understand that the metal

In Search of a Language for the Mind-Brain, ed. Saleemi, Bohn and Gjedde, *The Dolphin* 33 © 2005 by Aarhus University Press, Denmark. ISBN 87 7934 005 9.

ring is designed to hold the olive, and the lever lowers an X-shaped blade through one end, pushing the pit out through the other end. The shapes and arrangements of the springs, hinges, blades, levers, and rings all make sense in a satisfying rush of insight. We even understand why canned olives have an X-shaped incision at one end.

In the seventeenth century William Harvey discovered that veins had valves and deduced that the valves must be there to make the blood circulate. Since then we have understood the body as a wonderfully complex machine, an assembly of struts, ties, springs, pulleys, levers, joints, hinges, sockets, tanks, pipes, valves, sheaths, pumps, exchangers, and filters. Even today we can be delighted to learn what mysterious parts are for. Why do we have our wrinkled, asymmetrical ears? Because they filter sound waves coming from different directions in different ways. The nuances of the sound shadow tell the brain whether the source of the sound is above or below, in front of or behind us. The strategy of reverse-engineering the body has continued in the last half of this century as we have explored the nanotechnology of the cell and of the molecules of life. The stuff of life turned out to be not a quivering, glowing, wondrous gel but a contraption of tiny jigs, springs, hinges, rods, sheets, magnets, zippers, and trapdoors, assembled by a data tape whose information is copied, downloaded, and scanned.

The rationale for reverse-engineering living things comes, of course, from Charles Darwin. He showed how "organs of extreme perfection and complication, which justly excite our admiration" arise not from God's foresight but from the evolution of replicators over immense spans of time. As replicators replicate, random copying errors sometimes crop up, and those that happen to enhance the survival and reproduction rate of the replicator tend to accumulate over the generations. Plants and animals are replicators, and their complicated machinery thus appears to have been engineered to allow them to survive and reproduce.

Darwin insisted that his theory explained not just the complexity of an animal's body but the complexity of its mind. "Psychology will be based on a new foundation," he famously predicted at the end of *The Origin of Species*. But Darwin's prophecy has not yet been fulfilled. More than a century after he wrote those words, the study of the mind is still mostly Darwin-free, often defiantly so. Evolution is said to be irrelevant, sinful, or fit only for speculation over a beer at the end of the day. The allergy to evolution in the social and cognitive sciences has been, I think, a barrier to understanding. The mind is an exquisitely organized system that accomplishes remarkable feats no engineer can duplicate. How could the forces that shaped that system, and the purposes for which it was designed, be irrelevant to understanding it? Evolutionary thinking is indispensable, not in the form that many people think of - dreaming up missing links or narrating stories about the stages of Man - but in the form of careful reverse-engineering. Without reverse-engineering we are like the singer in Tom Paxton's "The Marvelous Toy," reminiscing about a childhood present: "It went ZIP! when it moved, and POP! when it stopped, and WHIRRR! when it stood still; I never knew just what it was, and I guess I never will."

Only in the past few years has Darwin's challenge been taken up, by a new approach christened "evolutionary psychology" by the anthropologist John Tooby and the psychologist Leda Cosmides. Evolutionary psychology brings together two scientific revolutions. One is the cognitive revolution of the 1950s and 1960s, which explains the mechanics of thought and emotion in terms of information and computation. The other is the revolution in evolutionary biology of the 1960s and 1970s, which explains the complex adaptive design of living things in terms of selection among replicators. The two ideas make a powerful combination. Cognitive science helps us to understand how a mind is possible and what kind of mind we have. Evolutionary biology helps us to understand *why* we have the kind of mind we have.

The evolutionary psychology of this book is, in one sense, a straightforward extension of biology, focusing on one organ, the mind, of one species, *Homo sapiens*. But in another sense it is a radical thesis that discards the way issues about the mind have been framed for almost a century. The premises of this book are probably not what you think they are. Thinking is computation, I claim, but that does not mean that the computer is a good metaphor for the mind. The mind is a set of modules, but the modules are not encapsulated boxes or circumscribed swatches on the surface of the brain. The organization of our mental modules comes from our genetic program, but that does not mean that there is a gene for every trait or that learning is less important than we used to think. The mind is an adaptation designed by natural selection, but that does not mean that everything we think, feel, and do is biologically adaptive. We evolved from apes, but that does not mean we have the same minds as apes. And the ultimate goal of natural selection is to propagate genes, but that does not mean that the ultimate goal of people is to propagate genes. Let me show you why not.

This book is about the brain, but I will not say much about neurons, hormones, and neurotransmitters. That is because the mind is not the brain but what the brain does, and not even everything it does, such as metabolizing fat and giving off heat. The 1990s have been named the Decade of the Brain, but there will never be a Decade of the Pancreas. The brain's special status comes from a special thing the brain does, which makes us see, think, feel, choose, and act. That special thing is information processing, or computation.

Information and computation reside in patterns of data and in relations of logic that are independent of the physical medium that carries them. When you telephone your mother in another city, the message stays the same as it goes from your lips to her ears even as it physically changes its form, from vibrating air, to electricity in a wire, to charges in silicon, to flickering light in a fiber optic cable, to electromagnetic waves, and then back again in reverse order. In a similar sense, the message stays the same when she repeats it to your father at the other end of the couch after it has changed its form inside her head into a cascade of neurons firing and chemicals diffusing across synapses. Likewise, a given program can run on computers made of vacuum tubes, electromagnetic switches, transistors, integrated circuits, or well-trained pigeons, and it accomplishes the same things for the same reasons.

This insight, first expressed by the mathematician Alan Turing, the computer scientists Alan Newell, Herbert Simon, and Marvin Minsky, and the philosophers Hilary Putnam and Jerry Fodor, is now called the computational theory of mind. It is one of the great ideas in intellectual history, for it solves one of the puzzles that make up the "mind-body problem": how to connect the ethereal world of meaning and intention, the stuff of our mental lives, with a physical hunk of matter like the brain. Why did Bill get on the bus? Because he wanted to visit his grandmother and knew the bus would take him there. No other answer will do. If he hated the sight of his grandmother, or if he knew the route had changed, his body would not be on that bus. For millennia this has been a paradox. Entities like "wanting to visit one's grandmother" and "knowing the bus goes to Grandma's house" are colorless, odorless, and tasteless. But at the same time they are *causes* of physical events, as potent as any billiard ball clacking into another.

The computational theory of mind resolves the paradox. It says that beliefs and desires are *information*, incarnated as configurations of symbols. The symbols are the physical states of bits of matter, like chips in a computer or neurons in the brain. They symbolize things in the world because they are triggered by those things via our sense organs, and because of what they do once they are triggered. If the bits of matter that constitute a symbol are arranged to bump into the bits of matter constituting another symbol in just the right way, the symbols corresponding to one belief can give rise to new symbols corresponding to another belief logically related to it, which can give rise to symbols corresponding to other beliefs, and so on. Eventually the bits of matter constituting a symbol bump into bits of matter connected to the muscles, and behavior happens. The computational theory of mind thus allows us to keep beliefs and desires in our explanations of behavior while planting them squarely in the physical universe. It allows meaning to cause and be caused.

The computational theory of mind is indispensable in addressing the questions we long to answer. Neuroscientists like to point out that all parts of the cerebral cortex look pretty much alike -- not only the different parts of the human brain, but the brains of different animals. One could draw the conclusion that all mental activity in all animals is the same. But a better conclusion is that we cannot simply look at a patch of brain and read out the logic in the intricate pattern of connectivity that makes each part do its separate thing. In the same way that all books are physically just different combinations of the same seventy-five or so characters, and all movies are physically just different patterns of charges along the tracks of a videotape, the mammoth tangle of spaghetti of the brain may all look alike when examined strand by strand. The content of a book or a movie lies in the *pattern* of ink marks or magnetic charges, and is apparent only when the piece is read or seen. Similarly, the content of brain activity lies in the patterns of connections and patterns of activity among the neurons. Minute differences in the details of the connections may cause similar-looking brain patches to implement very different programs. Only when the program is run does the coherence become evident. As Tooby and Cosmides have written,

> There are birds that migrate by the stars, bats that echolocate, bees that compute the variance of flower patches, spiders that spin webs, humans that speak, ants that farm, lions that hunt in teams, cheetahs that hunt alone, monogamous gibbons, polyandrous seahorses, polygynous gorillas. ... There are millions of animal species on earth, each with a different set of cognitive programs. *The same basic neural tissue embodies all of these programs*, and it could support many others as well. Facts about the properties of neurons, neurotransmitters, and cellular development cannot tell you which of these millions of programs the human mind contains. Even if all neural activity is the expression of a uniform process at the cellular level, it is the arrangement of neurons -- into bird song templates or web-spinning programs -- that matters.

That does not imply, of course, that the brain is irrelevant to understanding the mind! Programs are assemblies of simple information-processing units -- tiny circuits that can add, match a pattern, turn on some other circuit, or do other elementary logical and mathematical operations. What those microcircuits can do depends only on what they are made of. Circuits made from neurons cannot do exactly the same things as circuits made from silicon, and vice versa. For example, a silicon circuit is faster than a neural circuit, but a neural circuit can match a larger pattern than a silicon one. These differences ripple up through the programs built from the circuits and affect how quickly and easily the programs do various things, even if they do not determine exactly which things they do. My point is not that prodding brain tissue is irrelevant to understanding the mind, only that it is not enough. Psychology, the analysis of mental software, will have to burrow a considerable way into the mountain before meeting the neurobiologists tunneling through from the other side.

The computational theory of mind is not the same thing as the despised "computer metaphor." As many critics have pointed out, computers are serial, doing one thing at a time; brains are parallel, doing millions of things at once. Computers are fast; brains are slow. Computer parts are reliable; brain parts are noisy. Computers have a limited number of connections; brains have trillions. Computers are assembled according to a blueprint; brains must assemble themselves. Yes, and computers come in putty-colored boxes and have AUTOEXEC.BAT files and run screen-savers with flying toasters, and brains do not. The claim is not that the brain is like commercially available computers. Rather, the claim is that brains and computers embody intelligence for some of the same reasons. To explain how birds fly, we invoke principles of lift and drag and fluid mechanics that also explain how airplanes fly. That does not commit us to an Airplane Metaphor for birds, complete with jet engines and complimentary beverage service.

Without the computational theory, it is impossible to make sense of the evolution of the mind. Most intellectuals think that the human mind must somehow have escaped the evolutionary process. Evolution, they think, can fabricate only stupid instincts and fixed action patterns: a sex drive, an aggression urge, a territorial imperative, hens sitting on eggs and ducklings following hulks. Human behavior is too subtle and flexible to be a product of evolution, they think; it must come from somewhere else -- from, say, "culture." But if evolution equipped us not with irresistible urges and rigid reflexes but with a neural computer, everything changes. A program is an intricate recipe of logical and statistical operations directed by comparisons, tests, branches, loops, and subroutines embedded in subroutines. Artificial computer programs, from the Macintosh user interface to simulations of the weather to programs that recognize speech and answer questions in English, give us a hint of the finesse and power of which computation is capable. Human thought and behavior, no matter how subtle and flexible, could be the product of a very complicated program, and that program may have been our endowment from natural selection. The typical imperative from biology is not "Thou shalt ...," but "If ... then ... else."

The mind, I claim, is not a single organ but a system of organs, which we can think of as psychological faculties or mental modules. The entities now commonly evoked to explain the mind -- such as general intelligence, a capacity to form culture, and multipurpose learning strategies -- will surely go the way of protoplasm in biology and of earth, air, fire, and water in physics. These entities are so formless, compared to the exacting phenomena they are meant to explain, that they must be granted near-magical powers. When the phenomena are put under the microscope, we discover that the complex texture of the everyday world is supported not by a single substance but by many layers of elaborate machinery. Biologists long ago replaced the concept of an all-powerful protoplasm with the concept of functionally specialized mechanisms. The organ systems of the body do their jobs because each is built with a particular structure tailored to the task. The heart circulates the blood because it is built like a pump; the lungs oxygenate the blood because they are built like gas exchangers. The lungs cannot pump blood and the heart cannot oxygenate it. This specialization goes all the way down. Heart tissue differs from lung tissue, heart cells differ from lung cells, and many of the molecules making up heart cells differ from those making up lung cells. If that were not true, our organs would not work.

A jack-of-all-trades is master of none, and that is just as true for our mental organs as for our physical organs. The robot challenge makes that clear. Building a robot poses many software engineering problems, and different tricks are necessary to solve them.

Take our first problem, the sense of sight. A seeing machine must solve a problem called inverse optics. Ordinary optics is the branch of physics that allows one to predict how an object with a certain shape, material, and illumination projects the mosaic of colors we call the retinal image. Optics is a well-understood subject, put to use in drawing, photography, television engineering, and more recently, computer graphics and virtual reality. But the brain must solve the *opposite* problem. The input is the retinal image, and the output is a specification of the objects in the world and what they are made of -- that is, what we know we are seeing. And there's the rub. Inverse optics is what engineers call an "ill-posed problem." It literally has no solution. Just as it is easy to multiply some numbers and announce the product but impossible to take a product and announce the numbers that were multiplied to get it, optics is easy but inverse optics impossible. Yet your brain does it every time you open the refrigerator and pull out a jar. How can this be?

The answer is that *the brain supplies the missing information,* information about the world we evolved in and how it reflects light. If the visual brain "assumes" that it is living in a certain kind of world -- an evenly lit world made mostly of rigid parts with smooth, uniformly colored surfaces -- it can make good guesses about what is out there. As we saw earlier, it's impossible to distinguish coal from snow by examining the brightnesses of their retinal projections. But say there is a module for perceiving the properties of surfaces, and built into it is the following assumption: "The world is smoothly and uniformly lit." The module can solve the coal-versus-snow problem in three steps: subtract out any gradient of brightness from one edge of the scene to the other; estimate the average level of brightness of the whole scene; and calculate the shade of gray of each patch by subtracting its brightness from the average brightness. Large positive deviations from the average are then seen as white things, large negative deviations as black things. If the illumination really is smooth and uniform, those perceptions will register the surfaces of the world accurately. Since Planet Earth has, more or less, met the even-illumination assumption for eons, natural selection would have done well by building the assumption in.

The surface-perception module solves an unsolvable problem, but at a price. The brain has given up any pretense of being a general problem-solver. It has been equipped with a gadget that perceives the nature of surfaces in typical earthly viewing conditions because it is specialized for that parochial problem. Change the problem slightly and the brain no longer solves it. Say we place a person in a world that is not blanketed with sunshine but illuminated by a cunningly arranged patchwork of light. If the surface-perception module assumes that illumination is even, it should be seduced into hallucinating objects that aren't there. Could that really happen? It happens every day. We call these hallucinations slide shows and movies and television (complete with the illusory black I mentioned earlier). When we watch TV, we stare at a shimmering piece of glass, but our surface-perception module tells the rest of our brain that we are seeing real people and places. The module has been unmasked; it does not apprehend the nature of things but relies on a cheat-sheet. That cheat-sheet is so deeply embedded in the operation of our visual brain that we cannot erase the assumptions written on it. Even in a lifelong couch potato, the visual system never "learns" that television is a pane of glowing phosphor dots, and the person never loses the illusion that there is a world behind the pane.

Our other mental modules need their own cheat-sheets to solve their unsolvable problems. A physicist who wants to figure out how the body moves when muscles are contracted has to solve problems in kinematics (the geometry of motion) and dynamics (the effects of forces). But a brain that has to figure out how to contract muscles to get the body to move has to solve problems in *inverse* kinematics and *inverse* dynamics -- what forces to apply to an object to get it to move in a certain trajectory. Like inverse optics, inverse kinematics and dynamics are ill-posed problems. Our motor modules solve them by making extraneous but reasonable assumptions -- not assumptions about illumination, of course, but assumptions about bodies in motion.

Our common sense about other people is a kind of intuitive psychology -- we try to infer people's beliefs and desires from what they do, and try to predict what they will do from our guesses about their beliefs and desires. Our intuitive psychology, though, must make the assumption that other people *have* beliefs and desires; we cannot sense a belief or desire in another person's head the way we smell onions. If we did not see the social world through the lens of that assumption, we would be like the Samaritan I robot, which sacrificed itself for a bag of lima beans, or like Samaritan II, which went overboard for any object with a humanlike head, even if the head belonged to a large windup toy. (Later we shall see that people suffering from a certain syndrome lack the assumption that people have minds and *do* treat other people as wind-up toys.) Even our feelings of love for our family members embody a specific assumption about the laws of the natural world, in this case an inverse of the ordinary laws of genetics. Family feelings are designed to help our genes replicate themselves, but we cannot see or smell genes. Scientists use forward genetics to deduce how genes get distributed among organisms (for example, meiosis and sex cause the offspring of two people to have fifty percent of their genes in common); our emotions about kin use a kind of inverse genetics to guess which of the organisms we interact with are likely to share our genes (for example, if someone appears to have the same parents as you do, treat the person as if their genetic well-being overlaps with yours). I will return to all these topics in later chapters.

The mind has to be built out of specialized parts because it has to solve specialized problems. Only an angel could be a general problem-solver; we mortals have to make fallible guesses from fragmentary information. Each of our mental modules solves its unsolvable problem by a leap of faith about how the world works, by making assumptions that are indispensable but indefensible -- the only defense being that the assumptions worked well enough in the world of our ancestors.

The word "module" brings to mind detachable, snap-in components, and that is misleading. Mental modules are not likely to be visible to the naked eye as circumscribed territories on the surface of the brain, like the flank steak and the rump roast on the supermarket cow display. A mental module probably looks more like roadkill, sprawling messily over the bulges and crevasses of the brain. Or it may be broken into regions that are interconnected by fibers that make the regions act as a unit. The beauty of information processing is the flexibility of its demand for real estate. Just as a corporation's management can be scattered across sites linked by a telecommunications network, or a computer program can be fragmented into different parts of the disk or memory, the circuitry underlying a psychological module might be distributed across the brain in a spatially haphazard manner. And mental modules need not be tightly sealed off from one another, communicating only through a few narrow pipelines. (That is a specialized sense of "module" that many cognitive scientists have debated, following a definition by Jerry Fodor.) Modules are defined by the special things they do with the information available to them, not necessarily by the kinds of information they have available.

So the metaphor of the mental module is a bit clumsy; a better one is Noam Chomsky's "mental organ." An organ of the body is a specialized structure tailored to carry out a particular function. But our organs do not come in a bag like chicken giblets; they are integrated into a complex whole. The body is composed of systems divided into organs assembled from tissues built out of cells. Some kinds of tissues, like the epithelium, are used, with modifications, in many organs. Some organs, like the blood and the skin, interact with the rest of the body across a widespread, convoluted interface, and cannot be encircled by a dotted line. Sometimes it is unclear where one organ leaves off and another begins, or how big a chunk of the body we want to call an organ. (Is the hand an organ? the finger? a bone in the finger?) These are all pedantic questions of terminology, and anatomists and physiologists have not wasted their time on them. What is clear is that the body is not made of Spam but has a heterogeneous structure of many specialized parts. All this is likely to be true of

the mind. Whether or not we establish exact boundaries for the
components of the mind, it is clear that it is not made of mental
Spam but has a heterogeneous structure of many specialized
parts.

Our physical organs owe their complex design to the information
in the human genome, and so, I believe, do our mental organs. We
do not learn to have a pancreas, and we do not learn to have a
visual system, language acquisition, common sense, or feelings of
love, friendship, and fairness. No single discovery proves the
claim (just as no single discovery proves that the pancreas is
innately structured), but many lines of evidence converge on it.
The one that most impresses me is the Robot Challenge. Each of
the major engineering problems solved by the mind is unsolvable
without built-in assumptions about the laws that hold in that
arena of interaction with the world. All of the programs designed
by artificial intelligence researchers have been specially
engineered for a particular domain, such as language, vision,
movement, or one of many different kinds of common sense.
Within artificial intelligence research, the proud parent of a
program will sometimes tout it as a mere demo of an amazingly
powerful general-purpose system to be built in the future, but
everyone else in the field routinely writes off such hype. I predict
that no one will ever build a humanlike robot -- and I mean a
really humanlike robot -- unless they pack it with computational
systems tailored to different problems.

Throughout the book we will run into other lines of evidence
that our mental organs owe their basic design to our genetic
program. I have already mentioned that much of the fine
structure of our personality and intelligence is shared by identical
twins reared apart and hence charted by the genes. Infants and
young children, when tested with ingenious methods, show a
precocious grasp of the fundamental categories of the physical
and social world, and sometimes command information that was
never presented to them. People hold many beliefs that are at
odds with their experience but were true in the environment in

which we evolved, and they pursue goals that subvert their own wellbeing but were adaptive in that environment. And contrary to the widespread belief that cultures can vary arbitrarily and without limit, surveys of the ethnographic literature show that the peoples of the world share an astonishingly detailed universal psychology.

But if the mind has a complex innate structure, that does *not* mean that learning is unimportant. Framing the issue in such a way that innate structure and learning are pitted against each other, either as alternatives or, almost as bad, as complementary ingredients or interacting forces, is a colossal mistake. It's not that the claim that there is an interaction between innate structure and learning (or between heredity and environment, nature and nurture, biology and culture) is literally wrong. Rather, it falls into the category of ideas that are so bad they are not even wrong.

Imagine the following dialogue:

"This new computer is brimming with sophisticated technology. It has a 500 megahertz processor, a gigabyte of RAM, a terabyte of disk storage, a 3-D color virtual reality display, speech output, wireless access to the World Wide Web, expertise in a dozen subjects, and built-in editions of the Bible, the *Encyclopaedia Britannica, Bartlett's Famous Quotations*, and the complete works of Shakespeare. Tens of thousands of hacker-hours went into its design."

"Oh, so I guess you're saying that it doesn't matter what I type into the computer. With all that built-in structure, its environment can't be very important. It will always do the same thing, regardless of what I type in."

The response is patently senseless. Having a lot of built-in machinery should make a system respond *more* intelligently and flexibly to its inputs, not less. Yet the reply captures how centuries of commentators have reacted to the idea of a richly structured, high-tech mind.

And the "interactionist" position, with its phobia of ever specifying the innate part of the interaction, is not much better. Look at these claims.

The behavior of a computer comes from a complex interaction between the processor and the input.

When trying to understand how a car works, one cannot neglect the engine or the gasoline or the driver. All are important factors.

The sound coming out of this CD player represents the inextricably intertwined mixture of two crucial variables: the structure of the machine, and the disk you insert into it. Neither can be ignored.

These statements are true but useless -- so blankly uncomprehending, so defiantly incurious, that it is almost as bad to assert them as to deny them. For minds, just as for machines, the metaphors of a mixture of two ingredients, like a martini, or a battle between matched forces, like a tug-of-war, are wrongheaded ways of thinking about a complex device designed to process information. Yes, every part of human intelligence involves culture and learning. But learning is not a surrounding gas or force field, and it does not happen by magic. It is made possible by innate machinery designed to do the learning. The claim that there are several innate modules is a claim that there are several innate learning machines, each of which learns according to a particular logic. To understand learning, we need new ways of thinking to replace the prescientific metaphors -- the mixtures and forces, the writing on slates and sculpting of blocks of marble. We need ideas that capture the ways a complex device can tune itself to unpredictable aspects of the world and take in the kinds of data it needs to function.

The idea that heredity and environment interact is not always meaningless, but I think it confuses two issues: what all minds have in common, and how minds can differ. The vapid statements above can be made intelligible by replacing "How X works" with "What makes X work better than Y":

The *usefulness* of a computer depends on both the power of its processor and the expertise of the user.

The *speed* of a car depends on the engine, the fuel, and the skill of the driver. All are important factors.

The *quality* of sound coming from a CD player depends on two crucial variables: the player's mechanical and electronic design, and the quality of the original recording. Neither can be ignored.

When we are interested in *how much better* one system functions than a similar one, it is reasonable to gloss over the causal chains inside each system and tally up the factors that make the whole thing fast or slow, hi-fi or low-fi. And this *ranking* of people -- to determine who enters medical school, or who gets the job -- is where the framing of nature versus nurture comes from. But this book is about how the mind works, not about why some people's minds might work a bit better in certain ways than other people's minds. The evidence suggests that humans everywhere on the planet see, talk, and think about objects and people in the same basic way. The difference between Einstein and a high school dropout is trivial compared to the difference between the high school dropout and the best robot in existence, or between the high school dropout and a chimpanzee. That is the mystery I want to address. Nothing could be farther from my subject matter than a comparison between the means of overlapping bell curves for some crude consumer index like IQ. And for this reason, the relative importance of innateness and learning is a phony issue.

An emphasis on innate design should not, by the way, be confused with the search for "a gene for" this or that mental organ. Think of the genes and putative genes that have made the headlines: genes for muscular dystrophy, Huntington's disease, Alzheimer's, alcoholism, schizophrenia, manic-depressive disorder, obesity, violent outbursts, dyslexia, bed-wetting, and some kinds of retardation. They are *disorders*, all of them. There have been no discoveries of a gene for civility, language, memory, motor control, intelligence, or other complete mental systems, and there probably won't ever be. The reason was summed up by the politician Sam Rayburn: Any jackass can kick down a barn, but it takes a carpenter to build one. Complex mental organs, like complex physical organs, surely are built by complex genetic recipes, with many genes cooperating in as yet unfathomable ways. A defect in any one of them could corrupt the whole device, just as a defect in any part of a complicated machine (like a loose distributor cable in a car) can bring the machine to a halt.

The genetic assembly instructions for a mental organ do not specify every connection in the brain as if they were a wiring schematic for a Heathkit radio. And we should not expect each organ to grow under a particular bone of the skull regardless of what else happens in the brain. The brain and all the other organs differentiate in embryonic development from a ball of identical cells. Every part of the body, from the toenails to the cerebral cortex, takes on its particular shape and substance when its cells respond to some kind of information in its neighborhood that unlocks a different part of the genetic program. The information may come from the taste of the chemical soup that a cell finds itself in, from the shapes of the molecular locks and keys that the cell engages, from mechanical tugs and shoves from neighboring cells, and other cues still poorly understood. The families of neurons that will form the different mental organs, all descendants of a homogeneous stretch of embryonic tissue, must be designed to be opportunistic as the brain assembles itself, seizing any available information to differentiate from one another. The coordinates in the skull may be one trigger for differentiation, but the pattern of input firings from connected neurons is another. Since the brain is destined to be an organ of computation, it would be surprising if the genome did not exploit the capacity of neural tissue to process information during brain assembly.

In the sensory areas of the brain, where we can best keep track of what is going on, we know that early in fetal development neurons are wired according to a rough genetic recipe. The neurons are born in appropriate numbers at the right times, migrate to their resting places, send out connections to their targets, and hook up to appropriate cell types in the right general regions, all under the guidance of chemical trails and molecular locks and keys. To make precise connections, though, the baby neurons must begin to function, and their firing pattern carries information downstream about their pinpoint connections. This isn't exactly "experience," as it all can take place in the pitch-black womb, sometimes before the rods and cones are functioning, and many mammals can see almost perfectly as soon as they are born. It is more like a kind of genetic data compression or a set of internally generated test patterns. These patterns can trigger the cortex at the receiving end to differentiate, at least one step of the way, into the kind of cortex that is appropriate to processing the incoming information. (For example, in animals that have been cross-wired so that the eyes are connected to the auditory brain, that area shows a few hints of the properties of the visual brain.) How the genes control brain development is still unknown, but a reasonable summary of what we know so far is that brain modules assume their identity by a combination of what kind of tissue they start out as, where they are in the brain, and what patterns of triggering input they get during critical periods in development.

Our organs of computation are a product of natural selection. The biologist Richard Dawkins called natural selection the Blind Watchmaker; in the case of the mind, we can call it the Blind Programmer. Our mental programs work as well as they do because they were shaped by selection to allow our ancestors to master rocks, tools, plants, animals, and each other, ultimately in the service of survival and reproduction.

Natural selection is not the only cause of evolutionary change. Organisms also change over the eons because of statistical accidents in who lives and who dies, environmental catastrophes that wipe out whole families of creatures, and the unavoidable by-products of changes that *are* the product of selection.

But natural selection is the only evolutionary force that acts like an engineer, "designing" organs that accomplish improbable but adaptive outcomes (a point that has been made forcefully by the biologist George Williams and by Dawkins). The textbook argument for natural selection, accepted even by those who feel that selection has been overrated (such as the paleontologist Stephen Jay Gould), comes from the vertebrate eye. Just as a watch has too many finely meshing parts (gears, springs, pivots, and so on) to have been assembled by a tornado or a river eddy, entailing instead the design of a watchmaker, the eye has too many finely meshing parts (lens, iris, retina, and so on) to have arisen from a random evolutionary force like a big mutation, statistical drift, or the fortuitous shape of the nooks and crannies between other organs. The design of the eye must be a product of natural selection of replicators, the only nonmiraculous natural process we know of that can manufacture well-functioning machines. The organism appears as if it was designed to see well now because it owes its existence to the success of its ancestors in seeing well in the past. (This point will be expanded in Chapter 3.)

Many people acknowledge that natural selection is the artificer of the body but draw the line when it comes to the human mind. The mind, they say, is a by-product of a mutation that enlarged the head, or is a clumsy programmer's hack, or was given its shape by cultural rather than biological evolution. Tooby and Cosmides point out a delicious irony. The eye, that most uncontroversial example of fine engineering by natural selection, is not just any old organ that can be sequestered with flesh and bone, far away from the land of the mental. It doesn't digest food or, except in the case of Superman, change anything in the physical world. What does the eye do? The eye is an organ of information processing, firmly connected to -- anatomically speaking, a part of -- the brain. And all those delicate optics and intricate circuits in the retina do not dump information into a yawning empty orifice or span some Cartesian chasm from a physical to a mental realm. The receiver of this richly structured message must be every bit as well engineered as the sender. As we have seen in comparing human vision and robot vision, the parts of the mind that allow us to see are indeed well engineered, and there is no reason to think that the quality of engineering progressively deteriorates as the information flows upstream to the faculties that interpret and act on what we see.

The adaptationist program in biology, or the careful use of natural selection to reverse-engineer the parts of an organism, is sometimes ridiculed as an empty exercise in after-the-fact storytelling. In the satire of the syndicated columnist Cecil Adams, "the reason our hair is brown is that it enabled our monkey ancestors to hide amongst the coconuts." Admittedly, there is no shortage of bad evolutionary "explanations." Why do men avoid asking for directions? Because our male ancestors might have been killed if they approached a stranger. What purpose does music serve? It brings the community together. Why did happiness evolve? Because happy people are pleasant to be around, so they attracted more allies. What is the function of humor? To relieve tension. Why do people overestimate their chance of surviving an illness? Because it helps them to operate effectively in life.

These musings strike us as glib and lame, but it is not because they dare to seek an evolutionary explanation of how some part of the mind works. It is because they botch the job. First, many of them never bother to establish the facts. as anyone ever documented that *women* like to ask for directions? Would a woman in a foraging society *not* have come to harm when she approached a stranger? Second, even if the facts had been established, the stories try to explain one puzzling fact by taking for granted some other fact that is just as much of a puzzle, getting us nowhere. *Why* do rhythmic noises bring a community together? *Why* do people like to be with happy people? *Why* does humor relieve tension? The authors of these explanations treat some parts of our mental life as so obvious -- they are, after all, obvious to each of *us*, here inside our heads -- that they don't need to be explained. But *all* parts of the mind are up for grabs -- every reaction, every pleasure, every taste -- when we try to explain how it evolved. We *could have* evolved like the Samaritan I robot, which sacrificed itself to save a sack of lima beans, or like dung beetles, which must find dung delicious, or like the masochist in the old joke about sadomasochism (Masochist: "Hit me!" Sadist: "No!").

A good adaptationist explanation needs the fulcrum of an engineering analysis that is independent of the part of the mind we are trying to explain. The analysis begins with a goal to be attained and a world of causes and effects in which to attain it, and goes on to specify what kinds of designs are better suited to attain it than others. Unfortunately for those who think that the departments in a university reflect meaningful divisions of knowledge, it means that psychologists have to look outside psychology if they want to explain what the parts of the mind are for. To understand sight, we have to look to optics and computer vision systems. To understand movement, we have to look to robotics. To understand sexual and familial feelings, we have to look to Mendelian genetics. To understand cooperation and conflict, we have to look to the mathematics of games and to economic modeling.

Once we have a spec sheet for a well-designed mind, we can see whether *Homo sapiens* has that kind of mind. We do the experiments or surveys to get the facts down about a mental faculty, and then see whether the faculty meets the specs: whether it shows signs of precision, complexity, efficiency, reliability, and specialization in solving its assigned problem, especially in comparison with the vast number of alternative designs that are biologically growable. The logic of reverse-engineering has guided researchers in visual perception for over a century, and that may be why we understand vision better than we understand any other part of the mind. There is no reason that reverse-engineering guided by evolutionary theory should not bring insight about the rest of the mind. An interesting example is a new theory of pregnancy sickness (traditionally called "morning sickness") by the biologist Margie Profet. Many pregnant women become nauseated and avoid certain foods. Though their sickness is usually explained away as a side effect of hormones, there is no reason that hormones should induce nausea and food aversions rather than, say, hyperactivity, aggressiveness, or lust. The Freudian explanation is equally unsatisfying: that pregnancy sickness represents the woman's loathing of her husband and her unconscious desire to abort the fetus orally.

Profet predicted that pregnancy sickness should confer some benefit that offsets the cost of lowered nutrition and productivity. Ordinarily, nausea is a protection against eating toxins: the poisonous food is ejected from the stomach before it can do much harm, and our appetite for similar foods is reduced in the future. Perhaps pregnancy sickness protects women against eating or digesting foods with toxins that might harm the developing fetus. Your local Happy Carrot Health Food Store notwithstanding, there is nothing particularly healthy about natural foods. Your cabbage, a Darwinian creature, has no more desire to be eaten than you do, and since it can't very well defend itself through behavior, it resorts to chemical warfare. Most plants have evolved dozens of toxins in their tissues: insecticides, insect repellents, irritants, paralytics, poisons, and other sand to throw in herbivores' gears. Herbivores have in turn evolved countermeasures, such as a liver to detoxify the poisons and the taste sensation we call bitterness to deter any further desire to ingest them. But the usual defenses may not be enough to protect a tiny embryo.

So far this may not sound much better than the barf-up-your-baby theory, but Profet synthesized hundreds of studies, done independently of each other and of her hypothesis, that support it. She meticulously documented that (1) plant toxins in dosages that adults tolerate can cause birth defects and induce abortion when ingested by pregnant women; (2) pregnancy sickness begins at the point when the embryo's organ systems are being laid down and the embryo is most vulnerable to teratogens (birth defect – inducing chemicals) but is growing slowly and has only a modest need for nutrients; (3) pregnancy sickness wanes at the stage when the embryo's organ systems are nearly complete and its biggest need is for nutrients to allow it to grow; (4) women with pregnancy sickness selectively avoid bitter, pungent, highly flavored, and novel foods, which are in fact the ones most likely to contain toxins; (5) women's sense of smell becomes hypersensitive during the window of pregnancy sickness and less sensitive than usual thereafter; (6) foraging peoples (including, presumably, our ancestors) are at even higher risk of ingesting plant toxins, because they eat wild plants rather than domesticated crops bred for palatability; (7) pregnancy sickness is universal across human cultures; (8) women with more severe pregnancy sickness are less likely to miscarry; (9) women with more severe pregnancy sickness are less likely to bear babies with birth defects. The fit between how a baby-making system in a natural ecosystem ought to work and how the feelings of modern women do work is impressive, and gives a measure of confidence that Profet's hypothesis is correct.

The human mind is a product of evolution, so our mental organs are either present in the minds of apes (and perhaps other mammals and vertebrates) or arose from overhauling the minds of apes, specifically, the common ancestors of humans and chimpanzees that lived about six million years ago in Africa. Many titles of books on human evolution remind us of this fact: *The Naked Ape, The Electric Ape, The Scented Ape, The Lopsided Ape, The Aquatic Ape, The Thinking Ape, The Human Ape, The Ape That Spoke, The Third Chimpanzee, The Chosen Primate.* Some authors are militant that humans are barely different from chimpanzees and that any focus on specifically human talents is arrogant chauvinism or tantamount to creationism. For some readers that is a reductio ad absurdum of the evolutionary framework. If the theory says that man "at best is only a monkey shaved," as Gilbert and Sullivan put it in *Princess Ida*, then it fails to explain the obvious fact that men and monkeys have different minds.

We *are* naked, lopsided apes that speak, but we also have minds that differ considerably from those of apes. The outsize brain of *Homo sapiens sapiens* is, by any standard, an extraordinary adaptation. It has allowed us to inhabit every ecosystem on earth, reshape the planet, walk on the moon, and discover the secrets of the physical universe. Chimpanzees, for all their vaunted intelligence, are a threatened species clinging to a few patches of forest and living as they did millions of years ago. Our curiosity about this difference demands more than repeating that we share most of our DNA with chimpanzees and that small changes can have big effects. Ten megabytes of genetic information and three hundred thousand generations are enough to revamp a mind considerably. Indeed, minds are probably easier to revamp than bodies because software is easier to modify than hardware. We should not be surprised to discover impressive new cognitive abilities in humans, language being just the most obvious one.

None of this is incompatible with the theory of evolution. Evolution is a conservative process, to be sure, but it can't be all *that* conservative or we would all be pond scum. Natural selection introduces differences into descendants by fitting them with specializations that adapt them to different niches. Any museum of natural history has examples of complex organs unique to a species or to a group of related species: the elephant's trunk, the narwhal's tusk, the whale's baleen, the platypus' duckbill, the armadillo's armor. Often they evolve rapidly on the geological timescale. The first whale evolved in something like ten million years from its common ancestor with its closest living relatives, ungulates such as cows and pigs. A book about whales could, in the spirit of the human-evolution books, be called *The Naked Cow*, but it would be disappointing if the book spent every page marveling at the similarities between whales and cows and never got around to discussing the adaptations that make them so different.

To say that the mind is an evolutionary adaptation is not to say that all behavior is adaptive in Darwin's sense. Natural selection is not a guardian angel that hovers over us making sure that our behavior always maximizes biological fitness. Until recently, scientists with an evolutionary bent felt a responsibility to account for acts that seem like Darwinian suicide, such as celibacy, adoption, and contraception. Perhaps, they ventured, celibate people have more time to raise large broods of nieces and nephews and thereby propagate more copies of their genes than they would if they had their own children. This kind of stretch is unnecessary, however. The reasons, first articulated by the anthropologist Donald Symons, distinguish evolutionary psychology from the school of thought in the 1970s and 1980s called sociobiology (though there is much overlap between the approaches as well).

First, selection operates over thousands of generations. For ninety-nine percent of human existence, people lived as foragers in small nomadic bands. Our brains are adapted to that long-vanished way of life, not to brand-new agricultural and industrial civilizations. They are not wired to cope with anonymous crowds, schooling, written language, government, police, courts, armies, modern medicine, formal social institutions, high technology, and other newcomers to the human experience. Since the modern mind is adapted to the Stone Age, not the computer age, there is no need to strain for adaptive explanations for everything we do. Our ancestral environment lacked the institutions that now entice us to nonadaptive choices, such as religious orders, adoption agencies, and pharmaceutical companies, so until very recently there was never a selection pressure to resist the enticements. Had the Pleistocene savanna contained trees bearing birth-control pills, we might have evolved to find them as terrifying as a venomous spider.

Second, natural selection is not a puppetmaster that pulls the strings of behavior directly. It acts by designing the generator of behavior: the package of information-processing and goal-pursuing mechanisms called the mind. Our minds are designed to generate behavior that would have been adaptive, on average, in our ancestral environment, but any particular deed done today is the effect of dozens of causes. Behavior is the outcome of an internal struggle among many mental modules, and it is played out on the chessboard of opportunities and constraints defined by *other* people's behavior. A recent cover story in *Time* asked, "Adultery: Is It in Our Genes?" The question makes no sense because neither adultery nor any other behavior can be in our genes. Conceivably a *desire* for adultery can be an indirect product of our genes, but the desire may be overridden by *other* desires that are also indirect products of our genes, such as the desire to have a trusting spouse. And the desire, even if it prevails in the rough-and-tumble of the mind, cannot be consummated as overt behavior unless there is a partner around in whom that desire has also prevailed. Behavior itself did not evolve; what evolved was the mind.

Reverse-engineering is possible only when one has a hint of what the device was designed to accomplish. We do not understand the olive-pitter until we catch on that it was designed as a machine for pitting olives rather than as a paperweight or wrist-exerciser. The goals of the designer must be sought for every part of a complex device and for the device as a whole. Automobiles have a component, the carburetor, that is designed to mix air and gasoline, and mixing air and gasoline is a subgoal of the ultimate goal, carting people around. Though the process of natural selection itself has no goal, it evolved entities that (like the automobile) are highly organized to bring about certain goals and subgoals. To reverse-engineer the mind, we must sort them out and identify the ultimate goal in its design. Was the human mind ultimately designed to create beauty? To discover truth? To love and to work? To harmonize with other human beings and with nature?

The logic of natural selection gives the answer. The ultimate goal that the mind was designed to attain is maximizing the number of copies of the genes that created it. Natural selection cares only about the long-term fate of entities that replicate, that is, entities that retain a stable identity across many generations of copying. It predicts only that replicators whose effects tend to enhance the probability of their own replication come to predominate. When we ask questions like "Who or what is supposed to benefit from an adaptation?" and "What is a design in living things a design *for*?" the theory of natural selection provides the answer: the long-term stable replicators, genes. Even our bodies, our selves, are not the ultimate beneficiary of our design. As Gould has said, "What is the 'individual reproductive success' of which Darwin speaks? It cannot be the passage of one's body into the next generation -- for, truly, you can't take it with you in this sense above all!" The criterion by which genes get selected is the quality of the bodies they build, but it is the genes making it into the next generation, not the perishable bodies, that are selected to live and fight another day.

Though there are some holdouts (such as Gould himself), the gene's-eye view predominates in evolutionary biology and has been a stunning success. It has asked, and is finding answers to, the deepest questions about life, such as how life arose, why there are cells, why there are bodies, why there is sex, how the genome is structured, why animals interact socially, and why there is communication. It is as indispensable to researchers in animal behavior as Newton's laws are to mechanical engineers.

But almost everyone misunderstands the theory. Contrary to popular belief, the gene-centered theory of evolution does *not* imply that the point of all human striving is to spread our genes. With the exception of the fertility doctor who artificially inseminated patients with his own semen, the donors to the sperm bank for Nobel Prize winners, and other kooks, *no* human being (or animal) strives to spread his or her genes. Dawkins explained the theory in a book called *The Selfish Gene*, and the metaphor was chosen carefully. People don't selfishly spread their genes; genes selfishly spread themselves. They do it by the way they build our brains. By making us enjoy life, health, sex, friends, and children, the genes buy a lottery ticket for representation in the next generation, with odds that were favorable in the environment in which we evolved. Our goals are subgoals of the ultimate goal of the genes, replicating themselves. But the two are different. As far as *we* are concerned, our goals, conscious or unconscious, are not about genes at all, but about health and lovers and children and friends.

The confusion between our goals and our genes' goals has spawned one muddle after another. A reviewer of a book about the evolution of sexuality protests that human adultery, unlike the animal equivalent, cannot be a strategy to spread the genes because adulterers take steps to prevent pregnancy. But whose strategy are we talking about? Sexual desire is *not* people's strategy to propagate their genes. It's people's strategy to attain the pleasures of sex, and the pleasures of sex are the genes' strategy to propagate themselves. If the genes don't get propagated, it's because we are smarter than they are. A book on the emotional life of animals complains that if altruism according to biologists is just helping kin or exchanging favors, both of which serve the interests of one's genes, it would not *really* be altruism after all, but some kind of hypocrisy. This too is a mixup. Just as blueprints don't necessarily specify blue buildings, selfish genes don't necessarily specify selfish organisms. As we shall see, sometimes the most selfish thing a gene can do is to build a selfless brain. Genes are a play within a play, not the interior monologue of the players.

Notes
[1] That is, *How the Mind Works*, the original source of this chapter. – Editors.

References

Chomsky, N. 1975. *Reflections on language*. New York: Pantheon.

Chomsky, N. 1988. *Language and problems of knowledge: The Managua lectures*. Cambridge, Mass.: MIT Press.

Chomsky, N. 1991. Linguistics and cognitive science: Problems and mysteries. In A. Kasher (ed.), *The Chomskyan turn*. Cambrdige, Mass.: Blackwell.

Chomsky, N. 1993. *Language and thought*. Wakefield, R. I., and London: Moyer Bell.

Cosmides, L. 1985. Deduction or Darwinian algorithms? An explanation of the "elusive" content effect on the Wason selection task. Ph. D. dissertation, Department of Psychology, Harvard University.

Cosmides, L and J. Tooby. 1994. Beyond intuition and instinct blindness: Toward an evolutionarily rigorous cognitive science. *Cognition* 50: 41-77.

Darwin, C. 1859/1964. *On the origin of the species*. Cambridge, Mass.: Harvard University Press.

Dawkins, R. 1976/1989. *The selfish gene*. (New edition.) New York: Oxford University Press.

Dawkins, R. 1983. Universal Darwinism. In D. S. Bendall (ed.), *Evolution from molecules to man*. New York: Cambridge University Press.

Dawkins, R. 1986. *The blind watchmaker: Why the evidence of evolution reveals a universe without design*. New York: Norton.

Dawkins, R. 1995. *River out of Eden: A Darwinian view of life*. New York: Basic Books.

Fodor, J. A. 1968a. The appeal to tacit knowledge in psychological explanation. *Journal of philosophy* 65: 627-640

Fodor, J. A. 1975. *The language of thought*. New York: Crowell.

Fodor, J. A. 1981. The present status of the innateness controversy. In J. A. Fodor (ed), *RePresentations*. Cambridge, Mass.: MIT Press.

Fodor, J. A. 1983. *The modularity of mind*. Cambridge, Mass.: MIT Press.

Fodor, J. A. and commentators. 1985. Précis and multiple review of "The Modularity of Mind". *Behavioral and brain sciences* 8: 1-42.

Fodor, J. A. 1994. *The elm and the expert: Mentalese and its semantics*. Cambridge, Mass.: MIT Press.

Gould, S. J 1980b. Caring groups and selfish genes. In S. J. Gould, *The panda's thumb*. New York: Norton.

Gould, S. J. 1983b. What happens to bodies if genes act for themselves? In S. J. Gould, *Hen's teeth and horses toes*. New York: Norton.

Gould, S. J. 1992. The confusion over evolution. *New York Review of Books*, November 19.

Gould, S. J. and R. C. Lewontin. 1979. The spandrels of San Marco and the Panglossian program: A critique of the adaptationist prgramme. *Proceedings of the Royal Society of London* 205: 281-288.

Hamilton, W. D. 1996. *Narrow roads of gene land: The collected papers of W. D. Hamilton*, Vol. 1: *Evolution of social behavior*. New York: W. H. Freeman.

Minsky, M. 1985. *The society of mind*. New York: Simon and Schuster.

Minsky, M. and S. Papert. 1988b. Epilogue: The new connectionism. In M. Minsky and S. Papert, *Perceptrons: Expanded edition*. Cambridge, Mass.: MIT Press.

Newell, A. and H. A. Simon. 1981. Computer science as empirical science: Symbols and search. In Haugeland, 1981a.

Profet, M. 1992. Pregnancy sickness as adaptation: A deterrent to maternal ingestion of teratogens. In Barkow, Cosmides and Tooby, 1992.

Putnam, H. 1960. Minds and machines. In S. Hook (ed.), *Dimensions of mind: A symposium*. New York: New York University Pres.

Simon, H. A. and A. Newell. 1964. Information process in computer and man. *American scientist* 52: 281-300.

Symons, D. 1979. *The evolution of human sexuality*. New York: Oxford University Press.

Symons, D. 1992. On the use and misuse of Darwinism in the study of human behavior. In Barkow, Cosmides and Tooby, 1992.

Tooby, J. 1985. The emergence of evolutionary psychology. In D. Pines (ed.), *Emergence synthesis in science*. Santa Fe, N.M.: Santa Fe Institute.

Tooby, J. 1988. The evolution of sex and its sequelae. Ph.D. dissertation, Harvard University.

Tooby, J. and L. Cosmides. 1989. Adaptation versus phylogeny: The role of animal psychology in the study of human behavior. *International journal of comparative psychology* 2: 105-118.

Tooby, J. and L. Cosmides. 1990a. The past explains the present: Emotional adaptations and the structure of ancestral environments. *Ethology and Sociobiology* 11: 373-424.

Tooby, J. and L. Cosmides. 1992. Psychological foundations of culture. In Barkow, Cosmides and Tooby, 1992.

Turing, A. M. 1950. Computing machinery and intelligence. *Mind* 59: 433-460.

Williams, G. C. 1966. *Adaptation and natural selection: A critique of some current evolutionary thought*. Princeton, N.J.: Princeton University Press.

Williams, G. C. 1992. *Natural selection: Domains, levels, and challenges*. New York: Oxford University Press.

Language and the Brain[1]

Noam Chomsky

The right way to address the announced topic would be to review the fundamental principles of language and the brain and to show how they can be unified, perhaps on the model of chemistry and physics 65 years ago, or the integration of parts of biology within the complex a few years later. But that course I am not going to try to attempt. One of the few things I can say about this topic with any confidence is that I do not begin to know enough to approach it in the right way. With less confidence I suspect it may be fair to say that current understanding falls well short of laying the basis for the unification of the sciences of the brain and higher mental faculties, language among them, and that many surprises may lie along the way to what seems a distant goal — which would itself come as no surprise if the classical examples I mentioned are indeed a realistic model.

This somewhat skeptical assessment of current prospects differs from two prevalent but opposing views. The first holds that the skepticism is unwarranted, or more accurately, profoundly in error, because the question of unification does not even arise. It does not arise for psychology as the study of mind, because the topic does not fall within biology, a position taken to define the "computer model of mind" [1]; nor for language, because language is an extra-human object, the standard view within major currents of philosophy of mind and language, and also put forth recently by prominent figures in neuroscience and ethology. At least that is what the words seem to imply; the intentions may be different. I will return to some prominent current examples.

A contrasting view holds that the problem of unification does arise, but that the skepticism is unwarranted. Unification of the

In Search of a Language for the Mind-Brain, ed. Saleemi, Bohn and Gjedde, *The Dolphin* 33 © 2005 by Aarhus University Press, Denmark. ISBN 87 7934 005 9.

brain and cognitive sciences is an imminent prospect, overcoming Cartesian dualism. This optimistic assessment is expressed forthrightly by evolutionary biologist E. O. Wilson in a recent publication of the American Academy of Arts and Sciences devoted to the brain, summarizing the state of the art, and seems to be shared rather broadly: "Researchers now speak confidently of a coming solution to the brain-mind problem" [2]. Similar confidence has been expressed for half a century, including announcements by eminent figures that the brain-mind problem has been solved.

We can, then, identify several points of view with regard to the general problem of unification:

(1) There is no issue: language and higher mental faculties generally are not part of biology.

(2) They belong to biology in principle, and any constructive approach to the study of human thought and its expression, or of human action and interaction relies on this assumption, at least tacitly.

Category (2), in turn, has two variants: (A) unification is close at hand; (B) we do not currently see how these parts of biology relate to one another, and suspect that fundamental insights may be missing altogether.

The last point of view, (2B), seems to me the most plausible. I will try to indicate why, and to sketch some of the terrain that should be covered in a careful and comprehensive overview of these topics.

As a framework for the discussion, I would like to select three theses that seem to me generally reasonable, and have for a long time. I will quote current formulations by leading scientists, however, not my own versions from past years.

The first thesis is articulated by neuroscientist Vernon Mountcastle, introducing the American Academy study I mentioned. A guiding theme of the contributions, and the field generally, he observes, is that "Things mental, indeed minds, are emergent properties of brains," though "these emergences are not regarded as irreducible but are produced by principles that control the interactions between lower level events — principles we do not yet understand."

The second thesis is methodological. It is presented clearly by ethologist Mark Hauser in his comprehensive study *Evolution of Communication*.[3] Following Tinbergen, he argues, we should adopt four perspectives in studying "communication in the animal kingdom, including human language." To understand some trait, we should:

Seek the mechanisms that implement it, psychological and physiological; the *mechanistic* perspective
Sort out genetic and environmental factors, which can also be approached at psychological or physiological levels; the *ontogenetic* perspective
Find the "fitness consequences" of the trait, its effects on survival and reproduction; the *functional* perspective
Unravel "the evolutionary history of the species so that the structure of the trait can be evaluated in light of ancestral features"; the *phylogenetic* perspective

The third thesis is presented by cognitive neuroscientist C.R. Gallistel [4]: the "modular view of learning," which he takes to be "the norm these days in neuroscience." According to this view, the brain incorporates "specialized organs," computationally specialized to solve particular kinds of problems, as they do with great facility, apart from "extremely hostile environments." The growth and development of these specialized organs, sometimes called "learning," is the result of internally-directed processes and environmental effects that trigger and shape development. The language organ is one such component of the human brain.

In conventional terminology, adapted from earlier usage, the language organ is the *faculty of language* (FL); the theory of the initial state of FL, an expression of the genes, is *universal grammar* (UG); theories of states attained are *particular grammars*; the states themselves are *internal languages*, "languages" for short. The initial state is, of course, not manifested at birth, as in the case of other organs, say the visual system.

Let us now look more closely at the three theses—reasonable I think, but with qualifications—beginning with the first: "Things mental, indeed minds, are emergent properties of brains."

The thesis is widely accepted, often considered a distinctive and exciting contribution of the current era, if still highly controversial. In the past few years it has been put forth as an "astonishing hypothesis," "the bold assertion that mental phenomena are entirely natural and caused by the neurophysiological activities of the brain" and "that capacities of the human mind are in fact capacities of the human brain"; or as a "radical new idea" in the philosophy of mind that may at last put an end to Cartesian dualism, though some continue to believe that the chasm between body and mind cannot be bridged.

The picture is misleading, and it is useful to understand why. The thesis is not new, and it should not be controversial, for reasons understood centuries ago. The thesis was articulated clearly in the 18th century, and for compelling reasons—though controversially then, because of affront to religious doctrines. By 1750, David Hume casually described thought as a "little agitation of the brain."[5] A few years later the thesis was elaborated by the eminent chemist Joseph Priestley: "the powers of sensation or perception and thought" are properties of "a certain organized system of matter"; properties "termed mental" are "the result [of the] organical structure" of the brain and "the human nervous system" generally. Equivalently: "Things mental, indeed minds, are emergent properties of brains" (Mountcastle). Priestley of course could not say how this emergence takes place, nor can we do much better after 200 years.

I think the brain and cognitive sciences can learn some useful lessons from the rise of the emergence thesis in early modern science, and the ways the natural sciences have developed since, right up to the mid-20th century, with the unification of physics-chemistry-biology. Current controversies about mind and brain are strikingly similar to debates about atoms, molecules, chemical structures and reactions, and related matters, which were very much alive well into this century. Similar, and in ways that I think are instructive.

The reasons for the 18th century emergence thesis, recently revived, were indeed compelling. The modern scientific revolution, from Galileo, was based on the thesis that the world is a great machine, which could in principle be constructed by a master artisan, a complex version of the clocks and other intricate automata that fascinated the 17th and 18th centuries, much as computers have provided a stimulus to thought and imagination in recent years; the change of artifacts has limited consequences for the basic issues, as Alan Turing demonstrated 60 years ago. The thesis—called "the mechanical philosophy"— has two aspects: empirical and methodological. The factual thesis has to do with the nature of the world: it is a machine constructed of interacting parts. The methodological thesis has to do with intelligibility: true understanding requires a mechanical model, a device that an artisan could construct.

This Galilean model of intelligibility has a corollary: when mechanism fails, understanding fails. For this reason, when Galileo came to be disheartened by apparent inadequacies of mechanical explanation, he finally concluded that humans will never completely understand even "a single effect in nature." Descartes, in contrast, was much more optimistic. He thought he could demonstrate that most of the phenomena of nature could be explained in mechanical terms: the inorganic and organic world apart from humans, but also human physiology, sensation, perception, and action to a large extent. The limits of mechanical explanation were reached when these human functions are mediated by thought, a unique human possession based on a principle that escapes mechanical explanation: a "creative" principle that underlies acts of will and choice, which are "the noblest thing we can have" and all that "truly belongs" to us (in Cartesian terms). Humans are only "incited and inclined" to act in certain ways, not "compelled" (or random), and in this respect are unlike machines—that is, the rest of the world. The most striking example for the Cartesians was the normal use of language: humans can express their thoughts in novel and limitless ways that are constrained by bodily state but not determined by it, appropriate to situations but not caused by them, and that evoke in others thoughts that they could have expressed in similar ways—what we may call "the creative aspect of language use."

It is worth bearing in mind that these conclusions are correct, as far as we know.

In these terms, Cartesian scientists developed experimental procedures to determine whether some other creature has a mind like ours—elaborate versions of what has been revived as the Turing test in the past half century, though without some crucial fallacies that have attended this revival, disregarding Turing's explicit warnings, an interesting topic that I will put aside.[6] In the same terms, Descartes could formulate a relatively clear mind-body problem: having established two principles of nature, the mechanical and mental principles, we can ask how they interact, a major problem for 17th century science. But the problem did not survive very long. As is well known, the entire picture collapsed when Newton established, to his great dismay, that not only does mind escape the reach of the mechanical philosophy, but so does everything else in nature, even the simplest terrestrial and planetary motion. As pointed out by Alexander Koyr', one of the founders of the modern history of science, Newton showed that "a purely materialistic or mechanistic physics is impossible."[7] Accordingly, the natural world fails to meet the standard of intelligibility that animated the modern scientific revolution. We must accept the "admission into the body of science of incomprehensible and inexplicable 'facts' imposed upon us by empiricism," as Koyr' puts the matter.

Newton regarded his refutation of mechanism as an "absurdity," but could find no way around it despite much effort. Nor could the greatest scientists of his day, or since. Later discoveries introduced still greater "absurdities." Nothing has lessened the force of David Hume's judgment that by refuting the self-evident mechanical philosophy, Newton "restored Nature's ultimate secrets to that obscurity in which they ever did and ever will remain."

A century later, in his classic history of materialism, Friedrich Lange pointed out that Newton effectively destroyed the materialist doctrine as well as the standards of intelligibility and the expectations that were based on it: Scientists have since "accustomed ourselves to the abstract notion of forces, or rather to a notion hovering in a mystic obscurity between abstraction and concrete comprehension," a "turning-point" in the history of materialism that removes the surviving remnants of the doctrine far from those of the "genuine Materialists" of the 17th century, and deprives them of much significance.

Both the methodological and the empirical theses collapsed, never to be reconstituted.

On the methodological side, standards of intelligibility were considerably weakened. The standard that inspired the modern scientific revolution was abandoned: the goal is intelligibility of theories, not of the world — a considerable difference, which may well bring into operation different faculties of mind, a topic some day for cognitive science, perhaps. As the preeminent Newton scholar I. Bernard Cohen put the matter, these changes "set forth a new view of science" in which the goal is "not to seek ultimate explanations," rooted in principles that appear to us self-evident, but to find the best theoretical account we can of the phenomena of experience and experiment. In general, conformity to common sense understanding is not a criterion for rational inquiry.

On the factual side, there is no longer any concept of body, or matter, or "the physical." There is just the world, with its various aspects: mechanical, electromagnetic, chemical, optical, organic, mental — categories that are not defined or delimited in an a priori way, but are at most conveniences: no one asks whether life falls within chemistry or biology, except for temporary convenience. In each of the shifting domains of constructive inquiry, one can try to develop intelligible explanatory theories, and to unify them, but no more than that.

The new limits of inquiry were understood by working scientists. The 18th century chemist Joseph Black observed that "chemical affinity must be accepted as a first principle, which we cannot explain any more than Newton could explain gravitation, and let us defer accounting for the laws of affinity until we have established such a body of doctrine as Newton has established concerning the laws of gravitation." That is pretty much what happened. Chemistry proceeded to establish a rich body of doctrine; "its triumphs [were] built on no reductionist foundation but rather achieved in isolation from the newly emerging science of physics," a leading historian of chemistry observes.[8] In fact, no reductionist foundation was discovered. What was finally achieved by Linus Pauling 65 years ago was unification, not reduction. Physics had to undergo fundamental changes in order to be unified with basic chemistry, departing even more radically from common sense notions of "the physical":

Physics had to "free itself" from "intuitive pictures" and give up the hope of "visualizing the world," as Heisenberg put it,[9] yet another long leap away from intelligibility in the sense of the scientific revolution of the 17th century.

The early modern scientific revolution also brought about what we should properly call "the first cognitive revolution" — maybe the only phase of the cognitive sciences to deserve the name "revolution." Cartesian mechanism laid the groundwork for what became neurophysiology. 17th and 18th century thinkers also developed rich and illuminating ideas about perception, language, and thought that have been rediscovered since, sometimes only in part. Lacking any conception of body, psychology could then— and can today—only follow the path of chemistry. Apart from its theological framework, there has really been no alternative to John Locke's cautious speculation, later known as "Locke's suggestion": God might have chosen to "superadd to matter *a faculty of thinking*" just as he "annexed effects to motion which we can in no way conceive motion able to produce"—notably the property of attraction at a distance, a revival of occult properties, many leading scientists argued (with Newton's partial agreement).

In this context the emergence thesis was virtually inescapable, in various forms: For the 18th century: "the powers of sensation or perception and thought" are properties of "a certain organized system of matter"; properties "termed mental" are "the result [of the] organical structure" of the brain and "the human nervous system" generally.

A century later, Darwin asked rhetorically why "thought, being a secretion of the brain," should be considered "more wonderful than gravity, a property of matter."[10]

Today, the study of the brain is based on the thesis that "Things mental, indeed minds, are emergent properties of brains"

Throughout, the thesis is essentially the same, and should not be contentious: it is hard to imagine an alternative in the post-Newtonian world.

The working scientist can do no better than to try to construct "bodies of doctrine" for various aspects of the world, and seek to unify them, recognizing that the world is not intelligible to us in anything like the way the pioneers of modern science hoped, and that the goal is unification, not necessarily reduction. As the history of the sciences clearly reveals, one can never guess what surprises lie ahead.

It is important to recognize that Cartesian dualism was a reasonable scientific thesis, but one that disappeared three centuries ago. There has been no mind-body problem to debate since. The thesis did not disappear because of inadequacies of the Cartesian concept of mind, but because the concept of body collapsed with Newton's demolition of the mechanical philosophy. It is common today to ridicule "Descartes's error" in postulating mind, his "ghost in the machine." But that mistakes what happened: Newton exorcised the machine; the ghost remained intact. Two contemporary physicists, Paul Davies and John Gribbin, close their recent book *The Matter Myth* by making that point once again, though they misattribute the elimination of the machine: to the new quantum physics. True, that adds another blow, but the "matter myth" had been demolished 250 years earlier, a fact that was understood by working scientists at the time, and has become part of the standard history of the sciences since. These are issues that merit some thought, I believe.

For the rejuvenated cognitive science of the 20th century, it is also useful, I think, to pay close attention to what followed the unification of a virtually unchanged chemistry with a radically revised physics in the 1930s, and what preceded the unification. The most dramatic event that followed was the unification of biology and chemistry. This was a case of genuine reduction, but to a newly created physical chemistry; some of the same people were involved, notably Pauling. This genuine reduction has sometimes led to the confident expectation that mental aspects of the world will be reduced to something like the contemporary brain sciences. Maybe so, maybe not. In any event, the history of science provides little reason for confident expectations. True reduction is not so common in the history of science, and need not be assumed automatically to be a model for what will happen in the future.

Still more instructive is what was taking place just before the unification of chemistry and physics. Prior to unification, it was commonly argued by leading scientists that chemistry is just a calculating device, a way to organize results about chemical reactions, sometimes to predict them. In the early years of this century, molecules were regarded the same way. Poincar' ridiculed the belief that the molecular theory of gases is more than a mode of calculation; people fall into that error because they are familiar with the game of billiards, he said. Chemistry is not about anything real, it was argued: the reason is that no one knew how to reduce it to physics. In 1929, Bertrand Russell -- who knew the sciences well—pointed out that chemical laws "cannot at present be reduced to physical laws"[11]; not false, but misleading in an important way. It turned out that the phrase "at present" was out of place. Reduction was impossible, as was soon discovered, until the conception of physical nature and law was (radically) revised.

It should now be clear that the debates about the reality of chemistry were based on fundamental misunderstanding. Chemistry was "real" and "about the world" in the only sense of these concepts that we have: it was part of the best conception of how the world works that human intelligence had been able to contrive. It is impossible to do better than that.

The debates about chemistry a few years ago are in many ways echoed in philosophy of mind and cognitive science today— and theoretical chemistry, of course, is hard science, merging indistinguishably with core physics: it is not at the periphery of scientific understanding, like the brain and cognitive sciences, which are trying to study systems that are vastly more complex, and poorly understood. These very recent debates about chemistry, and their unexpected outcome, should be instructive for the brain and cognitive sciences. They suggest that it is a mistake to think of computer models of the mind that are divorced from biology—that is, in principle unaffected by anything that might be discovered in the biological sciences. Or Platonistic or other non-biological conceptions of language, also insulated from important evidence, to their detriment. Or to hold that the relation of the mental to the physical is not reducibility but the weaker notion of *supervenience*: any change in mental events or states entails a "physical change," though not conversely, and there is nothing more specific to say. The pre-unification debates over chemistry could be rephrased in these terms: those denying the reality of chemistry could have held that chemical properties supervene on physical properties, but are not reducible to them. That would have been an error: the right physical properties had not yet been discovered. Once they were, talk of supervenience became superfluous and we move towards unification. The same stance seems to me reasonable in the study of mental aspects of the world.

In general, it seems sensible to follow the good advice of post-Newtonian scientists, and Newton himself for that matter, and seek to construct "bodies of doctrine" in whatever terms we can, unshackled by common sense intuitions about how the world must be—we know that it is *not* that way—and untroubled by the fact that we may have to "defer accounting for the principles" in terms of general scientific understanding, which may turn out to be inadequate to the task of unification, as has regularly been the case for 300 years. A good deal of discussion of these topics seems to me misguided, perhaps seriously so, for reasons such as these.

There are other similarities worth remembering between pre-unification chemistry and current cognitive science. The "triumphs of chemistry" provided valuable guidelines for the eventual reconstruction of physics: they provided conditions that core physics would have to meet. In a similar way, discoveries about bee communication provide conditions that have to be met by some future account in terms of cells. In both cases, it is a two-way street: the discoveries of physics constrain possible chemical models, as those of basic biology should constrain models of insect behavior.

There are familiar analogues in the brain and cognitive sciences: the issue of computational, algorithmic and implementation theories emphasized by David Marr, for example. Or Eric Kandel's work on learning in marine snails, seeking "to translate into neuronal terms ideas that have been proposed at an abstract level by experimental psychologists," and thus to show how cognitive psychology and neurobiology "may begin to converge to yield a new perspective in the study of learning."[12] Very reasonable, though the actual course of the sciences should alert us to the possibility that the convergence may not take place because something is missing—where, we cannot know until we find out.

I have been talking so far about the first of the three theses I mentioned at the outset: the guiding principle that "Things mental, indeed minds, are emergent properties of brains." That seems correct, but close to truism, for reasons understood by Darwin and by eminent scientists a century earlier, and that followed from Newton's discovery of "absurdities" that were nonetheless true.

Let us turn to the second: the methodological thesis, quoted from Mark Hauser's *Evolution of Communication*: to account for some trait we must adopt the ethological approach of Tinbergen, with its four basic perspectives: (1) mechanisms, (2) ontogenesis, (3) fitness consequences, (4) evolutionary history.

For Hauser, as for others, the "Holy Grail" is human language: the goal is to show how it can be understood if we investigate it from these four perspectives, and only that way. The same should be true of vastly simpler systems: the "dance language" of the honeybee, to select the sole example in the animal world that, according to standard (though not uncontroversial) accounts, seems to have at least some superficial similarity to human language: infinite scope, and the property of "displaced reference"—the ability to communicate information about something not in the sensory field. Bees have brains the size of a grass seed, with less than a million neurons; there are related species that differ in mode of communication; there are no restrictions on invasive experiment. But basic questions remain unanswered: questions about physiology and evolution, in particular.

In his review of this topic, Hauser does not discuss mechanisms, and the few suggestions that have been made seem rather exotic; for example, mathematician/biologist Barbara Shipman's theory that the bee's performance is based on an ability to map a certain six-dimensional topological space into three dimensions, perhaps by means of some kind of "quark detector."[13] On evolution, Hauser has only a few sentences, which essentially formulate the problem. The same is true of other cases he reviews. For example, songbirds, which are "*the* success story in developmental research," although there is no "convincing scenario" about selection—or even an unconvincing one, it seems.

It should hardly surprise us, then, that questions about physiological mechanisms and phylogenesis remain so mysterious in the incomparably more difficult case of human language.

A closer look at Hauser's study gives some indication of the remoteness of the goal that he and others set—a worthy goal, but we should be realistic about where we stand in relation to it. First, the title of the book is misleading: it is not about the evolution of communication, a topic that receives only passing mention. Rather, it is a comparative study of communication in many species. That is made explicit in the comments in Derek Bickerton's review in *Nature* that are quoted on the jacket cover; and in the final chapter, which speculates about "future directions." The chapter is entitled "comparative communication," realistically; there is little speculation about evolution, a quite different matter. Rather generally, what Hauser and others describe as the record of natural selection turns out to be an account of the beautiful fit of an organism to its ecological niche. The facts are often fascinating and suggestive, but they do not constitute evolutionary history: rather, they formulate the problem to be solved by the student of evolution.

Second, Hauser points out that this comprehensive study of comparative communication is "irrelevant to the formal study of language" (an overstatement, I think). That is no small point: what he calls the "formal study of language" includes the psychological aspects of the first two perspectives of the

ethological approach: (1) the mechanisms of language, and (2)
their ontogenesis. And what is irrelevant to psychological aspects
is irrelevant to physiological aspects as well, since anything that
has bearing on physiological aspects imposes conditions on
psychological aspects. Accordingly, the first two perspectives of
the recommended approach of Tinbergen are effectively
abandoned, for human language. For similar reasons, the
comparative study may be "irrelevant," in the same sense, to
contemporary inquiry into bee communication, largely a richly
detailed variety of "descriptive linguistics." That seems a
plausible conclusion: a great deal has been learned about
particular species at a descriptive level—insects, birds, monkeys,
and others. But little emerges of any generality.

The "irrelevance" to human language is, however, far deeper.
The reason is that—as Hauser also observes—language is not
properly regarded as a system of communication. It is a system
for expressing thought, something quite different. It can of course
be used for communication, as can anything people do— manner
of walking or style of clothes or hair, for example. But in any
useful sense of the term, communication is not *the* function of
language, and may even be of no unique significance for
understanding the functions and nature of language. Hauser
quotes Somerset Maugham's quip that "if nobody spoke unless he
had something to say,...the human race would very soon lose the
use of speech." His point seems accurate enough, even apart from
the fact that language use is largely to oneself: "inner speech" for
adults, monologue for children. Furthermore, whatever merit
there may be to guesses about selectional processes that might, or
might not, have shaped human language, they do not crucially
depend on the belief that the system is an outgrowth of some
mode of communication. One can devise equally meritorious (that
is, equally pointless) tales of the advantage conferred by a series
of small mutations that facilitated planning and clarification of
thought; perhaps even less fanciful, since it is unnecessary to
suppose that the mutations took place in parallel in the group—
not that I am proposing this or any other story. There is a rich
record of the unhappy fate of highly plausible stories about what

might have happened, once something was learned about what did happen—and in cases where far more is understood.

In the same connection, it is noteworthy that human language does not even appear in Hauser's "taxonomy of communicative information" (mating, survival, identity of caller). Language can surely be used for alarm calls, identification of speaker, and so on, but to study the functioning of language in these terms would be hopelessly misleading.

A related difficulty is that Hauser restricts the functional perspective to "adaptive solutions." That sharply limits the study of evolution, a point that Darwin forcefully emphasized and is now much better understood. In fact, Hauser cites case after case of traits that have no adaptive function, so he argues—appearing only in contrived situations with no counterpart in nature.

These matters are barely discussed; what I have cited are scattered remarks, a sentence here and there. But they indicate the immensity of the gaps that we must contemplate if we take the ethological perspective seriously—as of course we should, so I believe, and have been arguing for 40 years.[14] Hauser's speculations about some future inquiry into the evolution of human language highlight the mystery. He refers to the two familiar basic problems: it is necessary to account for (1) the massive explosion of the lexicon, and (2) the recursive system for generating an infinite variety of meaningful utterances. For the latter, no speculation is offered. As for (1), Hauser reports that there is nothing analogous in the animal kingdom, including his own specialty (nonhuman primates). He observes that a precondition for the explosion of the lexicon is an innate human capacity to imitate, which he finds to be fundamentally different from anything in the animal world, perhaps unique. He was able to find only one possible exception: apes subjected to training. His conclusion is that "certain features of the human environment are required for engaging the capacity to imitate in apes," which, if true, would seem to imply that the capacity is not the result of the adaptive selection to which he and others insist we must restrict ourselves in studying evolution. As for the origins of the human capacity to imitate, he points out that we know nothing and may never be able to find out when - or for that matter how - it appeared in hominid evolution.

Furthermore, like many others, Hauser seriously underestimates the ways in which the human use of words to refer differs in its essential structural and functional properties from the rare examples of "referential signals" in other species, including some monkeys (possibly some apes, though the evidence, he says, is uncertain), a matter that goes well beyond the issues of displaced and situation-free reference. And he also seriously overstates what has been shown. Thus, citing some of Darwin's cautious speculations, he writes that "we thus *learn* two important lessons" about "human language evolution": that "the structure and function of human language can be accounted for by natural selection," and that "the most impressive link between human and nonhuman-animal forms of communication lies in the ability to express emotional state." Similarly, Steven Pinker "*shows* how a Darwinian account of language evolution is the only possible account,... because natural selection is the only mechanism that can account for the complex design features of a trait such as language" (my emphasis). It would be remarkable if something had been "shown" about the evolution of human language, let alone the vastly more ambitious claim cited; or if we could "learn" anything significant from speculations about the topic. Surely nothing so amazing has taken place. Cautious speculation and confident pronouncement do not *show* anything, and the most that we *learn* is that there might be a useful path to follow. Perhaps.

That aside, the conclusions that have supposedly been demonstrated make little sense, apart from a charitable reading; uncontroversially, natural selection operates within a space of options determined by natural law (and historical/ecological contingencies), and it would be the sheerest dogmatism to issue a priori proclamations on the role of these factors in what comes to pass. That is true whether we are considering the appearance of the Fibonacci series in nature, or human language, or anything else in the biological world. What has been "shown" or "persuasively argued" is that natural selection is plausibly taken to be a primary factor in evolution, as Darwin argued, and as no one (within the circles that Hauser considers) even questions; why he has decided that I (or anyone) have insisted that "natural selection theory cannot account for the design features of human language," he does not say (and it is manifestly untrue, under the charitable reading required to grant the statement some meaning). Beyond the generally shared assumptions about natural selection and other mechanisms in evolution, one tries to find out what took place, whether studying the eye, the giraffe's neck, the bones of the middle ear, mammalian visual systems, human language, or anything else. Confident pronouncement is not to be confused with demonstration or even persuasive argument.

Though I suppose Hauser would deny this, it seems to me that on a close look, his actual conclusions do not differ much from the extreme skepticism of his Harvard colleague, evolutionary biologist Richard Lewontin, who concludes — forcefully — that the evolution of cognition is simply beyond the reach of contemporary science.[15]

The remoteness of the proclaimed goals leads to what seem to me some strange proposals: for example, that "the human brain, vocal tract, and language appear to have co-evolved" for the purposes of linguistic communication. Hauser is borrowing the notion of co-evolution of language and the brain from neuroscientist Terrence Deacon.[16] Deacon argues that students of language and its ontogenesis — the first two perspectives of the ethological approach — are making a serious error when they adopt the standard approach of the neurosciences: seeking to discover a genetically-determined component of the mind/brain and the state changes it undergoes through experience and maturation. They have overlooked a more promising alternative: "that the extra support for language learning," beyond the data of experience, "is vested neither in the brain of the child nor in the brains of parents or teachers, but outside brains, in language itself." Language and languages are extra-human entities with a remarkable "capacity...to evolve and adapt with respect to human hosts." These creatures are not only extra-human, but apparently outside the biological world altogether.

What are these strange entities, and where did they come from? What they are is left unstated, except that they have evolved to incorporate the properties of language that have been mistakenly attributed to the brain. Their origin is no less mysterious, though once they somehow appeared, "the world's languages evolved spontaneously," through natural selection, in a "flurry of adaptation" that has "been going on *outside* the human brain." They have thereby "become better and better adapted to people" — like parasites and hosts, or perhaps prey and predator in the familiar cycle of co-evolution; or perhaps viruses provide the best analogy, he suggests. We also derive an account of language universals: they have "emerged spontaneously and independently in each evolving language... They are *convergent* features of language evolution," like the dorsal fins of sharks and dolphins. Having evolved spontaneously and acquired the universal properties of language by rapid natural selection, one of these extra-human creatures attaches itself to my granddaughter in New England, and a different one to my granddaughter in Nicaragua — actually she is infected by two of these mysterious viruses. It is a mistake to seek an explanation of the outcome in these and all other cases by investigating the interplay of experience and innate structure of the brain; rather, the right parasites attach themselves to hosts in a particular community in some mystical fashion — by a "magician's trick," to borrow Deacon's term for the ordinary assumptions of naturalistic science — yielding their knowledge of specific languages.

Deacon agrees, of course, that infants are "predisposed to learn human languages" and "are strongly biased in their choices" of "the rules underlying language," acquiring within a few years "an immensely complex rule system and a rich vocabulary" at a time when they cannot even learn elementary arithmetic. So there is "something special about human brains that enables us to do with ease what no other species can do even minimally without intense effort and remarkably insightful training." But it is a mistake to approach these predispositions and special structures of the brain the way we do other aspects of nature — the visual system, for example; no one would propose that insect and mammalian visual organs evolved spontaneously by rapid natural selection and now attach themselves to hosts, yielding the visual capacities of bees and monkeys; or that the waggle dance of bees or the calls of vervets are organism-external parasites that have co-evolved to provide the capacities of the host. But in the special case of human language, we are not to pursue the normal course of the natural sciences, seeking to determine the nature of the "predispositions" and "special structures" and the ways they are realized in brain mechanisms (in which case the extra-organic entities that have co-evolved with language vanish from the scene).

Since in this unique case extra-organic "viruses" have evolved that attach themselves to hosts in just the right way, we need not attribute to the child more than a "general theory of learning." So we discover once we overcome the surprising failure of linguists and psychologists to recognize that the languages of the world — in fact, the possible languages that are as yet unspoken — may have evolved spontaneously, outside of brains, coming to "embody the predispositions of children's minds" by natural selection.

There is, I think, a sense in which Deacon's proposals are on the right track. The idea that a child needs no more than a "general theory of learning" to attain language and other cognitive states can be sustained only with quite heroic moves. That is a basic thrust of the third of the framework theses introduced at the outset, to which we return directly. Much the same conclusion is illustrated by the extraordinarily rich innatist and modular assumptions embedded within attempts to implement what are often misleadingly presented as unstructured general learning theories, and the no less extraordinary assumptions about innate structure built into approaches based on speculative evolutionary scenarios that explicitly assume extreme modularity.[17]

The only real problem, Deacon argues, is "symbolic reference." The rest will somehow fall into place if we account for this in evolutionary terms. How the rest falls into place is not discussed. But perhaps that does not matter, because "symbolic reference" is also left as a complete mystery, in part because of failure to attend to its most elementary properties in human language. I have been giving quotes, because I have no idea what this means. And understanding is not facilitated by an account of "linguistics" (including views attributed to me) that is unrecognizable, with allusions so vague that it is often hard even to guess what might have been the source of the misunderstanding (sometimes it is easy; e.g., misunderstanding of terminology used in a technical sense, such as "competence"). Whatever the meaning may be, the conclusion seems to be that it is an error to investigate the brain to discover the nature of human language; rather, studies of language must be about the extrabiological entities that co-evolved with humans and somehow "latch on" to them. These proposals have been highly acclaimed by prominent evolutionary psychologists and biologists, but I do not see why. Taken at all seriously, they seem only to reshape standard problems of science as utter mysteries, placing them beyond any hope of understanding, while barring the procedures of rational inquiry that have been taken for granted for hundreds of years.

Returning to the methodological thesis that we should adopt an ethological approach, it is reasonable enough in principle, but the ways it is pursued raise many questions. As far as I can see, the renewed call to pursue this approach, as advocated 40 years ago in the critical literature on "behavioral science," leaves us about where we were. We can study the genetically-determined component of the brain — and maybe more than the brain — that is dedicated to the structure and use of language, and the states it attains (the various languages), and we can investigate the process by which the state changes take place (language acquisition). We can try to discover the psychological and physiological mechanisms and principles, and to unify them, standard problems of science. These inquiries constitute the first two perspectives of the ethological approach: the study of mechanisms and ontogenesis. Turning to the third perspective, the functional perspective, we can investigate the use of language by the person who has attained a particular state, though the restriction to effects on survival and reproduction is far too narrow, if we hope to understand much about language. The fourth perspective — phylogenesis — seems a remote prospect at best, and does not seem much advanced by the comparative study of communication, a wholly different matter.

Let us turn finally to the third thesis I mentioned, quoting Gallistel: the substantive thesis that in all animals, learning is based on specialized mechanisms, "instincts to learn" in specific ways; what Tinbergen called "innate dispositions to learn."[18] These "learning mechanisms" can be regarded as "organs within the brain [that] are neural circuits whose structure enables them to perform one particular kind of computation," as they do more or less reflexively apart from "extremely hostile environments." Human language acquisition is instinctive in this sense, based on a specialized "language organ." This "modular view of learning" Gallistel takes to be "the norm these days in neuroscience." He argues that this framework includes whatever is fairly well understood, including conditioning, insofar as it is a real phenomenon. "To imagine that there exists a general purpose learning mechanism in addition to all these problem-specific learning mechanisms...is like trying to imagine the structure of a general purpose organ, the organ that takes care of problems not taken care of by adaptively specialized organs like the liver, the kidney, the heart and the lungs," or a "general purpose sensory organ, which solves the problem of sensing" for the cases not handled by the eye, the ear, and other specialized sensory organs. Nothing like that is known in biology; "Adaptive specialization of mechanism is so ubiquitous and so obvious in biology, at every level of analysis, and for every kind of function, that no one thinks it necessary to call attention to it as a general principle about biological mechanisms." Accordingly, "it is odd but true that most past and contemporary theorizing about learning" departs so radically from what is taken for granted in the study of organisms—a mistake, he argues.

As far as I know, the approach Gallistel recommends is sound; in the special case of language, it seems to me to be adopted by all substantive inquiry, at least tacitly, even when that is heatedly denied. It is hard to avoid the conclusion that a part of the human biological endowment is a specialized "language organ," the faculty of language FL. Its initial state is an expression of the genes, comparable to the initial state of the human visual system, and it appears to be a common human possession to close approximation. Accordingly, a typical child will acquire any language under appropriate conditions, even under severe deficit and in "hostile environments." The initial state changes under the triggering and shaping effect of experience, and internally-determined processes of maturation, yielding later states that seem to stabilize at several stages, finally at about puberty. We can think of the initial state of FL as a device that maps experience into state L attained: a "language acquisition device" (LAD). The existence of such a LAD is sometimes regarded as controversial, but it is no more so than the (equivalent) assumption that there is a dedicated "language module" that accounts for the linguistic development of an infant as distinct from that of her pet kitten (or chimpanzee, or whatever), given essentially the same experience. Even the most extreme "radical behaviorist" speculations presuppose (at least tacitly) that a child can somehow distinguish linguistic materials from the rest of the confusion around it, hence postulating the existence of FL (= LAD)[19]; and as discussion of language acquisition becomes more substantive, it moves to assumptions about the language organ that are more rich and domain specific, without exception to my knowledge. That includes the acquisition of lexical items, which turn out to have rich and complex semantic structure, even the simplest of them. Knowledge of these properties becomes available on very limited evidence and, accordingly, would be expected to be essentially uniform among languages; and is, as far as is known.

Here we move to substantive questions within the first three perspectives of the ethological approach, though again, without restricting inquiry into language use to fitness consequences: survival and reproduction. We can inquire into the fundamental properties of linguistic expressions, and their use to express thought, sometimes to communicate, and sometimes to think or talk about the world. In this connection, comparative animal research surely merits attention. There has been important work on the problem of *representation* in a variety of species. Gallistel introduced a compendium of review articles on the topic a few years ago by arguing that representations play a key role in animal behavior and cognition; here "representation" is understood as isomorphism, a one-one relation between mind/brain processes and "an aspect of the environment to which these processes adapt the animal's behavior" — e.g., when an ant represents the corpse of a conspecific by its odor.[20] It is a fair question whether, or how, the results relate to the mental world of humans; in the case of language, to what is called "phonetic" or "semantic representation."

As noted, from the biolinguistic point of view that seems to me appropriate — and tacitly adopted in substantive work — we can think of a particular language L as a state of FL. L is a recursive procedure that generates an infinity of expressions. Each expression can be regarded as a collection of information for other systems of the mind/brain. The traditional assumption, back to Aristotle, is that the information falls into two categories, phonetic and semantic; information used, respectively, by sensorimotor systems and conceptual/intentional systems — the latter "systems of thought," to give a name to something poorly understood. That could well be a serious oversimplification, but let us keep to the convention. Each expression, then, is an internal object consisting of two collections of information: phonetic and semantic. These collections are called "representations," phonetic and semantic representations, but there is no isomorphism holding between the representations and aspects of the environment. There is no pairing of internal symbol and thing represented, in any useful sense.

On the sound side, this is taken for granted. It would not be false to say that an element of phonetic representation — say the internal element /ba/ in my language — picks out a thing in the world, namely the sound BA. But that would not be a helpful move, and it is never made. Rather, acoustic and articulatory phonetics seek to understand how the sensiromotor system uses the information in the phonetic representation to produce and interpret sounds, no trivial task. One can think of the phonetic representation as an array of instructions for the sensorimotor systems, but a particular element of the internal representation is not paired with some category of events in the outside world, perhaps a construction based on motions of molecules. Similar conclusions seem to me appropriate on the meaning side. It has been understood at least since Aristotle that even the simplest words incorporate information of many different kinds: about material constitution, design and intended use, origin, gestalt and causal properties, and much more. These topics were explored in some depth during the cognitive revolution of the 17th and 18th century, though much of the work, even including the well-studied British empiricist tradition from Hobbes to Hume, remains little known outside of historical scholarship. The conclusions hold for simple nouns, count and mass—"river," "house," "tree," "water," personal and place names—the "purest referential terms" (pronouns, empty categories), and so on; and the properties become more intricate as we turn to elements with relational structure (verbs, tense and aspect,...), and of course far more so as we move on to more complex expressions. As to how early in ontogenesis these complex systems of knowledge are functioning, little is known, but there is every reason to suppose that the essentials are as much a part of the innate biological endowment as the capacity for stereoscopic vision or specific kinds of motor planning, elicited in considerable richness and specificity on the occasion of sense, in the terminology of the early modern scientific revolution.

There seems nothing analogous in the rest of the animal world, even at the simplest level. It is doubtless true that the massive explosion of lexicon, and symbolic representation, are crucial components of human language, but invoking imitation or symbol-thing correspondence does not carry us very far, and even those few steps could well be on the wrong track. When we turn to the organization and generation of representations, analogies break down very quickly beyond the most superficial level.

These properties of language are almost immediately obvious on inspection—which is not to say that they are deeply investigated or well understood; they are not. Moving beyond, we find other properties that are puzzling. The components of expressions—their *features*, in standard terminology— must be interpretable by the systems that access them; the representations at the interface with sensorimotor and thought systems consist of interpretable features. One would therefore expect that the features that enter computation should be interpretable, as in well-designed artificial symbolic systems: formal systems for metamathematics, computer languages, etc. But it is not true for natural language; on the sound side, perhaps never true. One crucial case has to do with inflectional features that receive no semantic interpretation: structural case (nominative, accusative), or agreement features such as plurality (interpretable on nouns, but not on verbs or adjectives). The facts are not obvious in surface forms, but are reasonably well substantiated. Work of the past 20 years has provided considerable reason to suspect that these systems of uninterpretable features are quite similar among languages, though the external manifestation of the features differs in fairly systematic ways; and that a good deal of the typological variety of language reduces to this extremely narrow subcomponent of language. It could be, then, that the recursive computational system of the language organ is fixed and determinate, an expression of the genes, along with the basic structure of possible lexical items. A particular state of FL—a particular internal language—is determined by selecting among the highly structured possible lexical items and fixing parameters that are restricted to uninterpretable inflectional features and their manifestation. It could be that that is not a bad first approximation, maybe more than that.

It seems that the same uninterpretable features may be implicated in the ubiquitous *dislocation* property of natural language. The term refers to the fact that phrases are commonly articulated in one position but interpreted as if they were somewhere else, where they can be in similar expressions: the dislocated subject of a passive construction, for example, interpreted as if it were in the object position, in a local relation to the verb that assigns it a semantic role. Dislocation has interesting semantic properties. It may be that the "external" systems of thought (external to FL, internal to the mind/brain) require that FL generate expressions with these properties, to be properly interpreted. There is also reason to believe that the uninterpretable features may be the mechanism for implementing the dislocation property, perhaps even an optimal mechanism for satisfying this externally-imposed condition on the language faculty. If so, then neither the dislocation property nor uninterpretable features are "imperfections" of FL, "design flaws" (here using the term "design" metaphorically, of course). These and other considerations raise more general questions of optimal design: Could it be that FL is an optimal solution to interface conditions imposed by the systems of the mind/brain in which it is embedded, the sensorimotor and thought systems?

Such questions have been seriously posed only quite recently. They could not be raised before there was a fairly good grasp of the fixed principles of the faculty of language and the restricted options that yield the rich typological variety that we know must be rather superficial, despite appearances, given the empirical conditions on language acquisition. Though naturally partial and tentative, such understanding has increased markedly in the past 20 years. Now it seems that questions of optimal design can be seriously raised, sometimes answered. Furthermore, the idea that language may be an optimal solution to interface conditions, in nontrivial respects, seems a good deal more plausible than it did a few years ago. Insofar as it is true, interesting questions arise about the theory of mind, the design of the brain, and the role of natural law in the evolution of even very complex organs such as the language faculty, questions that are very much alive in the theory of evolution at elementary levels, in work of the kind pioneered by D'Arcy Thompson and Alan Turing that has been somewhat at the margins until recently. It is conceivable that the comprehensive ethological approach discussed earlier might be enriched in these terms, though that remains a distant prospect.

Still more remote are the fundamental questions that motivated the classical theory of mind — the creative aspect of language use, the distinction between action appropriate to situations and action caused by situations, between being "compelled" to act in certain ways or only "incited and inclined" to do so; and in general, the question of how "members of animal bodies move at the command of the will," Newton's phrase in his review of mysteries that remain unresolved, including the causes of interaction of bodies, electrical attraction and repulsion, and other basic issues that remained unintelligible, by the standards of the scientific revolution.

In some domains, inquiry into components of the mind/brain has made dramatic progress. There is justified enthusiasm about the promise of new technologies, and a wealth of exciting work waiting to be undertaken in exploring mental aspects of the world and their emergence. It is not a bad idea, however, to keep in some corner of our minds the judgment of great figures of early modern science—Galileo, Newton, Hume and others—concerning the "obscurity" in which "nature's ultimate secrets ever will remain," perhaps for reasons rooted in the biological endowment of the curious creature that alone is able even to contemplate these questions.

Notes

[1] Address at European Conference on Cognitive Science, 27th-30th October, 1999, Siena

References

[1] Ned Block (1990), "The Computer Model of the Mind," in D.N. Osherson and E. E. Smith, eds. An Invitation to Cognitive Science vol. 3, Thinking (Cambridge, MA: MIT press).

[2] "The Brain," Daedalus, Spring 1998.

[3] Mark Hauser (1998), The Evolution of Communication (Cambridge, MA: MIT press).

[4] C.R. Gallistel (1997), "Neurons and Memory," in M. S. Gazzaniga, Conversations in the Cognitive Neurosciences (Cambridge, MA: MIT press); (1999), "The Replacement of General-Purpose Learning Models with Adaptively Specialized Learning Modules," in M. S. Gazzaniga, ed., The Cognitive Neurosciences, 2nd edition (Cambridge, MA: MIT press).

[5] David Hume, Dialogue on Natural Religion.

[6] N. Chomsky (1990), "Language and Cognition," Conference of Cognitive Science Society, in D. Johnson and C. Emeling, eds. (1997), The Future of the Cognitive Revolution (New York: Oxford U. Press). Chomsky (1995), "Language and Nature," Mind 104.413: 1-61, Jan., reprinted in Chomsky (2000), New Horizons in the Study of Language and Mind (Cambridge: Cambridge U. press). See the latter collection for many sources not cited here.

[7]   Alexandre Koyr' (1957), From the Closed World to the Infinite Universe (Baltimore: Johns Hopkins U. press).

[8]   Arnold Thackray (1970), Atoms and Powers (Cambridge, MA: Harvard U. Press).

[9]   Cited by Gerald Holton, "On the Art of Scientific Imagination," Daedalus 1996, 183-208.

[10] Cited by V.S. Ramachandran and Sandra Blakeslee (1998), Phantoms in the Brain (London: Fourth Estate).

[11] Bertrand Russell (1929), The Analysis of Matter (Leipzig: B. G. Teubner).

[12] R.D. Hawkins and E.R. Kandel (1984), "Is there a cell-biological alphabet for simple forms of learning?," Psychological Review 91: 376-391.

[13] Adam Frank, Discover 80 (1997), Nov.

[14] N. Chomsky (1959), Review of B.F. Skinner, Verbal Behavior, Language 35.1, 26-57.

[15] Richard Lewontin (1990), in Osherson and Smith, op.cit.

[16] Terrence Deacon (1998), The Symbolic Species: The Co-evolution of Language and the Brain (New York: Norton, 1997).

[17] For current discussion of these topics, see, inter alia, Jerry Fodor (forthcoming), The Mind Doesn't Work That Way (Cambridge, MA: MIT press); Gary Marcus (1998), "Can Connectionism Save Constructivism?," Cognition 66: 153-182.

[18] See reference of note 14, and for more general discussion, focusing on language, Chomsky (1975), Reflections on Language (New York: Pantheon).

[19] On the nontriviality of this rarely recognized assumption, see Fodor, op. cit.

[20] C.R. Gallistel, ed. (1990), Animal Cognition, Cognition 37.1-2, Nov.

Subjectivity and the Self:
The Neurobiology of Consciousness

Albert Gjedde

Definitions

An important feature of consciousness is subjectivity. It refers the objects of the mind to a self. The mind is a four-dimensional virtual space in which selected elements of the bodily records of events become objects of consciousness by a process of mapping or projection. To be conscious is to be aware of these objects of the mind. The origin of the four-dimensional space is a locus, the self, to which all objects of the mind are referred. As the result of the mapping of objects onto the four-dimensional space, the self becomes a property of the mind.

As far as neurobiologists know, the mapping of objects onto consciousness is a process that occurs only in the brains of mammals, and in these brains only by the concerted action of specific populations of connected nerve cells. As such, the mind is the most advanced product of brain activity, among the multitude of brain functions established by evolution because they increased the probability of survival of the individual members of the species. Thus, the self is not the same as the mind, and the mind is not the same as consciousness: Consciousness is the state of being aware of the objects of the mind, which is a subjective space, and the self is a point to which the dimensions of the mind refer the objects of which we are consciously aware.

These definitions of conscious awareness of the objects of the mind generally agree with Sommerhoff's concept of an Integrated Global Representation (IGR) of selected elements of a Running World Model (RWM), and Baars' concept of a Global Workspace (GW). This World Registry, as I will call it, is composed from

In Search of a Language for the Mind-Brain, ed. Saleemi, Bohn and Gjedde, *The Dolphin* 33 © 2005 by Aarhus University Press, Denmark. ISBN 87 7934 005 9.

continuing records of events inside and outside of the body, as monitored by the senses and their receptors (Baars 1988, Sommerhoff 2000), although the objects of the mind do not qualify as 'representations', because no audience is present to observe the sources of the objects in the real world. The world is really there, of course, but it has no appearance and hence cannot reappear as a representation. Colours and sound and temperature and surface texture and weight and length and duration and speed and age are objects of the mind and hence parts of the world, whether I am consciously aware of them or not. To be consciously aware of the objects of the mind is to be in a state of open communication within the network of neurons in which the objects of the mind are realized, and within a vast system of other networks involved in the processing of the information communicated among the networks. The extent of conscious awareness in different species is likely to depend on the size of this system of communicating networks, and on the presence of the network in which the subjective mind is an activity.

As continuous projections of details of the bodily records of events, the objects of the mind are both interpretations of the events that left these records, and predictions of the records that future events are expected to leave. This is a process of continuous monitoring of the accuracy of the predictions, in an attempt to identify those events that leave records at variance with the predictions. Because of the predictive nature of the objects of the mind, the process in principle is a Darwinian solution to the otherwise impossible task of choosing *a priori* a single interpretation of events, which potentially satisfy an infinite number of interpretations. The winner of the Darwinian competition among interpretations builds on the past, but is no more than the first random extension which is not contradicted by the events of the future.

The process of testing and if necessary rejecting the projection of hypothetical objects of the mind is so fundamental that its absence frequently is deemed to be pathological. The attempt to falsify the projections of the hypothetical records left by future events is in essence a weighing of probabilities. Common sense is the realization that no hypothetical object of the mind can be trusted fully, although some objects in the four-dimensional space are a lot more probable than others. The weighing of probabilities, on which the fate of the objects depends, owes more to the principles of Bayesian inference from prior knowledge than to classical statistics (Lee 1997). This contrast may explain the peculiar propensity of humans to be fooled by the outcome of evaluations based on the rules of classical statistics, for example in games.

The converse conviction that an object of the mind is the only possible interpretation, i.e., that the projection is true in the sense that the probability of its rejection is zero, is generally deemed to be a sign of psychiatric pathology. A conviction is pathological if it is not open to the possibility, however remote, that it may be wrong. This conviction can be an important clue to the presence of psychosis or, in its more encapsulated form, to an *idée fixe*, an object of the mind of the truth of which the holder is absolutely convinced. The similarity with Popper's concept of scientific logic is no coincidence (Popper 1959).

Soul or Software?

There is no soul in the mechanisms outlined above. The definitions do not uphold the classical separation of form and function, ascribed to Plato and further developed by Descartes in terms of origin and extent. The neurobiological methods do not allow us to distinguish between, for example, consciousness as the function of the self and the self as the form of consciousness. Thus, there are no scientific reasons to uphold the separability of these two aspects of the same thing, and questions about the dualistic relations between soul and body cannot be answered because they refer to entities which are not separable. As described above, the self has a certain superficial similarity to the concept of soul introduced by Descartes. His soul is the immaterial observer of the world and mechanistic mover of the bodily machine (Descartes 1662). The claim that the similarity could be real has had scientifically respectable defenders even in recent years (e.g., Popper & Eccles 1977), but it is dismissed by the neuroscientists of today, who reject the view that the objects of the mind are presented to an observer, in part because this observer itself would need to contain another observer, to be observed by yet a third observer, and so forth, resulting in infinite regression (Dennett 1991). For the same reasons, the neuroscientists also dismiss as unfounded the similarities between Descartes' 'Cartesian' theater and the Global Workspace and Running World Models as entities, in which a play about the world is performed for the benefit of an audience of populations of nerve cells, which fill the roles of playwright, public, critic, censor, and editor. When neuroscientists inadvertently use the term 'representation' of the objects of the mind, they rather speak of the cartographic process of projection (Dretske 1997).

Modern neurobiologists have no need for immaterial observers and movers, because for them the mind is the framework of conscious awareness, generated as an activity of a network of neurons, with the self located at the origin of the axes of the four dimensions. Arguably, this definition of the subjective mind, i.e., as a framework referring to a fixed origin, suffers from 'property' dualism and requires the intervention of 'a ghost in the machine', or *deus ex machina*, because it is unclear how the mind can be a thing. The objection is usually countered by the argument that the objects of the mind exist in the cells in which the virtual space of the mind is an activity (Searle 1984). Consciousness is the state of being aware of the objects of the mind, organized in time and three-dimensional space relative to an origin, which is the self. The mind could be empty, of course, although it begs the question of the reality of a meditative state, of whether it is possible to be aware of absent objects.

It is not possible to say with certainty how and where the objects of the mind are realized in the brain. The uncertainty clearly is compounded by the role of conscious awareness as an interpreter of the bodily records of events. The interpretations have statistical weight but they are never certain and can never be fully verified, however often they have avoided rejection. In and of itself, the theory of conscious awareness of real objects residing in the virtual four-dimensional space of the subjective mind, with the self at its origin, is a conceptual hypothesis and hence an object of the mind. The hypothesis suffers from the same fundamental uncertainty that affects other objects of the subjective mind as interpretations of bodily records, and it is subject to the same experiential falsification and risk of rejection.

It is of interest to note in this context that the original Jewish, Christian and Muslim theologies had no concept of a soul. They spoke of the resurrection of the body. The soul is a philosophical tool that came to be used by Graeco-Roman philosophers and their followers to allow a compartmentalization of the objects of the subjective mind into those characterized by high predictability, forming by definition the material world, and those associated with low or no predictability, belonging to the remaining immaterial or spiritual realm.

Positions of the Self
Neurobiology is the science of the mechanisms underlying the brain's functions and work. Medical neurobiology focuses on the activities of the living human brain and its diseases. Conscious awareness is the activity of being aware of the objects of the subjective mind, as organized with reference to the orthogonal coordinates defining the mind's virtual space, originating in the self, which gives shape and direction to conscious awareness along three spatial dimensions and one temporal dimension. The temporal dimension provides chronological order to the objects of the mind. Vogeley et al. (2001) describe the self as a 'subjective experience of a multidimensional universe in time and space, in which the person of the observer is in the centre'. This context naturally invites the distinction between the 'minimal' self, which is the bare framework of the mind, and the extensive or 'narrative' self (Gallagher 2000), which allows the pure reason (Kant 1781) to be anchored firmly and constantly in time and space with reference to all previously experienced positions to the current position of the minimal self (egocentricity) and in respect of the current minimal self to the predicted positions of other selves (allocentricity). The narrative self is the superior or total framework comprising all of the frames adopted throughout the life of the individual.

Defined in this manner, the self is the origin of the framework of awareness of current behavior and sensations in relation to all previous origins of awareness, in the four directions of forward-backward, up-down, left-right, and before-after (Gallagher 2000). As the origin of the framework of a brain function with survival value, the self plays a practical role on the surface of a planet of the size of the Earth, on which the direction 'down' is defined by gravity, and 'North' is a place in the 'forward' direction when an observer looks towards the North Pole. 'East' and 'West' are then at right and left angles to 'North'. The framework applies equally well to other planets of approximately the same size as the Earth but would be of little use on a smaller planet with little gravity and surface. This restriction is not trivial because the axes of the mind cannot be fixed without reference to the importance of the physical relations of individuals to other objects of the mind in time and space. 'Left' and 'right' can only be fixed in relation to the movements of the individual (Campbell 1995), and the fixation is based on experience. Conscious awareness and the framework of the mind develop in parallel.

There are reasons to believe that the self as the origin of conscious awareness serves as the basis for exchange of information among members of a social network, which is why it is typically present in humans but undoubtedly also in mammals in general, albeit in varying amounts (Baars 2001). One reason is the apparent uselessness of a self in individuals who for all practical purposes are alone in the world. The neurobiological hypothesis can be summarized as the concept of consciousness as a simulator with (at least) two frames of reference: a current frame dictated by the present state of the individual (minimal self), and a more extensive frame positioning the current origin in a historical-cultural context (the narrative self).

Consciousness and Modern Cosmology
Modern physics has revealed that the conscious perception of objects in time and space is a fictional account of the properties of a quantum-mechanic field, which arose 15 billion years ago. This fiction is the reason for the conceptual gap between the quantum-mechanical description of the universe and the embedding of consciousness in a material self. The self assigns time, space and matter to the universe in the shape of a framework originating at a single point, where time began and from which space is

apparently still expanding. To inquire into events before the birth of the universe is as meaningless as searching for a place east of the sun and west of the moon. This contradiction in terms may have been at the core of the Inquisition's case against Galileo. It has been said that the inquisitor, Cardinal Bellarmin, could claim with some justification that not only the Earth's circling around the Sun but also the entire spatial description of the solar system and the universe could be one grand illusion, at variance with the function of consciousness in the interest of human beings; thus Galileo's claim could be considered dangerous to the daily lives of mankind, because it invited people to regard the world as an illusion and experience as a collection of hallucinations.

The conflict between the Church and Galileo raised the question of the discrepancy between pure and practical reason. To Kant, the self possessed a primary and primordial existence, which is the basis of all insights and experiences (Kant 1781). Thus, pure reasoning can contradict practical reasoning (Kant 1788) of a self built from, but not predating, experience. As consciousness based in the individual must have evolved because it increased the probability of survival of members of social groups, rejection of the insights of this consciousness may affect society adversely.

Then, as now, it was impossible to incorporate Galileo's or any other scientist's insight into the true relations among planets and stars into the objects of practical reason. This is true also of the few who travelled into space and cast off the bonds of gravity. Safe-navigation in a universal coordinate system requires lengthy exposure to the uses of instruments and computers. Even the greatest familiarity with the theory of relativity reveals that practical reason (consciousness) never fully appreciates that the subjective model of the world is an illusion (Einstein 1952). (The common use of the term 'matter' is ambiguous. Quantum physicists distinguish between 'matter' and 'field', and claim that the perception of matter is an illusory interpretation of a field, but naturally they do not claim that the universe and its field do not exist outside of consciousness or that they are illusory.)

Consciousness and Medical Neurobiology

The fundamental goal of medical neurobiology is to test the theory that the self is a property of consciousness, which is an awareness of constructed probable causes of the sensations that leave their marks on brain tissue by means of the mechanisms of memory. Where, how, or when, the self is established is not known with any certainty but recent results from neuroimaging techniques imply that nerve cells unite to form functional cell assemblies or modules, which collaborate on the storage, interpretation, and perception of sensations.

The forebrain has central nuclei of neurons wrapped in a cortex of other neurons. The cortex consists of two hemispheres, each of which is further subdivided in three sensory lobes -- the occipital, temporal, and parietal lobes -- and one executive lobe, namely, the frontal lobe. Each sensory lobe is a primary reception centre for one or more senses. The occipital lobe is the seat of the primary sense of vision, the temporal lobe houses the auditory sense, and the parietal lobe is the centre of the tactile senses and pain. Among the remaining classical senses, olfaction occupies a very special position because it appears to have direct access to neurons that form a ring of nuclei and to so-called 'old' (meaning primordial) cortical areas around the core of the brain, which branch into the two hemispheres. This ring ('limbus' or 'limbo') is known as the limbic system. The individual parts of the limbic system are believed to be involved in the selection of the material in the World Registry, which is projected into objects of the mind by a process of remapping ('remapping' has a different connotation in the field of plasticity research, in which it refers to the process of neuronal remodelling).

It is likely that the World Registry has different sizes and powers of resolution in different species, in relation to the size and development of the 'new' cortical areas or neocortex of the hemispheres. However, the brain function which projects selected items of the World Registry into objects of the mind from its seat in the limbic system is thought to be a very 'old' property of the brain. Reptilian forebrain consists almost entirely of the limbic cortex. Olfaction arises from the interaction between odor molecules and receptors in nose and throat. It is interesting to note that this sense has the most direct access to the oldest cortical areas. Other sensory stimuli undergo processes of computation and interpretation of the relevant internal or external messages, which lead to release of neurotransmitters, the molecules that cross the chasm between nerve cells as the bearers of information in the mechanism of neurotransmission. This translation does not appear to be necessary for the odour molecules; as preformed transmitters they may represent the earliest form of communication.

The integral parts of the limbic system are the hippocampus, the innermost layers of the temporal lobe shaped like a seahorse, the parahippocampal gyrus next to the hippocampus, the amygdala or amygdaloid nucleus, shaped like an almond, the cingulate gyrus, shaped like a belt which encircles the fibres between the hemispheres, and usually also the orbitofrontal cortex in the midline of the frontal lobe in front of the cingulate gyrus and just above the eye sockets -- and a few other smaller regions. While olfaction in reptiles appears to enjoy direct access to these areas of the limbic system without special selection or filtration, the subsequent evolution of the sensory lobes of mammals and the particularly marked development of the frontal lobes in primates including humans is evidence of the steadily more complex processing of other sensations as they contribute to the recording and elaboration of information about the internal and external milieux in the World Registry, from which the objects of the mind are selected.

The definition of a primary central seat of a sense is a cluster or an assembly of neurons which react specifically and adequately to stimulation of the sense's peripheral receptors. This definition should not be taken to mean that the relevant neurons react only passively to the adequate stimuli. On the contrary, the impulses appear to be directed to the secondary region common to and surrounded by the three sensory lobes, collectively known as the association cortex, to which the primary impulses are retransmitted and on which they converge. This direction resembles a mechanism of positive or negative feedback, depending on the anticipation of the most probable interpretation of the impulses.

The anticipated interpretation raises the important question of how consciousness knows where and how to perform the interpretation before it is realized to reveal the contents of the sensation. The question is a variation of the Darwinian objection to Lamarck's explanation of the giraffe's long neck as the product of an attraction towards the leaves at the top of trees: Neither the giraffe nor its neck could have known of the leaves before the neck had the required length. To the question of the interpreted sensations, the answer is that the limbic system is the source of the information, from which the sensations are selected. Templates of sensations are formed in the limbic system, and the templates guide the selection of the one particular sensation among the many in the World Registry, which subsequently reaches consciousness. The selection is undoubtedly a Darwinian struggle, in which the majority of possible sensations do not prevail because they do not fit the template. Consciousness is the assignment of form and content to the selected sensations in a steady flow of 'memories of the future' (Ingvar 1985).

Human Brain Mapping

Novel methods of brain imaging emerged after the Second World War. They contributed significantly to the localization of sites of activity in the living brain in many conditions and thus refined the theories of consciousness. The results form a kind of cerebral topography of tomographic maps (*tomos*, cut; *graphein*, inscription) of brain functions drawn by computer based on pictures of brain sections which are obtained by a special camera. The rush to create such maps is not new, however.

In the first half of the 19th century, a new theory of brain function, 'phrenology', arose from the urge to understand the relationship between the brain and the mind, based on attempts to make inferences about the functions of the living brain beneath the intact skull; this was done by means of techniques collectively known as 'cranioscopy'. Phrenology was intended as a science (*logos*) of the mind (*phren*), which has much in common with the modern practice of cerebral topography. The word *phren* is derived from the Greek word for the midriff, which Aristotle believed to be the supporter of the spirits of life emanating from the heart.

The German anatomist Franz-Joseph Gall (1757-1828) first presented the teachings of phrenology in Vienna in 1796. Gall gave private lessons in the organization of the mind under the influence of natural philosophy. He wished to map the functions of the brain to understand the mind, but he focused on what he believed to be the visible imprints of the gyri on the skull, because he could not reach the living gyri themselves. According to Gall, the number and size of these imprints reflect the activity in as many as 35 regions of the brain, with each region serving a particular brain function. Of these many regions, only the postulated language centre in region 33 of the frontal lobe has had any lasting, albeit coincidental, impact on the course of brain research. In the second half of the 20th century, several researchers, including Seymour Kety and Louis Sokoloff in Pittsburgh, Wilder Penfield, Donald Hebb and Brenda Milner in Montreal, and Noam Chomsky and Jerry Fodor in Boston, for entirely different reasons, revived or inspired a school of neurological localization in the form of a new theory of the functional modularity of the brain. The theory was in part based on the experiments with, or observations of, the causes and effects of brain disorders and diseases made by North-American neuropsychiatrists (Seymour Kety), neurophysiologists (Louis Sokoloff), neurosurgeons (Wilder Penfield), neuropsychologists (Donald Hebb and Brenda Milner), and philosophers (Jerry Fodor). Canadian and American brain researchers introduced novel tomographic methods of the phrenologically inspired mapping of centres active in the brain in the years after the Second World War. These methods were later brought to Scandinavia by the neurophysiologist Niels A. Lassen in Copenhagen and the neuropsychiatrist David H. Ingvar in Lund (Ingvar 1985).

The neophrenological maps meant a complete departure from the behaviourally and politically based associationism, according to which the manifestations of the mind can be neither subdivided nor explained by results from studies of the brain (Jørgensen 1963). The neophrenologists themselves differed as to whether the

functional organization of the brain was best understood
vertically as a system of columns reminiscent of Descartes'
mechanical links and Gall's 'organs' of the brain -- each serving a
specific and independent function (such as vision or motor
control), or horizontally as levels of ever more complex and
refined elaborations of incoming impulses by strata of cells
reminiscent of Victorian society (Hughlings Jackson) -- or as non-
stratified companies of cells ('assemblies') creating gradients of
activity with flexible boundaries (Donald Hebb).

Penfield and Jasper (1954) invented a method that enabled
them to distinguish between these possibilities. They electrically
stimulated the cortex of the brain of patients kept awake during
neurosurgical procedures. By means of tiny electrodes, they
showed that the cortex is the seat of somewhat poorly outlined
functional centres, areas which appear to activate specific
functions such as motion, sensation, or memory. Penfield and
Jasper discovered that motion arises from the posterior regions of
the frontal lobe, where every single muscle group is represented
in proportion to the degree of fineness of motor control. The
muscles of the finest motions have the greatest representation.
They also discovered that sensations arise in the parietal,
temporal and occipital lobes; tactile and painful sensations in the
parietal lobe, auditory sensations in the temporal lobe, and visual
sensations in the occipital lobe. These functional centres now are
known as modules, regardless of the extent of horizontal or
vertical integration.

Penfield's intraoperative mapping of modules in the brain has
been replaced by the less invasive mapping of active brain regions
by imaging of active brain regions, for instance, by means of
positron emission tomography (PET), functional magnetic
resonance imaging (fMRI) of changes in blood circulation in the
brain, as well as, in latter years, by registration of native or
provoked fluctuations of electrical (electrical encephalography or
EEG) or magnetic (magnetoencephalography or MEG) fields on
the surface of the brain. PET also makes it possible to map
changes of energy metabolism or transmitter release.

Maps of functional modules in brain reveal multiple specific
centres of sensory, motor, and cognitive activity, and they are

considerably more detailed than hitherto suspected. Superficially, the maps resemble the phrenological maps of Franz-Joseph Gall transposed to the cortex of the human brain, but the functional activities do not match a phrenological map's horizontal layers of higher and lower brain functions. On the contrary, it is evident that the pathology of many brain diseases is confined to specific brain regions or functional units, which trigger off distinct defects when they fail to execute their normal functions.

The Functions of Consciousness: Will and Conscience
The limbic system of reptiles receives olfactory impulses directly from the environment. The ensuing action on the part of the animal is not subject to detailed reflection other than as required for purposes of spatial orientation. The reptile has no choice other than to attack in the right direction and to fell the prey. People also have experiences of this kind. When you hear a word in your native language, you understand it and cannot choose not to understand. On the other hand, you can claim to be free to execute or not execute specific acts: You choose to cheat on your taxes or to turn down the next drink.

Several arguments militate against this appearance of free will. In part, they are based on the concept of causality in physics, and in part on the experiments of Libet (1993) and others, using the methods of functional tomography (Pedersen et al. 1998). These experiments reveal the presence of increased activity in the frontal lobe as early as a second or more before the onset of a voluntary movement, also when subjects declare not to be aware of the motion sooner than 200 milliseconds before its execution. In this sequence of events, separate centres in the cortex are activated sequentially on the way from prefrontal cortex to motor cortex. The last in the sequence is the primary motor centre in cerebral cortex, which engages the cells of motor cortex to execute the specific movement of selected skeletal muscle fibres.

There is still time to interrupt the motion, despite the delay of conscious awareness. It is the purpose of consciousness to place the motion in the wider context of time and space coordinates, selected from among the elements of the World Registry. Details of the past and the present are projected onto the future and the consequences are weighed. Reflection on the consequences involves a comparison of diverse projections, constructed from experiences listed in the World Registry. It is likely that the projections involve several sensory modalities in the World Registry, including the somatic markers of joy and sorrow, hunger and thirst, love and hate, and fear and loathing.

The projections of consciousness construct the dichotomy of either-or of the past or the future in the present. If an outcome were unpleasant in the past, it is likely to be unpleasant also in the future, and is presented as such to the consciousness of the present. The projection provides a context for the voluntary act. It is perhaps not a coincidence that the terms consciousness and conscience are related both as words and as concepts. The relation suggests that a major function of consciousness is to bring the consequences of future acts under the scrutiny of conscience, which in turn provides a context for the acts. In this sense conscience is a catalogue of precisely those experiences in the World Registry which add value to the projections of consciousness. There is evidence that the weight of the projections is established in orbitofrontal cortex in the middle of the anterior frontal lobe, which belongs to the limbic system. Damasio (1994) showed that patients who lose the activity in this part of the brain because of trauma or disease also lose the ability to review and reflect on the future consequences of current acts. They are victims of their own impulses and face an uncertain future, despite a preserved intellect.

A second perspective of the self is grounded in the consequences of individual acts to others. It appears that the human brain is capable of forming a theory of the contents of other people's minds, the so-called theory-of-mind perspective. This capacity of the self allows a person to predict the objects that are present in the minds of other humans and possibly also of some animals. This property of consciousness is based on the decoding of signals emanating from facial and bodily movements of people with whom we communicate, and it is accompanied by activity of the limbic system in the mid-anterior part of the frontal lobe and in the temporal lobe. Autists and individuals with sociopathic tendencies may suffer from reduced activity in the regions subserving this function of empathy (Happé et al. 1996).

Function of Self

The self is a scaffold for the objects of the mind wherein acts are contemplated and weighed. The self frames the objects of the mind in time and place. Without this prior fixation in time and place, projection of distant, past or future events cannot be distinguished from events within immediate sensory or executive range.

A basic function of the self is evident when the frame collapses. We experience the space around us as stationary when eye movements are executed by the brain, but the space immediately wobbles when the eye is moved by pressing on the eye ball with a finger. Kohler (1964) changed people's perception of the orientation of the world around them by giving them prisms instead of ordinary glasses. The subjects regained a normal perception of the world around them in a few days but only when they moved around in this world of their own accord. The reorientation did not happen if the subjects were moved by other individuals, for example by being confined to a wheelchair. Thus passive movements are of no use; the subjects must execute voluntary movements of their own accord (Sommerhoff 2000).

Activity in a certain region of the frontal lobe accompanies the voluntary movements of the eyes. The region is called the frontal eye fields. Brodmann assigned this part of the frontal lobe the number 8. It seems that all mammals move in a cognitive space with a stationary frame, which only fails when the body is exposed to sudden external motion. Deubel & Schneider (1996) showed that activity in the special attention centres of the frontal and parietal lobes accompanies movements of the body inside this stationary cognitive frame (Johannsen et al. 1999). There is evidence that the cognitive space extends only as far as the arms can reach.

The stationary frame established by the self is by definition first and foremost 'egocentric', but it specifically allows an evaluation of allocentric relations, that is, including the relations among the objects placed outside the frame, as shown by Rieser et al. (1986). The frame is updated continuously as we move around, even when blindfolded.

The activity in the centres of attention reveals that the frame is revised by means of information about the body of the individual and the world around it, which reaches specific regions of the cerebral cortex from the relevant sensors when attention is directed towards a particular aspect of the external world. At the same time it is continuously updated from the brain's World Registry when the focus of attention is directed elsewhere, as it often is. The revision is acutely felt when attention is focused on conditions that differ greatly from the running update provided by the World Registry. In principle this dramatic revision is the result of a falsification of a specific hypothesis of a detail in the world provided by the World Registry. It is also one of the greatest sources of excitement of the conscious mind, actively sought by artists and scientists. In the most coveted situations, the excitement can be either the excitation generated by a falsification, which involves subcortical mechanisms and monoaminergic neurotransmitters, or the ecstasy of a significant confirmation, which appears to emanate from the frontal lobes. These events are not unlike the phases of the reproductive act, in which subcortical activity accompanies the sexual excitation and frontal activity accompanies the orgasm.

The self generally provides a more or less hypothetical projection of details in the World Registry onto posited or expected elements of time and space, including the past and the future. Real revision of the objects of the mind referred to the past or the future is difficult, of course, as the attention cannot be directed to the world of the past or the future itself. The projection nonetheless allows attention to be focused on mental objects affected by the current hypothesis. Occasionally, historians and archeologists come across the real sources of their mental objects, and a glorious falsification or confirmation may ensue. Likewise, experimental science is the projection of future events that eventually may or may not happen the way the scientists predicted. Sending humans to the moon is perhaps the most dramatic act of conscious projection of future events ever performed, and it resulted in the most satisfactory confirmation of the objects of the mind that we know as Newton's laws of physics. There is evidence that the contents of the World Registry undergo revision only when a hypothetical projection has been made in advance. The revision is an interpretation that is not needed if the projection in principle cannot be falsified, but on the other hand the interpretation only occurs when a hypothesis is present.

Conscious objects of the past may undergo revision also when they are projected allocentrically onto the future as a kind of experimental archeology by which attention eventually may be directed towards the real source of the objects. This also means that new sensations do not necessarily make sense; the interpretation is selected from among a number (small or large) of proposals relevant to the source, which the sensation (conceptually as well as anatomically or geographically) is presumed to be a product of. The self is intimately linked to the mechanism that selects the possible interpretations (schemata) from among the many elements in the World Registry that are relevant under the circumstances. Brain imaging confirms that the brain figures out identical sensory stimuli differentially, depending on the experiences present in the World Registry. This mechanism of the self has received labels such as 'central command', 'anticipation', 'context', and most lately 'predictive coding'.

In their simplest form, experiences may be instructions given just prior to the sensation. A group of researchers led by Robert Zatorre of the Montreal Neurological Institute (Zatorre et al. 1992) asked volunteers to interpret words either in terms of spelling or in terms of pitch. Depending on the instruction, the identical stimuli led to increased activity either in Broca's language centre in the left frontal lobe or in the prosody center in the right frontal lobe. The activity of the centres could only have been recruited on the basis of experience, as the identical stimuli gave no indication of the differential processing required. This Darwinist mechanism of consciousness has the advantage that a specific sensation prevents the extinction of a randomly generated object (template) of the mind from among the many objects that face extinction by the shifting foci of attention. The mechanism has elements in common with Nobel laureate Niels Jerne's explanation of the ability of the immune system to fight off unknown microorganisms or chemicals. The only condition is that at least one of the many projections of the World Registry survives the continuing process of extinction. Consciousness depends on the existence of experiences that cover the objects of the mind which need interpretation. Experience precedes conscious insight, either as actual experience or as an inborn pattern of reactivity.

Anatomy of the Self
As a property (or framework) of consciousness, the self is not easy to map. Some neurobiologists regard the self as the result of an act of 'mind-reading' with elements in common with the mechanism of the theory of mind that we apply to other people. Here the self is an egocentred perspective, as opposed to the theory-of-mind one which somewhat imprecisely may be called an allocentred perspective. The objection can be made that the self as a framework of the objects of the mind plays a role that is not the same as that of a brain mechanism which serves to decode the contents of the mind of someone else. Despite this objection the question has been raised as to whether the self as a feature of consciousness arises from activity in the same area of the orbitofrontal cortex in the midventral part of the frontal lobe that is active during the formulation of theories of mind.

The team of Vogeley et al. (2001) tested whether brain activity arises in the same place during the scrutiny of ego- and allocentred conscious perspectives. In one case, volunteers were asked to evaluate the objects of their own mind, while in another they weighed the objects of other peoples' minds in relation to brief descriptions of everyday events. Both ego- and allocentred consciousness raised activity in the anterior cingulate gyrus of the limbic system, as well as respectively in right and left temporal lobes where meaning is thought to be assigned. Interestingly the attention centre in the right frontal lobe was active when subjects had to distinguish between the ego- and allocentred perspectives. Apparently, the perspectives of the self (i.e., the origin of the frame of the objects of the mind) and theories of mind are not identically represented in the brain.

Experimental lowering of consciousness is possible in attempts to reduce awareness of the objects of the mind. These experiments show that the activity of the anterior cingulate gyrus declines less than the activity in the rest of the brain when conscious awareness of the objects of the mind decreases (Figure 1). It is possible that the narrative self anchors the objects of the mind in this structure. Its activity is required to restore the continuity of the self after sleep and unconsciousness, and this activity may be the source of the perspective of the self.

One patient who lost the ability to recall events in the past and to fix new experiences in memory had a particularly high activity in this part of the brain when she tried and then failed to remember. The memory function was impaired by the presence of a subcortical tumor that exerted pressure on parts of the limbic system. Removal of the tumor restored the memory function and eliminated the activity of the anterior cingulate gyrus when the patient again correctly recalled specific experiences. Instead, the memory task raised the activity in orbitofrontal cortex in the midventral region of the frontal lobe.

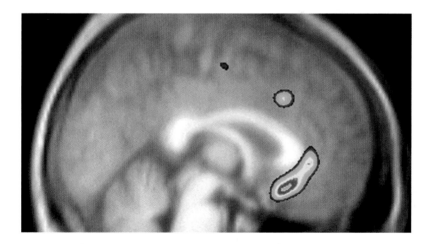

Figure 1 (For legend, see next page)

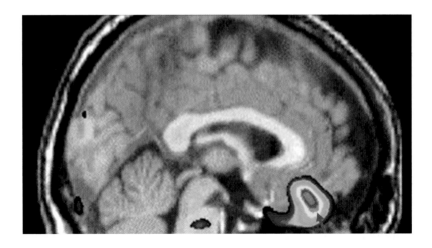

Figure 2

Legend to Figure 1: Elevated blood flow (shown as rainbow-color-coded activity) in the anterior cingulate gyrus and the anterior part of the frontal lobe during deep anesthesia of volunteers undergoing positron emission tomography at Aarhus Hospital of Aarhus University Hospitals. The anatomy of the brain is recorded by MRI. (Courtesy of Schlünzen et al., *Acta Anaesthesiol. Scand.* 2004).

Legend to Figure 2: A 53-year old woman lost the ability to form new memories (amnesia) because of a tumor in the third ventricle of the brain. The tumor compressed structures in the vicinity of the hippocampal formation. Neuropsychological testing and positron emission tomography during an associative memory test were completed before and 2 months after tumor removal. Brain imaging after the surgery did not show evidence of permanent damage to structures near the hippocampus. After tumor removal, the patient showed a complete recovery of the ability to form new memories. A significant decrease of blood flow indicative of reduced brain activity occurred in the ventromedial prefrontal cortex, consistent with the theory that this part of the brain is most active when the brain is in "default" mode, i.e., not engaged in goal-directed behavior. (Courtesy of Kupers, Fortin, Astrup, Gjedde & Ptito, 2004, *Arch. Neurol. 61: 1948-1952*)

These and other experiments show that the limbic system plays an important role in the generation of conscious awareness but they do not point to any obvious division of labor among the individual parts of the system. However, with regard to the amygdaloid nucleus we know that it contributes to the creation of emotional quality of the objects of the mind, while the hippocampus contributes to the creation of episodic memories and, particularly in its posterior extremity, to the recall of spatial relations. Collectively, the limbic system is the rudimentary forebrain. In primates and other mammals it collaborates with an enormously expanded forebrain with the necessary networks for construction of the conscious details of the World Registry.

It is improbable that conscious recall occurs by storage and research of materials in an archive, as in a filing cabinet. It is more likely that anticipated or hypothetical details undergo construction, with the assistance of the amygdaloid nucleus, in networks of the common association area of the three primary sensory cortices (posterior operculum). The pertinent sections of the archive are created on demand. This creation is the act of recall. The construction is challenged when impulses from the world outside the brain fail to confirm the prediction. To understand this process better, it may be of value to consider a metaphor: The construction appears to occur much like the creation of music by means of a piano. Use of the keyboard activates a vast repertory of mechanisms that work to create objects of the mind. The World Registry is the totality of sheet music available to the pianist. The notes are read in the frontal lobe, the combination of hands and keyboard is implemented in the limbic system, and the combination of the hammers and the strings in the resonator is the polymodal association cortex in the back of the forebrain.

Origin and Development of the Self: Plasticity of the Brain

It is not known with certainty when the framework which is the self is established during infancy and childhood. New sensations and their recruitment into conscious awareness is an important clue to the function of the self. New sensations are typical of early development but they also arise in adulthood, for example when a sense which previously did not work suddenly comes to life, by surgery on the blind or the deaf, or when new abilities are acquired. In contrast to brains of other mammals, the human brain undergoes a massive expansion after birth; at the second anniversary, the human brain has already tripled in size.

This astonishing development takes place under the constant bombardment of new sensations, by a combination of cell division, migration, sprouting and arborization, during which each neuron makes a contact, known as the synapse, with as many as 10,000 other neurons. This process reaches its maximum at the ages of 6-8 when a total of more than 10^{15} points of contact connect more than 10^{11} neurons. The number of contacts is so vast that it would take more than 300 million years to count one every second.

The number of contacts is reduced after the age of the maximum expansion. This process of pruning occurs by regression of sprouts (mostly in humans) or removal of whole cells (mostly in other mammals). The remaining nerve fibres envelop themselves in a fatty insulation in a process known as myelinization. This first phase of development is complete at the end of puberty, when the brain weight has quadrupled since birth.

The reason for the regression is not known. For the individual layers of the cortex, it does not appear to depend on external stimuli. The relations among different regions of the cortex, on the other hand, are clearly influenced by the types of stimuli received from the world outside the brain, or perhaps just outside specific parts of the brain. The total number of contacts may be excessive if some contacts are non-functional because they do not connect the right partners. The team of development neurobiologists headed by Greenough (1987) makes a distinction between two kinds of plasticity in the undeveloped brain: the general plasticity shared by all members of a species (experience-expectant) and the specific plasticity of each individual member (experience-dependent). The former is directed by inborn mechanisms evolved to deal with universal conditions of the species and occurs predominantly by regression of contacts, while the latter is shaped by individual challenges by an extension of contacts. It is the latter type that seems to be most important to the generation of conscious awareness.

Elbert et al. (1995) used MEG to show that training of musical skills affects the location and topographical extent of the primary sensory hand area in the postcentral gyrus in proportion to the years of training. The only connection between the hemispheres of the brain is the bundle or bridge of 200 million nerve fibres called the corpus callosum (literally 'callous body'). The number of fibres continues to grow until the age of 25, but MRI (magnetic resonance imaging) reveals a greater expansion of the anterior part of the corpus callosum, which connects brain regions involved in motor activity in musicians who play the piano or the violin, especially if they had started practicing before the age of seven (Schlaug et al. 1995).

The plastic reconstruction of the connections among neurons probably continues everywhere in the brain after the end of puberty, but in certain regions the neurons retain the ability to replicate themselves. Eleanor Maguire and her co-workers (1997, 2000) showed that cab drivers in London not only exhibit a higher activity in the right hippocampus when they imagine specific routes but also that the posterior portion of the hippocampus increases in size relative to the average population, and in proportion to the number of years of driving a cab in that city. In the metaphorical piano introduced above, it appears that the keyboard (the limbic system) is expanded by tuning the music (the activity in the posterior operculum) to the demands of the notes (activity in the frontal lobes).

Learning and Skills

Images of brain activity show that conscious awareness of motor acts fades when they become highly skilled through learning. The acquisition of motor skills is assisted by the work of the basal ganglia in the subcortical interior of the forebrain. During skill learning, neurons in the basal ganglia communicate by means of the neurotransmitter dopamine. The cells in the basal ganglia appear to mediate the automation of motor acts and their subsequent loss to conscious awareness. They also seem to mediate the sensations of initial excitement and subsequent euphoria that follow the successful execution of highly skilled motor acts. The sensations constitute a reward and they undoubtedly serve to motivate further learning.

Dopamine is made in the neurons that have their origin in the midbrain and send their fibres to the basal ganglia. The dopamine neurons are exquisitely sensitive to lack of oxygen, and the release of dopamine fails to a greater or lesser extent in pathological conditions, some of which may be the result of oxygen deprivation.

The best known condition of inadequate dopamine release is the one that occurs in Parkinson's disease, but recently depletion has also been seen long after difficult births and after exposure to environmental toxins and homemade ('designer') drugs of abuse. When dopamine is lost, communication ceases among the cells that depend on the signal transmitted by dopamine, and the triad of skill learning, automation, and reward is disrupted. Familiar acts no longer generate the same release of dopamine as in the average population. This loss plays a very important role in the pathology of psychiatric diseases and disorders of behaviour. Learning deficits may ensue in the young. Hyperactivity, drug abuse, smoking, pathological gambling, bulimia and anorexia, and violent behaviours may all reflect the sufferers' frantic attempts to relieve a state of dopamine deficient reward generation. Thus, these conditions may all share the characteristic that they are dopamine deficiency disorders. The loss of rewarding skills is strongly felt, and many who suffer from the alleged dopamine deficiency soon discover that certain abnormal or deviant activities increase what in reality is an effect of dopamine, and they quickly learn to compensate to a greater or less extent for the lack of natural reward by engaging in these artificial activities as a kind of self-medication. Cocaine and amphetamine both increase the effects of dopamine. However, they commonly do so excessively, with eventual devastating results in the form of permanent psychotic loss of the ability to distinguish between reality and fantasy.

Stimulated by dopamine, the basal ganglia free the mind of the clutter of objects such as acts and patterns of motor activity which prove to be perfectly matched to the contents of the World Registry. The more firmly a pattern of motor activity depends on activity in the basal ganglia, the more difficult it appears to dislodge it from the grip of the dopamine and again place it under conscious scrutiny of its relations to the world outside the brain. The automation limits the ability of the individual to distinguish between obsolete or undesirable skills and the challenges of novel circumstances, and it eliminates the distinction between fantasy (the old) and reality (the new).

Dissolution of the Self

As the solitary framework of consciousness, the self would seem to be susceptible to disruption due to the loss of the link between the hemispheres, i.e., the calossal body. Apparently this is not the case. People born without the corpus callosum enjoy generally normal conscious and unitary awareness of the objects of the mind, despite the missing link between the hemispheres, although it is occasionally possible to observe very discrete functional deficits (Springer & Deutsch 1998). These patients do not regard themselves as two persons in one body. The same fortunately seems to be the case for patients in whom the link between the hemispheres is surgically severed to prevent otherwise intractable epileptic seizures. There is no agreement on this point, however. Only few of these so-called split-brain patients have sufficient linguistic abilities in the right hemisphere to allow the hemispheres to communicate individually with the outside world. In one such patient, the personalities of the hemispheres were so different that it seemed justifiable to speak of two persons in this single brain (LeDoux et al. 1977). The case of this patient may perhaps be explained by the selection of the details in World Registry by separate attention centres in the hemispheres. If attention centres of the two hemispheres select different details from the World Registry, it is possible that the frameworks of the conscious awareness of separate objects are duplicated and hence constitute two selves.

Some diseases lead to more or less complete dissolution of the self. So-called 'out-of-body' experiences may follow when entries in the World Registry disappear, for example when information about the state of the body (proprio- and interoception) fails to register and the framework that is the self no longer can be anchored in the body itself. Near-death experiences and psychotic depersonalization may be of this kind. Loss of information about the environment (exteroception) may lead to hallucinations or other dream-like experiences based exclusively on the proprio- and interoceptive senses.

Conclusion

Neurobiologists use the concept of the self when they describe conscious awareness of the objects of the mind as the work of the brain. Consciousness results from the work of certain neurons in certain networks in the brain. Consciousness is the scrutiny of a rational and practical projection of certain hypothetical details in the registry of sensations from the world outside the brain. From this projection arises a framework which fixes the objects of the mind in relation to time and place. The self is the origin of the awareness of the axes of space and time. The dimensions of the conscious awareness of the objects of the mind, and their relations to the origin of these dimensions, explain many of the functions of the brain in healthy or diseased human beings.

References

Baars, B. J. 2001. There are no known differences in fundamental brain mechanisms of consciousness between humans and other mammals. *Animal welfare* 10: 31-40.

Baars, B. J. 1988. *A cognitive theory of consciousness.* Cambridge: Cambridge University Press.

Campbell, J. 1995. *Past, space, and self.* Cambridge, MA: The MIT Press.

Damasio, A. R. 1994. *Descartes' error.* New York: Avon Books.

Dennett, D. C. 1991. *Consciousness explained.* Boston: Back Bay Books/Little, Brown and Company.

Descartes, R. 1662/1991-1995. *De homine.* Leyden, Leffen & Moyardus, Fol. 118, Fig. LIII. Leiden: Peter Leffen and Franciscus Moyard.

Deubel, H., and W. X. Schneider. 1996. Saccade target selection and object recognition: Evidence for a common attentional mechanism. *Vision res.* 36: 1827-1837.

Dretske, F. 1997. *Naturalizing the mind.* Cambridge, MA: The MIT Press.

Einstein, A. 1916/1952/1961. *Relativity: The special and the general theory.* New York: Crown Trade Paperbacks.

Elbert, T., C. Pantev, C. Wienbruch, B. Rockstroh, and E. Taub. 1995. Increased cortical representation of the fingers of the left hand in string players. *Science* 270: 305-307.

Gallagher, S. 2000. Philosophical conceptions of self: Implications for cognitive science. *Trends cog. sci.* 4: 14-21.

Greenough, W. T., J. E. Black, and C. S. Wallace. 1987. Experience and brain development. *Child dev.* 58: 539-559.

Happé, F., S. Ehlers, P. Fletcher, U. Frith, M. Johannson, C. Gillberg, R. Dolan, R. Frackowiak, and C. Frith. 1996. 'Theory of mind' in the brain: Evidence from a PET scan study of Asperger syndrome. *Neuroreport* 8: 197-201.

Ingvar, D. H. 1985. Memory of the future: An essay on the temporal organization of conscious awareness. *Hum. neurobiol.* 4: 127-136.

Johannsen, P., J. Jakobsen, P. Bruhn, and A. Gjedde. 1999. Cortical responses to sustained and divided attention in Alzheimer's disease. *NeuroImage* 10: 269-281.

Jørgensen, J. 1963. *Psykologi paa biologisk grundlag.* Munksgaard.

Kant. 1781. *Kritik der reinen vernunft.*

Kant. 1788. *Kritik der praktischen vernunft.*

Kohler, I. 1964. The formation and transformation of the perceptual world. *Psychological issues* 3: 1-173.

Kupers, R. C., A. Fortin, J. Astrup, A. Gjedde and M. Ptito. 2004. Recovery of anterograde amnesia in a case of craniopharyngioma. *Arch Neurol.* 61:1948-1952.

LeDoux, J. E., D. H. Wilson, and M. S. Gazzaniga. 1977. A divided mind: Observations on the conscious properties of the separated hemispheres. *Ann. neurol.* 2: 417-421.

Lee, P. M. 1997. *Bayesian statistics: An introduction* (2nd ed.). London: Arnold.

Libet, B. 1993. The neural time factor in conscious and unconscious events. In *Experimental and theoretical studies of consciousness* (CIBA Foundation Symposium 174). New York: John Wiley & Sons.

Maguire, E. A., R. S. Frackowiak, and C. D. Frith. 1997. Recalling routes around London: Activation of the right hippocampus in taxi drivers. *J. neurosci.* 17: 7103-7110.

Maguire, E. A., D. G. Gadian, I. S. Johnsrude, C. D. Good, J. Ashburner, R. S. Frackowiak, and C. D. Frith. 2000. Navigation-related structural change in the hippocampi of taxi drivers. *Proc. natl. acad. sci. USA* 97: 4398-4403.

Pedersen, J. R., P. Johannsen, C. K. Bak, B. Kofoed, K. Saermark, and A. Gjedde 1998. Origin of human motor readiness field linked to left middle frontal gyrus by MEG and PET. *NeuroImage* 8: 214-220.

Penfield, W., and H. Jasper. 1954. *Epilepsy and the functional anatomy of the human brain.* Boston: Little, Brown and Company.

Popper, K. R. 1959. *The logic of scientific discovery.* London: Hutchinson.

Popper, K. R., and J. C. Eccles. 1977/1983. *The self and its brain.* London & New York: Routledge.

Rieser, J. J., D. A. Guth, and E. W. Hill. 1986. Sensitivity to perspective structure while walking without vision. *Perception* 15: 173-188.

Schlaug, G., L. Jancke, Y. Huang, J. F. Staiger, and H. Steinmetz. 1995. Increased corpus callosum size in musicians. *Neuropsychologia* 33: 1047-1055.

Schlünzen, L., M. S. Vafaee, G. E. Cold, M. Rasmussen, J. F. Nielsen, A. Gjedde 2004. Effects of subanaesthetic and anaesthetic doses of sevoflurane on regional cerebral blood flow in healthy volunteers: A positron emission tomographic study. *Acta Anaesthesiol. Scand.* 48: 1268-76.

Searle, J. R. 1984. *Minds, brains, and science.* Cambridge, MA: Harvard University Press.

Searle, J. R. 1997. *The mystery of consciousness.* London: Granta Books.

Sommerhoff, G. 2000. *Understanding consciousness: Its function and brain processes.* London: SAGE Publications.

Springer, S. P., and G. Deutsch. 1998. *Left brain, right brain: perspectives from cognitive neuroscience.* New York: Worth Publishers.

Vogeley, K., P. Bussfeld, A. Newen, S. Herrmann, F. Happé, P. Falkai, W. Maier, N. J. Shah, G. R. Fink, and K. Zilles. 2001. Mind reading: Neural mechanisms of theory of mind and self-perspective. *NeuroImage* 14: 170-181.

Zatorre, R., A. C. Evans, E. Meyer, and A. Gjedde. 1992. Lateralization of phonetic and pitch discrimination in speech processing. *Science* 256: 846-849.

Minimalist Visions[1]

Martin Atkinson

In a series of papers, produced during the last decade, Chomsky has developed an approach to syntactic theory framed in terms of what is known as the Minimalist Programme. While this approach has stimulated a good deal of research, it is certainly true that its principal tenets, often presented somewhat opaquely, are considered suspect by many syntacticians. From one perspective, this is puzzling. If we consider a lengthy and detailed textbook introduction to minimalism (Radford, 1997), in the Glossary and Abbreviations, we find as the entry for 'Minimalism/Minimalist Program (p. 515):

> 'A theory of grammar ... whose core assumption is that grammars should be described in terms of the minimal set of theoretical and descriptive apparatus necessary.'

Radford's text provides ample illustration of this 'core assumption,' but what is of interest is the entirely uncontroversial nature of this characterisation. It appears to suggest that there might be theories of grammar around which do not adopt this assumption and which, knowingly or otherwise, do not adhere to Occam's Razor, happily embracing theoretical constructs which serve no necessary function. In short, Radford's characterisation looks like little more than a formulation of what it means to do responsible science, and if this were all there were to minimalism, it is difficult to see how anyone could rationally object to the programme.[2]

Chomsky himself might be regarded as contributing to this view, when he says (1998, 5, n13):

In Search of a Language for the Mind-Brain, ed. Saleemi, Bohn and Gjedde, *The Dolphin* 33 © 2005 by Aarhus University Press, Denmark. ISBN 87 7934 005 9.

'It is a misunderstanding to contrast "minimalism and X," where X is some theoretical conception (Optimality Theory, Lexicalism, etc.). X may be pursued with minimalist goals, or not.'

Undoubtedly, it is the case that alternative approaches to syntactic theory can be scientifically responsible or not, but, as I hope to show, the Chomskian slant on the enterprise has *substantive* elements, taking it beyond an entirely orthodox reliance on minimising theoretical vocabulary, maximising the scope of principles, etc. The extent to which there is genuine conflict between minimalism and X, then, will depend on the extent to which X is aligned with these additional, substantive elements. If this diagnosis is correct, it follows that there is more to minimalism than Radford's glossary entry suggests, and one of the purposes of this paper is to try to clearly spell out what this additional substance consists of.

I believe that this is urgent in a context where I take it as uncontroversial that Chomsky's ideas have provided the inspiration for a great deal of work in related areas of cognitive enquiry over the last 30 years or so, most particularly from my perspective, first language acquisition. In a paper presented at the University of Essex in 1998, Ray Jackendoff, a scholar who has been broadly sympathetic to the Chomskian approach throughout his career, indicated that he feels that recent developments have lost touch with the wider field of cognitive science, and that the approach to syntactic theory I shall be focusing on currently runs the risk of being regarded as a colossal irrelevance. The last decade of acquisition research might be regarded as giving the lie to this view, with leading scholars such as Ken Wexler, Nina Hyams and Tom Roeper enthusiastically signing up to a minimalist approach (see, for example, Pöppel and Wexler, 1993; Wexler 1994; Harris and Wexler, 1996; Wexler, 1999; Hoekstra and Hyams, 1994; Hyams 1996; Roeper, 1996). As is well known, Wexler and Hyams in particular embed their commitment to minimalism within an approach to acquisition that adopts the Continuity Hypothesis - the view that the child's grammar is identical to that of the adult in significant respects right from the beginnings of the production of structured speech. I have nursed a number of reservations about continuity for a number of years (Atkinson, 1996), and one intriguing prospect (for me) is that an understanding of minimalism that goes beyond the exploitation of its technology might be compatible with, or even demand, a discontinuous approach to acquisition. To the extent that this is true, it raises fundamental questions about developmental processes, and the concluding section of this paper offers some tentative suggestions on how this line of enquiry might proceed.

In what follows, I shall try to set out in Section 1 what seem to me to be the foundational aspects of minimalism, as these are presented and developed in Chomsky (1995a, 1995b, 1998, 1999). Section 2 will illustrate the application of these principles with respect to the overall architecture of the theory. In Section 3, I shall focus on phrase structure, outlining how the basic stipulations of this core part of syntactic theory might be derived from minimalist principles. Because I am concerned to have approachable exemplification, I shall here ignore observations in Chomsky (1998), which suggest that some of this reasoning is redundant in the light of more recent developments. Section 4 will introduce the crucial concept of 'imperfections,' the strategy of regarding imperfections as 'apparent' and an airing of what seems to me to be the major question faced by current versions of minimalism. This will enable me to formulate the acquisition issues with which I am concerned, and Section 5 will offer a first pass at how these issues might be approached.

1. Fundamental Aspects of Minimalism

In the introduction to Chomsky (1995b, 1), minimalism is characterised as a response to a pair of questions:[3]

> '[(i)] What conditions on the human language faculty are imposed by considerations of virtual conceptual necessity? [(ii)] To what extent is the language faculty determined by these conditions, that is, how much special structure does it have beyond them? The first question ... has two aspects: what conditions are imposed on the language faculty by virtue of (A) its place within the array of cognitive systems of the

mind/brain, and (B) general considerations of simplicity, elegance and economy that have some independent plausibility?'

How this passage should be interpreted is not immediately obvious. Let's first focus on (ii), which is fairly straightforward. The sense is that 'special structure' is to be avoided if possible, with the nature of the language faculty being determined by whatever conditions emerge from consideration of (i).[4] Putting it simply, extensive 'special structure', assuming we can attach content to this phrase, would signal the demise of minimalism. Given this interpretation, it is of interest that Chomsky himself appears to be pessimistic about the prospects of avoiding 'special structure' entirely. In Chomsky (1999, 1), we find:

'The strongest minimalist thesis SMT would hold that language is an optimal solution to [legibility] conditions. ... *While SMT cannot be seriously entertained*, there is now reason to believe that in nontrivial respects some such thesis holds ...' (my italics – MA)

Setting aside the notion of 'optimality' and the reference to 'legibility conditions' to which we shall return, Chomsky here appears to be acknowledging that minimalism could be correct *in certain respects* but inappropriate in others. In my view, this is a worrying concession, since it raises the spectre of vacuity. Specifically, we might ask how it is different from the proposition that minimalism is correct except when it isn't.[5] It is not difficult to envisage that the modifier 'weak' will at some point find itself collocated with 'minimalism,' and since I firmly believe that positions in cognitive science prefaced by 'weak' are usually associated with lack of content, I shall regard the above remark as one which Chomsky would be advised to withdraw. So, we have the proposition that the language faculty has *no* special structure.[6]

We now turn to the more puzzling (i), and I believe that there are three issues which merit discussion. Let's start by considering (A) from the cited passage, initially ignore the modifier 'virtual' and concentrate on 'conceptual necessity.' For the last forty years or so, linguists working within the Chomskian approach have been committed to the study of the language faculty as abstract inquiry into the nature of one aspect of the mind/brain (see Chomsky, 2000b, for a collection of essays from the last decade defending and developing this view). With this commitment, comes the assumption that such enquiry, with its attendant idealisations, is scientifically legitimate, along with the recognition that the language faculty must interact with other cognitive systems. Standardly, these latter are viewed as including systems of articulation and acoustic perception (for the case of spoken language) and general conceptual-intentional systems.[7] Now, this way of looking at things can be regarded as a conceptual scheme, and, *given this particular scheme*, certain consequences follow. For instance, the interaction between the language faculty and other cognitive systems will require that there be at least two *interfaces* mediating this interaction. Thus, the existence of these interfaces becomes a matter of conceptual necessity - within this approach, It is not possible that such interfaces do not exist. Immediately, then, we see that whereas there is no need for the linguist working within this framework to *justify* interface levels of representation, such justification, in the form of empirical argument, is necessary for any other level of representation, a point to which I shall return in Section 2.

The interfaces alluded to above will have properties, and it ought to be possible to examine the role, if any, that such properties play in the structure and operation of the language faculty itself. That such properties exist is again conceptually necessary in the context of this specific approach to the nature of the language faculty, and properties of the language faculty that somehow *serve* these interface properties themselves become conceptually necessary from this perspective. Thus, we see that conceptual necessity with respect to (A) is to be viewed as necessity relativised to a way of viewing the nature of language, as a biological object embedded in a mind/brain consisting of a number of interacting systems, and the idealisations appropriate to its study.

Of course, it must be acknowledged that different conceptual schemes could be appropriate for guiding the study of language.

For instance, it might be maintained that the idealisation involved in the recognition of a separate language faculty is misguided, and that language should be approached as just another aspect of 'general cognition.' From this perspective, there will be no interface between the language faculty and general conceptual systems - indeed, there will be no language faculty in the sense assumed by the Minimalist Programme - and there will be no corresponding interface properties within this scheme. Recognition of the existence of such possibilities provides the motivation for the modifier preceding 'conceptual necessity'; the belief that pursuit of these has failed to yield significant insights justifies that modifier being 'virtual.'

Different kinds of alternative are provided by approaches to the study of language that remove it entirely from the cognitive context. For instance, Katz (1980) maintains that it is necessary to regard the proper objects of linguistic study as 'abstract,' transcending any instantiation in individual minds. Or the focus may be on the computationally effective characterisation of the properties of sets of expressions, and a rather explicit commitment to this, eschewing cognitive speculation, can be found in the early work on Generalised Phrase Structure Grammar (Gazdar *et al.*, 1985).[8]

Next, consider (B). Here, there is scope for confusion, as Chomsky's reference to 'elegance, simplicity and economy' could be regarded as expressing nothing more than adherence to the principles of 'good science,' that have already been discounted as providing the distinctive character of minimalism. However, in later discussion, Chomsky makes it clear that he has something different in mind. He says (1998, 5, n12):

> 'Note further that the question of optimal design is not that of "best theory" for [the faculty of language], however intricate and "imperfect" the design of the system.'

This remark indicates that it is taken for granted that linguists will practise 'good science,' with the requirements of 'elegance, simplicity and economy' always informing theory construction. The real issue is substantive and concerned with the *object of enquiry* itself, viz. the language faculty. No matter how 'poorly designed' the latter is, it will be incumbent on the linguist to seek to produce the best theory characterising it, with such a best theory displaying as much elegance, etc. as possible.[9] Now, while conceptual necessity is plausibly ascribed to those epithets that are characteristic of 'good science,' it is far from clear that the same goes for the properties of the object of enquiry itself. It could, indeed, turn out to be the case that this object is well designed (whatever that may mean), but, as Chomsky himself has repeatedly emphasised, this would be an *empirical* outcome, and a *surprising* one.[10] That it would be surprising immediately indicates that other outcomes are readily *conceivable* within the conceptual scheme that Chomsky takes for granted, and from this it follows that the applicability of 'conceptual necessity' to this sort of consideration is contentious. Be that as it may, what Chomsky is trying to achieve is clear. On the one hand, we have conditions imposed on the language faculty by virtue of it being required to interface with other cognitive systems; on the other, we have conditions imposed by considerations of 'good design.' While the notion of 'good design' awaits elucidation, the proposition that the language faculty is responsive to these two types of constraints (and nothing else, by virtue of an appropriate answer to question (ii)) is intelligible, even if we choose to withhold 'virtual conceptual necessity' from the design constraints.[11]

The third issue which demands attention is, then, the notion of 'good design' itself, and here we can take account of a remark from Chomsky (1999, 1):

> '"Good design" conditions are in part a matter of empirical discovery, though within general guidelines of an *a prioristic* character, a familiar feature of rational enquiry.'

Thus, it is not maintained that minimalist theorising is straitjacketed by some set of inviolable principles of 'good design' - there are no such principles. We might anticipate that whatever 'design sense' we bring to our activity will confront cases where it is immediately satisfied (or affronted), but other cases will not be transparent. For these latter, empirical considerations will hold sway, and illustration of precisely this situation will be provided in Section 2.[12]

Having sought to clear away some possible sources of misunderstanding, we can now proceed to a more explicit formulation of minimalism, specifically the Strong Minimalist Thesis (see above). In this connection, the (simplified) evolutionary fable provided by Chomsky (1998, 5) may be helpful:

> 'Imagine some primate with the human mental architecture and sensorimotor apparatus in place, but no language organ …. Suppose some event reorganizes the brain in such as way as, in effect, to insert [the faculty of language]. To be usable, the new organ has to meet certain "legibility conditions." Other systems of the mind/brain have to be able to access expressions generated by states of [the faculty of language] … to "read" them and use them as "instructions" for thought and action.'

It is worth pausing on this to get as clear a picture as possible of its significance. To suggest that our primate has 'the human mental architecture' appears to include the proposition that it controls a combinatorial system allowing it to entertain (though not express) 'complex' thoughts. Chomsky himself suggests that crediting his fictional primate with a Language of Thought, in the sense of Fodor (1975), might not be far off the mark. Suppose that we regard expressions in such a system as arrangements of 'semantic/conceptual features.' Since the system is combinatorial, subsets of such features will be isolable as recurrent packages. Additionally, our primate may be assumed to have access to systems enabling it to construct and perceive sound sequences, and so we might suppose that one consequence of the insertion of a language organ is that the primate acquires the ability to construct a 'protolexicon' exhibiting Saussurean arbitrariness with sets of 'sound features' associated with sets of 'semantic/conceptual features.' Arguably, the boundary conditions for the functioning of a language system are now set -

our primate has a lexicon, and the task is to devise a computational system which will take elements from this lexicon and construct 'complex objects' which will be *interpretable* by the system of thought and the sensorimotor systems. Given this perspective, *legibility* of the complex objects being presented to the interfaces is a minimal design condition to impose on the newly constructed language faculty. If objects arrive at the interfaces littered with the wrong (uninterpretable) sort of information, the objects will not be *usable* by the systems beyond the interfaces. Accordingly, *usability* by the interfacing cognitive systems is the driving design condition, and an immediate consequence of this is legibility.

Suppose, then, that we have a language faculty in the sense of Chomsky's fable in place, and that it operates by taking items from the protolexicon (in some manner to be made precise) and combining them (in some manner to be made precise) to produce 'complex' objects that are interpretable at the interfaces. Furthermore, suppose that these procedures of selection and combination are in some sense *optimal*, where optimality now joins *legibility* as a constraint on the system. The Strong Minimalist Thesis (SMT) can now be formulated as in (1) (Chomsky, 1998, 6):

(1) Language is an optimal solution to legibility conditions[13]

At this stage, and still within the context of the fable, we can begin to reflect on what properties an 'optimal solution' to the conditions posed by the legibility requirements might have. We have supposed that at the interfaces and appearing in the protolexicon we have arrangements of 'semantic/conceptual' and 'sound' features. Obviously, these are required by design considerations, but such considerations do *not* immediately require other types of feature. Thus, a plausible condition following from the design stance is the Interpretability Condition in (2) (cf. Chomsky, 1998, 27):[14]

(2) The language faculty, including lexical items, operates exclusively with features that are interpretable at the interfaces

Next, reflection on the process of producing complex interface representations from selections of lexical items suggests the design attractiveness of the Inclusiveness Condition in (3) (cf. Chomsky, 1995b, 225; 1998, 27):

(3) The production of complex interface representations involves only features that are supplied by the lexical items involved in the process.

The introduction of features that are interpretable at the conceptual-intentional interface would prejudice the compositional nature of interpretation; the introduction of features that are not interpretable at this interface would lead to representations that are not usable (but see Section 4). Accordingly, 'complex' representations should ideally be nothing more than re-arrangements of the features supplied to the computation by lexical items, and 'new' features should not be added as the computation proceeds.[15]

In considering (1), it is important to understand that it contains an implicit commitment to the view that *nothing* beyond legibility conditions and optimality constrains the nature of language; as a consequence, it is an extraordinarily strong hypothesis. To appreciate this, suppose that we construct an account of a language that includes (4) among its consequences:

(4) ⟨cats chase mice, MICE CHASE CATS⟩

This is intended to represent a pair of objects such that the first member of the pair is interpretable at the sensorimotor interface and the second at the conceptual-intentional interface, i.e. both objects, we suppose, are legible at the appropriate interfaces. As is immediately clear, such an account is empirically wrong. Quite simply, it pairs *inappropriate* interface representations. Or, to take an example akin to one considered by Chomsky himself (1998, 8), suppose our account yields the consequences in (5):

(5) (a) ⟨John is easy to catch, IT IS EASY TO CATCH JOHN⟩

(b) ⟨John is easy to be caught, IT IS EASY TO CATCH JOHN⟩

Again, legibility conditions are satisfied by both pairs of objects, we suppose, and this account is adequate for (5a) in pairing representations such that the first is interpreted as having the meaning of the second. However, while it may be the case that if *John is easy to be caught* means anything at all, its meaning corresponds to IT IS EASY TO CATCH JOHN, it is undeniable that this sentence is deviant in some way, and the mere need to satisfy legibility conditions does not, in itself, capture this deviance.

From examples such as the above, it is apparent that satisfaction of legibility conditions alone is not sufficient for the adequacy of a theory. The essence of SMT is that supplementing legibility requirements with 'good design' requirements *and nothing more* will be sufficient to avoid consequences such as these.

We can thus formulate a provocative consequence of SMT for sound-meaning pairs in (6):

(6) If SMT is correct, a theory of a language which satisfies good design conditions will produce pairs (π, λ) such that:
(a) π is legible at the sensorimotor interface.
(b) λ is legible at the conceptual-intentional interface.
(c) π means λ.

Note that (6) indicates that, *in principle*, resort to data such as 'the sentence ... means ...' is not necessary in theory construction, although it may prove to be indispensable in practice.[16]

Now, of course, if it transpires that optimally designed accounts yield consequences such as (4) and (5), then, it becomes necessary to move away from optimality and introduce complexity in the form of *special* structure or constraints.[17] As Chomsky puts it (1998, 8):

'Suppose all "best ways" to satisfy legibility conditions yield incorrect associations. Then departure from optimal design is required.'

We are now in a position to outline the first step of the research strategy which minimalism demands. Suppose that P is some 'property' that appears in our account of L. The correctness of SMT requires that P is a (possibly trivial) consequence of a set of 'axioms' which express either (a) legibility conditions, or (b) a commitment to some defensible notion of 'good design' (but cf. n12 above). We shall shortly turn to some simple examples where this strategy appears to be instantiated.

Before closing this section, I want to raise two further general issues, one of which amounts to at least a procedural difficulty and at worst a crippling handicap to the fulfilment of minimalist goals. The second focuses on an aspect of Chomsky's exposition of minimalism that raises interesting issues regarding explanation.

The procedural difficulty is easy to appreciate. We are confronted with constructing theories that answer to two sorts of conditions. Firstly, they rely on having a grasp of what 'good design' involves. As we have noted, Chomsky is optimistic that, while some negotiation around this concept is almost inevitable (cf. phrases like '*an* optimal design' and '*all* "best ways"'), there is no reason to doubt that substantial agreement can be reached, at least in the case of core instances. Secondly, they must respond to conditions imposed by the interfaces, and the difficulty here is that knowledge of these conditions is rudimentary to say the least. Thus, we appear to be in the unenviable position of seeking to solve for the values of $n+m$ variables where we have only n equations at our disposal. It is undisputable that this is an accurate characterisation of our condition, but despair is not the only response. As Chomsky puts it (1998, 7):

'Suppose we understood external systems well enough to have clear ideas about the legibility conditions they impose. Then the task at hand would be fairly straightforward .... But life is never that simple. The external systems are not well

understood. Progress in understanding them goes hand-in-
hand with progress in discovering the language systems that
interact with them.'

Putting a more positive gloss on this, we might note that while
our knowledge of interface systems is sparse, it is not nonexistent. There is an area of enquiry, cognitive psychology, where
questions of the appropriate type are sometimes posed, and it
would be rash to suppose that nothing of value can be gleaned
from this field regarding the nature of the conceptual-intentional
interface.[18] And for vocal-auditory linguistic systems, one very
obvious, and uncontroversial, property on which I shall have
occasion to rely below is linearisation. Thus, while the conditions
to which we need to refer are certainly incomplete and, in many
respects, extremely tentative, they are not totally lacking in
content. Arguably, this takes on added significance if we compare
minimalism with other approaches to syntactic theory that do not
operate within a cognitive framework.[19]
     The final point to which I wish to draw attention here
concerns the *outcomes* of minimalist enquiry, and an asymmetry
that Chomsky links to such outcomes. He says (1999, 1):

> 'Tenable or not, SMT sets an appropriate standard for true
> explanation: anything that falls short is to that extent
> descriptive, introducing mechanisms that would not be found
> in a "more perfect" system satisfying just legibility conditions.
> If empirical evidence requires mechanisms that are
> "imperfections," they call for some independent account:
> perhaps path-dependent evolutionary history, properties of
> the brain, or some other source.'

This statement asks us to consider an outcome according to which
parts of the language system are 'well designed' while other parts
are not, and Chomsky seems to be suggesting that explanation
stops here for the first category, but not for the second. I believe
that this suggestion raises a number of issues. First, there is a clear
sense in which Chomsky is surely right here. If we propose that
the language faculty operates with a feature that is legible at the

conceptual-intentional interface, say [±plural], this latter fact is the only explanation we need for the former. Such a case exploits the legibility requirement, but turning to good design (an essential component of SMT), matters are less clear. Suppose, for instance, that we are persuaded that all grammatical processes satisfy some locality condition or other, and we advertise this as an aspect of good design. Unless this can itself be somehow linked to legibility, it seems to me that the asymmetry to which Chomsky refers is not operative here. Whatever is discovered about the language faculty in this respect will invite enquiries at other levels, e.g. brain evolution (note 'invite' and not 'require,' since I don't believe that there is any reason to suppose that enquiry further down will necessarily produce insight). In short, if parts of the language faculty are, or are not, well designed, it is open for brain historians to try to figure out how the parts came to be, or not be, well designed, and I don't see any justification for an asymmetry of effort here. Furthermore, anti-reductionism is at least consistent with the notion of good design not surviving the move to lower levels. It's interesting that there have been instances over the years when Chomsky has hinted at being attracted by reductionism, although I'm not familiar with any explicit discussion of the matter by him. Obviously, he manages to combine this attraction (if, indeed, he feels it) with a large dose of scepticism about the significance of what is currently going on in brain science (see, for example, Chomsky, 1995c).

With the general principles of minimalism now in place, we turn to considerations of aspects of minimalist accounts of language, beginning with the overall architecture suggested by the minimalist stance. Throughout the following two sections, the emphasis is on examining the extent to which 'properties' of minimalist accounts can be argued to follow from no more than the requirement to satisfy legibility conditions and some notion of 'good design.'

2. The Architecture of Minimalist Theories

It is relatively easy to see how the considerations outlined in the previous section have as consequences a number of architectural features of minimalist accounts. Consider first the distinction between the lexicon and the computational system (CHL). The need to make this distinction follows immediately from the fact that a language is viewed as a combinatorial system, although even here, it is possible to raise an issue which bears on 'good design.' Suppose that the raw material with which the language faculty operates is features, a cover term for properties which are linguistically relevant in some way or other. Given this perspective, one task involved in 'fixing' a language can be viewed as that of assembling sets of such features into lexical items, with the set of assembled lexical items then comprising the lexicon of the language (see the discussion of a simplified view of this, yielding a protolexicon, in the previous section). But, of course, this is not *logically* necessary, and an alternative would be to regard the set of features provided by the language faculty as freely available for the assembly of lexical items, the chosen assemblies varying from one occasion to another. To the extent that the lexicon of a language appears to be relatively fixed, the empirical evidence does not favour this second possibility, but we might also be persuaded that considerations of 'good design' militate against it, as it requires continued access to the complete set of features and invocation of the assembly operations every time the language faculty is engaged. A better designed system, it might be supposed, will make a once-and-for-all selection from the set of available features, with any subsequent lexical creativity being constrained at least to this extent.

Continuing with this theme, and now taking the distinction between lexicon and computational system as given, there must be some operation, SELECT, which extracts an item from the lexicon and makes it accessible to the computational system. Somewhat less obviously, we can maintain that intervening between the lexicon and the computational system is a set of selected lexical items, a lexical array or a numeration, on which the computational system operates without further recourse to the lexicon.[20] According to this view, then, two selection operations are required, the first to compose a lexical array or numeration, and the second to make items from this object available to C_{HL}. An immediate issue that arises is that of justification for such a two-stage process of selection.

It is of some interest that Chomsky uses the question of the existence of lexical arrays/numerations to argue for the *insufficiency* of conceptual arguments in establishing a particular design stance. He points out that conceptual arguments against embracing lexical arrays/numerations are easy to formulate: *ceteris paribus*, a theory which does not employ a construct is better designed than an otherwise identical one that does. However, things are not always equal, and this simple perspective can be countered by the observation that 'If the derivation accesses the lexicon at every point' – a consequence of selection not producing a lexical array/numeration to which the computation is subsequently restricted – 'it must carry along this huge beast, rather like cars that have to replenish fuel supply constantly.' (1998, 13). Ultimately, Chomsky concludes, the issue must be viewed as empirical.[21]

What we have, then, up to now argues for a preliminary architecture along the lines of (7):

(7) LEXICON $\rightarrow$ LEXICAL ARRAY/NUMERATION $\rightarrow$ C_{HL}
        SELECT$_1$ SELECT$_2$

Moving into C_{HL}, it is uncontroversial that some type of merger operation forms part of this system. This again follows from the fact that a language is being regarded as a combinatorial system, whereby complex expressions are constructed out of their component parts. Arguably, it might also be seen as a consequence of legibility conditions at LF, and the Principle of Integration stating that at LF (the linguistic side of the conceptual-intentional interface) every category (except the root) must be contained in another category. (Collins, 1995, 69) offers a formulation of such a condition.[22]

It was because of the 'conceptual necessity' associated with merger that Chomsky (1995b) felt that he could regard tokens of the operation as 'costless' in computations of economy of derivations, a strategy which immediately underwrites the system's preference for Merge over Move. As we shall see in Section 4, later developments ground this preference in complexity considerations, relying on the observation that any token of Move contains a token of Merge as a proper component.

The requirement that a language be responsive to legibility conditions at the interfaces immediately motivates a further operation of C_{HL}, Spell-Out. It is generally regarded as obvious that what is legible at the conceptual-intentional interface (LF) is illegible at the sensorimotor interface (PF) and vice versa. It follows that features that are legible at one interface must not be presented to the other if legibility conditions are not to be violated. If merger produces complex objects that are perhaps no more than rearrangements of the features entering C_{HL} from the lexicon (cf. the Inclusiveness Condition), it is essential that these features are effectively partitioned by the system. This is achieved by the operation of Spell-Out, which in Chomsky (1995b) is presented as a single operation, demarcating overt and covert syntactic processes.[23]

In contrast to Spell-Out, an operation that is necessary to satisfy the demands of the interfaces, the levels of linguistic representation familiar from Principles and Parameters Theory, d-structure and s-structure, have no such motivation. Accordingly, the starting point of minimalism is that these levels of representation do not exist.[24]

Bringing the discussion of this brief section together, then, we arrive at an overall (incomplete) architecture along the lines of (8):[25]

(8)
LEXICON →LEXICAL ARRAY/→ C_{HL}(= MERGE, ...)→SPELL-
OUT→LF
     NUMERATION   ↓
SELECT₁   SELECT₂   PF

All aspects of this architecture can be seen as responsive to the general requirements that were formulated in Section 1. We turn next to some rather more specific aspects of minimalist theorising.

3. Bare Phrase Structure

Chomsky (1995b, 249) concludes his discussion of phrase structure with the following characterisation of Bare Phrase Structure. It is:

'... essentially "given" on grounds of virtual conceptual necessity,' [and] 'structures stipulated in earlier versions are either missing or reformulated in elementary terms satisfying minimalist conditions, ... Stipulated conventions are derived.'

This is a very positive diagnosis, and it suggests that phrase structure is an area ripe with the sort of argumentation that concerns me. We begin with a brief indication of the content of 'earlier versions,' so we can get a sense of what is 'reformulated' or 'derived'. A popular precursor to Bare Phrase Structure was some version or other of X-bar Theory, subscribing to principles such as those in (9), ignoring the role of adjuncts:

(9) XP = (YP) - X'
   X' = X - (YP)
   (order not specified)

Typically (9) has been supplemented by some version of the Extended Projection Principle (EPP) along the lines of (10):

(10) Spec, IP is obligatory (all clauses have subjects)

From (9), we can immediately see that its implicit stipulations include: (a) all branching is (at most) binary; (b) all projections are headed. From (10), focusing on A-movement, it is apparent that the position to which an item moves under A-movement in, for example, a raising construction, is already supplied by the EPP. As a consequence, taking I as the 'target' of such movement, a natural assumption in a framework in which features of I and of the moved expression need to enter a relation in which Case and agreement can be 'checked,' we can see that the identity of the constituent which results from an instance of A-movement is determined by the target - it is IP rather than, say a D- or N-projection. Equally, in cases of head movement, where, say, a V targets a higher I position, the resulting configuration has been assumed to be (11a) and not (11b):

(11) a. [$_I$ V - I]
    b. [$_V$ V - I]

Here, (11a) again subscribes to projection of target, and in this case the assumption is entirely implicit, i.e. there is nothing like the EPP to underwrite this conclusion in this case. Thus, we can add to our set of stipulations: (c) in cases of movement, the target of movement projects. We shall now take these stipulations in turn and see how they can be 'derived' without offending minimalist sensibilities.[26] We begin with a 'proof' that all tokens of Merge are binary, with the consequence that reconstructing Bare Phrase Structure into traditional tree notation would yield only binary branching.[27]

A published 'proof' of the binarity of Merge appears in Collins (1995). In fact, Collins starts from the proposition that Merge is unrestricted with respect to the number of arguments it can take, and seeks to establish the conclusion that economy considerations require that *any legitimate token* of Merge will be binary. We are to suppose that we need to merge α, β and γ. If we assume unrestricted Merge, there are two ways we can do this. First, we could allow Merge to operate as a ternary operation, yielding (12):

(12) Merge $(\alpha, \beta, \gamma) = \{H, \{\alpha, \beta, \gamma\}\}$

Here, I diverge from Collins in allowing H to designate the 'label' of the merged object, i.e. whatever it is that gives it its syntactic character - we make no assumptions about headedness at this stage. Alternatively, we could have two applications of binary Merge, as indicated in (13) (obviously, we could also effect two binary mergers in different orders, but such options are irrelevant to the issue under discussion):

(13) Merge $(\alpha, \beta) = \{H', \{\alpha, \beta\}\}$
    Merge $(\gamma, \{H', \{\alpha, \beta\}\}) = \{H'', \{\alpha, \beta, \gamma\}\}$

Now, Collins observes that (12) is preferred to (13) by virtue of the length of the derivation. But 'length of derivation' is a 'global' economy condition, and Collins is seeking to restrict economy issues to 'local' choices at specific points in derivations. From this latter perspective, he maintains that (13) is preferred to (12), since 'the first step of [13] is simpler than the first step in [12].' (*op. cit.,* 75). Overall, this appears to say little more than that a binary operation is 'simpler' than a ternary operation, and apart from its relationship to the proposition that 2 is smaller than 3, this doesn't immediately strike me as convincing. It is therefore appropriate to ask whether there is an alternative 'proof' of binarity, more properly engaging the issues we have explored in Section 1.

We start from a remark appearing in Chomsky (1998, 12):

'Relations which enter into C_{HL} either (i) are imposed by legibility conditions, or (ii) fall out in some natural way from the computational process.'

We should already have a sense of what the first disjunct here requires, so I shall focus on the second. 'Falling out' of operations of Merge (which, at this stage, we assume not to be restricted to a binary operation) are the relations 'sister-of' and 'immediately contains,' where the latter is the set-theoretic analogue of the more familiar 'immediately dominates.' Given any token of Merge applied to syntactic objects α and β to produce the syntactic object K, α and β are in the sister-of relation and both K and α and K and β are in the immediately-contains relation. Thus, we may suppose that these are 'given,' and inherit their conceptual necessity from the conceptual necessity of Merge itself.[28]

If we now suppose that the immediately given relations can be composed, it is easy to see how we can define 'contains' (equivalent to the more familiar 'dominates') and 'c-command.' For the former, we can use the definition in (14):

(14) α contains β iff α immediately contains β or there is a sequence $(\gamma_1, \ldots \gamma_n)$ $(n \geq 1)$, such that γ_i immediately contains

γ_{i+1} $(1 \leq i \leq n - 1)$, α immediately contains γ_1 and γ_n immediately contains β.

For c-command, (15) will serve our purposes:

(15) α c-commands β iff there is a γ such that α is a sister of γ and γ contains β

Because of the availability of simple definitions like these, Chomsky is happy to regard c-command as 'falling out' of the operation of the computational system in a natural way.[29]

With this much established, we can now construct a 'proof' that Merge is binary, by relying on Kayne (1994). The 'proof' is set out in (16):

(16) (i)   terminal strings are linearly ordered at PF;
     (ii)   The syntactic objects produced by C_{HL} do not contain order information;
     (iii) The phonological component must impose this linear ordering on the basis of information which is supplied by C_{HL} (i.e., there must be some relation R, accessible to C_{HL}, such that L(a, b) iff R(a, b), where L is a linear ordering);[30]
     (iv)   asymmetric c-command is accessible to C_{HL};
     (v)   asymmetric c-command is (locally) total only if branching is binary.

Taking these steps in turn, (16i) is a straightforward statement of a PF-legibility condition. I suppose that it could be argued that (16ii) embodies an empirical hypothesis, but I would prefer to interpret it as being indicative of 'good design.' There are no LF-legibility conditions requiring that syntactic objects should be ordered; therefore, it would be poor design to build a representational property into objects that is not necessary for interpretation. Given (16i) and (16ii), (16iii) follows. As argued above, c-command is available to C_{HL}, and asymmetric c-command merely requires access to this relation and its complement. Thus, it is not unreasonable to suggest that asymmetric c-command 'falls out' of the operation of C_{HL}. Finally, (16v) is established by Kayne (1994). We can thus see that the binarity of Merge follows from a simple legibility condition (16i), a principle of 'good design' (16ii), and the accessibility of a simple relation that 'falls out' of the operation of Merge itself.[31]

Consider next headedness. Adopting the view that syntactic objects are just sets of features, and supposing that any complex syntactic object bears a *label* to indicate its syntactic 'character,' we need to establish (17):

(17) Merge $(\alpha, \beta) = \{\alpha, \{\alpha, \beta\}\}$ or $\{\beta, \{\alpha, \beta\}\}$

The 'proof' of (17), based directly on Chomsky (1995b, 244), appears in (18):

(18) (i) The output of Merge applied to α and β must involve minimally $\{\alpha, \beta\}$, the 'simplest' construct out of α and β;

 (ii) However, $\{\alpha, \beta\}$ is not sufficient for this purpose, since the interfaces interpret, e.g. nominal and verbal projections, differently;

 (iii) No elements are introduced to the derivation by C_{HL};

 (iv) The manner of indicating the 'character' of $\{\alpha, \beta\}$ can use only the feature sets α and β themselves;

 (v) We thus need to consider the possible set-theoretic operations on α and β yielding α, β, $\alpha \cap \beta$, $\alpha \cup \beta$ as candidates for the label of Merge (α, β);

 (vi) Both $\alpha \cap \beta$ and $\alpha \cup \beta$ lead to violations of legibility conditions, via 'emptiness' or 'contradictoriness';

 (vii) Thus, Merge $(\alpha, \beta) = \{\alpha, \{\alpha, \beta\}\}$ or $\{\beta, \{\alpha, \beta\}\}$

There are two propositions embedded in (18i). Firstly, the idea that the combination of α and β should be some function of α and β, rather than having a value which does not acknowledge these components is simply an acknowledgement of compositionality. Secondly, (18i) explicitly, and uncontroversially, claims that the simplest construct out of two objects is the set containing the two objects. Legibility conditions provide the basis for (18ii), and again the intuitions behind this step look sound. One way to put it is that there is a fundamental distinction between predicates and those of which they are predicated, a distinction that is represented in some way in any system that is designed to make contact with the way we think. Now, some expressions correspond to predicates, whereas others function as arguments of these predicates, and there is every reason to believe that the LF-interface and the interpretive systems beyond require information about this contrast. In (18iii), we see a simple statement of the Inclusiveness Condition, a 'good design' condition characteristic of the derivation to the LF-interface, although, it seems, not holding of the derivation to PF (cf. n15). Given (18iii), (18iv) is an immediate consequence, and with (18v) we consider the space of possibilities for defining a label designating the syntactic 'character' of Merge (α, β) in terms of α and β. Now, α and β are each sets of features, so it is natural to consider the standard class of operations on two sets in contemplating what the label might be. These are the identity operations for each of the two sets, set intersection and set union. These possibilities are merely enumerated in (18v).[32] In (18vi), the space enumerated in (18v) is reduced by invoking legibility conditions. The issue here can easily be illustrated with a simple example such as *read books*. There is no reason to believe that the lexical entries for *read* and *books* have anything in common. If, therefore, we rely on set intersection to compute the label for the phrase, this will yield the empty set and presumably the complex object corresponding to *read books* will be wrongly predicted to be uninterpretable at LF. To demonstrate the inappropriateness of set union, adopting familiar views on categorial features, we will suppose that the lexical entry for *read* contains, *inter alia*, [–N] and [+V], whereas that for *books* contains [+N] and [–V]. Then, the union of the two sets of features will contain contradictory features, and again it seems uncontroversial to conclude that LF will not be able to interpret such objects. Thus, we reach the desired (18vii).

Once more, it is instructive to clearly spell out the status of the hypotheses that justify this conclusion. Both (18i) and (18iii) rely on considerations of 'good design,' whereas (18ii) and (18vi) invoke legibility requirements.

The last topic I wish to consider in this section is the 'proof' that target projects. Chomsky (1995b) contains a long (and distributed) discussion of this 'theorem,' and Atkinson (1998) is the first stage of an attempt to unpack this discussion and to try to clearly set out and assess the minimalist credentials of the 'proof.'[33] Recall that the stipulation we are trying to deal with in this connection is that formulated in the Extended Projection Principle (see 10 above and Chomsky and Lasnik, 1995, 55). The 'proof' is set out in (19):

(19) (i)   Move raises α to a position β only if morphological properties of α itself would not otherwise be satisfied in the derivation;

(ii) Checking of morphological properties takes place only in checking domains;

(iii) Intermediate projections are not relevant at the LF interface, and *therefore* are not visible to CHL;

(iv) Suppose α raises targeting β and α projects;

(v) α must be maximal or minimal in its original site;

(vi) If α is maximal, then α is intermediate (after projection) and invisible for feature checking *in situ* or for further movement;

(vii) If α is minimal and projects, the targeted category becomes a complement of α in its raised position and no checking relation is established;

(viii) β projects.

We again proceed to discuss this 'proof' line by line. In (19i), we see a formulation of the Principle of Greed, which was a feature of the systems presented in Chomsky (1995a, b). From one perspective, this looks like a straightforward implementation of 'good design' conditions, with movement only being called on when necessary. However, it also incorporates a 'look ahead' facility, as satisfaction of the relevant properties of α may occur only at some later point in a derivation, and this has led to the abandonment of Greed in Chomsky's later work.[34] Since we are painting fairly broad strokes here, let us assume that 'good design' considerations are what motivate (19i). Turning to (19ii), its status is perhaps less clear. The checking domain of a head includes the head's specifier and various adjoined positions (see Nunes and Thomson, 1998, for a formal definition), and perhaps the important point to make clear is that it is clearly differentiated from a head's complement domain, which is the locus of argument selection.[35] Suppose, then, that selection and checking are important and essential operations of C_{HL} that serve quite different purposes in the grammar. Arguably, this could be used to motivate different domains in which they operate. Let us suppose that this is so, and conclude that (19ii) can again be grounded in 'good design' considerations.[36]

We next turn to (19iii), and this too is not unproblematic. It actually consists of two assertions. The first is the bald statement that intermediate projections are not relevant at LF. Chomsky (1995b, 242) asserts this, but in an accompanying footnote indicates that (382): '... [it] depends on properties of phrases that are still unclear.' Against the background of this uncertainty, it is interesting that Chomsky (1999, 32) is prepared to give up the assumption, saying ' ... the assumption that X' is not interpreted at LF ... is questionable and in fact rejected in standard approaches.' The second statement embodied in (19iii) is that irrelevance at LF has invisibility to CHL as a consequence, and while it is easy enough to sympathise with the spirit of this remark, it is difficult to regard it as an instantiation of any general principle. Indeed, if we identify lack of relevance with uninterpretability (possibly justified on the basis of Chomsky's remark that 'X' is not interpreted at LF'), we need only note the status of uninterpretable features in CHL to be persuaded that we are some way from general principles. By definition, such features are uninterpretable at LF, yet they play a major role in the operation of CHL. It is thus apparent that in general invisibility to CHL is *not* a consequence of LF-uninterpretability; accordingly, this second part of (19iii) takes on the air of an uncomfortable stipulation.

Whether the above diagnosis of the status of (19iii) is appropriate is perhaps not too important in the context of the current discussion. It is reasonably clear that (19iii) seeks to allude to both legibility (in the first statement) and 'good design' (in the second), so its intended credentials are clear enough. From hereon, the argument is straightforward. In (19iv), we meet the *reductio* premise, and (19v) follows from (19iii) - if α is to be raised, it must be visible to CHL, i.e. via (19iii), it must be maximal or minimal. The next two propositions, (19vi) and (19vii), simply take the two cases originating from (19v) and show that both of them lead the derivation to crash. In the case of (19vi), this conclusion follows again from (19iii), the invisibility to CHL of intermediate projections; for (19vii), it follows from (19ii). We can thus deny the *reductio* premise and conclude (19viii).

Before closing this section, it is important to be clear on what its aims have been. I do not wish to suggest that any of the three arguments analysed in some detail in (16), (18) and (19) are beyond reproach. Indeed, I have drawn attention to what appear to be some fairly major flaws in the reasoning. I suggest, however, that they do purport to be the *type* of argument that it is necessary to formulate if minimalism is to succeed, and they lend *some* credence to the remarks of Chomsky (1995b) with which I opened this section. To the extent that such arguments are sound, we might be persuaded that phrase structure is 'perfect,' constituting the optimally designed response to legibility conditions. In the next section, we turn to what are undoubtedly *prima facie* imperfections in language systems.

4. 'Apparent' Imperfections

An important distinction in the domain of features is first systematically discussed in Chomsky (1995b). This is the distinction between *interpretable* and *uninterpretable* features, where the notion of interpretability refers to the LF interface.[37] To illustrate, categorial features are uncontroversially regarded as interpretable: whether a token of *walk* is to be interpreted as verbal or nominal is clearly a matter of importance for LF. Equally, features of number and person in the nominal system are interpretable, signalling the difference between *book* and *books* or between *me* and *you*. Collectively, such nominal features are referred to as φ-features, and the general claim is that the φ-features of nominals are interpretable. By contrast, the Case features of nominals, which clearly play a part in the operation of C_{HL}, are deemed to be uninterpretable, and evidence for this can be gleaned from the examples in (20):

(20) a. John believes that *he* is a liar
     b. John believes *him* to be a liar

Here, we see the nominative and accusative forms of the pronoun *he/him*, but whatever difference in interpretation accrues to the sentences in (20) is not down to the role that these expressions play in the interpretation - in both cases, the property of being a liar is predicated of a third person singular referent, with the resulting proposition being the object of John's belief. Additionally, the agreement features of verbs (their φ-features) are uninterpretable because they are redundant. Invoking the traditional asymmetric claim that verbs agree with nominals suggests that the locus of person and number interpretation is at the nominal and not at the verb.

With even this much in place, it is easy to raise the spectre of the language system containing imperfections. Recall the Interpretability Condition (2) from Section 1, which requires that the features associated with lexical items should, from a design stance, be uniformly interpretable at one or the other interface. The recognition of the need to incorporate uninterpretable features such as the above within the theory of grammar immediately challenges (2).

An additional issue arises once we recognise that a constant theme in Chomsky's recent work has been the involvement of uninterpretable features in accounts of movement. Thus, consider (21):

(21) John seems to be awake

The derivation of this sentence assumes the intermediate structure in (22):

(22) T seems [John to be awake]

Assuming the technology of Chomsky (1995b), in this structure, T has uninterpretable φ-features matching those of *seems*, and *John* has an uninterpretable Case feature. Movement of *John* to [Spec, TP] sees *John* enter the checking domain of T, and in this configuration, the various uninterpretable features are checked (deleted), allowing the derivation to converge at LF.[38]

An extension to these ideas in Chomsky (1995b) is the notion, based on 'good design' principles, that since the function of movement appears to be that of ensuring that uninterpretable features are deleted in the course of a derivation, canonical instances of movement will be non-overt and simply involve the movement of features. What is at issue here can be readily illustrated by standard examples such as those in (23):

(23)   a. There seems to be a problem
       b. There seem to be some problems

The facts here are that the verb forms *seems* and *seem* agree with *a problem* and *some problems*, respectively, and Chomsky's response to this was to suggest that, by virtue of being uninterpretable, the Case feature associated with *problem/problems* undergoes covert feature movement (Move F, later Attract F when the process is re-conceptualised as driven by features of the target of movement) into the checking domain of finite T in the main clause. Furthermore, it is assumed that Move/Attract F 'automatically carries along FF(LI)' (*op. cit.,* 265), where FF(LI) refers to the set of 'formal features of LI,' including interpretable φ-features. Thus, this movement ensures that all uninterpretable features enter into appropriate checking relations and are deleted. Additionally, it is taken as axiomatic that T has an uninterpretable EPP-feature, which is satisfied (and deleted) by the merger of expletive *there* in [Spec, TP].[39]

The account I have just caricatured gives rise to a number of technical difficulties, which there is not space to go into here. An important feature of Chomsky (1998, 1999) is that he develops a somewhat different perspective, while claiming that it avoids these complexities.[40] To move towards the issues I wish to focus on in this section, it is necessary to have some appreciation of this alternative.

Consider, then, the examples in (24), noting that (24b) exhibits exactly the same kind of 'long distance' agreement between matrix T and a lower constituent (in this case *prizes*) that we have seen in (23):

(24)   a. several prizes are likely to be awarded
       b. there are likely to be awarded several prizes

For (24a), we can consider the intermediate stage in the derivation represented in (25):

(25)   T be awarded [several prizes]

Two assumptions, not adopted in Chomsky (1995b), are important. The first is that the infinitival T that appears in raising (and ECM) structures contains a *defective* uninterpretable φ-set, which comprises only the feature [person]. Uninterpretable features are deemed to be *active* in the derivation (visible to CHL), and this enables the [person] feature of T to function as a *probe*, seeking a matching *goal*. The lexical item *prizes* contains an uninterpretable Case feature that renders it active, and this enables the [person] feature of T to identify the interpretable [3person] feature of *prizes* as a goal.[41] This process of an active probe identifying an active goal and evaluating whether the latter contains interpretable features matching the uninterpretable features of the former is the first stage of the operation *Agree*, which replaces Move/Attract F. The consequences of successful matching, which complete the operation Agree, can now be set out. They are: (a) the uninterpretable [person] feature of T is deleted (as far as the syntactic derivation is concerned) under matching with the [3person] feature of *prizes*, while being simultaneously *valued* for the operation of the phonological component;[42] (b) the uninterpretable Case feature of *prizes*, however, is *not* deleted, since Chomsky stipulates (1998, 40; 1999, 4) the proposition in (26), which comprises the second innovation when compared to Chomsky (1995b):

(26) α must have a complete set of φ-features (it must be φ-complete) to delete uninterpretable features of the paired matching element β

A consequence of this is that *prizes* remains active for future operations of CHL.[43]

Additionally, T is stipulated as containing an uninterpretable EPP-feature (cf. n39), a feature which in order to be deleted requires that an expression with appropriate characteristics merges with (25), thereby creating [Spec, TP]. If no suitable candidate remains in the numeration to satisfy this EPP-feature via Merge, it is necessary to move *several prizes* to yield the intermediate structure (27):[44]

(27) [several prizes][T be awarded t]

Clearly illustrated in this account is the proposition that Move is a more complex operation than Merge. Not only does it include a token of Merge, but it also presupposes a token of Agree and of whatever operation is necessary to determine that *several prizes* (rather than just *prizes*) is the expression undergoing movement. Thus, this 'additive' notion of complexity of Move when compared to Merge supplements the purely conceptual considerations from Chomsky (1995b), where it is noted that it is a characteristic of *any* combinatorial system that it includes an operation akin to Merge (cf. above), which is not the case for Move.

From (27), the derivation proceeds by merger of *likely* followed by matrix T to give (28):

(28) [T likely [several prizes [T be awarded t]]]

Unlike raising T, matrix T is assumed to host a complete, uninterpretable φ-set, and this again acts as a probe, identifying the still active φ-set of *prizes* as a goal. Matching of φ-sets leads to the deletion of the φ-features of T, as far as the syntactic derivation to LF is concerned, *and* deletion of the uninterpretable Case feature of *prizes*.[45] Again, T is assumed to have an uninterpretable EPP-feature, and the only candidate for satisfying this is *prizes* (expanded to *several prizes* under the pied-piping mechanisms, whatever these may be). Thus, we get to (29):

(29) [several prizes][T likely [t [T be awarded t]]]

In (29), all uninterpretable features have been deleted, and the derivation converges.

Now consider (24b), starting again at the intermediate stage of the derivation in (25). Everything proceeds as for (24a) until we raise the question of satisfying the uninterpretable EPP-feature of T. Supposing now that the expletive *there* is available in the numeration and is appropriate to satisfy this feature, we invoke the principle that CHL prefers a token of (pure) Merge to a token of Move. Thus, given the choice between merging *there* and moving *several prizes*, CHL opts for the former, giving (30):[46]

(30) there T be awarded [several prizes]

Next, we proceed as before, first merging the adjective *likely* with (30) followed by merger of (φ-complete) T with the A-projection, giving (31):

(31) T likely [there [T be awarded several prizes]]

The uninterpretable φ-set of matrix T acts as a probe and locates the active [person] feature of *there* as goal. Because the φ-set of *there* is incomplete, it will not delete the φ-set of matrix T under (26), and the latter remains active. Matrix T, just like raising T, has an uninterpretable EPP-feature, and now, unlike what we have supposed for raising T, the numeration does *not* contain a suitable expression to delete this EPP-feature via pure Merge. Thus, Move is called upon, locating the 'closest' suitable expression to satisfy this EPP-requirement. This expression is *there*, and, as a consequence, we derive (32):

(32) there T likely [t [T be awarded several prizes]]

We are not quite finished. Recall that the complete φ-set of matrix T remains undeleted by virtue of the φ-incompleteness of matching *there*, so it must act as a probe again, locating the φ-set of the still active *prizes* as a matching goal. This latter expression does have a complete φ-set, so it deletes the uninterpretable φ-set of matrix T and simultaneously values this φ-set for PF-purposes, i.e. we have agreement between matrix T (ultimately signalled on the verb) and *prizes*. Additionally, the appropriate feature of matrix T deletes (and values for PF-purposes) the uninterpretable Case-feature of *prizes* as nominative. Now, all uninterpretable features have been deleted, and the derivation converges at LF.

From the above discussion, the major differences between Chomsky (1995b) and Chomsky (1998, 1999) should be reasonably clear. In the earlier work, the theory of Case-agreement and the theory of movement are inextricably linked, and a consequence of this is that even when Case-agreement is operative without any overt movement, as in examples including expletives, it is necessary to postulate non-overt movement (Move/Attract F) to produce a consistent account. In the later papers, however, Chomsky treats Case-agreement and movement as quite independent. The former is dealt with via the operation Agree, whereas the latter is a response to an independent EPP-feature.[47] The consequences of Move/Attract F (F a feature) in Chomsky (1995b) are now dealt with by a matching/deletion operation (Agree) that applies to expressions *in situ*. Whether a token of Move (now restricted to overt movement) is contingent on an application of Agree is entirely determined by whether the configuration contains an appropriate EPP-feature. As Chomsky (1998, 41) puts it, using the vocabulary of Chomsky (1995b):

> '... elements merge in checking domains for reasons independent of feature checking; and feature checking takes place without dislocation to a checking domain.'

An example such as (24b) illustrates both possibilities. Merger of *there* in the specifier position of the raising T in this case has nothing to do with the 'checking' (i.e. deletion of uninterpretable Case-agreement features).[48] Equally, the operation of Agree that

takes the φ-set of matrix T as a probe and that of *prizes* as a goal
eliminates ('checks') the uninterpretable features at these two sites
without invoking overt or non-overt dislocation.

The important issues to be clear on for the subsequent
discussion are (a) while a token of Agree does not entail a
corresponding token of Move, any token of Move *does*
presupposes a token of Agree, and (b) Agree is normally triggered
by sets of uninterpretable features in a probe seeking sets of
matched interpretable features in an active goal (although, see
n46).

Whatever the correct technology turns out to be, what must be
stressed is that what we find in these versions of Chomsky's
minimalism is two challenges to the proposition that the language
faculty exhibits 'good design.' As noted at the outset of this
section, while interpretable features inherit their legitimacy from
the fact that they are legible at the interfaces, uninterpretable
features have no such credentials. And while the operation of
Merge, or something similar, appears to be conceptually
necessary in characterising the nature of any combinatorial
system, this is not the case for Move, as witnessed by the fact that
it finds no place in the artificially constructed systems of logic and
mathematics.[49] Chomsky's way of approaching such phenomena
is as follows (1998, 27):

> 'The research strategy is to seek "imperfections" of language
> ... Apparent imperfections come in several varieties. Given
> some apparent property P of language, we may find:
> (i) P is real, and an imperfection
> (ii) P is not real, contrary to what had been supposed
> (iii) P is real, but not an imperfection; it is part of a best way to
> meet design specifications.'

Examples intended to illustrate outcome (ii) have already been
encountered in our discussion of Bare Phrase Structure. Thus,
such 'imperfections' as the stipulations that all phrases are headed
or that target projects can be argued to be 'not real' in the sense
that they can be derived by relying only on sets of assumptions
which satisfy minimalist requirements. Obviously, outcome (i) is

damaging to minimalism, with the extent of the damage perhaps depending on whether the programme can tolerate systems that exhibit 'good design' but only partially (cf. discussion in Section 1). We are now faced with uninterpretable features and movement instantiating outcome (i), and it is difficult to be sanguine about the prospects for minimalism if this diagnosis is confirmed.

There remains, however, outcome (iii), and arguably the most intriguing aspect of Chomsky (1998) is that he takes the first steps towards suggesting that this is the correct outcome for our two delinquent properties. There are two stages to the argument, with the first seeking to reduce two 'apparent' imperfections to one. Starting with overt movement and recognising that embedded in any token of Move there is a token of Agree, we observe that Agree is triggered only by the presence of uninterpretable features which render an item 'active' and visible to the computational system. So the way is open to suggest that uninterpretable features are nothing more than the *mechanism* used by the language faculty to implement the dislocation property. As Chomsky (1998, 36) puts it:[50]

'The distinction is familiar. We may say that the function of the eye is to see, but it remains to determine the implementation; a particular protein in the lens that reflects light, etc. ... Perhaps [uninterpretable features] are used to yield the dislocation property. If so, then the two imperfections might reduce to one, the dislocation property.'

If we accede to this line of thought, we must focus our attention on dislocation.[51] This takes us back to the Strong Minimalist Thesis in (1), repeated as (33):

(33) Language is an optimal solution to legibility conditions

If dislocation is an 'apparent' imperfection, it follows that it must constitute part of such an 'optimal solution.' So, we might expect that tokens of dislocation will be answerable to either PF-legibility conditions or LF-legibility conditions. If the former is the case, we would expect the dislocation in question to be located in the PF-component of the grammar, whereas the latter would commit us to accommodating the dislocation in the derivation to LF, what Chomsky refers to as the 'narrow syntax.' We can thus formulate the fundamental questions posed by SMT as (34):

(34) (a) what LF-legibility conditions motivate cases of syntactic dislocation?
(b) what PF-legibility conditions motivate cases of 'phonological dislocation'?

It is apparent that (34) raises the question of the criteria we might employ in recognising instances of syntactic or phonological dislocation. Getting an initial grip on this is reasonably straightforward. The reference in (34a) to LF-legibility conditions indicates that a token of movement to which this question applies must be responsive to an interpretive requirement: LF presents an interpretation problem that is insoluble without the movement in question. In implementing the movement, the system solves the interpretation problem, and it follows that the movement must have consequences for interpretation.[52] By exclusion, we can then maintain that any token of movement which does *not* have such consequences will constitute an instance of phonological dislocation.[53]

The remainder of this section consists largely of exemplifications of approaches to these questions in Chomsky (1999), beginning with his discussion of the rule of Thematisation/Extraposition (TH/EX), a movement rule Chomsky takes to belong to the phonological component. We begin with the phenomenon.

It appears to be a fact about English that the internal argument in an expletive passive construction cannot remain *in situ* adjacent to its selecting verb:

(35) *there were donated several books to the bazaar

However, alongside (35), we have (36a, b), where the internal argument *several books* has been moved to a 'peripheral' position:

(36) a. there were several books donated to the bazaar
    b. there were donated to the bazaar several books

Here, (36b), while not entirely idiomatic, is a considerable improvement on (35), and (36a) is totally unexceptionable. In connection with the operation producing such examples, Chomsky says (*op. cit.*, 16): '[It] is reminiscent of normal displacement of subject and object, both to edge positions, but it differs in not yielding the normal surface semantic effects.'

The 'normal surface semantic effects' for subjects alluded to here have given rise to considerable speculation for a number of years. Continuing to focus on expletives, they are most directly revealed by the Definiteness Effect, illustrated in (37) (Milsark, 1974; Jenkins, 1975; Reuland and ter Meulen, 1987):

(37) a. there is a man in the garden
    b.?there is the man in the garden
    c. the man is in the garden

Here, (37b) does not admit of a straightforward 'existential' reading, but only what Milsark first referred to as a 'list' reading. An entirely unexceptionable structure is produced by raising the definite expression to subject position, as in (37c), and this provides evidence that there is at least some 'affinity' between subject position and a definite argument.

Chinese provides a very clear demonstration of the interaction between position and interpretation, as, setting numerous complications aside, it does not allow indefinites in subject position. Aoun and Li (1989, 141) cite the examples in (38):

(38) a. *san-ge   ren   lai-le
       three-CL   man   come-LE
    b. you   san-ge   ren   lai-le
       have   three-CL   man   come-LE
       'there are three men who came'

Indeed, as observed by Huang (1987, 238), the converse situation also exists in Chinese, as overtly definite expressions are ruled out in existential sentences directly following *you* 'have':

(39) a. you   yi-ben   shu   zai   zhuo-shang
         have one-CL book at   table-top
         'There is a book on the table'

      b. *you nei-ben shu   zai   zhuo-shang
         have that-CL book at   table-top
         'There is that book on the table'

A related point can be made in terms of the interpretation of bare nouns in Chinese, which can be interpreted as indefinite, definite or generic in postverbal position, but only as definite or generic if they appear preverbally. The examples in (40), based on Cheng and Sybesma (1999, 510) illustrate this:

(40) a. Hufei mai shu   qu-le
         Hufei buy book go-LE
         'Hufei went to buy a book/the book/books'
      b. gou   yao   gao   malu
         dog   want cross road
         'The dog wants to cross the road,' but not 'A dog wants to cross the road'
      c. gou   ai   chi   rou
         dog   love eat   meat
         'The dog loves/Dogs love to eat meat,' but not 'A (specific) dog loves to eat meat'

Returning to English, one further confirmation of the interpretive importance of the subject being displaced to a peripheral position is provided by such pairs as (41):

(41) a. many students are in all the classes
      b. there are many students in all the classes

For (41a), two interpretations are possible, corresponding to the familiar scope ambiguity induced by the quantifiers. However, the interpretation where there are many individual students each of whom attends all the classes is not readily available for (41b), which illustrates a strong preference for the wide scope reading for *all the classes*.

With a sense of what is intended by the claim that movement to the traditional subject position has interpretive consequences in place, we return to TH/EX. What Chomsky has in mind is illustrated by the examples in (42):

(42) a. *there were donated those books to the bazaar
      b. *there were those books donated to the bazaar[54]
      c. *there were donated to the bazaar those books
      d. those books were donated to the bazaar

Here, it appears that a definite, specific internal argument of the passive participle *donated* cannot be 'saved' by TH/EX, as is indicated by (42b, c). However, as we might expect, it can be saved by raising to subject, as in (42d), suggesting that this raising interacts in some way with the referential status of the argument. Thus, the positions targeted by TH/EX appear not to be associated with interpretive consequences in the sense that they can no more accommodate a definite, specific argument than can the canonical internal argument position. The target position of subject raising, however, is quite different in this respect.

For object displacement, Chomsky is concerned with the process of Object Shift, to which we will turn presently. For now, all we need to note is that *by virtue of its not having interpretive consequences*, TH/EX is a candidate for a phonological displacement rule.

In support of this conclusion, Chomsky develops an argument to show that *wh*-movement, taken to be undisputably a narrow syntactic operation, cannot interact with TH/EX in ways that would be predicted if the latter were also an operation in narrow syntax. Outlining this argument, consider (43):

(43) what did they donate [several books about t] to the
      bazaar?

Here, we see extraction of a *wh*-expression from the phrase *several
books about what* when this phrase occurs as internal argument of
active *donate*. However, this extraction is not possible if the
containing phrase constitutes the internal argument in an
expletive passive construction:

(44) *what were there donated [several books about t] to the
      bazaar?

In order to derive (44), two conditions would need to be satisfied:
we would have to extract *what* from the phrase *several books about
what*, an extraction (43) shows to be legitimate in other contexts,
and *several books about what* would have to remain *in situ*. This
second condition is not satisfied if TH/EX is an obligatory
phonological process, so (44) is not a legitimate PF.[55]

What about the positions to which TH/EX moves phrases?
The relevant structures are (45a, b):

(45) a. there were [several books about what] donated to
         the bazaar
      b. there were donated to the bazaar [several books
         about what]

Intriguingly, extraction of the *wh*-expression in either of these
structures appears to be impossible:

(46) a. *what were there [several books about t] donated
         to the bazaar?
      b. *what were there donated to the bazaar [several
         books about t]?

It seems, then, that we can add the output configurations of
TH/EX to the input configuration for the process - both somehow
block the application of *wh*-movement - and we have the general
conclusion that TH/EX and *wh*-movement are incompatible. For

output configurations, however, we have something more than this. Focusing on these, we now explicitly assume that TH/EX is a phonological movement process. What this means is that, *as far as the narrow syntax is concerned*, no movement takes place. As a consequence, the structures in (45a, b) are never visible to the narrow syntax, and, as *wh*-movement is assumed to be a narrow syntactic process, it will never have access to structures that would enable it to produce the outputs in (46).[56]

Let's suppose, then, that the above persuades us that TH/EX is appropriately located in the phonology. It is at this point that the concerns raised in n53 become urgent. The conclusion that TH/EX is in the phonology is motivated entirely by the fact that its application has no interpretive consequences, but this tells us nothing about the phonological factors to which it must be responding if SMT is correct. Unfortunately, there appears to be nothing in Chomsky's own discussion which bears on this issue, so what I am taking to be the fundamental challenge faced by minimalism is not met in this case: for TH/EX, we have no answer to (34b).[57]

We now turn to the case of Object Shift. The account Chomsky (1999) offers of this phenomenon is involved and programmatic in a number of ways, and it would not be appropriate to try to engage all of these complexities here. What I shall do, then, is seek to distil the essential aspects of this account into a form that will enable me to make use of it in the final section of this paper. It may be that, in so doing, I seriously misrepresent aspects of Chomsky's proposal, but I don't believe this to be the case.

There are three core observations that need to be taken into account (for extensive discussion of these observations, see, for example, Bobaljik, 1995). These are set out in (47):

(47) a. Object Shift occurs in Germanic languages other than English;

   b. Object Shift in SVO Germanic languages (e.g. Icelandic) appears to be contingent on verb raising (Holmberg's Generalisation);

   c. Object Shift is linked to interpretive issues, with the
       shifted object requiring a specific or definite
       interpretation.

To illustrate (47c), consider the contrast between (48a, b) in
Icelandic, cited in Bobaljik (*op. cit.*, 76):

   (48) a. Í fyrra   máluðu stúdentarnir ekki hús
             last year   painted students.the not   house
             'The students didn't paint a house last year'

         b. Í fyrra   máluðu stúdentarnir húsið   ekki
             last year   painted students.the house.the not
             'The students didn't paint the house last year'

Taking the negative *ekki* 'not' as defining the left edge of the VP,
we see that *hús* 'a house' remains inside the VP in (48a) but *húsið*
'the house' is moved to a pre-VP position in (48b). That this shift
is not simply linked to grammatical definiteness in Icelandic is
argued by observations of Diesing (1995), cited in Bobaljik (*op. cit.*,
345):

   (49) a. Hann les   lengstu bókina   sjaldan
             He   reads longest book.the seldom
             'He seldom reads the longest book'

         b. Hann les   sjaldan lengstu bókina
             He   reads seldom   longest book.the
             'He seldom reads the longest book'

While the English glosses for (49a, b) are identical, this conceals a
difference in interpretation which Diesing characterises as a *de
re/de dicto* distinction. Thus, (49a) requires the existence of a
specific longest book which he seldom reads, whereas (49b)
would be used to assert only that he seldom reads whatever
happens to be the longest book.
      In general, it appears that shifted objects are linked to
referentiality, specificity and old information, while the

interpretation of their non-shifted counterparts is not constrained in this way. For notational convenience, Chomsky refers to the set of properties including referentiality, etc. as INT and their complement as INT'.[58]

Suppose, then, that we have the configuration in (50):

(50) [$_v$ P SUBJ v [VP V OBJ]]

If the v - V complex raises, SUBJ raises to T and there is no Object Shift, LF will be presented with the configuration in (51):

(51) ... [$_v$ P tSUBJ t$_v$ - V [VP tV OBJ]]

In this configuration, OBJ occurs at what Chomsky calls the *phonological border* of vP, and he proposes (52) as the parameter which characterises Object Shift languages (1999, 28):[59]

(52) At the phonological border of vP, XP is assigned INT'[60]

This constraint is not operative in a non-Object Shift language, so in such a language (as well as in an Object Shift language, where the object is not at the phonological border of vP because the v - V complex has not raised), the object can be freely assigned INT or INT'.

Now, suppose that we have an object (for example, a definite pronoun), which, by virtue of its inherent semantic features, requires the interpretation INT. In a language characterised by (52), if the subject and verbal complex have raised, the non-shifted object will be assigned INT' and an interpretive anomaly will result. However, we can contemplate saving such a situation by subscribing to the statement in (53) (*ibid*), which is taken to be universal:[61]

(53) The EPP position of v is assigned INT

Thus, so long as v has an EPP feature, SPEC-v will provide a position for a shifted object to move to and a consequence of this movement will be the assignment of INT to the shifted object without interpretive anomaly. In short, there will be interpretive consequences of the movement.

On this account, we can see how Object Shift is contingent on raising of the v - V complex in SVO languages. Only if this raising occurs, will the conditions be created to trigger (52) with the object at the phonological border of vP. Equally, we can see how Object Shift does not require raising of the verbal complex in SOV languages – for such languages, subject raising will be sufficient to locate the object at the phonological border of vP, and this will in turn bring (52) into play.

There is a deeper observation which links the above to one of the topics discussed in the next section. The view that the EPP-feature of v (and C) is optional is a theme that runs through Chomsky's recent work (see, for example, Chomsky 1998, 23). The factor that determines the exercising of this option can now be formulated as (54):

(54) v is assigned an EPP-feature only if that has an effect on outcome

The outcome in question here is the shift from anomaly to non-anomaly in an Object Shift language in which the object inherently requires INT and, by virtue of other movement processes, finds itself at the phonological boundary of vP, where, because of (52), it can only be assigned INT'. Therefore, the interpretive motivation for movement is inextricably linked to the interpretive motivation for the uninterpretable feature that drives it, a clear illustration of the principle that uninterpretable features are only 'apparent' imperfections in that they serve to drive tokens of movement which, if they did not occur, would fail to resolve an interpretive anomaly at LF.[62] Equipped with this example of an answer to (34a), in the last section of this paper, I shall explore whether the ideas discussed in this section can be put to use in the study of first language acquisition.[63]

5. The Acquisition Perspective: Dynamic Minimalism?
In this section, I wish to briefly pursue some of the consequences of taking SMT seriously in the context of first language

acquisition.[64] That SMT might have such consequences is suggested by the following remark from Chomsky (1998, 9):

> 'Suppose that FL satisfying legibility conditions in an optimal way satisfies all other empirical conditions too: acquisition, processing, neurology, language change ... Then the language organ is a perfect solution to minimal design specifications. That is, a system that satisfies a very narrow subset of empirical conditions in an optimal way – those it must satisfy to be usable at all – turns out to satisfy all empirical conditions.'

It is not entirely clear what it means for an FL 'satisfying legibility conditions in an optimal way' to also satisfy acquisition as an 'empirical condition,' but some sense of what might be involved can be gleaned by rehearsing what we have already observed for sound-meaning pairs in (6) above. The observation that π means λ is an empirical observation which, if SMT is correct, is a also a *consequence* of a theory satisfying legibility and 'good design' conditions, and nothing more. Obviously, *empirical observations* about acquisition abound, and a straightforward interpretation of what Chomsky has in mind might be that the content of these observations too will be derivable consequences of a minimalist account.[65]

Now, the sort of observation that we meet in studies of first language acquisition typically takes the form that some property, P_1, of the emerging system is in place before some other property P_2, this being what gives accounts their *developmental* flavour. Accordingly, we might be attracted by the prospect of reflecting on developmental orders, and seeing whether these can, in any sense, be grounded in minimalist thinking. Alternatively, we might take the minimalist framework, as outlined in earlier sections of this paper, and examine whether there are any theory internal grounds on which we might base developmental predictions. In what follows, I shall briefly pursue this second possibility, acknowledging that the speculations need to be embedded in a set of observations from acquisition.

To get us started, we can attend to a further remark of Chomsky (1998, 12-13):

'UG makes available a set F of features (linguistic properties) and operations C_{HL} (the computational procedure for human language) that access F to generate expressions. The language L maps F to a particular set of expressions EXP. Operative complexity is reduced if L makes a one-time selection of a subset [F] of F, dispensing with further access to F. It is reduced further if L includes a one-time operation that assembles elements of F into a lexicon LEX, with no new assembly as computation proceeds. On these (conventional) assumptions, acquiring a language involves at least selection of the features [F], construction of lexical items LEX, and refinement of C_{HL} in one of the possible ways - parameter setting.'

This remark makes clear that we are justified in focusing attention on the developmental status of *features* and it is important to observe that much of the recent literature on early clause structure, particularly that arguing for the correctness or otherwise of the Continuity Hypothesis, has been concerned with the presence or absence in child grammars of grammatical *categories* (see, for example, Radford, 1990; Pöppel and Wexler, 1993; Wexler, 1994, Hyams, 1994). A popular variant of the continuity position has maintained that such categories, including the complete set of functional categories, are intact from the earliest stages of word combination, while certain features, such as Tense in its adult form, are not. However, in the Bare Phrase Structure framework embraced by minimalism (as, indeed, in earlier versions of Principles and Parameters Theory), categories are nothing more than convenient abbreviations for sets of features. Given this, there is something quite puzzling about maintaining that an adult category, lacking one or more of the features that comprise the category, exists in the child's grammar. By definition, distinct feature sets comprise distinct syntactic objects, and it follows that child collocations of features that do not correspond exactly to the appropriate adult collocations signal a *grammatical* difference between child and adult. Thus, the postulation of missing, or underspecified features in child grammars (e.g. in the work of Schütze and Wexler, 1996), far from being consistent with continuity, would appear to provide *prima facie* evidence for a discontinuity position.[66]

As we have seen, a fundamental distinction in recent varieties of minimalism is that between interpretable (at LF) and uninterpretable features, and it is this distinction that may be exploitable in a developmental context. We have also seen that there is a clear sense in which minimalism requires the language faculty to comprise an optimal response to problems posed by the PF- and LF-interfaces. Suppose that these problems are fixed once and for all; then, there is no reason to ascribe a developmental dimension to minimalism.[67] Alternatively, suppose that the cognitive systems 'beyond' the interfaces are themselves subject to developmental considerations, i.e. it is not the case at the outset of acquisition that the sensorimotor system and the 'system of thought' are in the final, adult state. If we further assume that developments in these domains are 'qualitative' in some sense we would like to make precise, a consequence would appear to be that PF and LF themselves are subject to development - they are, after all, interfaces, and their character must be sensitive to the nature of the systems they are interfacing. On these assumptions, it follows that the problems posed to the language faculty are not fixed, but change in reponse to the developing demands of the interfaces. Taking the minimalist perspective to this conclusion yields what we might call the Thesis of Dynamic Minimalism (TDM) in (55):

(55) At any point in development, the child's language system is an optimal solution to legibility problems posed by the interfaces

In other words, the child's language is always 'perfect,' but it can deviate from the adult system to the extent that it comprises a solution to a different set of problems to those confronted by the fully developed system.[68] An immediate consequence of taking TDM seriously concerns the popular strategy of seeking to locate what at first sight appear to be significant changes in the child's grammar in some other aspect of development, a strategy which has found a home among supporters of the Continuity Hypothesis.

To take an example, Wexler (1994) in his discussion of the optional infinitive stage, argues against the view that this stage reflects any significant *grammatical* immaturity on the part of the child. The details of Wexler's preferred account of optional infinitives need not concern us here, but it is important that he locates the source of children's difficulties in their non-adult representation of tense. Arguably, the options here are stark: the child's deficit is either grammatical, denying the correctness of the continuity position, or semantic/pragmatic, relegating it to some location outside the grammar. Obviously, Wexler has to select the latter alternative, and it is noteworthy that he seems happy to contemplate genuine development, in the form of maturation, in this domain, saying (*op. cit.*, 340):

> 'Why does T take a while to develop? We have no particular answer to this; perhaps the values of T mature …'

From the minimalist stance, however, it is not clear that this second alternative is available. Supposing that we are, indeed, talking about developments in the child's representations of temporal relations and this development takes place outside the grammatical system. On our current assumption, such developments may well have consequences for the LF-interface and there is no *a priori* reason to suppose that the nature of the problems presented to the grammar will not change in non-trivial ways in response to the child's maturing sytstem of knowledge about temporal relations. But then there is no reason to suppose that the grammar itself will not change substantially, while continuing to satisfy a 'good design' condition. Given this, it is at least possible that the postulation of substantive developmental changes beyond the interfaces is unlikely to provide much succour for the continuity position.[69]

Supposing, then, that a minimalist approach justifies a focus on the development of features, it seems to me that there are at least three types of consideration that might be of interest. These are listed in (56):

(56) (a) the emergence of interpretable features;
(b) the developmental relationship between interpretable and uninterpretable features;
(c) the question of *why* uninterpretable features enter the language system at all.

Of these, arguably (56c) raises the most searching issues. I shall now take them in turn.

We begin by examining (56a) in the light of TDM, paying due attention to the remarks of Chomsky cited above. Suppose that the set of features F provided by UG is not given in its entirety at the outset of acquisition. Has this assumption any *prima facie* plausibility? Restricting attention to LF-interpretability, I maintain that it would be premature to suppose that it does not. If a feature is LF-interpretable, this requires that it provides 'instructions' (Chomsky, 1998, 3) to 'systems of thought.' But if a 'system of thought,' by virtue of its immaturity, does not make certain distinctions, TDM requires that the language system *not* incorporate features that would provide the 'instructions' relevant to such distinctions. The alternative would be to allow the grammar to contain features that *will* become interpretable at LF at the point at which the cognitive system beyond LF requires the relevant distinction to be made; however, at the stage being contemplated, these features are not interpretable and will not play any part in convergent derivations. But minimalist thinking suggests that such features will not be part of the child's grammar at this stage - to embrace a feature that does not respond to legibility problems (directly or indirectly) would be to engage in 'bad' design. As development takes place beyond the the LF-interface, the nature of the problems posed to the language faculty will necessitate expansion of the features made available by UG, and the possibility of an incremental approach to (interpretable) feature acquisition begins to look credible.[70]

To give a flavour of what is at stake here, Radford (2000) has recently speculated that in the domain of *interpretable* φ-features, [person] is cognitively more complex than [number]. If this is correct, we might anticipate that the *linguistic* (interpretable) [number] feature is in place before the (interpretable) [person] feature, and Radford cites evidence from Alison Bloom at ages 1;8 and 1;10 which suggests that this is not an idle speculation. Specifically, he notes that at this stage in development Alison used a range of singular nouns along with their appropriate plural forms as well as a small number of irregular plurals, such as *children*. By contrast, during the same period, she uses names for both self-reference and addressee-reference, producing such forms as *wiping baby chin* (with reference to her own chin) and *eating mommy cookie* (when addressing her mother). Thus, there is *prima facie* evidence to indicate that Alison's grammar contains no [person] feature, and this is exactly what TDM would predict if there were independent grounds for supposing that the child's 'system of thought' is indifferent to person distinctions at this stage.[71]

As regards the basis for his cognitive complexity claim, Radford notes that [person] and [number] can be distinguished in terms of the former being inherently *relational*, while the latter is not, and it is not my intention here to seek to evaluate this claim.[72] If, however, our best accounts of cognitive development subscribe to the view that children have access to some 'concepts' before others, the research programme suggested by these speculations is clear: we need to carefully examine what is known about the earliest stages of cognitive development and assess its significance for the child's inventory of LF-interpretable features.[73]

The above has not sought to engage the question of uninterpretable features raised in (56b), so let us now see whether it is possible to begin to provide any developmental perspective here. If we focus on the functioning of the grammar, it appears that a set of simple generalisations can be formulated quite easily. So, consider a situation in which a numeration contains a set of lexical choices each of which consists of only interpretable features. Whether a convergent derivation can be constructed from such a numeration will, of course, depend on the precise nature of the selection and the way in which interpretive features function in regulating the operation of (pure) Merge.[74] Let us suppose that such convergent derivations are available in principle.[75]

Next, consider a lexical selection that includes tokens of uninterpretable features. In terms of the framework developed in Chomsky (1998, 1999) the latter can be seen as belonging to one of three sets.[76] Firstly, we have the φ-features of T, which are uninterpretable and enter into *matching* relationships with the interpretable φ-features of nominals. Without these nominal φ-features, no matching will take place, the uninterpretable φ-features of T will survive in the derivation which, as a consequence, will not converge. The appropriate generalisation is formulated in (57):

(57) Uninterpretable φ-features require matching interpretable φ-features if a derivation is to converge

Secondly, consider the Case feature of nominals. This too is uninterpretable and must be deleted for convergence. However, unlike the φ-features of T, the Case feature of a nominal does not delete under *matching*: rather, it requires the presence of a specific interpretable feature in the probe which *assigns* an appropriate Case (cf. n41)[77] Despite this difference in the relation which must obtain if deletion is to proceed (matching *versus* some stipulated pairing of features), the consequence of the Case feature not having available its interpretable mate is exactly the same as for φ-sets: the derivation will not converge. We thus have (58):

(58) Uninterpretable Case features require the presence of appropriate interpretable features if a derivation is to converge.

Finally, there is the EPP-feature of v and T, the feature which requires movement of an appropriate category so as to be deleted. While there is considerable obscurity surrounding the precise nature of this feature, it is possible to maintain that it too requires the presence of a 'matching' interpretable feature to ensure its deletion. In Chomsky (1995b), this feature was regarded as categorial, a D- or N-feature of the moved item, and in Chomsky

(1998, 1999), there is the speculation that perhaps it is no more than a [person] feature.[78] Whatever, the details, it is clear that again the availability of an uninterpretable feature in the grammar will ensure non-convergent derivations, unless the appropriate interpretable features are present. So, we also have (59):

> (59) Uninterpretable EPP-features require the presence of appropriate interpretable features if a derivation is to converge.

Putting (57) – (59) together, we can move to the conclusion that, while a grammar can give rise to convergent derivations while containing only interpretable features, this is not the case for one containing 'unmatched' uninterpretable features. Developmentally, then, it follows that we can at least contemplate the possibility that interpretable features will enter the system before their 'matching' counterparts.[79]

The above discussion has indicated that an acquisition course in which uninterpretable features are acquired later than their interpretable analogues is at least consistent with TDM. The obvious question posed by such a perspective is: what is the nature of a computational system that, while including an interpretable feature, does not include the matching uninterpretable feature? To get a sense of the issues raised by this question, let us first focus on the Case-agreement system, and consider the configuration in (60):

$$(60) \dots T \dots [\dots \quad N \dots]$$
$$[\varphi]$$

Here, we suppose that T contains no uninterpretable φ-features and N contains no uninterpretable Case feature. Obviously, in such circumstances, Agree will not apply in the derivation, and it will be possible for (a) correct agreement inflections to not appear on the verb; (b) correct Case inflections to not appear on the nominal. If we interpret this as a developmental prediction, it is, of course, somewhat akin to the situation described for English acquisition by Radford (1990), and of course one burden of supporters of the Continuity Hypothesis has been to dispute its correctness, initially on the basis of acquisition data from languages displaying more inflectional richness than English (see, for example, Phillips, 1996) and extended to English by Harris and Wexler (1996). This is not the place to review this dispute in detail (see Atkinson, 1996 for cautionary remarks). Suffice it to say that I believe that the quality of data on which continuity claims have been based leaves something to be desired and, until the difficulties this gives rise to are properly addressed, the issue of the early emergence of fully-fledged Case-agreement systems remains more open than continuity supporters appear to believe. For the purposes of the present discussion, it is sufficient for me to establish that a system containing structures like (61) is at least possible in the context of TDM.

The structure in (60) is also intended to signal the lack of an uninterpretable EPP-feature in T, and we again observe that this appears to be a genuine possibility in the sense that a grammar with this deficit would not, as a consequence, be doomed to produce non-convergent derivations. The EPP-feature's formal function is, of course, to trigger overt movement, so once more it is possible to make contact with the claims of Radford (1990), viz. that in the earliest stages of English word combination, subjects are not raised from their VP-internal position, a claim which has again been disputed by those attracted by continuity.[80]

The above speculations have sought to establish that it is at least intelligible to suppose that uninterpretable features enter the child's grammar later than 'matching' interpretable features. They say nothing about the issue raised in (56c), i.e. why do uninterpretable features enter the child's system at all? To close I shall offer some speculations on this which, if they can be developed and substantiated, would pose a further challenge to the continuity position. As for (56b), there is a set of specific questions that can be formulated:

(61) a. Why do EPP-features enter the child's grammar?
　　 b. Why do P- (for 'peripheral') features enter the child's grammar?

    c. Why do the uninterpretable features involved in Case-agreement enter the child's grammar?

It is quite likely that these questions will turn out to be improper, and certainly I have no answers to them that do not rely on what are almost certainly illegitimate assumptions. Nonetheless, having come this far, I feel that it is incumbent on me to try to give a sense of what answers might look like. I shall first say a little about (61a), adopting a simplified view of the discussion of Object Shift that was outlined in the previous section.

    Recall that Chomsky supposes that an interpretive complex that he designates INT is associated with 'peripheral' positions, notably (Spec, vP), and for simplicity, let us suppose that the complement of INT, INT' is associated with the internal argument position.[81] Suppose further that the contrast between INT and INT' is not made in the child's 'system of thought' at the earliest stages of acquisition. If this is the case, TDM will require that an optimally designed system will not signal this contrast to the interface. Accordingly, the option of introducing an EPP-feature in (54) will never be exercised, and there will be no role for an EPP-feature in the child's grammar. When the INT/INT' contrast becomes of significance to the child, the existing grammar is no longer adequate, and some device must be incorporated which enables the interface to be provided with appropriately partitioned information.[82] It should go without saying that such speculation is far from compelling. It does, however, raise the possibility of a serious rapprochement between research in general cognitive development and attempts to understand linguistic development, and I for one would like to be persuaded that this rapprochement is not worth serious consideration The 'simple' question posed is: do we have evidence from general cognitive development bearing on the availability of the INT/INT' contrast and if we do, what is the nature of this evidence? Serious pursuit of an answer to this question will undoubtedly require refinement of what is encoded by INT, but that is going to be necessary anyway.

    It may well be that the question in (61b) concerning A'-movement is closer to traditional concerns in cognitive developmental psychology. If we suppose that 'quantification' is a cognitively later development than basic propositional structure, this might provide the basis for a relatively late emergence of P-features. This is potentially interesting in the light of a proposal first made by Borer and Wexler (1987) and recently developed by Babyonyshev *et al.* (2000). This proposal is that the child's ability to represent A-chains is one aspect of UG that is not available from the outset of acquisition, and it is recruited to account for a range of observations, of which the most important in Borer and Wexler (1987) is the fact that children's initial passives can all be construed as 'adjectival' and therefore not requiring a movement analysis. In Babyonyshev *et al.* (2000), 'adjectival' passives are described as syntactic (s-) homophones of their verbal correlates, i.e. strings which, while PF-identical to verbal passives, have quite distinct structural characteristics.[83] As regards reasons for A-chains being delayed in development, it is suggested that children are unable to assign θ-roles 'non-locally,' with the result that any derivation including a token of A-movement results in a violation of the θ-Criterion, which is taken to be innate. I do not intend to try to systematically evaluate these suggestions here, but it is noteworthy that the perspective raised in the previous paragraph may provide an alternative way of thinking about the delayed development of A-chains. If we suppose that A-movement, and its triggering EPP-feature, enters the child's grammar only in response to a novel problem posed by the LF-interface and if we have independent evidence to suggest that this problem arises relatively late in the child's development, we can see how TDM might be able to come to terms with the claims made about passives, etc.

It is also the case that TDM can dissociate the emergence of A'-movement and A-movement, since the emergence of EPP-features and P-features might be responses of the developing linguistic system to *different* interface requirements. As is well-known, Borer and Wexler (*op. cit.*) are at pains to point out that tokens of A'-movement are attested in child corpora some time before clear examples of verbal passives, and if cognitively driven P-features enter the system before cognitively driven EPP-features, this is precisely what we would expect.[84]

Finally, what of (61c)? It is difficult to even begin to guess why the uninterpretable features in the Case-agreement system enter the child's grammar. What could be the problems posed by a developing interface that promote this development? One possibility might be related to developments in the child's 'system of thought' involving the emergence of *n*-ary predication. Supposing that the Case-agreement system provides a way of keeping track of the relationships between arguments and predicates (see Baker 1988, 114ff. for more general remarks along these lines). This system becomes necessary only at a point at which the child controls (cognitive) predicates which co-occur with more than one argument - if there is only one argument for a predicate, it seems reasonable to suppose that the predicate-argument construction can be fully interpreted on the basis of inherent semantic properties of the items involved. There is at least one immediate difficulty with this suggestion in terms of Chomsky's (1998, 1999) framework. As I understand it, an operation of Agree (without an associated movement) does not, in itself, provide any information for LF - uninterpretable features are deleted, but there is nothing to indicate to LF that Agree has taken place between two syntactic objects. In response to this, it is tempting to consider whether the suggestion aired in n49, viz. that Agree is an LF-directed process, the consequences of which *should* be 'visible' to LF, possibly via the 'apparent imperfection' of co-indexation.

For me, what is attractive about the speculations offered in this section is that in principle they provide a theoretically justified means of reviving the developmental aspect of the study of child language acquisition. I have been (almost) unreservedly impressed by the results of bringing a strong linguistic focus to acquisition research. However, a price that has been paid as a consequence of these moves has been a lack of useful contact between acquisition theorists and those working on general cognitive development. It may be that this lack of contact is itself principled, with cognitive developmental psychology having nothing to offer the linguist. But it may not, and the context of minimalism, specifically the suggestion that key aspects of languages can be understood as responses to problems arising from the fact that languages are embedded in a rich array of cognitive systems, provides the stimulus to at least have a good look at what cognitive developmental psychology has to offer. That is the next step!

Notes

1 I am grateful to members of the University of Essex Language Acquisition and Universal Grammar Research Group for their discussion of, and comments on, an earlier version of this paper. Parts of the paper have formed sections of presentations at the University of Essex and the University of Cambridge.

2 This characterisation should not be regarded as critical of what Radford achieves in his text. As an introductory discussion of a wide range of data and complex technology for accommodating these data, it is a model of clarity. However, in my view, it never seeks to seriously engage the foundational aspects of the Minimalist Programme, because the uncontroversial methodological principle cited in the text is never embedded in the substantive assumptions that, I maintain, give minimalism its character.

3 It should be observed that minimalism, with its emphasis on 'economy' and 'good design,' acknowledges its roots in numerous developments that took place within the earlier government-binding and principles and parameters frameworks. Commenting on this, Chomsky (1998, 12) says:
'Possibilities that have been investigated ... include constraints barring PF-vacuous overt movement ... An LF counterpart is that covert operations are allowed only if they have an effect on interpretation at LF. Another category seeks to reduce "search space" for computation: "shortest move/attract," successive cyclic movement (relativized minimality, subjacency) ...'
Much of the agenda for minimalism can be viewed as driven by the necessity to incorporate the descriptive insights associated with topics such as those listed in this statement into a system observing a more 'principled' set of assumptions.

4 It is of some interest to consider this commitment to 'no special structure' in the context of earlier views of modularity, such as those debated in Piattelli-Palmarini (1980). In the discussions reported there, Chomsky, with extensive support from Fodor, argues against conceptions of language inspired by Piagetian psychology, whereby its essential features can be regarded as linked to, and ultimately

derived from, aspects of general intelligence. The substance of the Chomsky-Fodor case was partly based on the implausibility of any analogue of such syntactic constraints as the Specified Subject Condition finding a niche in accounts of general intelligence. Of course, the Specified Subject Condition, along with a basket of similar principles, has been consigned to history, but, as we shall see, a core minimalist strategy is (and has to be) one of locating the justification for some property or other of the language faculty at its interface with what Chomsky calls the 'conceptual-intentional system' or sometimes 'systems of thought.' This might be regarded as an immediate challenge to modularity and a recognition that something like 'general intelligence' does, indeed, provide a foundation for language systems. However, it is important to acknowledge a distinction between the *requirements* imposed by an interface and the *mechanisms* used by the language faculty to satisfy these requirements. While the requirements might be regarded as imposing boundary conditions on the mechanisms, they do not determine the actual form of the latter. A way of putting this, exploiting the terminology of Fodor (1983), is to maintain that interface representations do not 'penetrate' the operations of the language faculty, which rely on domain specific vocabulary and processes. To this extent, then, the computational mechanisms of the language faculty can retain their modular character, while serving the requirements of other cognitive systems. This issue will be touched on again in Section 5.

5 One issue which is raised by the proposition that minimalism is correct except when it isn't is its relationship to 'exceptionful laws' in the special sciences. It's sometimes seen as a bit of a mystery that 'laws' can have exceptions, and it's something that Fodor (1975, 1978) discusses at length in developing his arguments for a non-reductionist stance as regards the mind/brain relationship. My feeling is that with minimalism we have something rather different to this situation, and that whereas counterexemplification of a law in a special science doesn't (necessarily) prejudice the status of the law, little parcels of 'chaos' in the language faculty would signal the demise of the minimalist approach. Anticipating discussion of 'good design,' another way to express this concern is that it seems to me likely that *any* moderately serious syntactic theory could point to aspects of the mechanisms on which it relies and maintain that they exhibit good design. If this in itself qualified such a theory as minimalist, we would

once again be left wondering what all the fuss is about (cf. observations on the passage cited from Radford above).

6 Here, we must acknowledge that a constant theme throughout the development of minimalism has been the view that phonology is different, permitting violation of a range of considerations and providing ample *prima facie* evidence that it is not consistent with fundamental minimalist principles. It is, of course, not clear whether the 'apparent imperfection' strategy which we will be meeting later (Section 4) can be recruited in phonology (cf. Chomsky, 1998, pp. 32-33 for this possibility), but for the purposes of my discussion, and supposing that the distinction between phonology and other aspects of the computational system is principled, I shall set these concerns aside. It may, of course, be possible to make *principled* distinctions in syntax too, which could then be invoked to draw the line between those areas of language structure that succumb to minimalist analysis and those that don't. I take this prospect as sufficiently remote at the moment to justify adopting the 'no special structure' position as a working hypothesis.

7 Almost certainly, this characterisation is grossly oversimplified for a number of reasons. Specifically, there is no guarantee that a single interface will serve both articulation and acoustic perception, and it is necessary to also take account of languages that are 'realised' in media other than the vocal-auditory (e.g. Sign Languages). Recognition of this raises the possibility that there may also be a multiplicity of interfaces with conceptual-intentional systems (which may themselves be differentiated). Again, I shall offer one or two further remarks in this connection in Section 5 (see also Platzack, 1999).

8 It should be increasingly apparent why it is necessary to be cautious about Chomsky's remark that minimalist considerations can be extended to other theories of grammar. If such a theory does not even share a 'cognitive' slant, it is unclear what minimalism could amount to for such a theory, beyond reliance on Occam's Razor and other principles of 'good science.'

9 For explicit discussion of this issue in terms of a contrast between *methodological* and *substantive* miminalism, see Chomsky (2000a). My point, and Chomsky's if I understand him correctly, is that minimalism claims no special status from a methodological point of view.

[10] Chomsky says (1998, 6): ' ... language design may really be optimal in some respects, ... The conclusion would be surprising, hence interesting if true.'

[11] Johnson and Lappin (1997), in the context of a detailed critique of certain aspects of the Minimalist Programme, take issue with Chomsky's view that the 'good design' of the human language faculty, if demonstrated in some significant sense, would raise concerns for biologists. They maintain that what is currently known about biological systems suggests that they do not generally display such 'good design'; rather, they are 'messy' and sport redundancy as their trademark. If theories of the language faculty are to be construed as part of theoretical biology, this looks like *prima facie* evidence that either the Minimalist Programme's commitment to 'good design' or much of current biological theorising is misguided. Johnson and Lappin see selection of the latter of these alternatives as unjustified. Observations suggesting that the issue is not as clear-cut as Johnson and Lappin maintain appear in Uriagareka (1998) and Chomsky (2000a).

[12] It is in this connection that it is perhaps easiest to appreciate Chomsky's characterisation of minimalism as a *programme* and not a *theory* (cf. 1998, 5). There are no sharp principles of good design that might constitute the 'axioms' of a theory; rather, there are vaguely formulated intuitions that enable questions to be posed.

[13] An obvious question that arises in connection with (1) is the referent of 'language' here. Typically, Chomsky aims his discussion at the 'language faculty,' and this raises the issue of the status of individual languages with respect to optimal design. Chomsky (2000a) acknowledges the matter and speculates that *all* individual languages might fall under (1), with the distinction between individual languages and the language faculty reducing in significance. An immediate consequence of this is that different values of parameters yield systems which exhibit good design in equal measure. This may not be as far-fetched as it sounds, since parameters must be set on the basis of primary linguistic data, and their effects will be 'visible' at the sensorimotor interface. Accordingly, the 'problems' posed to a language, viewed as a system linking interface representations, will vary, and what is optimal in the face of one such problem may not have this property when confronted by another. The ideas I will explore in Section 5 are consistent with this speculation, although it

would be premature to suggest that the questions it raises have been seriously thought through.

[14] As we shall see in Section 4, it appears to be impossible to maintain (2) in the light of empirical observations, but for now I am merely concerned to use (2) as an uncontentious example of what 'good design' could encompass.

[15] As already observed, an often-repeated assertion in Chomsky's recent work is that phonology provides ample *prima facie* evidence to embarrass 'good design' conditions. This is readily apparent with (3) if we consider, say, intonation. Presumably, information about intonation is supplied to, and interpreted by, the sensorimotor interface, although this information does not enter the system via the lexical entries of individual lexical items. The reference to compositionality in the text might be thought to pose serious difficulties for (3). It is customary for beginning students in linguistics to be exposed to a version of the Principle of Compositionality along the lines of: the interpretation of a complex expression is determined by the interpretation of its component expressions *along with the syntax of the expression*. And there is nothing in (3) which appears to take account of the italicised phrase. Note, however, that our assumptions about the lexicon see it as populated by *sets* of features. If we construe re-arrangement as nothing more than the construction of sets, then it is at least conceivable that the syntax we need for compositionality can be represented in terms of the properties of such sets. The theory of Bare Phrase Structure (cf. Section 3) is an attempt to implement this idea.

[16] This conclusion is reminiscent of one debated extensively some years ago concerning the practising linguist's reliance on judgements of deviance, ambiguity, paraphrase, etc. As there is no evidence that systematic information about these properties of linguistic expressions is available in the child's primary linguistic data, it follows that, *in principle*, theory construction ought to be able to proceed without resort to such information. Of course, recognition of this did not require linguists to cease to rely on such information (for relevant discussion in connection with ungrammaticality, see, for example, Baker, 1979).

A further perspective which deserves to be mentioned in passing here is the issue of *epistemological priority* and so-called 'semantic bootstrapping' in the initial stages of acquisition (see, for example, Pinker, 1984). Seeking to provide the child with a way into syntax, many acquisition theorists have been attracted by the view that the *meanings* of some utterances occurring in the child's environment are transparent, and that children can use this transparency to establish sound-meaning correspondences that enable them to 'bootstrap' their way into syntax. Indeed, this perspective also informs the classic learnability work of Wexler and Culicover (1980). If it transpires that reliance on optimal design (coupled to legibility) is all that is needed to guarantee correct sound-meaning associations, it is at least conceivable that resort to bootstrapping with respect to the structural aspects of interpretation can be entirely avoided. I hope to be able to pursue the consequences of this line of thought elsewhere.

[17] This need not be the only response to the sort of outcome we are now considering. As the notion of 'good design' is not given in any definitive way, there may always be room for manoeuvre regarding how this idea is to be interpreted (cf. the reference to '*all* "best ways" to satisfy legibility conditions' in the citation from Chomsky immediately below in the text). Clearly, however, there must be limits to the employment of such a strategy if minimalism is not to be devoid of content.

[18] This issue will be of considerable importance when I seek to formulate some developmental implications of minimalist thinking in Section 5. From a quite different perspective, Chomsky (2000a, 30) speculates that various topics which have been studied as belonging to 'core' syntax (e.g. the properties of antecedent contained deletions) may be more properly viewed as revealing aspects of 'thought systems ... at the point near the language faculty.'

[19] There may be an interesting set of issues here, concerning ways in which we evaluate minimalism with respect to such other approaches. Suppose, for the sake of argument, that there's nothing to choose between minimalism and X as far as 'good science' goes, i.e. practitioners of both varieties of theory behave responsibly with respect to elegance, simplicity, etc. And suppose further that there's nothing between minimalism and X as far as empirical results are concerned, i.e. it is possible to produce coherent accounts of the same range of data in both frameworks. It could be maintained that minimalism operates within a further set of constraints, viz. those provided by legibility and 'good design,' and that these are substantial, even if not understood in detail. By contrast, X has no such additional obligations. A confrontational way to phrase the question suggested by these remarks is: what is X about?

20 The distinction between lexical array and numeration is of some importance, although it is not clear which, if either, of these constructs is appropriate. A lexical array is simply a set of lexical items, while a numeration consists of a set of pairs, the first member of each pair being a lexical item and the second an integer indicating the number of occasions the paired item has been selected from the lexicon - equivalently, we could regard a lexical array as a set of lexical *types*, while a numeration is a set of lexical *tokens*. The choice of appropriate construct is linked to the need to keep track in a derivation of distinct selections of the same lexical item, an issue that appears to require a violation of the Inclusiveness Condition in (3) via the use of indices as the tracking mechanism. Consider the representation in (i) (Chomsky, 1998, 35):

(i) Whom did everyone talk to whom about whom

Given the copy theory of movement, as it stands, this could correspond to either (iia) or (iib):

(ii) a. Whom did everyone talk to about whom
    b. Whom did everyone talk to whom about

These can be distinguished in a representation like (i) if we allow the different selections of *whom* to bear distinct indices, as in (iiia, b):

(iii) a. Whom$_i$ did everyone talk to whom$_i$ about whom$_j$
    b. Whom$_j$ did everyone talk to whom$_i$ about whom$_j$

Chomsky (1999, 8) appears to suggest that resort to such indices is not necessary, but it is difficult to see the justification for such optimism.

21 Despite this uncontroversial conclusion, Chomsky offers no empirical arguments in favour of lexical arrays/numerations at this point in his discussion. This is quite possibly because he proceeds to argue for a further refinement of the relationship between the lexicon and the computational system, whereby lexical arrays/numerations are further structured into *phases*, with the computational system operating on a 'one phase at a time' basis. I do not propose to discuss phases in any detail here, but it is important that in this connection, Chomsky *does* offer empirical observations for their being required. And it is easy to see how these might be recruited in defence of lexical arrays/numerations against access to the complete lexicon. Specifically, given the preference for Merge over Move, something to which we return, if the whole lexicon remained accessible throughout a derivation, movement would *never* be called on in the absence of look ahead. Given an uninterpretable EPP-feature needing to be deleted to ensure convergence, the lexicon will always provide a

suitable argument expression if the position in question is a θ-position ([Spec, *v*P]) or an expletive if it is not ([Spec, TP] or [Spec, CP]). Thus, consider a simple sentence like (i):

(i) John has caught a fish

At an intermediate stage of the derivation, we will have the structure in (ii):

(ii) [$_{TP}$ has [$_{vP}$ John [$_{VP}$ caught a fish]]]

Agreement between features in the T head of TP and features of *John* will proceed in the manner sketched in Section 4 with all relevant uninterpretable features being deleted. If T contains an EPP-feature and the lexicon is available in its entirety, the preference for Merge over Move will ensure that *there* is inserted into the derivation as [Spec, TP]. Then, given the assumptions in Chomsky (1998, 1999), the derivation will converge as (iii) and (i) will be underivable :

(iii) *there has John caught a fish

22 I confess to being less than compelled by this sort of consideration, which doesn't seem to me to demand merger. Thus, the Principle of Integration could be satisfied by selecting items individually from the lexical array/numeration and submitting them to LF. As each would arrive at LF as a root (root here being understood as the root of a structure), the Principle of Integration would be vacuously satisfied. Presumably, what Collins has in mind is a requirement that the members of a lexical array/numeration must be composed into a *single* representation in order to be LF-interpretable, an idea that can also be found in Chomsky (1995b, 226). If the Principle of Integration is driven by LF-legibility conditions, it would appear to follow that unintegrated items are not LF-legible. But this looks like an unattractive constraint (cf. Chomsky, 1998, 8) for relevant discussion.

23 In Chomsky (1998, 1999), this view is substantially revised in the phase-based approach to derivations alluded to in n21. According to this approach, a lexical array/numeration is partially accessed, with a subset of items being selected. This subset of items forms the basis for a sub-derivation that constitutes a phase. At a point after this phase is 'complete,' Spell-out operates, allowing the phonological component to determine an appropriate PF for the phase independently of other aspects of the derivation. Thus, Spell-Out itself now becomes cyclic. Not surprisingly, there are many unresolved and complex issues surrounding the idea of phase-based derivations, so I shall not seek to extend the discussion to take account of this innovation here (see Atkinson, 2000, for some relevant observations).

24 As Chomsky observes (1998, 27), a consequence of this rejection is that '... everything accounted for in these terms has been misdescribed and is better understood in terms of legibility conditions at the interface,' and he goes on to point out that the empirical evidence pointing to the importance of these levels of representation is extensive. In the context of these remarks, it may be worth contrasting this summary dismissal of intermediate linguistic levels ('imperfections' if they exist because they are not motivated in terms of the interfaces) with the attitude Chomsky adopts to other 'imperfections.' As we shall see in Section 4, these latter include uninterpretable features and the operation Move, and he goes to considerable lengths to establish the possibility that these 'imperfections' are only 'apparent.' Without wishing to suggest that the task is even meaningful, it does strike me as odd for similar considerations not to be raised in connection with d-structure and s-structure. Of course, this is not to avow any personal attraction for these constructs, but it is to plead for a level playing field in getting to show whether your lack of 'perfection' is merely 'apparent' or not. The brief observations in nn29 and 82 below may perhaps also be relevant to this perspective.

25 Obviously, this sketch does not attempt to represent the structural intricacies of C_{HL}, merely displaying those aspects of the system that are straightforwardly derivable from minimalist assumptions.

26 The arguments that follow are not compelling at every stage. They do, however, illustrate the style of reasoning to which a minimalist account of phrase structure subscribes.

27 Unary branching is not permitted in Bare Phrase Structure. Since all projections consist of nothing more than a rearrangement of the features constituting the expressions that produce the projection, it would be an entirely vacuous operation. It is of note that even as recently as Freidin (1997), it was maintained that the binariity of Merge/branching was stipulated, merely being a consequence of the stipulated binarity of Generalised Transformation (Chomsky 1995b, p. 191).

28 For relevant discussion, see Chomsky (1998, 31). Chomsky treats 'immediately contains' as a reflexive relation, but since this has no consequences for the issues under discussion, I shall not follow him in this respect.

29 An issue that is puzzling concerns the pariah status Chomsky attaches to government in his recent work. In Chomsky (1998, 28), we find the phrase 'the relations provided *directly* by the indispensable

computational operation Merge,' which is what is being explored in the text above. Unfortunately, I don't know what the precise force of 'directly' is supposed to be, but it is clear that we can at least conclude that government is *less* directly available than, say, c-command. However, in itself this presents a problem, since if we are given c-command, then there doesn't appear to be any obstacle to defining m-command and government - the only additional notions needed are maximal projection (certainly definable relationally in the Bare Phrase Structure framework of Chomsky, 1995b, as illustrated by Nunes and Thompson, 1998) and intervention. Then, the question becomes: why should government offend minimalist principles when c-command doesn't? Neither is primitive in the same way as immediate containment or sisterhood, and it doesn't strike me as a sensible exercise to try to draw a line between concepts that are distinguished only in terms of the differential complexity of their definitions. Primitive vs. defined is fine by me, but less complex definition vs. more complex definition looks like a recipe for drawing the line exactly where it suits.

[30] As Bob Borsley has pointed out to me, the parenthesis here is an appropriate amplification of (16iii) only if we suppose that ordering is determined by reference to a *single* relation accessible to C_{HL}. Linear ordering could be achieved, for example, if the phonology had access to a *set* of ordering constraints based on categorical information. The soundness of the argument, therefore, depends on an additional assumption that reliance on a single relation is to be preferred to reliance on a set of category specific constraints.

[31] Of course, Kayne (1994) already contains a 'proof' that branching is binary. In (16) this is simply set alongside the argument that asymmetric c-command is an accessible relation in the system, a necessary additional step if we are to be rigorously minimalist.

[32] Two observations should be made here. First, if we were seeking to be exhaustive, it might be considered necessary to also include the complements of α and β and the two differences, $\alpha-\beta$ and $\beta-\alpha$, in the space of possibilities. We could quickly rule out the former on the grounds that any complementary set of features will be a large heterogeneous set, uninterpretable at LF. For the differences, we can simply note that $\alpha-\beta = \alpha \cap \beta'$, where β' designates the complement of β. Thus differences are definitionally more complex than unions and intersections, and will therefore not be relied on in a well-designed system if there is a simpler alternative. Of more concern, it is open to

someone to maintain that the features determining the label of $\{\alpha, \beta\}$ should, in some cases, be a *selection* of features from α and from β. Clearly, this option does not have the necessary consequence that the selection is contradictory and uninterpretable. By failing to take account of this possibility, the argument in (18) is incomplete in a quite serious way. I am grateful to Bob Borsley for drawing this difficulty to my attention.

[33] Atkinson (1998) is concerned exclusively with the simpler case of movements that involve 'substitution' in terms of the principles and parameters framework. I subsequently proceeded to consider the various sub-cases of adjunction discussed in Chomsky (1995b), and as that work approached conclusion, Chomsky (1998) appeared. There, Chomsky discusses the same issue, although he presents it as consideration of the predictability of labels, and concludes (*op. cit.*, 51, n105): 'An elaborate argument to guarantee projection of the target in [Chomsky, 1995b] is superfluous, under this reanalysis.' The reanalysis in question is, in some respects, rather simple, but it also depends on implementations of selection and θ-theory which are far from clear in my mind. For this reason, I have decided to reproduce here a sketch of the argument from Chomsky (1995a), which differs in a number of respects from that appearing in Chomsky (1995b). It has the virtue of being reasonably transparent. Even if it transpires that what follows in the text is 'superfluous,' it will nonetheless provide a further instantiation of the sort of deductive process I am concerned to illustrate in this section. The second (unpublished) part of my discussion of adjunction is too involved to merit inclusion in this paper.

[34] Paraphrasing Chomsky (1998, 42), in this later work, movement is driven by properties of the target (now referred to as a probe). By contrast, Greed was driven by properties of the moved item. I shall say a little more about the technology of the later system in Section 4.

[35] An important exception to this generalisation is provided by the selection of the 'external' argument of v, which, in traditional terms, merges the argument in [Spec, vP]. For the purposes of this discussion, I shall ignore this exception.

[36] The argument here is far from compelling for reasons that are not difficult to articulate. Checking (with or without attendant movement) is itself motivated by the requirement to rid a derivation of *uninterpretable* (at the LF-interface) features. As we shall see in the next section, the presence of such features in language provides a

prima facie counterexample to the claim that the language faculty exhibits 'good design.' Thus, an adequate discussion of the status of (19ii) requires an elaboration of the issues discussed later. For present purposes - trying to expose the logical structure of a specific argument - what we have in the text should suffice.

37 The features briefly discussed below are obviously not interpretable at the PF-interface. For observations on the uninterpretability at PF of phonological features linked to the assertion that phonology provides *prima facie* evidence for the wholesale violation of the Interpretability Condition in (2), see Chomsky (1998, 32-3; 1999, 3).

38 I am quite deliberately offering a crude and imprecise version of the checking mechanisms developed in Chomsky (1995b), as my major concern in what follows will be the rather different system presented in Chomsky (1998, 1999).

39 To my mind, the status of EPP-features throughout the recent developments of minimalism remains problematic. Recall from Section 3, the observation that the Extended Projection Principle itself is regarded as a stipulation, the consequences of which should be derived from fundamental minimalist principles. In Section 3, I did not seek to do this, but merely sketched a 'proof' that target projects in cases where movement ('substitution') occurs. However, this does not impinge on the underlying motivation for overt movement to [Spec, TP] itself, nor on the general requirement that [Spec, TP] be occupied. To say that this is because of the presence of an uninterpretable EPP-feature in T seems to be entirely equivalent to the assertion that TPs must have subjects. I shall return to this difficulty below, when we shall see that Chomsky's most recent work takes on the problem of 'motivating' EPP-features. For proposals that seek to account for the properties of raising constructions without invoking EPP-features, see Epstein and Seeley (1999).

40 The complexities in question include those arising from the need to have a precise definition of checking domain and the status of 'feature chains.' As we shall see, an intuitively attractive manoeuvre, replaces checking by matching *in situ*, and this certainly obviates the need for checking domains to be formally defined. However, whether feature chains present the difficulties Chomsky suggests is not clear to me. As Chomsky discusses it (1998, 34), the issue revolves around the need to distinguish *occurrences* of features, and the interaction of this problem with the definition of a chain as a set of occurrences of the same object. Chomsky indicates that *some* instances of occurrence identification can

be dealt with via reference to categorial information. Thus one occurrence of, say, a [person] feature can be distinguished from another by virtue of the fact that the former belongs to a nominal feature set, whereas the latter is verbal. So, the occurrence identification problem appears to arise only if we are concerned to distinguish two occurrences of, say, [person], which are both, say, verbal. Suppose that we accept the need to embrace numerations, with indexing being used to mark distinct selections of the same lexical item from the numeration (cf. Section 2). Of course, lexical items are just sets of features, and we can ask what it means for a selection of a lexical item to bear an index. One possibility would be for the index to just be a feature added on selection from the numeration, but another would be for the index to be distributed across the full set of features comprising the lexical item at this stage. It's difficult to see why C_{HL} should care either way – both are violations of Inclusiveness - but it is noteworthy that if we adopt the latter view, the problem Chomsky is seeing for feature chains seems not to arise. A feature chain, a sequence of occurrences of the same feature(s), will be (F_i , F_i) and a sequence of occurrences of identical (say, agreement) features will be (F_i, F_j). Nor is there a problem in distinguishing the *occurrences* of F_i in the first of these representations – this can be done via the identification of an occurrence of X with the sister of X, since Chomsky (1998, 32) explicitly extends the definition of sisterhood to include features. Of course, if Chomsky's suggestion that indexation linked to selection is not necessary can be maintained, this manoeuvre will not be available.

[41] There are a number of complexities that are being glossed over here. For instance, Chomsky introduces matching as involving feature identity, an intuitively clear notion. However, he goes on to suggest that uninterpretable features (φ-features associated with T and the Case feature of nominals) are *unvalued* at this point in the derivation; thus the required notion of identity must abstract away from the values of features and operate entirely on their substance. A number of complications that arise in connection with feature deletion under matching are discussed in Atkinson (1999, 2000).

[42] In the case of finite clauses, this notion of 'valuation' has obvious PF-consequences in the form of the verb. Consistency suggests extending the notion to the non-finite case, even though there is no reflex of this valuation at PF.

[43] Chomsky (1999, 34, n7) refers to the plausibility of (26) being derivable from more fundamental properties of the language faculty. In Chomsky (1998, 40), (26) is referred to as being 'in the same spirit' as the proposal that 'deletion is a "one fell swoop" operation, dealing with the φ-set as a unit.' Unfortunately, there is no development of the plausibility claim in the later paper, and it is difficult to see the earlier remark as other than rhetorical. We must, therefore, acknowledge that the status of (26) remains uncertain.

[44] There are mysteries here that Chomsky nowhere adequately resolves. For instance, he maintains that it is *prizes* that carries the uninterpretable Case feature into the derivation and that this Case feature somehow determines that *several prizes* will be pied-piped to satisfy the EPP-feature of raising T. The mechanics of this 'generalised pied-piping' are not addressed in Chomsky (1998, 1999). Pesetsky and Torrego (2000) assume that uninterpretable Case features are a property of D, an assumption that allows Case to be a feature of DP in the Bare Phrase Structure framework.

[45] In parallel with the valuation (for PF-purposes) of the uninterpretable φ-features of T, the uninterpretable [Case] feature of *prizes* becomes specified as [nominative] by virtue of an interpretable feature of finite T. Again, this information is assumed to be available only to the phonology from hereon. It is potentially interesting that feature valuation under matching appears to be a heterogeneous process, sometimes involving *copying* in the case of φ-sets and sometimes something more akin to *assignment* as exemplified by Case (cf. n78 for an observation that this distinction may have empirical consequences)

[46] A technical problem arises at this point, since Chomsky maintains that the 'pure expletive' *there* contains only an uninterpretable [person] feature. In Chomsky (1998), he proposes to deal with this by treating *there* as a head which can function as a probe. A difficulty which immediately arises in the 1998 framework is that by the time *there* enters the derivation, the matching [person] feature of defective T has already been deleted via matching with the [3person] feature of *prizes*; the more detailed discussion of 'phases' in Chomsky (1999) can be seen as addressing this issue directly, but this in turn raises the difficulty that there is something conceptually odd about matching an *un*interpretable probe with an *un*interpretable goal. It is interesting that Chomsky (1999, 3) introduces Agree as 'holding between α and β, where α has interpretable inflectional features and β has uninterpretable ones.' It may be that 'inflectional' here enables

Chomsky to escape a charge of inconsistency with regard to his subsequent practice, but he goes on to maintain that within 'Case-agreement and related systems ... probe and goal match *if features are valued for the goal and unvalued for the probe.'* (*op. cit.* 4, my emphases – MA). This is worded in such a way as to suggest that uninterpretable probe and interpretable goal provides a necessary condition for matching, a natural enough suggestion. Thus, the feeling of unease regarding uninterpretable goal matching uninterpretable probe persists. This set of issues is discussed more fully in Atkinson (1999, 2000)

[47] The status of EPP-features is an issue to which I have already drawn attention (n39). It is of some interest that Chomsky (1999, 6) briefly considers the idea that the presence of EPP-features can be linked to the notion of φ-completeness. In the context of outlining an alternative account of Case-agreement to that sketched above, he speculates that: 'It is tempting to associate EPP with φ-completeness.' It is easy to see the attractiveness of this idea in a system where EPP-features appear to be stipulated, although arguably it would only push the hard question back to: what determines the property of φ-completeness? Chomsky proposes that C is always φ-complete, but that T has this property only when necessary, and he offers some programmatic remarks extending these considerations to v and V. Since I suspect that major inconsistencies follow from these suggestions, and as Chomsky himself does not pursue this alternative for long, I shall not seek to evaluate it more seriously here. A different question concerns whether the suggestion we shall meet towards the end of this section that EPP-features are 'driven' by LF-requirements (and, therefore, not stipulated) could be in any way connected to this link between such features and φ-completeness.

[48] It is, of course, required by the assumed EPP-feature of raising T. This indicates that it is necessary to restrict the notion of 'feature checking' in the citation from Chomsky (1998) to the checking of Case-agreement features.

[49] An issue that deserves serious consideration is the status of Agree with respect to this distinction. There is, it seems to me, a clear sense in which Agree and Move can be viewed as similar from the design perspective: both serve to establish dependencies between two positions in a syntactic structure. In the case of Move this dependency is overtly coded in the system, by virtue of the item *in situ* and the moved item constituting two occurrences of the same object. However,

in the case of Agree, there is no overt coding of the dependency, even though in the case of φ-sets there is a sense in which the interpretable features of the goal are copied into the probe position. In fact, this 'copying' produces PF-relevant valuations of the φ-features that are *not* visible to the computation to LF. Thus, in the case of (24b), after Agree has operated with matrix T as a probe and *prizes* as a goal, the phonology is provided with the information which enables it to produce the third person plural form *seem*, but there is nothing in the derivation which proceeds to LF indicating that Agree has linked these two sites. A speculation that might be worth pursuing is that Agree is the LF-driven 'dislocation' property, whereas overt movement is a response to problems posed by PF. Thus, if an application of Agree were accompanied by a signal that a dependency has been established (say, by co-indexation, introducing a violation of Inclusiveness which might be reduced to the status of an 'apparent' imperfection by relying on the strategy we are going to be considering shortly), it could be maintained that LF is indifferent to whether or not some expression moves overtly. From one perspective, this speculation might look like a sharpening up of the independence of Case-agreement and overt movement briefly described in the text: Case-agreement (mediated by Agree) is an LF-directed strategy, whereas overt movement is a response to PF-requirements. However, we shall see shortly that Chomsky (1998, 1999) takes a quite different view on these matters, so I shall not pursue this speculation further here. It is, however, noteworthy that Chomsky (1999, 3) explicitly introduces Agree as an apparent imperfection, saying '... that [it] may be part of an optimal solution to minimal design specifications by virtue of [its] role in establishing the property of "displacement".' But this can't be a completely accurate characterisation, since, as we have noted, there are tokens of Agree which are not embedded in tokens of overt movement. Thus, it seems more appropriate to regard uninterpretable features as providing the mechanism that serves *both* Agree and Move, rather than to see uninterpretable features and Agree as serving Move.

[50] At this point, it may not be inappropriate to speculate about functions and implementations in a way that is familiar in cognitive science (see, for example, Marr, 1982, Fodor and Pylyshyn, 1988). So the grammar must compute a function in which expressions get moved around, or, more neutrally, related to some other location in a structure. However, the *way* the grammar does this is of no interest to the function, being an implementation question. Setting aside fundamental questions

about whether the cognitive stance on the nature of language is appropriate, one could envisage that the apparent imperfections of uninterpretable features and movement in the Minimalist Programme is matched by the apparent imperfection of, for instance, slash categories in HPSG. Nigel Duffield (p.c.) has suggested a further perspective on this, noting that experimental psycholinguistics, with its emphasis on *process*, could perhaps focus more explicitly on *representation*, with a view to determining how the abstract function is implemented in the human mind.

[51] It seems to me that the considerations raised in n49 are potentially urgent here. Overt A-movement in Chomsky (1998, 1999) is driven *entirely* by EPP-features, so it cannot be maintained that by focusing on such movement, we are encompassing the full complement of uninterpretable features. If the strategy outlined in the text is correct, we need to take seriously the observation that the residue of uninterpretable features serves Agree. For this strategy to work, then, Agree *must* enter the set of 'apparent' imperfections. In what follows in the text, I shall continue to adopt Chomsky's own emphasis, and apart from speculative remarks in Section 5, reserve further discussion of the status of Agree for another time.

[52] As regards (34a), we can discern the first formulation of a relevant principle in Chomsky (1995b, 294). There, we meet the phrase 'effect on output,' and in the current context this gives us the conclusion that a token of dislocation will occur in the narrow syntax only if it has an effect on interpretation at LF (for relevant discussion in connection with Quantifier Raising, see Fox, 1995).

[53] Note that an asymmetry enters the picture at this point. In identifying the interpretive consequences of a movement in the narrow syntax, we necessarily go some way towards identifying the LF-pressures to which the movement is a response. However, this is not the case for PF-movement, which at this stage is identified simply in terms of it not having interpretive consequences. The nature of the PF-problem that drives the movement is completely untouched by such a characterisation.

[54] Note that (42b) (although not 42a, nor, indeed, 42c) again appears to be acceptable on a 'list' reading, where it might occur in response to a question such as 'Can you think of anything we might give to Bill?' In such circumstances, it appears that even number agreement between T and its associate can be dispensed with, giving *there's those books*

donated to the bazaar (See Chomsky 1995, 384, n43 and 1998, 44, n91 for inconclusive discussion).

55 Presumably, taking account of the argument that follows, the derivation which would yield (44) converges at LF.

56 Chomsky's discussion appears to be inconsistent with respect to the assumptions he makes about the relevant properties of the structures to which narrow syntax has access. On the one hand, he says (1999, 16): 'The narrow syntactic computation ... proceeds on course with [the input to TH/EX] unchanged except that the trace of TH/EX is phonologically empty even prior to the strong phase level, at which point the position would have become phonologically empty even if not subject to TH/EX.' This appears to be committing him to the view that narrow syntax has access to the output of phonological processes. However, he also says (*ibid.*): 'The English constructions reach LF in the same form as in similar languages, as we would expect if LF-external systems of interpretation are essentially language-independent ....' But presumably for the 'similar languages' to which he refers (Italian, Dutch), there is no question of trace appearing at the original position of a phrase analogous to one undergoing TH/EX in English, since, as Chomsky points out, structures analogous to (35) are well-formed in these languages. The criterion of 'LF-identity' thus requires that the English phrase remain *in situ* in narrow syntax, and there seems to be no reason to complicate the picture by supposing that the computation to LF has access to the output of PF processes. That Chomsky might be attracted by this perspective is indicated by his later remark (*op. cit.*, 18): 'A simpler alternative is that the ... output of TH/EX is immune to all narrow-syntactic or LF-interface operations, and that the operations that apply (Agree, or those at the LF-interface) are accessing the trace left by TH/EX.' This is entirely compatible with the account I favour, except that I see no necessity for a reference to 'the trace left by TH/EX' – the *in situ* original phrase can perform the required function.

57 The nearest we get to relevant discussion in Chomsky (1999, 18) is: 'TH/EX moves [a phrase] rightward or leftward leaving a copy without phonological features, presumably adjunction to *v*P and substitution in SPEC-*v*, if a weak phase has a phonological counterpart to EPP.' Setting aside whether it is sensible to suppose that a trace created by PF-movement is accessible to the narrow syntax, all this does is identify target sites for TH/EX and, for the leftward version, raise the spectre of a 'phonological' EPP-feature. As the EPP-feature of

narrow syntax has already been identified as somewhat problematic in status, I am not attracted by the importing of analogous notions into phonology. We can use Chomsky's observation that Dutch and Italian do not have TH/EX to sharpen up the point raised in the text. What *phonological* difference between English and these languages could be responsible for this difference with respect to TH/EX? I take it that minimalism has to offer *something* on this if it is to be taken seriously. An important property of PF is, of course, its linear character, and one issue that could be re-addressed from this point of view is clitic movement in the context of a Bare Phrase Structure version of Kayne's (1994) Linear Correspondence Axiom. Chomsky (1995b, 337-8) contains remarks relevant to this topic. But it is currently difficult to see how considerations such as these could be extended to the case at hand. Naturally, this is not an argument for abandoning the analysis - questions of this nature are being posed for the first time, and we should not be surprised to conclude that current understanding falls well short of even beginning to answer them.

[58] It must, of course, be acknowledged that there is no serious theory at this point. INT is merely a label for a set of poorly understood notions. And it is probably more in the spirit of what Chomsky intends to construe INT' as the relative complement of INT with respect to a relatively small set of properties linked to specificity, etc.

[59] Phonological border (of HP) is introduced as referring to 'a position not c-commanded by phonological material within HP.' (*op. cit.*, 27). In a footnote, Chomsky suggests that this definition should perhaps utilise c-command *from the left*. This appears to be necessary in order to account for Object Shift in SOV languages. The positions filled by trace in (51) are taken to be voided of phonological content by cyclic Spell-Out operating in a phase-based model.

[60] In fact, Chomsky refers to the phonological border of v^*P in his formulation of this principle, where v^*P is a particular type of vP with complete argument structure. I do not believe that failure to engage this distinction here affects the outline of the argument I am presenting.

[61] Introducing this possibility, Chomsky (199, 27) says: 'We assume that INT is assigned to the peripheral configuration universally, adopting [53], probably a subcase of a more general principle governing peripheral non-theta (EPP) positions including SPEC-T - a traditional idea, still somewhat obscure.' The observations about subject raising

made earlier are consistent with this 'traditional idea' while not pretending to dilute its obscurity.

62 It is here that we can reconsider the problematic status of EPP-features raised in n47. What we now appear to be meeting is the suggestion that an EPP-feature is nothing more than a response to the need to clearly signal to LF an interpretive distinction, crudely that between INT and INT'. It must be noted, though, that this sort of characterisation of the role of the EPP-feature of v doesn't appear to generalise easily. As observed in the brief discussion of subject raising earlier in this section, there appears to be some connection between Spec, TP and something similar to INT. However, the fact that the EPP-feature of T can be deleted via pure merger of the LF-uninterpretable expletive *there*, suggests that it would be a mistake to identify the roles of these two peripheral positions. Additionally, of course, unlike the EPP-features of v and C, that of T is taken to be obligatory, and it may be that this difference, if properly understood, would enable an account of other differences in these positions to be developed. For the moment, however, little more than acknowledgement of the preliminary and programmatic nature of the proposals is justified.

63 The notion of 'interpretational motivation' in this discussion is not straightforward. To see this, we can contrast Chomsky's position to one that simply links the internal argument position to INT' and the Spec-v position to INT. From this latter perspective, any argument which inherently requires INT will need to move to Spec-v to avoid anomaly, whereas any which requires INT' must remain *in situ*, and there is a direct correlation between movement and INT interpretation. Another way of putting this is that the EPP-feature of v and the movement that takes place to satisfy it are a direct consequence of the LF-imposed requirement to clearly signal the INT/INT' contrast. In Chomsky's account, however, both INT and INT' are compatible with the position of the internal argument in a non-Object Shift language, so it is not possible to maintain that configurations created by movement are necessary so that narrow syntax can clearly signal distinctions required at LF. In the final section of this paper, I shall suppose that something more akin to the simpler situation described in this note obtains, but it may well be that this constitutes a damaging oversimplification.

64 For some suggestions as to how minimalism may be interpreted in the context of L2 acquisition, see Hawkins (2000)

65 While empirical observations abound, I take it as given that not all of these will impose a predictive burden on an optimal (or, indeed, any) account of the language faculty. If we focus on naturalistic, longitudinal studies of language development, we are faced with linguistic corpora and all the well-known difficulties of dealing with such corpora. For example, if the object of our interest is the child's internalised system, we must not be seduced by odd examples of production which constitute routines, performance errors, or whatever; nor must we be immediately persuaded that a significant numerical disparity in favour of utterance type X over utterance type Y can substitute for an adult linguistic intuition, yielding the conclusion that X is well-formed according to the child's internalised system but Y isn't. In short, if we seek to pursue the consequences of minimalism seriously in the acquisition domain, we will meet the familiar interplay between theory and observation, to which it will be necessary to respond responsibly.

66 The sort of issue to which I am alluding here can be discerned most clearly in Schütze and Wexler's (1996, 679) suggestions which are intended to account for genitive subjects in child speech, exemplified by *my going in, my had a tape recorder*, etc. They pose the question as to 'which case an NP subject gets when there are *no Tense or Agr INFL features present...*' (my italics - MA), and noting the behaviour of gerunds in English, they propose that the answer is genitive. However, if we suppose, as is traditional, that INFL is the locus of *only* tense and agreement features, we must face the issue of the nature of this INFL that lacks these features. If there is no independent INFL category, as suggested in the text, the lack of tense and agreement indicates that there is no position in clausal architecture corresponding to that standardly occupied by INFL. It follows that on Schütze and Wexler's own account, child utterances with genitive subjects are inconsistent with the continuity position to which they subscribe.

67 It is, I suppose, conceivable that the 'logic' of the optimal solution imposes some constraints on the way in which the solution is arrived at. However, I shall not pursue this speculation further here.

68 At this point, the issues briefly raised in n13 are obviously significant.

69 For a different attempt to account for optional infinitives in terms of emergent properties of tense, see Hyams (1996), and for observations on this approach, Atkinson (1996)

70 In terms of the framework offered by Chomsky, I am supposing that it makes sense to at least consider the possibility that F, the set of

linguistic features, is itself subject to developmental expansion. Obviously, we might expect the membership of [F], the set of features 'operative' in a specific language L to shift as development proceeds, as the child comes to know (by whatever means) that such-and-such a distinction is or is not operative in L, although, given the lack of evidence, there would appear to be little scope for variation here as far as LF-interpretable features are concerned (for a somewhat enigmatic aside touching on this matter, see Chomsky, 1998, 3, n3).

71 Radford goes further to link the absence of a [person] feature to the absence of determiners in Alison's speech, invoking the notion, developed in Abney (1987), that the position occupied by determiners is the position which hosts [person] in adult grammars.

72 It might be suspected that the 'egocentric stage' from Piagetian thinking will provide the required independent grounds. Here, however, I am concerned only to establish the possibility of taking a certain perspective seriously; pursuit of the evidence bearing on the correctness of the perspective is for another occasion.

73 To allay any possible misunderstandings, I should re-iterate a point I made much earlier (n4). This suggestion that language development theory should look to non-linguistic cognitive development in no sense prejudices the view that the linguistic system is modular, since the operations that the language system performs on its features can be significantly different from anything assumed to take place in general cognition. In Atkinson (1982), I developed a detailed critique of what I referred to as 'cognitive reductionism,' viz. the view that an understanding of first language acquisition can be gleaned from careful consideration of the child's cognitive system, and I am no more attracted to this position now than I was 20 years ago. However, rejection of cognitive reductionism does not entail that what is known about cognitive development cannot inform our understanding of language acquisition in certain specific respects, viz. with respect to the developmental properties of those linguistic objects (features) which, by definition, interface with 'systems of thought.' Indeed, Chomsky himself acknowledges as much when he says (1998, 10): 'Suppose we understood external systems well enough to have clear ideas about the legibility conditions they impose. Then the task at hand would be fairly straightforward ...' He goes on to note that the external systems are *not* well understood, but this is not to say that nothing is known about them; and if anything is known, there is every reason to avail ourselves of this knowledge. In my earlier work, I

regarded it as a truism that children's semantic knowledge requires that they control an appropriate inventory of concepts, and this truism is re-appearing here with respect to the *substance* of LF-interpretable features.

74 Chomsky (1998, 50-1) offers a somewhat programmatic discussion of such issues. There, he seeks to assimilate *pure* Merge (that is, Merge which is not a component of Move) to Agree to the extent of maintaining that it is an *asymmetric* operation requiring a selector (analogous to a probe) and an item selected (analogous to a goal), which must match it in some way. The motivation for imposing asymmetry in this fashion is located in the need to be able to predict the label of the merged object without stipulation (cf. discussion of projection of target in Section 3, to which this motivation relates). Chomsky proceeds to suggest that an important distinction between the selector in Merge and the probe in Agree is that the former is a semantic (hence interpretable) feature that does not delete as a consequence of the operation. However, there is no discussion of the status of the matching feature in the selected item. If this too is an interpretable feature, as suggested by Chomsky's occasional reliance on the term 's-selection,' there would appear to be no principled obstacle to the production of a convergent derivation that does not contain any tokens of uninterpretable features.

75 That convergence can be a property of derivations containing only interpretable features is suggested by Chomsky's (1998, 8) remark that 'the 'property *converges at I[nterface] L[evel]* may hold of an expression formed in the course of a derivation that then proceeds on to IL. If, say, particles or adverbs have only LF-interpretable features, then they converge at LF when extracted from the lexicon and at every subsequent stage of derivation.'

76 Chomsky (1998, 1999) occasionally speculates on the nature of the features (interpretable and uninterpretable) that provide the mechanism for the displacement of *wh*-items and other items instantiating A'-movement. Since these speculations are not developed and would not, I believe, require a form of argument distinct to that in the text, I will not refer to them further at this point.

77 This observation *may* provide an additional source for developmental predictions, as it seems appropriate to suppose that the formal operations underlying matching and assignment are distinct. It is, therefore, conceivable that a system could contain one without the other, and this may provide a way of coming to terms with the data

reported for German-speaking SLI children by Clahsen, Bartke and Eisenbeiss (2000), which indicate intact Case-marking but large numbers of agreement errors (but see n79 below). The system for handling case presented in Pesetsky and Torrego (2000) is rather different. They regard (nominative) case as an uninterpretable tense feature which is *matched* by T itself (where T is regarded as interpretable). It is not clear what these authors would say about the difference between nominative and null case, where the latter is assumed to appear on the null subjects of control infinitivals (Chomsky and Lasnik, 1995). Within Chomsky's system, it is possible to suppose that these case differences arise via distinct interpretable properties of finite T and the non-finite T occurring in control clauses.

78 This speculation arises in the context of Chomsky briefly considering whether categorial features are, in fact, needed in grammars (see, for example, Chomsky, 1999, 5). Note, however, that the [person] feature of *there* is deemed to be uninterpretable, and if this is the case, the generalisation that EPP features require the presence of appropriate interpretable features cannot be maintained in maximally general form.

79 There are a couple of observations that bear further on this suggestion. Firstly, while the logic of the argument is consistent with interpretable features preceding their corresponding uninterpretable features, it does not demand it; the logic is equally consistent with *simultaneous* emergence of the relevant objects. Secondly, what is being contemplated is not as gross as an interpretable feature *stage* preceding an uninterpretable feature *stage*. Specifically, while we might be persuaded that whatever interpretable feature of T it is that values the uninterpretable [Case] feature of nominals as nominative must be present if the [Case] feature itself is present, nothing follows immediately from this regarding the presence or absence of other interpretable and uninterpretable features. The close relationship between Case and agreement signalled by Chomsky's (1998, 37) view that 'structural Case [is] a reflex of an uninterpretable φ-set' may be consistent with a more 'connected' view of the developmental possibilities. However, I shall not seek to explore this further here.

80 It is perhaps worth noting a developmental possibility that becomes apparent as soon as we clearly separate the Case-agreement system and movement operations. With this separation, we can contemplate a developmental dissociation as follows: if the uninterpretable φ-set of T and the uninterpretable Case feature of N enter the child's system

before the uninterpretable EPP-feature of T, we should see Case and agreement inflections in place with no overt movement. What about the converse possibility, i.e. the EPP-feature of T enters the system before the φ-set of T and the Case feature of N? In fact, nothing of interest follows since (a) it is possible to satisfy the EPP-requirement of T by pure Merge; (b) satisfaction of this requirement via overt movement only takes place if it is linked to a token of Agree which itself requires the uninterpretable φ-set of T.

[81] The simplification, as noted at the end of Section 4, is potentially damaging. It is not adopted by Chomsky and it appears that in English an argument can be interpreted as either INT or INT' in internal position without anomaly. Furthermore, whatever is designated by INT appears to be quite complex, running together a set of properties covering definiteness, specificity, topicalisation, focus, etc. My aim is merely to establish the *prima facie* plausibility of bringing a specific perspective to acquisition questions, and from the perspective of this aim, the simplification may be justified.

[82] Elaborating a little, we might adopt Chomsky's version of Hale and Keyser's (1993) configurational account of θ-roles, with the LF-interface reading the thematic properties of an argument from the foot of the chain in which it occurs. Now, arguments are interpretively multi-faceted, with their thematic properties constituting only one part of their overall interpretation. Added to these are discourse/referential properties along the lines signalled by Chomsky's distinction between INT and INT' and 'logical' properties, notably scope. Suppose, then, that there is something like a (1-1) relation between configurations presented to the LF-interface and the aspects of interpretation which the systems beyond LF can derive from these configurations, a suggestion which itself might be seen as embodying 'good design.' It would follow that multi-faceted interpretation of arguments requires multiplicity of configurations, with different aspects of interpretation being 'read off' different configurations. It is tempting to speculate that this avenue is worth exploring in connection with *wh*-movement, where *wh*-items, by virtue of having both thematic *and* quantificational properties, must be associated with multiple configurations. The speculation briefly described here continues to maintain that there is a *single* interface between the grammar and the 'system of thought'; an alternative might partition the different aspects of interpretation in the grammar itself, so that the 'system of thought' is presented with a multiplicity of

objects, each defining a distinct interface. Something along these lines is proposed by Platzack (1999). Indeed, the final sections of Chomsky (1999), where he distinguishes between 'syntactic objects' (bearing some resemblance to traditional D-structures) and 'occurrence lists' (records of the movement history of specific items) might also be seen as moving in the direction of multiple interfaces between the grammar and the 'system of thought.'

[83] Borer and Wexler (1987) also contains discussion of passives in Hebrew and causatives in both English and Hebrew. The main focus in Babyonyshev *et al.* (2000) is on unaccusatives and their interaction with the genitive of negation in Russian.

[84] An immediate difficulty raised by this suggestion concerns the status of simple clauses in the context of the VP-internal Subject Hypothesis, which is, of course, adopted in Chomsky's minimalist framework. Raising of subject to (Spec, T) is itself triggered by an EPP-feature of T and, while I am happy to suggest that very early subjects may remain *in situ*, it appears to be uncontroversial that subjects are raised long before children overcome their difficulties with passives. For now, I have nothing of interest to say about this, but it is worth observing that Babyonyshev *et al.* (2000) must also confront this problem. Their response is to suggest that a simple clause like (i) has the s-homophone in (ii):

(i) Mary$_i$ T [t$_i$ speaks French]
(ii) Mary$_i$ T [PRO$_i$ speaks French]

Children's simple clauses are then regarded as tokens of (ii) rather than (i). Careful reflection on this suggestion must await another occasion.

References

Abney, S. P. 1987. The English Noun Phrase in its Sentential Aspect. PhD Dissertation. MIT.

Aoun, J. and Y.-H. Li. 1989. Scope and constituency. *Linguistic Inquiry* 20: 141-172.

Atkinson, M. 1982. *Explanations in the Study of Child Language Development*. Cambridge: Cambridge University Press.

Atkinson, M. 1996. Now hang on a minute: some reflections on emerging orthodoxies. In H. Clahsen (ed.), *Generative Perspectives on Language Acquisition*. Amsterdam: John Benjamins.

Atkinson, M. 1998. Some reflections on Bare Phrase Structure and projection of targets. *Essex Research Reports in Linguistics: Special Issue: Essays on Language Presented to Keith Brown*: 49-68.

Atkinson, M. 1999. There seem to be likely to be some problems. Ms. University of Essex.

Atkinson, M. 2000. Uninterpretable feature deletion and phases. *Essex Research Reports in Linguistics*, 00: 000-000.

Babyonshev, M., R. Fein, J. Ganger, D. Pesetsky and K. Wexler 2000. The maturation of grammatical principles: evidence from Russian unaccusatives. Ms. MIT and Microsoft Corporation.

Baker, C. L. 1979. Linguistic theory and the Projection Problem. *Linguistic Inquiry* 10: 533-81.

Baker, M. 1988. *Incorporation: A Theory of Grammatical Function Changing*. Chicago: University of Chicago Press.

Bobaljik, J. D. 1995. Morphosyntax: The Syntax of Verbal Inflection. PhD Dissertation. MIT.

Borer, H. and K. Wexler. 1987. The maturation of syntax. In T. Roeper and E. Williams (eds), *Parameter Setting*. Dordrecht: Reidel.

Cheng L. L.-S. and R. Sybesma. 1999. 'Bare and not-so-bare nouns and the structure of NP.' *Linguistic Inquiry* 30: 509-542.

Chomsky, N. 1986. *Barriers*. Cambridge, Mass.: MIT Press.

Chomsky, N. 1995a. Bare Phrase Structure. In G. Webelhuth (ed.), *Government and Binding Theory and the Minimalist Program*. Oxford: Blackwell.

Chomsky, N. 1995b. *The Minimalist Program*. Cambridge, Mass.: MIT Press,

Chomsky, N. 1995c. 'Language and Nature,' *Mind* 104: 1-61.

Chomsky, N. 1998. Minimalist Inquiries: The Framework. *MIT Occasional Papers in Linguistics* 15.

Chomsky, N. 1999. Derivation by Phase. Ms. MIT.

Chomsky, N. 2000a. An interview on minimalism. (with A. Belletti and L. Rizzi). University of Siena, Ms.

Chomsky, N. 2000b. *New Horizons in the Study of Language and Mind*. Cambridge: Cambridge University Press.

Chomsky, N. and H. Lasnik 1995. The theory of Principles and Parameters (Chapter 1 of Chomsky 1995b). Modified version of article of same title published in J. Jacobs, A. von Stechow, W. Sternefeld and T. Venneman (eds), *Syntax: An International Handbook of Contemporary Research*. Berlin: de Gruyter.

Clahsen, H., S. Bartke and S. Eisenbeiss. 2000. Case-marking and agreement in German-speaking SLI children: evidence for a selective linguistic impairment. Ms. University of Essex.

Collins, C. 1995. Toward a theory of optimal derivation. In R. Pensalfini and H. Ura (eds), *Papers on Minimalist Syntax. MIT Working Papers in Linguistics* 27.

Epstein, S. and D. Seeley. 1999. SPEC-ifying the GF "subject," eliminating A-chains and the EPP with a derivational model. Ms. University of Michigan.

Fodor, J. 1975. *The Language of Thought*. Hassocks: Harvester.

Fodor, J. 1978. Computation and reduction. In W. C. Savage (ed.), *Perception and Cognition: Minnesota Studies in the Philosophy of Science: 9*. Minneapolis: University of Minnesota Press.

Fodor, J. 1983. *The Modularity of Mind*. Cambridge, Mass.: MIT Press.

Fodor, J. and Z. Pylyshyn 1988. Connectionism and cognitive architecture: a critical analysis. *Cognition* 28: 3-71.

Fox, D. 1995. Economy and scope. *Natural Language Semantics*, 3: 283-341.

Freidin, R. 1997. Review of Chomsky (1995b). *Language* 73: 571-582.

Gazdar, G., Klein, E., Pullum, G. and I. Sag (1985). *Generalized Phrase Structure Grammar*. Cambridge, Mass.: Harvard University Press.

Hale, K. and J. Keyser. 1993. On argument structure and the lexical expression of semantic relations. In K. Hale and J. Keyser (eds), *The View from Building 20*. Cambridge, Mass.: MIT Press.

Harris, T. and K. Wexler. 1996. The Optional Infinitive Stage in Child English: evidence from negation. In H. Clahsen (ed.), *Generative Perspectives on Language Acquisition*. Amsterdam: John Benjamins.

Hawkins, R. 2000. Persistent selective fossilisation in second language acquisition and the optimal design of the language faculty. Ms. University of Essex.

Huang, C.-T. J. Existential sentences in Chinese and (in)definiteness. In E. Reuland and A. ter Meulen (eds).

Hyams, N. 1994. V2, null arguments and COMP projections. In T. Hoekstra and B. Schwarz (eds), *Language Acquisition Studies in Generative Grammar*. Amsterdam: John Benjamins.

Hyams, N. 1996. The underspecification of functional categories in early grammars. In H. Clahsen (ed.), *Generative Perspectives on Language Acquisition*. Amsterdam: John Benjamins.

Jenkins, L. 1975. *The English Existential*. Tübingen: Max Niemeyer Verlag.

Johnson, D. and S. Lappin 1997. A critique of the Minimalist Program. *Linguistics and Philosophy* 21: 273-333.

Katz, J. J. 1980. *Language and Other Abstract Objects*.

Kayne, R. 1994. *The Antisymmetry of Syntax*. Cambridge, Mass.: MIT Press.

Marr, D. 1982. *Vision: a Computational Investigation into the Human Representation and Processing of Visual Information*. San Francisco: W. H. Freeman.

Milsark, G. L. 1974. Existential Sentences in English. MIT Doctoral Dissertation.

Nunes, J. and Thomson 1998. In J. Uriagareka. *Rhyme and Reason*. Cambridge, Mass.: MIT Press.

Pesetsky, D. and E. Torrego 2000. T-to-C movement: causes and consequences. Ms. MIT and Umass.

Phillips, C. 1996. Syntax at age two: cross-linguistic differences. *MIT Working Papers in Linguistics* 26: 1-58.

Piattelli-Palmarini, M. (ed.) 1980. *Language and Learning: The Debate between Jean Piaget and Noam Chomsky*. Cambridge, Mass: MIT Press.

Pinker, S. 1984. *Language Learnability and Language Development*. Cambridge, Mass.: Harvard University Press.

Platzak, C. 1999. Multiple interfaces. Ms. Lund University.

Pöppel, D. and K. Wexler, 1993. The Full Competence Hypothesis of clause structure in early German. *Language* 69: 1-33.

Radford, A. 1990. *Syntactic Theory and the Acquisition of English Syntax: The Nature of Early Child Grammars of English.* Oxford: Blackwell.

Radford, A. 1997. *Syntactic Theory and the Structure of English: A Minimalist Approach.* Cambridge: Cambridge University Press.

Radford, A. 2000. Child language: a minimalist perspective. Ms. University of Essex.

Reuland, E. and A. ter Meulen (eds). 1987. *The Representation of (In)definiteness.* Cambridge, Mass.: MIT Press.

Roeper, T. 1996. The role of Merger Theory and formal features in acquisition. In H. Clahsen (ed.), *Generative Perspectives on Language Acquisition.* Amsterdam: John Benjamins.

Schütze, C. T. and K. Wexler 1996. Subject Case licensing and English root infinitives. In A. Stringfellow et al. (eds), *Proceeedings of Boston University Conference on Language Development 20: 670-81.*

Uriagareka, J. 1998. *Rhyme and Reason.* Cambridge, Mass.: MIT Press.

Wexler, K. 1994. Optional infinitives, head movement and the economy of derivations. In D. Lightfoot and N. Hornstein (eds), *Verb Movement.* Cambridge: Cambridge University Press.

Wexler, K. 1999. Maturation and growth of grammar. In W. Ritchie and T. Bhatia (eds), *Handbook of Child Language Acquisition.* San Diego, Ca.: Academic Press.

Wexler, K. and P. Culicover 1980. *Formal Principles of Language Acquisition.* Cambridge, Mass.: MIT Press.

A Fond Farewell to the Critical Period Hypothesis for Non-primary Language Acquisition

Ocke-Schwen Bohn

Abstract

Since its formulation 35 years ago, Lenneberg's Critical Period Hypothesis (CPH) has had an enormous influence on psycholinguistic research. In a nutshell, the CPH posits that languages can be successfully acquired only within a maturationally defined period of cerebral plasticity for the allocation of language functions. This chapter reviews the evidence for and against the CPH from research on non-primary (L2) acquisition of spoken language. The evidence suggests that age of learning is the most important determinant of L2 (speech) learning success in terms of ultimate attainment. However, the evidence from research carried out over the last ten years does not support the claims of the CPH that a) there is a well defined critical period during which native-like ultimate attainment is possible, b) that there is a sharp drop in language-learning abilities at around the onset of puberty, and c) that age-of-learning effects can be related to some kind of atrophy, or loss of plasticity, of the biological hardware that is necessary for language learning. Instead, this research suggests that language learning abilities remain intact across the life span, and that age affects are either due to the interaction of coexisting linguistic systems in the minds of multilingual speakers or to confounds with experiential variables.

In Search of a Language for the Mind-Brain, ed. Saleemi, Bohn and Gjedde, *The Dolphin* 33 © 2005 by Aarhus University Press, Denmark. ISBN 87 7934 005 9.

0. Introduction

The Critical Period Hypothesis for language learning (CPH) is one of the most influential hypotheses in psycholinguistics, and it is clearly the most influential hypothesis in second language acquisition research, as witnessed by the very large body of research which it has generated since its formulation 35 years ago. Building upon the aphasiological work of Penfield & Roberts (1959), Lenneberg (1967) described the critical period for language acquisition as that period during which the individual "appears to be most sensitive to stimuli ... and to preserve some innate flexibility for the organization of brain functions to carry out the complex integration of subprocesses necessary for the smooth elaboration of speech and language. After puberty, the ability for self-organization and adjustment to the physiological demands of verbal behavior quickly declines. The brain behaves as if it has become set in its ways ..." (Lenneberg 1967, 158). Like other influential hypotheses, the CPH is attractive in a number of ways. It addresses basic research issues in that it links language learning to a biological substrate (i.e., neurophysiological maturation), and it seems to provide an explanation for the sometimes painfully obvious differences between child and adult language learners. Common wisdom has it that children learn languages rapidly, without much effort, and that they are ultimately fully competent in the language(s) they are learning, whereas language learning in adulthood is perceived to be slow and effortful, and the ultimate result is often a far cry from what younger learners can achieve. These differences between child and adult language learners seem paradoxical. We like to believe (and, I would like to maintain, we are correct in assuming) that the cognitive abilities of children are somewhat inferior to those of adults, yet children seem to outperform adults when it comes to learning the most complex product of the human mind, language.

This chapter is organized as follows: Section 1 briefly presents an overview of how the CPH accounts for the apparently superior language learning abilities of children as opposed to adults, and it does so by referring to the characteristics of critical periods in general. Section 2 briefly discusses two types of pseudo-counterevidence on the CPH, and Section 3 presents the results of recent research that questions the validity of the CPH. Section 4 concludes with an evaluation of the CPH in the light of this recent evidence.

1. Characteristics of critical periods in general and of the CPH

In general, a critical period can be defined as a period of heightened sensitivity to certain types of environmental stimuli in the development of a species. In the narrower sense, a critical period is defined as the only period during which an organism is sensitive to a specific stimulus, with zero sensitivity outside the critical period. The classical case of a critical period in this narrow sense is presented by imprinting in certain avian species (see Figure 1), in which the stimulus characteristics and the behavioral pattern as a consequence of imprinting are well-defined, and in which the critical period has a sharply defined onset and terminus.

(Adapted from Riedl 1979, p. 58)

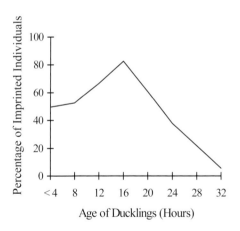

Figure 1: Imprinting in ducklings

A distinction is sometimes made between a critical period in this narrow sense (the strong version) and the weaker versions of a sensitive (Fox1970) or an optimal (Moltz 1973) period (see also

Oyama 1978). A sensitive period is characterized by a more gradual onset and terminus, and an optimal period by a relatively heightened sensitivity to environmental stimuli. In this chapter, the term critical period will be used in the general sense as a cover term for both a sensitive and an optimal period, partly to reflect general usage and partly because the strong version of the CPH has never seriously been entertained, simply because it is evidently wrong.[1]

Following Colombo (1982), any critical period, no matter whether it attempts to account for the ontogenesis of behavioral patterns or sensory abilities in humans or non-human animals, should make or actually does make claims about the *onset* and the *terminus* of the critical period, about the *intrinsic* (maturational) *component* and about the *extrinsic component* (i.e., the stimuli to which the organism is selectively sensitive), about the *system that is affected* by stimulation during the critical period, and about the *ultimate causes* (the functions and benefits) and the *proximate causes* (the mechanisms that regulate growth and decline of sensitivity) of the critical period.

With respect to the CPH, Lenneberg's (1966, 1967) claims were as follows: He suggested as the *onset* for the CPH the age of 2 years, probably because he equated language development with morphosyntactic development. Indeed, the evidence from language production that children start to use combinatorial rules could lead one to posit that morphosyntactic development starts at around age 2. However, it appears somewhat odd that Lenneberg chose the age of 2 years as the onset for the CP, given that phonological and lexical development is well under way at that age. As for lexical development, Lenneberg apparently did not consider this area to be affected by age constraints. As for phonological development, it remains a mystery why this area was excluded from defining the onset of the CP, given that Lenneberg claimed that this area would be affected by a CP (see below).[2]

The *terminus* of the CP, according to Lenneberg, is the onset of puberty (see also the quotation above). Lenneberg based his claim with regard to the terminus to a large extent on his interpretation of the evidence from a number of pathologies such as the arrest of language development in Down syndrome and on the prognosis for recovery from acquired aphasia. Based on the work of Penfield and Roberts (1959), he claimed that language functions that had become lost due to brain trauma before puberty could be allocated to brain areas that had not previously been used for language, whereas aphasics who had suffered trauma at a postpubescent age could not reallocate language functions because of a maturationally conditioned lack of plasticity.

The arguments for placing the terminus at the onset of puberty make it clear that the *intrinsic component* of the CPH is the maturation of the brain. In Lenneberg's view, it is only during the period of brain maturation that the brain is sufficiently plastic to host new language functions. Once the brain has (almost) reached adult levels of neurophysiological maturity, "the brain behaves as if it has become set in its ways ..." (Lenneberg 1967, 158), which means that it is unable to serve as efficiently and successfully as the substrate for language acquisition.

A close reading of Lenneberg's CPH in both the 1966 chapter and the 1967 monograph does not reveal any claims as to the nature of the *extrinsic component*. However, Lenneberg is quite explicit about the *systems that are affected* by stimulation during the CP: These are morphosyntax and phonetics and phonology; the lexicon is seen as being exempt from maturational constraints.

Concerning the *ultimate causes*, Lenneberg does not engage in any speculations with regard to the functions and benefits of the CP. However, the CPH has inspired such speculations, which have led some authors to the surprising conclusion that the inability of adults to learn additional languages fully successfully would represent an evolutionary advantage (e.g., Hurford 1992, Pinker 1994). Finally, the *proximate cause* which regulates the growth and decline of the ability to learn language(s) successfully is the plasticity of the brain, as is clear from Lenneberg's view on the intrinsic component of the CPH (see also above).

A considerable amount of the evidence by which the claims of the CPH can be judged comes from studies of language acquisition outside the period during which children normally acquire their first language. Three types of studies can be distinguished: First, studies of delayed first language acquisition in feral children (e.g., Curtiss, Fromkin, Krashen, Rigle & Rigler 1974, Grimshaw, Adelstein, Bryden & MacKinnon 1998). Even though these studies provide interesting insights on the dissociation of linguistic and cognitive abilities, they are of limited value as evidence for the CPH because of their necessarily anecdotal nature, which makes any generalization problematic. Secondly, there are a few studies of sign language acquisition which directly compared native signers to delayed learners (deaf children growing up in hearing environments) and to older sign learners with acquired deafness (e.g., Mayberry & Eichen 1991, Newman, Bavelier, Corina, Jezzard & Neville 2001). The third type of evidence is the one on which this chapter will focus: the very large number of studies of L2 (and second dialect) acquisition of spoken language in naturalistic settings.

Until the early 1990s, the existing evidence – primarily from L2 acquisition - was in most reviews interpreted as supporting the claims of the CPH (e.g., Long 1990, Pinker 1994). However, many of the findings from research on L2 speech learning and cross-language speech perception that have accumulated over the past 30 years have been at odds with some of the claims of the CPH. This evidence, as well as evidence on L2 speech learning and the acquisition on L2 morphosyntax that has accumulated over the past decade, lead to the conclusion that the CPH, which has guided psycholinguistic research for a third of a century, is no longer tenable.

The remainder of this chapter is organized as follows: First, there will be a brief section on pseudo-counterevidence to the CPH, followed by the main section which presents on overview of the most damaging counterevidence to the CPH. The conclusion will relate these findings from L2 acquisition research to the claims of the CPH as presented in this section.

2. Two pieces of pseudo-counterevidence to the CPH
2.1 "Older is better"
Given the everyday experience of, on the one hand, immigrant children who become fully proficient in the language of their new community and, on the other hand, ultimately less successful adult immigrants, it comes as a surprise that a review of the CPH

concludes that "older children and adults reveal their potential for fast, natural, and successful language learning ... The 20-year old, who by anyone's estimate is beyond the period of brain growth, equipotentiality, or plasticity, is ceteris paribus a better language learner than the 3-year-old or the 6-year-old." (Snow 1987).[3] Snow bases her assertions primarily upon a series of studies which examined various aspects of Dutch language proficiency in child, adolescent, and adult American immigrants to Holland during the first year of their stay. In this study, Snow & Hoefnagel-Höhle (1978) reported that adolescents (12-15 year old) outperformed all other age groups an almost all tests (on areas such as L2 morphosyntax, L2 speech, and translation tasks). In general, the adult group performed slightly less well than the adolescents, and for the three child groups (3-5 year olds, 6-7 year olds, and 8-10 year olds), age was positively related to test performance (i.e., younger was worse). The authors concluded that "these data do not support the critical period hypothesis for language acquisition" and interpreted their findings as "basis for rejecting the hypothesis that the period 2-12 years constitutes an optimal age for language acquisition" (Snow & Hoefnagel-Höhle 1978, 1114 and 1122).

The main problem with the Snow & Hoefnagel-Höhle study is that it is *not* a test of the CPH. The CPH makes predictions about *ultimate attainment*, that is, the final stage (or, perhaps more appropriately, the asymptote) of language learning beyond which learners make no or minimal progress. What Snow & Hoefnagel-Höhle examined was, however, *rate of learning* during the first months of L2 exposure. While age differences with respect to rate of learning certainly merit attention and require explanation, they are irrelevant as (counter-) evidence for the CPH which does not make predictions about age-related rate-of-learning differences during the first stages of L2 acquisition.

2.2 Exceptional learners

The second type of pseudo-counterevidence comes from studies which report to have identified adult L2 learners whose "phenomenal success" (Ioup et al. 1994, 91) seems to present an exception to the CPH. Any case of a fully successful adult L2 learner would indeed present a serious problem for the CPH. However, close examination of studies on so-called "exceptional" learners reveals that there are three good reasons for rejecting these learners as presenting counterevidence to the CPH. First, some of these studies are flawed either because the non-natives' performance was not compared to native speakers, or because native speakers were not consistently identified as native speakers (e.g. Bongaerts et al. 1997). Without such controls, studies on "exceptional" learners are simply inconclusive. Second, even though some adults may qualify as "exceptional" learners because they reach a very high level of proficiency in their second language, it needs to be emphasized that a near-native-level of proficiency is not the same as a native-like level of proficiency (as in the Ioup et al. 1994 study). Third, there exists (as yet) no study that has identified an adult learner who meets the only true criterion that would present counterevidence to the CPH, namely, passing "for native 100% of the time in all areas for which native speakers pass for native 100% of the time" (Major & Kim 1996, 466).

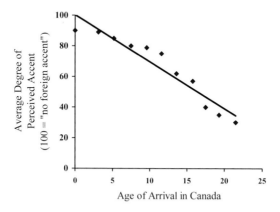

Figure 2: Mean foreign accent ratings of English sentences spoken by 240 L1 Italian speakers and a group of 24 native English speakers (AOA = 0) in the Flege et al. (1995) study. [4]

3. Evidence

Having established that two types of alleged counterevidence to the CPH are not valid because of methodological and/or logical flaws, this section turns to recently accumulated evidence on the CPH from L2 acquisition research which primarily addresses questions surrounding the terminus and the intrinsic (maturational) component of this hypothesis, but which also has implications for an evaluation of the system that is hypothesized to be affected by a CP, and for the hypothesized proximate causes of a CP.

The first piece of evidence comes from a series of studies that Flege and his collaborators conducted to assess the relationship between the degree of perceived foreign accent and a number of variables of which age of first exposure to the L2 (indexed as age of arrival in the L2 speech community) was the primary focus. For example, in the Flege, Munro & MacKay (1995) study, 240 native Italian speakers, who had arrived in Canada between the ages of 2 and 23 years, and who had been living in Canada for at least 15 years at the time of the study, were recorded producing simple sentences like *He turned to the right* and *I can read this for you*.

These sentences (as well as sentences produced by a native English control group) were presented to a panel of 10 native English speaking judges, who rated the sentences for foreign accentedness on a continuous (sliding) scale. As shown in Figure 2, Flege et al. (1995) found a strong negative correlation ($r = -0.845$) between the age of arrival (AOA) in Canada and the degree of perceived foreign accent. The results of Flege at al. (1995) also indicated that a foreign accent is detectable in individuals who started learning their L2 before the onset of puberty, and that there is a continuous postpubescent decline in speech learning abilities as measured in terms of perceived foreign accent.

These results have been corroborated and extended in studies which have used similar methodologies with large number of speakers covering AOAs from 2 years well into the third decade of life (Flege & Fletcher 1992, Flege et al. 1999, Yeni-Komshian et al. 2000). Taken together, the results of these studies present direct counterevidence to the CPH with respect to its alleged terminus, and they present indirect counterevidence with respect to the intrinsic component and the proximate causes of the CPH. Concerning the terminus, these studies have shown that a foreign accent is detectable in non-native speakers who started learning their L2 during childhood, several years before the onset of puberty. Contrary to the predictions of the CPH, none of these studies have identified a nonlinearity on the relation between degree of perceived foreign accent and age of learning. On the contrary, this relationship is quite linear even for learners in their third decade of life. This presents a major problem for the CPH because the hypothesized intrinsic component and the proximate cause of the CP is cerebral maturation. However, the documented postpubescent decline in speech learning abilities excludes such an account.

Having established that the phonetic and phonological component of L2 competence is strongly influenced by the age factor, but not in the way and not for the causes as hypothesized by the CPH, it needs to be determined whether the CPH fares more successfully when it comes to the learning of L2 morphosyntax. The findings of three studies will be presented which examined the influence of a number of variables, including age, on the ability to judge L2 English sentences for their grammaticality. Johnson & Newport (1989) is perhaps the most frequently cited study of age effects on the learning of L2 morphosyntax. The authors obtained grammaticality judgements from a group of 46 L1 speakers of Korean and Chinese whose AOA covered the range of 3 to 39 years, and who had resided in the USA between 3 and 26 years. In addition, a group of 23 native English speakers provided baseline data. Johnson & Newport presented the subjects with 276 sentences which were either grammatical examples of 12 rule types of English morphosyntax (e.g., plural, particle movement, yes/no questions), or their ungrammatical countertypes.

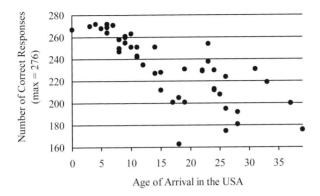

Figure 3: Number of correct responses to 276 grammatical and ungrammatical English sentences by 46 L1 Korean and native Chinese speakers differing in AOA and by 23 L1 English speakers (AOA = 0) in the Johnson & Newport (1989) study. [5]

Figure 3 shows the results of the Johnson & Newport study by plotting the measure of proficiency in L2 morphosyntax (number of correct grammaticality judgments) as a function of AOA. The figure indicates that non-natives who had started to learn English before the age of 8 years exhibited native-like judgment abilities. However, starting at an AOA of 8 years and extending throughout adolescence, AOL and grammatical judgment ability are strongly negatively correlated (Johnson & Newport report r = -.87 for this group of learners), which is consistent with the assumption that the acquisition of L2 morphosyntactic abilities is subject to maturational influences. The adult age group (age 17 and above) performed significantly worse that the younger subjects, and there was no siginificant correlation between AOL and judgment ability for the adult subjects, which suggests that adults' learning of morphosyntax is not influenced by maturational factors. These and other aspects of their study led Johnson & Newport (1989, 60) to conclude that "the results support the conclusion that a critical period for language acquisition extends its effects to second language acquisition".

Until quite recently, Johnson & Newport's interpretation was generally accepted and propagated in reviews (e.g., Pinker 1994) and textbooks (e.g., Lighbown & Spada 1999) as clear evidence for a critical period for L2 acquisition, even though problematic aspects of Johnson & Newport's data analysis had been pointed out by, e.g., Bialystok & Hakuta (1994). However, a recent replication study seriously questions Johnson & Newport's conclusion. Birdsong & Molis (2001) used the same materials and procedure as Johnson & Newport (1989), the only important difference being the subjects' L1, which was Spanish (n = 61) in the Birdsong & Molis study. From the viewpoint of the CPH, a reasonable expectation for learners with an L1 that is typologically more similar to English than Chinese and Korean is that the results would be qualitatively similar (e.g., age effect for young learners, no age effect for adults), but pehaps quantitatively different (e.g., with attenuated age effects). However, this is not at all what Birdsong & Molis found.

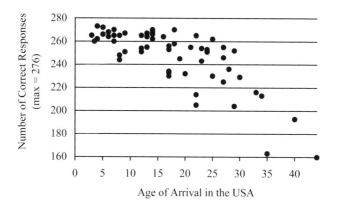

Figure 4: Number of correct responses to 276 grammatical and ungrammatical English sentences by 61 native Spanish speakers differing in AOA in the Birdsong & Molis (2001) study. [6]

Figure 4 (above) shows the results of the Birdsong & Molis (2001) study using the same coordinates as for the Johnson & Newport study in Figure 3. It is immediately apparent that the results for the L1 Spanish speakers of Birdsong & Molis are qualitatively different from those for the L1 Korean and Chinese speakers of Johnson & Newport. Differing from any prediction made by the CPH, and differing from the findings of Johnson & Newport, Birdsong & Molis found NO age effect for those L1 Spanish speakers who had started to learn English between the ages of 3 and 16. (Birdsong & Molis report a nonsignificant negative correlation of r = -.24 between judgment accuracy and age for this younger age group.) The very good performance of this younger age group suggests a ceiling effect, which, in and of itself, does not present countervidence to the CPH because the task may have been much simpler for L1 Spanish speakers than for L1 speakers of Korean or Chinese (see also McDonald 2000). The one aspect of the Birdsong & Molis study that is most damaging for the CPH is that age and judgment accuracy are highly significantly correlated (r = - .69) for learners with an AOA of 17 and above. Clearly, an age effect on the ability to judge L2 sentences for their grammaticality that extends from the second to the fifth decade of life is incompatible with a maturational account.

To sum up so far, the Johnson & Newport and the Birdsong & Molis studies used the same materials and procedures to examine age effects on judgment accuracy for L2 morphosyntactic phenomena. Contrary to the predictions of the CPH, the locus of the age effect seems to depend on the learners' L1: For L1 Chinese and Korean speakers, judgment accuracy is correlated with age up to an AOA of 15 (according to Johnson & Newport) or, in the reanalysis of Johnson & Newport's data by Bialystok and Hakuta (1994), an AOA of 20. For L1 Spanish speakers, on the other hand, judgment accuracy is correlated with age only for adult learners. The conclusion from these two studies, that age effects are a function of the L1 and that they may extend through several decades of adult life, are incompatible with the maturational account of the CPH.

Still more damaging for the CPH are the results of a recent study by Flege, Yeni-Komshian & Liu (1999), which strongly suggests that previous reports of age effects on grammaticality judgment accuracy may have been obtained because variables confounded with AOA were not sufficiently controlled. Flege et al. (1999) examined both pronunciation ability (through ratings of foreign accent) and morphosyntactic knowledge (through a grammaticality judgment task) of 240 L1 Korean speakers of L2 English who had arrived in the US between the ages of 1 and 23, and whose mean length of residence was 15 years at the time of testing.

The results of the foreign accent ratings of this group of learners (and a group of 24 English speakers) were quite similar to those obtained in previous studies by Flege and his collaborators (e.g., Flege & Fletcher 1992, Flege et al. 1995, see Figure 3) with L1 Italian speakers, the only important difference being that all L1 Korean speakers, even those who had arrived in the US at a very early age, received accentedness ratings that differed significantly from the L1 English speakers.

The grammaticality judgment task in the Flege et al. (1999) study used a set of items that was similar to the one used by Johnson & Newport (1989). Interestingly, the test items were designed to allow for the separate assessment of two types morphosyntactic knowledge: rule based knowledge (as e.g. in *Three boys played on the swings in the park* vs. **Three boy played on the swings in the park*) and lexically based knowledge in which the substitution of the verb (e.g., *expect* for *hope*) would turn the ungrammatical sentence into a grammatical sentence (e.g., *The farmers were hoping for rain* vs. **The farmers were hoping rain*).

The overall results for all grammatical test items (testing rule based and lexically based knowledge) agreed closely with the results of Johnson & Newport in that those native Korean speakers who had arrived in the US at a very early age (> 6 years of age) did not differ significantly from the L1 English subjects, whereas all subjects with higher AOAs performed at significantly lower levels. Like Johnson & Newport, Flege et al. (1999) reported a siginificant correlation between AOL and accuracy scores for the younger learners. However, Flege et al. (1999) also reported a significant correlation between AOL and accuracy scores for the older learners (irrespective of whether AOL was above 12 years or above 15 years), which differs from the findings of Johnson & Newport but agrees with those of Birdsong & Molis.

Perhaps the most interesting results of the Flege et al. (1999) study derive from detailed data analyses which the authors conducted to examine whether the age effects would hold up if other variables which are typically confounded with AOA (such of use of the L1 and the L2) were controlled. These analyses revealed that AOA had a significant, indepenent effect on just the foreign accent ratings, not on judgment accuracy for rule based or lexically based aspects of English morphosyntax. Separate analyses of the scores obtained for grammaticality judgments revealed that both types of morphosyntactic knowledge varied as a function of experiential factors. Specifically, knowledge of rule-based aspects of English morphosyntax was influenced significantly and independently by the amount of education in the L2 community (i.e., years of education in the US), whereas knowledge of lexically based aspects of English morphosyntax depended on how much the subjects used their L1 Korean.

Flege et al. (1999, 78) suggested as the conclusion from their study that "age constrains the learning of phonology but not the learning of morphosyntax". This difference across linguistic domains is consistent with the assumptions of a number of psycholinguistic theories which either postulate the use of different neural substrates for phonological versus morphosyntactic processing and learning (e.g., Liberman & Mattingly 1985) and/or the use of different mental modules (e.g., Fodor 1983).

One important question that remains concerns the nature of the age effect on L2 pronunciation ability which has been documented in a number of studies. Two interpretations have been entertained in L2 research: One of these attempts to explain age effects as being due to the passing of a critical period for language learning. However, as summarized above, the studies conducted by Flege and his collaborators (Flege et al. 1995, Flege et al. 1999) were not consistent with the predictions of the CPH. Specifically, there are three important findings of the Flege et al. studies that present counterevidence to the CPH: Flege et al. did not find any nonlinearities in L2 pronunciation ability that would mark the age range of the critical period for the acquisition of L2 phonetics and phonology, Flege et al. found that a foreign accent is detectable even in L2 speakers with very low AOAs, and they found that age effects extend far beyond the age range during which it would make sense to postulate maturational constraints on language learning.

A recent study by Yeni-Komshian, Flege & Liu (2000) was designed to test an alternative account of age effects on L2 pronunciation. Yeni-Komshian et al. hypothesized that "L2 learning ... may be influenced by the interaction ... between the L1 and L2 of bilinguals". The interaction hypothesis predicts that bilinguals, regardless of AOA, will not pronounce their L2 in the same way as monolinguals of the target L2, and it also predicts that the L2 will exert an influence on the production of the L1. The hypothesized mutual influence of L2 on the L1, and of L1 on the L2, was examined by Yeni-Komshian et al. (2000) in the first study that examined in detail not just the effects of age on L2 learning, but also the effects of L2 learning on the L1. The same 240 L1 Korean speakers as in the Flege et al. (1999) study produced simple sentences in L2 English and in L1 Korean. The English sentences were then judged for foreign-accentedness by a panel of 10 monolingual L1 English speakers (who also judged sentences produced by 24 L1 English speakers), and the Korean sentences were likewise judged for foreign-accentedness by a panel of 10 monolingual L1 Korean speakers (who also judged sentences produced by 24 L1 Korean speakers).

Figure 5 presents an overview of the results of the Yeni-Komshian et al. study. The figure shows an inverse relationship between pronunciation proficiency in L1 Korean and L2 English, which is precisely what was predicted by the interaction hypothesis. Except for those learners with an AOA of ca. 10 years, who pronounced English and Korean equally well (but with a detectable foreign accent in both languages), all bilinguals pronounced one language significantly better than the other. Younger learners were better at pronouncing L2 English than L1 Korean, and, inversely, older learners were better at pronouncing L1 Korean than L2 English. The findings present clear evidence against the notion of a balanced bilingual ("The bilingual is not two monolinguals in one person", Grosjean 1989). Rather, linguistic systems interact in the mind of the bilingual, and they do so irrespective of the age of learning.

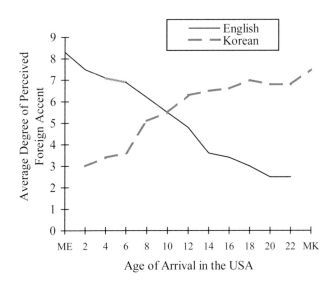

Figure 5: Average degree of perceived foreign accent in L2 English (solid line) and in L1 Korean (broken line) with 9 = "no accent" and 1 = "very strong accent". ME: Monolingual English speakers, MK: Monolingual Korean speakers [7]

4. Conclusion

Based on the brief review of influential and recent studies which have examined age effects on L2 learning, this section will evaluate the claims of the CPH by referring to the characteristics of the CPH as presented in section 1. Specifically, this section will summarize what is known about the onset and the terminus of age effects, about the intrinsic and extrinsic components, about the system that is affected, and about the ultimate and the proximate causes of age effects.

4.1 The onset of a hypothesized CP was not the focus of this review, but it is clear from L1 acquisition research that language acquisition starts before age 2 as originally hypothesized by Lenneberg. Neonates show a prenatally acquired sensitivity to intonation patterns of the ambient language (Mehler, Jusczyk, Lambertz, Halsted, Bertoncini & Amiel-Tison 1988), and parsing skills necessary for the acquisition of the lexicon and morphosyntax emerge during the first year of life (Jusczyk, Hirsh-Pasek, Kemler, Kennedy, Woodward & Piwoz 1992, Jusczyk, Cutler & Redanz 1993), as does the shift from language-general to language-specific speech perception (e.g., Werker & Tees 1984). Clearly, infants are very much engaged in language acquisition long before their second birthday.

4.2 Concerning the terminus of the CPH, none of the studies reviewed here (and, in fact, no other study that has come to my attention) has shown a loss or reduced ability to acquire an L2 at the onset of puberty. What is more, no study has demonstrated the existence of a "critical" period in the sense of dramatic differences in language learning abilities within and outside a hypothetical CP.

For phonetics and phonology, the available evidence suggests that a foreign accent is detectable in very young learners (Flege et al. 1999), which would put the terminus for L2 acquisition at some age in the preschool years. Also, young learners have been shown to pronounce their L1 with a detectable foreign accent, which is not something that the CPH would predict. Age effects on L2 speech have been shown to continue throughout the second and third decade of life, at which age a maturational component can be safely excluded. And, finally, quite a large number of studies on L2 speech (which have not been reviewed in the chapter) now suggest that there is no age limit for speech learning. These studies, which have examined L2 and or second dialect production and/or perception in adults, have shown that "production and perception of speech sounds remains subject to adaptation across the life span" (Munro et al. 1999, 401). Even adults who have long passed an assumed CP for language acquisition can modify their speech as a result of experience with a second dialect or L2. Furthermore, detailed studies of L2 speech learning in adults (e.g., Flege 1987, Bohn & Flege 1992, Flege, Bohn & Jang 1997) strongly suggest that learning and processing mechanisms for speech do not change across the life span. What does change as a function of age are the interactions between the phonetic systems of the language which the bilingual is exposed to. As described in detail in Flege's Speech Learning Model (Flege 1995) and as supported by a large number of studies (e.g., Flege, MacKay & Meador 1999), the nature of these interactions varies as a function of the state of the development of the L1 phonetic system when L2 learning begins. It also bears some note that a number of recent studies have highlighted the importance of language use patterns in shaping the strength of a foreign accent in the L1 or the L2 (e.g., Piske, MacKay & Flege 2001, Meador, Flege & MacKay 2000). For age effects on L2 learning of morphosyntax, the review of the literature has pointed to conflicting findings. However, the available evidence suggests that it is possible for young L2 learners (Johnson & Newport 1989, Flege et al. 1999) and even for postpubescent learners (Birdsong & Molis 2001) to acquire some morphosyntactic skills that do not differ from those of native speakers. The age effects that have been observed affect learners in their second, third, and even fourth decade of life, which is incompatible with the maturational account of the CPH. A recent factor analytic study of L2 morphosyntax learning strongly suggests that previous reports of age effects have been due to the confound of variables. Flege, Yeni-Komshian & Liu (1999) found that only experiential variables contributed independently and significantly to the measures of morphosyntactic knowledge of their subjects. In conclusion, the studies of age (and other) effects on L2 morphosyntactic knowledge reviewed here indicate that this knowledge is not maturationally controlled.

4.3 Concerning the intrinsic (maturational) component, it follows from the above that there is no identifiable biological correlate for the age effects that have been observed. The age effects that have been reported start during childhood and extend throughout the next several decades of life. Even a cursory glance at the literature on neurophysiological maturation will reveal that these age effects cannot be due brain maturation as posited by the CPH.

4.4 As pointed out in Section 1, the CPH does not make claims as to the nature of the extrinsic component. To the best of my knowledge, research that has addressed the question of selective sensitivity of L2 learners to specific types of stimuli as a function of age does not exist. The fairly large body of literature on the perception of native speech sounds does not in any way suggest that age-dependent changes are biologically controlled (for a review, see Bohn 2000).

4.5 Concerning the system that is affected by stimulation during the critical period, the Flege, Yeni-Komshian & Liu (1999) study suggests that unconfounded age effects can only be observed for L2 speech, not for L2 morphosyntax. However, as pointed out before, these age effects are not caused by some kind of neuro-sensory atrophy, there is no sharply defined period of sensitivity (as claimed by the CPH), and the reciprocal effects of L2 experience on L1 pronunciation ability for childhood learners speak against a maturational account (and support an interactionist account) of L2 speech learning.

4.6 The ultimate causes, the functions and benefits of the observed age effects, have not been reviewed. However, the Yeni-Komshian et al. (2000) study as well as other studies which have examined the effect of language use patterns on the proficiency of bilinguals suggest that age effects are ultimately due to the fact bilinguals process the dominant language (which is not necessarily the L1) rapidly and efficiently, which is likely to affect the processing of the nondominant language adversely. As for any potential benefit of being able to process only one (i.e. the dominant) language maximally efficiently, there is no indication in the literature (and indeed no reasonable speculation) why this should be beneficial. Certainly, the ability to process at most one language maximally efficiently does not convey an evolutionary advantage.

4.7 Concerning the proximate causes, the mechanisms that regulate the effects that have been observed, the evidence points against maturational causes and speaks clearly in favor of primarily (if not purely) experiential causes. As reviewed above, the apparently age-related decline in morphosyntactic skills is more appropriately accounted for in terms of experiential factors (with which age is confounded). Concerning L2 speech learning, the well-documented age-related decline in the ability to pronounce an L2 without a foreign accent is best accounted in terms of Flege's Speech Learning Model, which posits that the ability to form new categories for speech sounds diminishes as a function of experience with speech sounds in the dominant language. The experiential account of the effects found receives additional support from neuroimaging studies of bilinguals. Abutalebi, Cappa & Perani (2001, 179) summarize their review of fMRI and PET studies by stating that "consistent results indicate that attained proficiency, and maybe language exposure, are more important than age of acquisition as a determinant of cerebral representation of languages in bilinguals/polyglots".

In conclusion, this review has revealed that the CPH for non-primary acquisition of spoken languages is not tenable. Empirical evidence has shown that claims about the onset and the terminus of the CPH are wrong. There is no indication that a maturational component is involved in the effects that have been observed. The only linguistic system that is independently affected by the age of the learner is L2 speech, but the causes of the age effects are experiential, not maturational. However, just about anything that is known today about age effects in language learning is ultimately due to attempts to test the predictions of the CPH. Even though the CPH must be dismissed, it deserves a fond farewell because it has stimulated such a large body of research on one of the most fascinating questions in psycholinguistics.

Notes

[1] It is, for instance, evidently wrong to claim that there is any period in the life span of humans during which language learning is totally impossible.

2 This mystery is not truly resolved if one considers that research on the speech perception abilities of infants and young children was virtually nonexistent at the time when Lenneberg proposed the CPH in the 1960s.

3 Snow has more recently repeated claims to the same effect, e.g. Snow (1998).

4 Figure 2 is redrawn and converted to a scale with the endpoints of "no foreign accent" (100) and "strongest foreign accent" (0) based on figures in Flege et al. 1995 and Flege 1995. Each data point represents the ratings for 24 speakers, based on 150 ratings (15 sentences x 10 listeners) per speaker.

5 Plotting of the data points in Figure 3 is based on visual inspection of the two panels in Figure 2 of Johnson & Newport (1989).

6 Plotting of the data points in Figure 4 is based on visual inspection of the two panels of Figure 2 in Birdsong & Molis (2001).

7 Plotting of the data points in Figure 6 is based on visual inspection of Figure 1 and Figure 2 in Yeni-Komshian et al. (2000).

References

Abutalebi, J., Cappa, S. F. & Perani, D., 2001, The bilingual brain as revealed by functional neuroimaging. *Bilingualism: Language and Cognition 4*, 179-190.

Bialystok, Ellen & Hakuta, K., 1994, *In other words: The science and psychology of second- language acquisition.* New York, NY: Basic Books.

Birdsong, D. & Molis, M., 2001, On the evidence for maturational constraints in second-language acquisition. *Journal of Memory and Language* 44, 235-249.

Bohn, O.-S., 2000, Linguistic relativity in speech perception: An overview of the influence of language experience on the perception of speech sounds from infancy to adulthood. In: Niemeier, S. & Dirven, R., eds., *Evidence for Linguistic Relativity.* Amsterdam and Philadelphia: J. Benjamins, 1-28.

Bohn, Ocke-Schwen & Flege, James Emil, 1992, The production of new and similar vowels by adult German learners of English. *Studies in Second Language Acquisition* 14, 131-158.

Bongaerts, T., Summeren, C. van, Planken, B. & Schils, E., 1997, Age and ultimate attainment in the pronunciation of a foreign language. *Studies in Second Language Acquisition* 19, 447-465.

Colombo, John, 1982, The critical period concept: Research, methodology, and theoretical issues. *Psychological Bulletin* 91, 260-275.

Curtiss, Susan, Fromkin, Victoria, Krashen, Stephen, Rigier, David & Rigler, Marilyn, 1974, The linguistic development of Genie. *Language* 50, 528-554.

Flege, James Emil, 1987, The production of "new" and "similar" phones in a foreign language: Evidence for the effect of equivalence classification. *Journal of Phonetics* 15, 47-65.

Flege, James Emil, 1995, Second-language speech learning: Theory, findings, and problems. In.: Strange, W., ed., *Speech perception and linguistic experience: Theoretical and methodological issues*. Timonium, MD: York Press, 233-277.

Flege, James Emil, Bohn, Ocke-Schwen & Jang, Sunyoung, 1997, The production and perception of English vowels by native speakers of German, Korean, Mandarin, and Spanish. *Journal of Phonetics* 25, 437-470.

Flege, James Emil & Fletcher, Kathryn L., 1992, Talker and listener effects on degree of perceived foreign accent. *Journal of the Acoustical Society of America* 91, 370-389.

Flege, James Emil, MacKay, Ian R. A. & Meador, Diane, 1999, Native Italian speakers' perception and production of English vowels. *Journal of the Acoustical Society of America* 106, 2973-2987.

Flege, James Emil, Munro, Murray J. & MacKay, Ian R. A., 1995, Factors affecting strength of perceived foreign accent in a second language. *Journal of the Acoustical Society of America* 97, 3125-3134.

Flege, James Emil, Yeni-Komshian, Grace H. & Liu, Serena, 1999, Age constraints on second-language acquisition. *Journal of Memory and Language* 41, 78-104.

Fodor, J., 1983, *The modularity of mind: An essay on faculty psychology*. Cambridge, MA: MIT Press.

Fox, R. W., 1970, Overview and critique of stages and periods in canine development. *Developmental Psychobiology* 4, 37-54.

Grimshaw, G. M., Adelstein, A., Bryden, M. P. & MacKinnon, G. E., 1998, First-language acquisition in adolescence: Evidence for a critical period for verbal language development. *Brain and Language* 63, 237-255.

Grosjean, F., 1989, Neurolinguists beware! The bilingual is not two monolinguals in one person. *Brain and Language* 36, 3-15.

Hurford, J. R., 1991, The evolution of the critical period for language acquisition. *Cognition* 40, 159-201.

Ioup, G., Boustagui, E., Tigi, M. E. & Moselle, M., 1994, Reexamining the critical period hypothesis: A case study of successful adult SLA in a naturalistic environment. *Studies in Second Language Acquisition* 16, 381-411.

Johnson, Jacqueline S. & Newport, Elissa L., 1989, Critical period effects in second language learning: The influence of maturational state on the acquisition of English as a second language. *Cognitive Psychology* 21, 60-99.

Jusczyk, Peter W., Hirsh-Pasek, Kathy, Kemler Nelson, Deborah G., Kennedy, Lori, Woodward, Amanda & Piwoz, Julie, 1992, Perception of acoustic correlates of major phrasal boundaries by young infants. *Cognitive Psychology* 24, 252-293

Jusczyk, Peter W., Cutler, Anne & Redanz, Nancy J., 1993, Infants' preference for the predominant stress patterns of English words. *Child Development* 64, 675-687

Lenneberg, Eric H., 1966, The natural history of language. In: Smith, Frank & Miller, George A., eds., *The genesis of language: A psycholinguistic approach.* Cambridge, MA: MIT Press, 219-252.

Lenneberg, Eric H., 1967, *Biological foundations of Language.* New York, NY: Wiley.

Liberman, A. & Mattingly, I., 1985, The motor theory of speech perception revised. *Cognition* 21, 1-36.

Lightbown, Patsy M. & Spada, Nina, 1999, *How languages are learned.* Oxford, UK: OUP.

Long, Michael H., 1990, Maturational constraints on language development. *Studies in Second Language Acquisition* 12, 251-285.

Major, R. C. & Kim, E., 1996, The Similarity Differential Rate hypothesis. *Language Learning* 46, 465-596.

Mayberry, R. I. & Eichen, E. B., 1991, The long-lasting advantage of learning sign language in childhood: Another look at the critical period for language acquisition. *Journal of Memory and Language* 30, 486-512.

McDonald, Janet L., 2000, Grammaticality judgments in a second language: Influences of age of acquisition and native language. *Applied Psycholinguistics* 21, 395-423

Meador, Diane, Flege, James E. & MacKay, Ian R. A., 2000, Factors affecting the recognition of words in a second language. *Bilingulalism: Language and Cognition* 3, 55-67

Mehler, Jacques, Jusczyk, Peter W., Lambertz, Ghislaine, Halsted, Nilofar, Bertoncini, Josiane, & Amiel-Tison, Claudine, 1988, A precursor of language acquisition in young infants. *Cognition* 29, 143-178

Miller, Joanne L., Kent, Raymond D. & Atal, Bishnu, eds., 1991, *Papers in speech communication: Speech perception.* New York: Acoustical Society of America.

Moltz, H., 1973, Some implications of the critical period hypothesis. *Annals of the New York Academy of Science* 223, 144-146.

Munro, M. J., Derwing, T. M. & Flege, J. E., 1999, Canadians in Alabama: A perceptual study of dialect acquisition in adults. *Journal of Phonetics* 27, 385-403.

Newman, Aaron, Bavelier, Daphne, Corina, David, Jezzard, Peter & Neville, Helen J., 2001, A critical period for right hemisphere recruitment in American Sign Language processing. *Nature Neuroscience* 5, 76-80.

Oyama, Susan, 1978, The sensitive period and comprehension of speech. Working Papers in Bilingualism 16, 1-16. Repr. in: Krashen, Stephen D., Scarcella, Robin C. & Long, Michael H., eds., 1982, *Child-adult differences in second language acquisition.* Rowley, MA: Newbury House, 39-52.

Penfield, W. & Roberts, L., 1959, *Speech and brain mechanisms*. Princeton, NJ: Princeton University Press.

Pinker, Steven, 1994, *The language instinct*. New York, NY: William Morrow.

Piske, Thorsten, MacKay, Ian R. A. & Flege, James E., 2001, Factors affecting degree of foreign accent in an L2: A review. *Journal of Phonetics* 29, 191-215.

Riedl, R., 1979, *Biologie der Erkenntnis: Die stammesgeschichtlichen Grundlagen der Vernunft*. Berlin: Parey.

Snow, C., 1998, Bilingualism and second language acquisition. In: Berko Gleason, J. & Bernstein Ratner, N., eds., *Psycholinguistics*, 453-481.

Snow, Catherine E. & Hoefnagel-Höhle, Marian, 1977, Age differences in the pronunciation of foreign sounds. *Language & Speech* 20, 357-365.

Snow, Catherine E. & Hoefnagel-Höhle, Marian, 1978, The critical period for language acquisition- Evidence from second language learning. *Child Development* 49, 1114-1128.

Snow, Catherine, 1987, Relevance of the notion of a critical period to language acquisition. In: Bornstein, M. H., ed., *Sensitive periods in development: Interdisciplinary perspectives*. Hillsdale, NJ: Erlbaum, 183-210.

Werker, Janet F. & Tees, Richard C., 1984, Cross-language speech perception: evidence for perceptual reorganization during the first year of life. *Infant Behavior and Development* 7, 49-63.

Yeni-Komshian, G. H., Flege, J. E. & Liu, S., 2000, Pronunciation proficiency in first and second languages of Korean-English bilinguals. *Bilingualism: Language and Cognition* 3, 131-149.

Biology, Culture and the Emergence and Elaboration of Symbolization

Chris Sinha

1. Introduction

The human language capacity presents biological and cognitive sciences with a striking paradox, since this capacity is unique, even though its biological, cultural and communicative foundations are in large measure shared with non-human species. It is widely known that humans share around 95% of their genetic material with their closest primate relatives, chimpanzees. We also know, since the publication of the initial results of the human genome project, that the linguistic gulf separating the human species from other closely related species is not correlated with a difference of any substantial order of magnitude in the available quantity of genetic material for directly coding the language capacity. This does not falsify claims for such a direct coding, but should at least give pause for thought.

Language, it is plausibly maintained by anthropologists and other human scientists, is the basis of human cultural transmission and of the construction of human societies as symbolic and symbolically mediated orders. However, it has also been shown that culture is not a specifically human achievement. Culture can minimally be defined as the existence of intra-species group differences in behavioural patterns and repertoires, which are not directly determined by ecological circumstances (such as the availability of particular resources employed in the differing behavioural repertoires), and which are learned and transmitted across generations. On such a definition, there is ample evidence of culture and cultural differences in foraging strategies, tool use and social behaviours in chimpanzees (Whiten *et al.* 1999). Such a

In Search of a Language for the Mind-Brain, ed. Saleemi, Bohn and Gjedde, *The Dolphin* 33 © 2005 by Aarhus University Press, Denmark. ISBN 87 7934 005 9.

definition will also qualify, for example, epigenetically learned intra-species dialect differences between songbird communities as cultural and culturally transmitted behaviour.

Human natural languages are communicative systems, and the primary use of language is to communicate. The extent and nature of the relationship between the communicative functions, and the systemic properties, of natural languages may be disputed, but what cannot be disputed is that language is a vehicle for human communication. Studies of non-human communication systems have revealed not only the ubiquity of communication in the animal world, but also unsuspected complexity in some naturally occurring systems of non-human communication. A now-classic example is the communication system of the vervet monkeys studied by Cheney and Seyfarth (1981). These monkeys employ a system of warning calls in which each of three call-types codes for the presence of a particular predator (snake, eagle, leopard). Animals hearing a call respond with behaviour that is appropriate to the danger posed by the predator: hearing an eagle call, they descend from a tree, hearing a snake call they ascend a tree.

The capacity to use elements of, or corresponding to, the lexicons of human natural languages communicatively is certainly not unique to humans. People have communicated with domestic animals for countless generations. However, non-human animals can do more with human natural languages than respond to simple instructions. When raised in an environment broadly resembling the cultural and communicative settings in which human infants acquire language, bonobos (*Pan paniscus*) can apparently acquire extensive receptive and productive lexicons, use them combinatorially in ways which involve quite complex event characterization, and apparently spontaneously teach such uses to their offspring (Savage-Rumbaugh and Fields, 2000). African grey parrots, when participating in structured communication settings, can also learn extensive vocabularies and employ them for cross-classification of objects according to different object attributes (Pepperberg, 1999).

Given these findings, would it be correct to conclude, as some have, that the human language capacity is, after all, not species unique? Such an argument would hold that the evident continuity we can observe between humans and non-humans in genetic makeup, capacity for culture, and capacity to use language-like signs communicatively, justifies the "gradualist" conclusion that the difference in complexity between human natural languages, and the communication systems and abilities of non-human animals, is non-qualitative. I will present some arguments why this is not the case. My argument will not focus solely or primarily upon the unique grammatical properties of human natural languages, although it is clear that these exist. My argument is rather that, in contrast to non-human *signal systems* of communication, human natural languages are *symbol systems*. The evolutionary transition from signal to symbol usage, and the exo-somatic, culturally-driven elaboration of symbol usage into language, accounts for the unique complexity of human language (including grammar). This emergent complexity, I suggest, has, in the course of evolution co-opted or captured a suite of cognitive capacities that are uniquely developed (but not unique) in humans. There is no contradiction, I am claiming, between recognizing *both* the qualitative uniqueness of human language, *and* the essential continuity between human and non-human neurobiology. After fleshing out my account of the emergence and elaboration of symbolization, I discuss the wider implications of this evolutionary and developmental approach for our understanding of the mind-brain relation in the human species.

The account I offer of the human language capacity is neither nativist nor empiricist, but one based upon *the epigenetic emergence and elaboration of symbolization*. Each of the terms in this delineation of my approach is technical, and all of them are disputed. Hence, I conclude this Introduction by providing definitions of how I shall use the terms *epigenesis* (and epigenetic), *emergence, elaboration* and *symbolization*.

Epigenesis

Contemporary theories of epigenesis in biological and psychological development build upon the pioneering accounts of Waddington (1975) and Piaget (1979). Epigenetic naturalism

(Sinha, 1988) proposes a constructivist account of the interaction between genotype and somatic and extra-somatic environment in organismic development. The claim that such an interaction exists is, as such, trivial and undisputed, since everyone agrees that phenotype is co-determined by genes and environment. There are two particularly important characteristics of epigenesis that I wish to highlight here.

The first is that the role of the environmental factors is *constructive* rather than, or in addition to, being *selective*. Nativist approaches to the developmental interaction between genotype and environment stress the role of specific input either in permitting a developmental process to unfold, or in parametrically selecting a particular variant of development. An example of the former would be phenomena such as "imprinting", where an innate and fully endogenous process of development is "triggered" by an environmental event during a critical developmental window. An example of the latter would be the role hypothesized by generative linguists to be played by typological characteristics of target languages in setting parameters and thereby permitting the child non-inductively to acquire the grammar of the target language (Chomsky, 2000). In neither of these cases does the environmental information add any higher *level of organization* to the genetically coded information. That is to say, the pathway along which the behaviour develops, and its terminal structural complexity, are assumed already to be directly encoded in genes.

By contrast, in epigenesis the developmental pathway and final structure of the behaviour that develops are a consequence as much of the environmental information as of the genetically encoded information. For example, the development of birdsong seems to involve reproduction by imitative epigenetic learning, rather than selection from amongst pre-established alternatives (Marler and Peters, 1982). Fledglings not exposed to a model do develop birdsong, but it is impoverished or unelaborated relative to that of those individuals developing in a normal environment in which models are available.

The second key characteristic of epigenesis is, accordingly, that a genetically specified developmental envelope or window specifies an initial behavioural (or perceptual) repertoire that is subsequently elaborated through experience of a relevant environment. This process of elaboration is directional (see below), and once it has taken place the initial plasticity of the embryonic, or unelaborated, repertoire is lost. A typical example is the development in human infancy of speech sound perception (Bohn, this volume), in which the "universal" initial processor is transformed into a "language-specific" processor in a process that is probably analogous with that of the development of birdsong. We can note here that an epigenetic account of this process differs from a nativist, parameter-setting process inasmuch as no assumption is made that the infant brain is innately equipped with an inventory of all possible natural language phonemes (Characteristic 1, above). Equally, however, it differs from a classical learning account, inasmuch as epigenesis depends upon the elaboration of an initial repertoire which itself is not learned, in a process which cannot be re-run—the initial, unelaborated capacity cannot be re-accessed after the epigenetic developmental process has taken place, as all second language learners come rapidly to realise. In other words, the process of developmental elaboration implies in epigenetic development a transition from relative plasticity and informational openness to relative rigidity and informational closure.

There are two other characteristics of epigenesis that are particularly relevant to human development. One is its neurobiological basis in "Neural Darwinism", the selective stabilization of synaptic connections during ontogenesis (Changeux, 1985). The other is the role of ontogenesis itself in canalizing phylogenesis, through Baldwin effects and genetic assimilation.

Emergence

The "emergentist" hypothesis has received considerable attention recently as an alternative (closely allied with epigenetic theories) to nativism (MacWhinney, 1999). I will use *emergence* to mean, quite widely, the development of new properties and/or levels of organization of behavioural and cognitive systems as a consequence of the operation or cooperation of simpler processes.

Epigenesis is thus a special case of emergence. In this paper, I focus on *symbolization* as a phylogenetically emergent property of communication, as well as upon its epigenetic development in infancy.

Elaboration

By *elaboration* I mean the process whereby development gives rise to increased complexity of organism, behaviour and cognition. Increase in complexity usually involves both form and function. A crucial distinction between Darwinian natural selection and epigenetic development is that the latter, but not the former, *implies* elaboration. In ontogenesis, some instances of elaboration are under more or less direct genetic control, others may be epigenetically driven, and still others may be emergent consequences of the elaboration of subsystems. I will not make a strong distinction between emergence (new properties) and elaboration (greater complexity), which I see as two aspects of the underlying directionality of developmental change. Although it is appropriate to reject teleological explanations for Darwinian evolution, and teleology is not inherent in emergence, teleology is inherent in elaboration as a directional process whose "aim" is the increase in the spatio-temporal extent of the lived and cognized environment.

Symbolization

This is the central topic of this chapter, and I shall restrict myself here to some brief remarks which I shall elaborate below. The epigenetic development of symbolization involves the emergence of symbol usage from communicative signal usage. Whereas a communicative signal can be viewed as an instruction (perhaps coded) to *behave*, the use of symbols involves two emergent properties, *reference* and *construal*. Reference and construal are the basic functional components of the representational function of language, and the development of symbolization is essentially the process of the elaboration of the representational function.

2. Signals and Symbols
Signals and signal sensitivity

Sensitivity to signals is as basic a property of life as the ability to reproduce. All organisms are able to detect signals indicating (indexing) the presence of conditions hospitable to survival (including metabolisation) and reproduction. The more complex the organism, the greater the range of signals to which it is sensitive, and the more complex its behaviours both in response to, and in the active search for, life-relevant signals. So basic is sensitivity to signals to our understanding of life, that we are hesitant to attribute life to self-reproducing biological systems that display this capacity in only a very limited degree, such as prions. In the most general terms life might be defined as the possession by self-organizing systems of the dynamic and mutually influencing emergent properties of reproduction and signal sensitivity, which together provide the basic conditions for the organismic "value system".

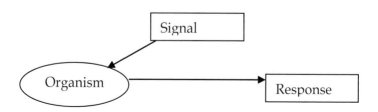

Figure 1: A non-communicative signal

The functional characterization of simple, non-communicative signals is essentially identical to that of the S-R link of classical learning theory, although the responsivity of the organism may be either innately determined or learned. It is diagrammed in Fig. 1.

Signals, in social animals, may also be used to communicate (Fig. 2). Social, communicative signals may be *systematic* and *coded*, that is, the same communicative modality may support a variety of coded instructions (as, we may hypothesize, in the vervet monkey alarm calls studied by Cheney and Sefarth), and it is even possible for them to support a simple "code-syntax". This does not, however, provide any criterion of symbolicity. In the familiar Peircian semiotic categorization, communicative signals, like all signals, are strictly *indexical*, even if they possess internal structure.

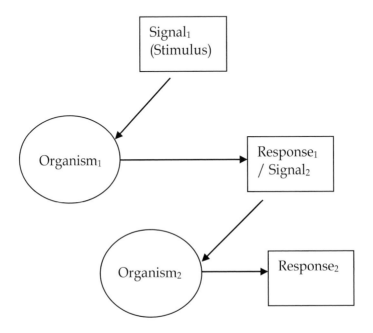

Figure 2: A communicative signal

In the case of communicative signals, the only *necessary* attentional relationships are between the sender and the *stimulus* (signal1), and the receiver and the *behaviour* (signal2) of the sender. The social exchange of communicative signals does not require *intentionality*. The sender does not have to emit the communicative signal purposively, since the signal may simply be an innate or learned response to a stimulus. The receiver does not have to direct its attention either to the sender, or to the original stimulus (signal$_1$) that causes the sender to emit the communicative signal, but only to the communicative signal emitted by the sender. The sender is not signifying or representing a "referent" for the receiver, and no mutual awareness of the cognitive viewpoint of sender and receiver is implied in the exchange.

The social exchange of signals, therefore, does not involve *intersubjectivity*, since there is no shared world of joint attention and reference. Communicative signals are therefore not *conventional*. They do not depend upon a socially shared world of joint reference, and it cannot be said that there is a shared convention of a sign "standing for" a referent or class of referents, since the receiver does not refer the communicative signal to the stimulus causing the sender to emit it. The mechanism underpinning the social exchange of signals is neither intersubjectivity nor social convention, but simple *co-ordination* of individual organismic behaviour (which may, indeed, be complex, arising like many complex behaviours from natural selection).

Symbols and symbolization

Symbols, on the other hand, are truly *conventional*, resting upon shared understanding that the symbol is a token *representing* some referential class, and that the *particular* token represents a *particular* (aspect of) a shared universe of reference and, ultimately, discourse.

Conventional symbol systems are *grounded* in an *intersubjective* meaning-field in which speakers *represent*, through symbolic action, some segment or aspect of reality for hearers. This representational function is unique to symbolization, and is precisely what distinguishes a symbol from a signal. A signal can be regarded as a (possibly coded) *instruction to behave* in a certain way. A symbol, on the other hand directs and guides, not the *behaviour* of the organism(s) receiving the signal, but their *understanding (construal)* or (minimally) their *attention*, with respect to a shared referential situation.

In this way, we can unpack and understand the concept of intentionality, widely understood to be intrinsic to symbol usage, but used in several different ways. For current purposes we can distinguish three meanings (or related aspects) of intentionality:

Intentionality₁. Purposiveness or goal-directedness.
Intentionality₂. Orientation to others as "minded" beings.
Intentionality₃. Directedness to the world, or reference.

I suggest that these different aspects of intentionality are inter-related in symbol usage, which involves the purposive use by a speaker of a symbolic sign to manipulate or direct the mental orientation (construal, or, minimally, attention) of a hearer with respect to an intersubjectively shared aspect of reality *(joint reference)*. N.B. — "speaker" and "hearer" should be understood as producer and interpreter of a symbolic sign in any modality, "reality" should be understood as any aspect of the shared universe of discourse.

It is important to emphasize here that symbolicity is here defined in terms of the semiotic and pragmatic *logic of communicative representation*, not on the specific typology, in the Peircian sense, of the relationship between sign and object (Sinha, 1988). Even an indexical sign, such as simple pointing, provided it is intentionally produced in an intersubjective field of joint reference, can be regarded as a kind of "proto-symbolic" communication, and the intentional and conventional production and comprehension of iconic representations such as maps clearly fall under this pragma-semiotic definition of symbolization.

My claim here is that the first criterion for symbolization, or the existence of a symbolic capacity in any organism or simulated organism, is *reference*. It is, however, important to specify that reference, in this definition, is not a property of signs or symbols "in themselves": symbols refer only by "inheriting" the referential function intended by their users — senders or receivers. The criteriality of reference to true symbolization has been pointed out by several authors, including by John Searle in his famous "Chinese room" thought experiment (Searle, 1980). However, Searle does not locate his argument in an analysis of the logic of communicative representation as grounded in an intersubjective field of *joint reference*, and his account can be criticized for locating referentiality (mysteriously) in the "mind/brain" of the individual speaker/hearer. The account I offer here and elsewhere (Sinha, 1999) is based instead upon a cognitive-functional or *usage-based* analysis of reference as communicative action.

Reference, however, is only the first of two criteria for fully developed, or "true", symbolization. I will claim that joint reference is the criterial basis for the *emergence* of symbolization, while the second criterion, which I shall call following (Langacker, 1987) *construal*, constitutes the set of cognitive operations which underpin the *elaboration* of proto-symbolic joint reference into true symbolization.

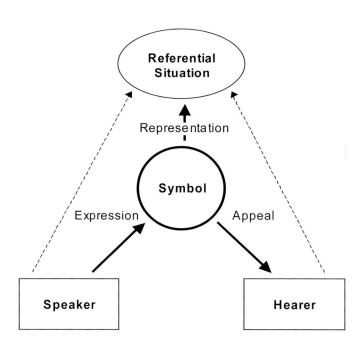

Figure 3: Symbolic communication
(A modified version of Bühler's Organon model of language. Broken lines represent joint attention.)

Simple, unadorned joint reference, such as implied by the production and comprehension of an indexical pointing gesture, serves to orient the attention of the receiver, but does not (in the general case) direct the receiver to any particular *understanding* or *conceptualization* of what is being referred to. The use of a truly symbolic sign, such as a word, however, at the very least implies a categorization of the referent, and may involve complex manipulations of perspective and Figure-Ground relations. This cognitive-functional analysis of symbol usage is essentially the same as that advanced by Karl Bühler (Bühler, 1990 [1934]) in his "Organon theory" of language (Fig. 3).

3. The emergence of symbolization
It is possible to envisage an evolutionary scenario for the phylogenetic emergence of symbolic communication from signal communication. We may hypothesize the following steps:

1. The receiver comes to pay attention to the sender as the source of communicative signals.
2. The sender comes to pay attention to the receiver as a recipient of communicative signals.
3. The receiver comes to pay attention to the evidential reliability of the sender's communicative signals as a source of information, by checking what the sender is paying attention to, or doing.
4. The sender comes to pay attention to the receiver's readiness to reliably act upon the information communicated, by paying attention to what the receiver is paying attention to, or doing.

The first two steps of this sequence do not involve intersubjective "sharing" by the communicating organisms of a referential world, but they do require orientation towards, or social referencing, of a communication partner either as a source of information or as an actor whose behaviour can be influenced. This level of communicative competence is probably widespread amongst mammals, underpinning complex signal-mediated social behaviours. Not only communication between conspecifics, but also communication between humans and domesticated or working animals such as dogs, horses and elephants often seems to involve an understanding on the part of the domesticated animal that the human can both send and receive signals. My young border collie, for example, brings a ball and nuzzles me with it, while looking at me, when she wants to play (an instance of Step 2 above). This can be considered an elementary instance of Communicative Intentionality, in the sense that the dog is able to treat communication as a means to indirectly achieve goal directed action (Intentionality$_1$).

A communicative signal indexing a non-communicative intention (such as a wish to engage in play, grooming, or any other social behaviour) often has its origins in an initiatory segment of the behaviour, which may be abbreviated or stylized in shifting its status from "just behaviour" to signal. It is the understanding by each of the communication partners that the other can both send and receive such signals that constitutes the mastery of Steps 1 and 2 above. Communication, with the achievement of Steps 1 and 2, remains strictly signal-based, but it implies the establishment of a first or primary level of intersubjectivity, consisting of a recognition by each communication partner of the other as a communication partner, and the recognition by each partner of the other as an agent capable of acting as initiator or mediator of goal directed action.

In phylogenesis, then, the basis of intersubjectivity is (I hypothesize) constructed through the mediation of goal directed social behaviours by signals, and the understanding of the communicative partner as a potential agent. The ontogenesis of intersubjectivity in humans follows a different route: primary intersubjectivity appears to be innate (Fig. 4).

Caretakers (usually mothers) and infants engage from a very early age in episodes of "communication" in which the bodily movements, facial expressions and vocalizations of the two participants provide the signals necessary for the maintenance of the communicative channel or intersubjective "we" formed by the dyad. The real time temporal meshing by the mother of her actions with those of the baby is of fundamental importance to the maintenance of intersubjectivity (Trevarthen and Hubley, 1978), indicating the emergence of a psychologically real "ontology of the social".

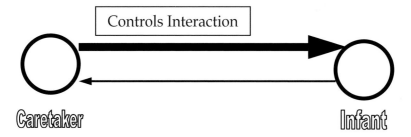

Figure 4: Primary Intersubjectivity
(Caretaker-neonate interaction from 3 weeks.)

In taking Steps 3 and 4, the sender and/or receiver develop the capacity to understand that a signal indexes an intention, rather than the action intended. With this, the possibility is opened for deception and suspicion regarding intentions. The most basic level of understanding of the communicative partner not just as a potential agent, but as an experiential subject within the intersubjective field, is the ability to follow gaze, as evidenced by human infants form about 6 mo. of age (Butterworth and Jarrett, 1991) and by a number of other species (Fig. 5).

Gaze following allows the receiver to monitor the activity and attention of the communicative partner, but not to manipulate as sender the attention of the receiver to a specific object or referent. The existence of spontaneous productive pointing even in our closest primate relatives is disputed, and probably occurs in the wild only intermittently, unsystematically and unreliably.

The ontogenetic development of this capacity has been well researched in the past couple of decades. From around nine or ten months of age human infants "begin to engage with adults in relatively extended bouts of joint attention to objects ... In these triadic interactions infants actively co-ordinate their visual attention to person and object, for example by looking to an adult periodically as the two of them play together with a toy, or by following the adults gaze. Infants also become capable at this age of intentionally communicating to adults their desire to obtain an object or to share attention to an object, usually through non-linguistic gestures such as pointing or showing, often accompanied by gaze alternation between object and person." (Tomasello, 1996: 310). The achievement of joint reference in human infancy establishes the "referential triangle" (Fig. 6), also referred to as "secondary intersubjectivity" (Trevarthen and Hubley, 1978).

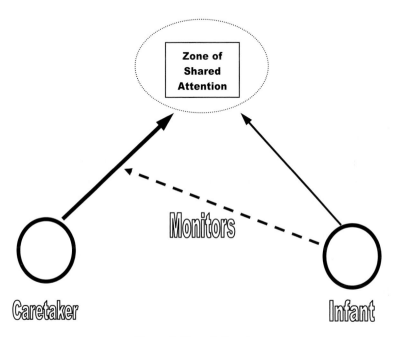

Figure 5: Gaze following
(Human infants 6 mo., chimps, dolphins, sheepdogs.)

The emergence of the "referential triangle" marks the emergence of the first criterion for symbol usage, namely reference in intersubjective field. From this point until about 14 mo. of age, infants increasingly mediate the manipulation of the field of joint attention by manipulating objects in give-and-take routines, and early in the second year of life they begin to demonstrate active mastery of the conventional or canonical usage of objects in play situations, their usage of such objects being dominated by the cultural specification of conventional

function until well into the third year of life (Sinha, 1988; Sinha
and Jensen de López, 2000). It seems to be a well-founded
conclusion that by early in the second year of life, the basic
foundations of symbolization in intersubjectivity, and in an
understanding of conventionality, have been laid.

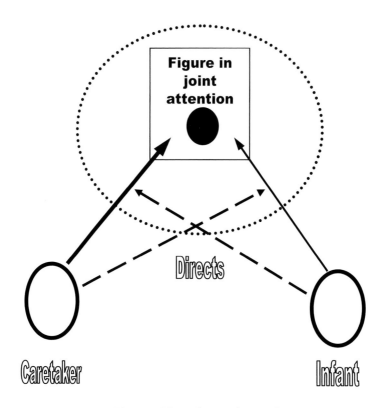

Figure 6: The referential triangle
(Joint reference at 9-10 mo. in human infancy, chimps (?), bonobos.)

4. The elaboration of symbolic representation

The classical definition of the sign—*aliquid stat pro aliquo*—
specifies very clearly that fully developed symbol usage depends
upon the mastery of symbolic material, and in the case of natural
languages, a symbolic system. Formalist theories in cognitive
science, influenced by generative linguistics, identify the criterion

of fully-developed symbolization with the productive and combinatorial properties of language-like symbol systems, and it is often claimed that the structural and systemic properties of such conventional systems are *arbitrary* with respect to their functional and cognitive properties.

Such approaches overlook the fundamental *motivation* of the elaboration of conventionalized symbol usage by cognitive and functional factors, and the basis of this motivation in the communicative requirement for *flexible construal* of referential situations.

The notion of construal (Langacker, 1987) can be simply illustrated by example. Any referential situation which requires characterization in terms of the relationships obtaining between more than one entity may so be characterized in more than one way. I can say, for example, that the cup is on the saucer, or that the saucer is under the cup. In the first case, the cup is the Figure (or Trajector), and the saucer the Ground (or Landmark) in relation to which the location of the cup is specified. In the second case, these cognitive roles are reversed. Similarly, the lexicalization "father of" represents the same relationship as the lexicalization "child of", but the two lexicalizations are perspectivized or profiled from different points of view.

Without going into details, we can say that the *elaboration* of symbolization into grammar involves the mastery of natural language subsystems that functionally permit flexible construal, and that this is the essential cognitive-functional motivation underlying the evolution and acquisition of language by humans.

Linguistic complexity is, on this view, the structural consequence of the operation of cognitive-functional principles for motivating construction that have been extensively studied in recent years by cognitive and functional linguists.

The main principles of motivation are:

Iconicity and Analogy (including specific motivations by: *embodiment, image schematization, force dynamics, cultural schematization*)
Figure-Ground articulation.
Topic-Comment articulation.

Perspective and Profiling.

Fig. 7 diagrams the semiotic structure resulting from the elaboration of joint reference into linguistic (symbolic) conceptualization via the mastery of symbolic vehicles enabling flexible construal. Fig. 7 is also to be understood as an elaboration, based upon cognitive-functional linguistic principles, of the Organon-model diagrammed in Fig. 3. In Fig. 7, the broken lines no longer represent merely joint attention, but the mutual construal of a referential situation by speaker and hearer within an intersubjectively shared universe of discourse.

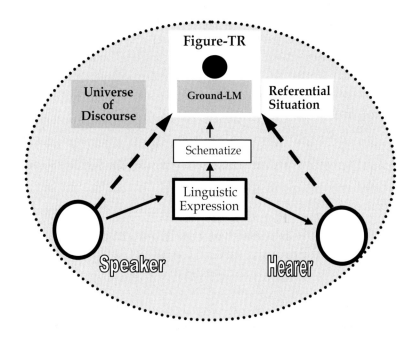

Figure 7: Semiotic mediation
(Linguistic conceptualization as symbolic construal.)

5. Infancy, evolution and culture

There is a common epigenetic logic to the phylogenetic and ontogenetic development of symbolization. The logic is one of process, from signals to the emergence and elaboration of symbols. This logic involves the following sub-processes, which significantly temporally overlap but which emerge in the order of mentioned below:

> *Intentionality and intersubjectivity.*
> *Conventionalizaton based in intersubjectivity.*
> *Structural elaboration yielding flexible construal.*

It should be emphasized that there is no claim here that ontogenesis necessarily involves, within any one of these processes, the recapitulation in ontogenesis of stages passed through in phylogenesis. Although we can observe analogous phenomena in (for example) the communication strategies of human children and non-human primates, there are also many differences. We have seen, for example, that primary intersubjectivity appears to be innate in humans, while it is hypothesized to be emergent in phylogenesis from the mediation by communicative signals of non-communicative social behaviours. Similarly, although it is plausible to draw very general analogies in terms of principles of motivation between grammaticalization processes in historical language change, and the acquisition by the child of the constructional resources of grammar, the stages and strategies characterizing each of these processes are very different (Slobin, 1997).

Commonalities in developmental logic do not, therefore, imply that ontogenesis recapitulates phylogenesis. Instead, I would like to suggest that ontogenesis—and in particular the ecological niche of infancy—played a crucial role in the evolutionary development of the human symbolic capacity. Human infants, as has often been pointed out, are extraordinarily well adapted to the demands of enculturation and the acquisition of symbolic communication (Tomasello, 1999). I would suggest that this is because, once established, the emergent social ontology of intersubjectivity and conventionalization sets up new parameters for the selection of context-sensitive and socially situated learning processes, rather than "content-dedicated" cognitive mechanisms. In such an evolutionary process, a major role might have been played by "Baldwin effects" (genetic assimilation) that lend a teleological directionality to natural selection through the developmental mimesis of the inherent teleology of the elaboration of symbolic communication (see Section 1).

Such an account is quite different from not only modularity theories of language, but the entire logic of currently popular "evolutionary psychology" narratives of origin. The traditional and still-dominant view of evolution and development is one in which the development of "higher" levels of organization is dependent upon prior developments in "lower" levels of organization. In particular, the priority of individual organismic properties is assumed to carry over from the level at which natural selection occurs to the level of psychological processes. Even if the existence of emergent, higher level (socio-cultural) properties is conceded, the autonomy of these levels is continually undermined by theories that reduce them to the causal properties of supposedly "more basic" levels.

An alternative view, consistent with recent findings in cultural primatology, stresses the emergence of the first foundation of symbolization and language not in individual organismic modules, but in the quintessentially social realm of intersubjectivity and normativity (including conventionalization).

According to such an alternative account, the emergence of what we can designate, in general terms, an emergent socio-cultural level of organization, set the stage for subsequent genetic selection (and epigenetic development)—rather than the other way round. The difference between the traditional and the alternative views is diagrammed in Fig. 8.

Fig. 8 is not intended to model actual evolutionary and developmental processes, but to illustrate different ways of conceptualizing directions of causality and dependency between "levels of analysis". In the traditional view, the "biological" causes (or is identical with) the "psychological", these two levels together being referred to as the "Mind/Brain." The (uniquely?)

human Mind/Brain, the "organ of cognition", in turn causes the emergence of the "social" level. Because each higher level is dependent upon the lower ones, the traditional view lends itself readily to epiphenomenal and reductionist interpretations of the higher levels.

In the alternative view, the socio-cultural level is emergent from the biological one, relatively autonomously from (but acting back upon by "capturing") the "psychological" level (which is non-autonomously emergent from the biological level). In this view, there is no "Mind/Brain", since "mind" is co-constituted by the biological and social.

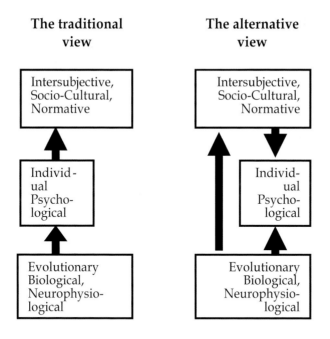

Figure 8: Two views of evolution and development

Although the illustration is deliberately simplistic (to avoid the confusing device of bidirectional "interaction arrows"), it is drawn so as to emphasize the resistance of the alternative view to the kind of reductionist interpretations which are the inevitable accompaniment of the traditional view.

6. Reflections on the mind and the brain

The "Mind/Brain" is the modern, neuro-computational avatar of the Cartesian "I." It inherits the latter's universal, rationalist and individualist character, but suggests (by dint of typographic convention) that the dualism of its original has been overcome: the mind is the brain. In quite which way the mind "is" the brain is disputed by eliminativists, functionalists, and other philosophers of mind, but the identity-mapping signalled by the typography is agreed on by an otherwise diverse group of thinkers. A "clear and distinct idea" the "Mind/Brain" seems not to be, but such is the power of the Cartesian paradigm that this hybrid creature seems almost impossible to evade, and an alternative difficult to formulate. I conclude this chapter by unpacking as simply as possible the contradiction inherent in the notion of the "Mind/Brain."

The brain is an organ of an individual organism. Your brain and my brain are different and non-interchangeable parts of each of our separate bodies: we cannot share our brains. It is seductively easy to assume that the mind is just the cognitive reflex or counterpart of this individual organ. After all, it is the very fact that my thoughts present themselves to me as *mine*, and mine alone (you cannot "read my mind" any more than you can share my brain), that provided Descartes with the foundation of his method of doubt.

Thoughts, however, unlike brains, *can* (if the thinker so chooses) be shared (most obviously, through the medium of language). Much of our ordinary discourse about communication employs a "conduit metaphor" (Reddy, 1978) in which utterances are conduits or containers by means of which thoughts are transferred from one individual mind to another. Given this picture of linguistic communication—which can be traced back at least to Aristotle—it is easy to envisage brains as somehow "containing" minds, in the same way that linguistic expressions "contain" thoughts. The "Mind/Brain" tends then to be seen as the "mental/physical" organ of thought, just as in traditional linguistics the linguistic sign unites the concept (content) with its physical-acoustic expression.

What is wrong with this picture of the "mind/brain" is that it assumes a pre-existing individual mind which only secondarily, *via* a kind of *ur*-Social Contract, reaches out to make contact with "Other Minds" – an assumption which carries in its train a host of well-rehearsed philosophical snares and diversions which eventuate, against everyone's better intentions and intuitions, in a despairing (or, even worse, triumphantly proclaimed) neural solipsism.

There is an alternative. The alternative is to view the human mind as grounded in an intersubjectively shared, ecologically real world: a world populated and animated by artefacts, symbols, conventions, and intersubjectively shared meanings. This alternative view is wholeheartedly materialist, and is fully committed to understanding the biological foundations of human cognition. It differs from the neo-Cartesian narrative of the "mind/brain" in that it embraces the materiality of the *products* of human cognition, and their formative role in the constitution of the developing human organism, as well as the materiality of the developmental, organismic processes which support the enculturation and self-enculturation of human beings.

As yet, we know too little to accept or reject hypotheses regarding the innateness of a specifically syntactic component of the human language faculty. I certainly would not wish to reject the possibility that the epigenetic processes selected for in human evolution include a predisposition for learning language, although this does not necessarily imply that any such predisposition is or was "dedicated" from the start exclusively to language. I would, however, venture to predict that, in the not too distant future, currently fashionable versions of evolutionary psychology, predicated upon a once-and-for-all fixing of the human mind in adaptations to hypothesized proto-hominid environmental conditions, will seem as quaint and outdated as behaviourist reductions of human cognition to stimulus (signal) – response contingencies.

The human brain is not infinitely plastic, but nor is it a mere Swiss-Army-Knife assemblage of primordial content-dedicated modules. Plasticity is real and, though cumulatively constrained by epigenetic development and experience, it is manifest throughout the human lifespan. Environments do not hold a magic key to the "engineering of the human soul", but this does not have to lead to the conclusion that human agency is reducible to, and negated by, a "pre-programmed" biology. What we make, and have made, has made and does make *us* human. To reduce the totality of human cognition, feeling, and behaviour to an invariant set of once-adaptive but outlived mechanisms violates our ethical and political sense of our own freedom, responsibility, and accountability. We need to cultivate such a sensibility. A science of mind that harmonizes with this ethical need is plausible, possible and necessary.

References

Bühler, K. (1990 [1934]) Theory of Language: The Representational Function of Language. Amsterdam: John Benjamins.

Butterworth, G. & N. Jarrett (1991) What minds have in common is space: spatial mechanisms serving joint visual attention in infancy. British Journal of Developmental Psychology 9. 55-72.

Changeux, J.-P. (1985) Neuronal Man: The Biology of Mind. Oxford: Oxford Uinversity Press.

Cheney, D.L. & Seyfarth, R.M. (1981) Selective forces affecting the predator alarm calls of vervet monkeys. Behaviour 76: 25-61.

Chomsky, N. (2000) The Architecture of Language (eds. N. Mukherji, B.N. Patnaik & R.K. Agnihotri). New Delhi: Oxford University Press.

Langacker, R.W. (1987) Foundations of Cognitive Grammar Vol. 1, Theoretical Prerequisites. Stanford: Stanford University Press.

MacWhinney, B. (1999) (Ed.) The Emergence of Language. Mahwah, NJ: Lawrence Earlbaum.

Marler, P. & Peters, S. (1982) Developmental overproduction and selective attrition: Newe processes in the epigenesis of birdsong. Developmental Psychobiology 15: 369-378.

Pepperberg, I. (1999) The Alex Studies. Cambridge, MA: Harvard University Press.

Piaget, J. (1979) Behaviour and Evolution. London: Routledge and Kegan Paul.

Reddy, M. (1978) The conduit metaphor: A case of frame conflict in our language about language. In A. Ortony (ed.) Metaphor and Thought. Cambridge: Cambridge University Press.

Savage-Rumbaugh, E.S. & Fields, W.M. (2000) Linguistic, cultural and cognitive capacities of bonobos (Pan paniscus). Culture and Psychology 6: 131-153.

Searle, J.R. (1980) Minds, brains and programs. Behavioral and Brain Sciences 3. 417-424.

Sinha, C. (1988) Language and Representation: A Socio-Naturalistic Approach to Human Development. Hemel Hempstead: Harvester-Wheatsheaf.

Sinha, C. (1999) Grounding, mapping and acts of meaning. In Theo Janssen, Gisela Redeker (Eds.) Cognitive Linguistics: Foundations, Scope and Methodology. Berlin: Mouton de Gruyter.

Sinha, C. & Jensen de López, K. (2000) Language, culture and the embodiment of spatial cognition. Cognitive Linguistics 11, 17-41.

Slobin, D.I. (1997) The origins of grammaticizable notions: beyond the individual mind. In Dan I. Slobin (Ed.) The Crosslinguistic Study of Language Acquisition Vol. 5: Expamding the Contexts. Mahwah, N.J.: Lawrence Earlbaum Associates.

Tomasello, M. (1996) The child's contribution to culture: A commentary on Toomela. Culture and Psychology 2: 307-318.

Tomasello, M. (1999) The Cultural Origins of Human Cognition. Cambridge, MA: Harvard University Press.

Trevarthen, C. & P. Hubley (1978) Secondary intersubjectivity: confidence, confiding and acts of meaning in the first year In A. Lock (Ed.) Action, Gesture and Symbol: the emergence of language. London: Academic Press.

Waddington, C.H. (1975) The Evolution of an Evolutionist. Edinburgh: Edinburgh University Press.

Whiten, A., J. Goodall, W.C. McGrew, T. Nishida, V. Reynolds, Y. Sugiyama, C.E.G. Tutin, R.W. Wrangham & C. Boesch (1999). Cultures and chimpanzees. Nature 399: 682-685.

A Simple Vocabulary for Planning and Deliberation: Risk, Complexity and Knightian Uncertainty

Jamsheed Shorish

Introduction

Why do individuals deliberate before making a decision? What is the reason that humans, collectively as a species, are able to weigh different options and evaluate or measure the effect of their actions to select the 'best' one? What is the 'act of deliberation' and why does it separate us from other species which appear to act solely upon 'instinct'?

In a sense the questions posed are all incomplete: our conventional wisdom, for example, points to our consciousness or 'thought' as the prerequisite for consideration of various alternatives, or deliberation, and hence the question might perhaps be better posed as dealing with consciousness in general. At the same time, it is reasonable to imagine a situation in which 'active' thought or consciousness is not used as a predicate for action at all. A stimulus-response mechanism, or a set of instinctive responses, does not fit into the framework of deliberation or thinking about the action – the action is simply performed according to the stimulus. In addition, thought may simply have a passive role, i.e. the focus of thought is not to generate an action (e.g. imagination or daydreaming). Consciousness and thought are perhaps too general to be used as a starting point for understanding deliberation.

It would probably not be far wrong to assume that there is some consensus about what it means to 'think things over' before committing to an action, i.e. to deliberate. We will apply a more formal (yet restrictive) definition of deliberation in what follows,

In Search of a Language for the Mind-Brain, ed. Saleemi, Bohn and Gjedde, *The Dolphin* 33 © 2005 by Aarhus University Press, Denmark. ISBN 87 7934 005 9.

in order to provide a simple groundwork for a *vocabulary* to discuss deliberation. This vocabulary will be based upon three determinants (by no means exhaustive) which form key components of the concept and action of deliberation: risk, uncertainty, and complexity. Each of these determinants provides a method of measuring degrees of deliberation, at least at the heuristic level given here. Constructing this vocabulary may provide common ground for discussing the act of deliberation, its causes and implications, and its distinct relationship from the act of instinctive response.

In constructing this vocabulary the primary vehicle for analysis is a collection of simple applications from formal models of decision-making in economics and financial economics. We use these models both to set the stage for what deliberation and planning (as the outcome of deliberation) are, and also to explore the foundations of deliberation in humans. It is not intended to promote any one decision-theoretic school of thought over any other, even if the economic examples may owe more to e.g. Arrow (1953), Savage (1954) and Debreu (1959) than to von Neumann and Morgenstern (1944). Rather, the focus is to highlight the usefulness of thinking about a decision problem 'in economic terms' without being weighed down by the complicated technical language in which such problems are usually framed. To this end I have attempted to keep the following observation of Alfred Marshall in mind:

> '[Y]et it seems doubtful whether any one spends his time well in reading lengthy translations of economic doctrines into mathematics, that have not been made by himself.' (1878, ix-x)

Heedful of this observation, three broad determinants of deliberation and planning may be defined. First and most important, a comparison of the relative risk between alternatives may involve a 'weighing' of alternatives under a known (or assumed) description of uncertainty in the environment. This weighing is a deliberative action. In addition, for those environments where the uncertainty itself cannot be adequately described, Knightian uncertainty may be a large factor in constructing alternative plans where the possible outcomes may not even be defined. And finally, computational complexity may be a non-trivial determinant of deliberation and planning, especially since finding the mapping between one's actions and the resultant outcomes may be a large and involved task. These three determinants serve as a rough base for building a vocabulary discussing how individuals form plans, and how they deliberate over alternatives — in the last part of the monograph we show how these simple determinants may be used to visualize deliberation time in a heuristic fashion.

1. Planning

The concept of a 'plan' does not usually need a definition — it is typically self-evident. But below the conceptual level it is prudent to place at least one definition upon this concept, as it will be useful in drawing parallels between human deliberation and economic decision-making (to be made shortly). For this reason we define a plan in the following manner:

> A **plan** is a collection of feasible actions to be taken over a given time period, in which one or more actions correspond to each state that an individual finds, or will find, his- or herself in during the given time period, such that the actions are mutually consistent.

Note that to keep the level of technical formalism to a minimum the definition is presented in an informal fashion — but formal definitions of 'state', 'time', '(feasible) actions', and 'mutually consistent' are all possible, and many such definitions (not necessarily in agreement with each other!) have been used extensively in the economics and finance literature, as well as the decision sciences literature.

A plan, then, requires several components, without any of which it would cease to be a plan. Consider the following simple examples:

1. "If it rains, I will carry an umbrella. If it is not raining, but is expected to rain today, I will carry an umbrella. If it is not raining and rain is not expected then I will not carry an umbrella."
2. "I cannot teleport. I do not have 25 trillion dollars. If it rains, I will teleport to Mars. If it is not raining, but is expected to rain today, I will donate 25 trillion dollars to the World Wildlife Fund. If it is not raining and rain is not expected then I will not carry an umbrella."
3. "If it is raining I will carry an umbrella. If it is raining I will not carry an umbrella."
4. "Just in case Martians come to my door to watch the Super Bowl, I will purchase an extra case of beer. If Martians are allergic to beer, I will give them umbrellas."

Using the earlier definition the first and last examples correspond to plans, while the second and third do not. The second example violates the feasibility of the actions under consideration—indeed the actions of teleportation and giving a huge sum of money are ruled out by the initial state (note in passing that an *attempt* is a feasible action—it is not the feasibility of a final action which is considered here, but only whether or not the mapping yields a feasible attempt). The third example violates the consistency of a plan, as the same state will lead to two contradictory actions which are mutually exclusive.

The *mapping* between state(s) and feasible action(s), such that the resulting collection of actions is mutually consistent, is what characterizes the formation of a plan. Humans have the ability to recognize states of the world, in the past, present and future. They have the ability to link states of the world to actions that occur. Is this sufficient to define a plan? Consider the following:

"If the rabbit runs across the field, the dog will chase it. If the dog sees a piece of meat, the dog will try to eat it. If the cat smells a dog, the cat will hide."

Are these examples of plans? Most people would not categorize such behavior on the part of animals as plans, but rather as instinct. What is the difference between the two? One possible distinction might be that:

Instinct maps a state to one and only one action. If the state should reoccur, all other things equal, precisely the same action will be performed as before.

I will not attempt to delve any deeper into a definition of instinct (or 'evolved psychological mechanisms'—for one viewpoint see e.g. Crawford and Krebs 1998). The issue here is simply (and rather coarsely) to highlight the fact that human beings often consider a *collection* of actions for each unique state, while animals—acting under instinct—appear to consider only one. Another way to put this would be in terms of states themselves: for animals there is a sharp distinction between primary and secondary states—the primary state is usually the current state ("what's going on right now"), while the secondary state is the previous state ("what just happened before"). The action taken is usually conditional upon the primary state *alone*. Future states are considered after the current state actions are completed, i.e. a future state only gains attention once it becomes a primary state, i.e. once it attains immediacy. It would appear that the purpose of instinct is to attempt to provide the most desired future state with the least amount of deliberation time (e.g., to maximize the chances of survival in a hostile encounter, when to delay may mean injury or death). In such an environment, the minimization of deliberation time is achieved by drastically reducing the set of states which an action is linked to, or conditioned upon.

For humans, on the other hand, the distinction between primary and secondary states, or even states in general, is often undefined. The current state, collections of previous states, and even expectations about future states are all weighed and assessed, often simultaneously, to arrive at an action. Indeed, it would appear that people often weigh many different states in an incredibly complex fashion, so that two different people, faced with apparently the same collection of states, end up taking different actions. The primacy, or hierarchy, of states (if any) is thus much more idiosyncratic for humans than for a given species of animal.

It must be stressed that any hidden states, which cannot be observed and hence not conditioned upon, are not assumed to be the focus of this difference of action. If they were, then the simple distinction between plan and instinct shown here would vanish. In this idealized framework, then, we presume that hidden states are not the sole determinant of heterogeneity of action, and will not discuss the effects of 'initial conditions' upon the mapping between states and actions.

2. Causality and Deliberation

Planning as defined requires a time horizon, a collection of states, and a feasible collection of actions which do not contradict each other, such that each state carries with it perhaps several feasible actions. But why do such plans exist? Why not remain content with e.g. 'see meat-eat meat' type of responses, which all humans might simply carry around 'in the back of the mind'? Surely deliberation is (at the very least) expensive in terms of the time lost deliberating—in the case of instinctive survival responses, this lost time might even be fatal for the individual.

One suggestion is that it is the recognition of *causality* which has allowed humans to move beyond instinct or stimulus response, toward developing plans. Instinct and causality appear to be too closely intertwined at the moment of execution of an action to allow causality between states to be recognized. If an individual does recognize the causality between states which is brought about by an action, i.e. that in such-and-such a state, a particular action brings about (or is at least consistent with) such-and-such a result, then this information can be coded into a plan. A simple instinctive response, by contrast, has the causality embedded within it, and does not allow for this sort of 'introspection'.[1]

One might argue that a recognition of causality must be one of the consequences of self-consciousness—if one has an active measure of what constitutes 'I' or 'myself' then perhaps it is easier to 'see the forest for the trees' and infer *personal* consequences of an action. In this case, plans are not only a consequence of consciousness, but are also derived from a combination of factors involving learning from others, observation of the environment, trial-and-error, and perhaps extensions of instinctive response. In general, however, planning is an *introspective* action. The individual posits a model of reality in which states, actions and consequences are identified, and the possible outcomes from various alternatives are 'weighed' until an 'optimal' plan is chosen. It is the weighing of alternative plans that truly separates deliberation from instinct. Instinctive responses are (as defined above) single-valued, one-to-one mappings between states and actions. By contrast, plans are 'multiple-valued maps' (mathematically speaking, they are correspondences) between various possible states and actions. They are *contingencies*, in that they specify a course of action in case certain future states actually obtain.

Is there a way in which 'degrees' of deliberation or introspection may be introduced into this specification of plans, as introspection over contingencies? To put it another way, in what sense is the process of deliberation *measurable*? As we have argued that an implication of consciousness and self-awareness is planning behavior, any measurement of deliberation may then itself be used as a descriptive lexicon for traits of consciousness.

Let us suppose that the instinctive actions available to us as individuals are somehow 'hard-wired' in the brain, and then expressed in the mind. They are passed down to us generation after generation, and are part of the evolution of our genetic makeup. By contrast, the most natural place for planning and deliberation to appear would be the mind itself, the conscious part of the brain that contains self-awareness. It would appear that one trait is perhaps more fundamental than the other—instincts are often referred to as our 'primitive' responses, which are 'rash' or 'impulsive', while deliberation is the product of a 'thoughtful', a 'cautious' or even a 'rational' mind. As we have argued to this point, it would appear that although instincts are a very limited sort of plan, 'real' plans are far richer, more complicated instruments for undertaking decisions.

3. Measuring Deliberation

Deliberation consists of the time taken, or 'thought devoted' to the resolution of a problem or attainment of a goal, before the action used to resolve the problem or attain the goal is actually implemented. The problem or goal is usually stated in the form of a plan as we have defined it. 'Which car should I buy with the money I have?' 'Will I sue or won't I?' 'Should I bring children into this world?' are all examples of goals or problems whose resolution or attainment depends upon a plan. The states may not be well-identified in such problems (to be addressed shortly) but the action mappings usually are. The 'weight functions' for alternative plans, however defined, often resolve themselves into emotional content. One plan 'feels better' than another, or 'feels right'. Humans never seem to judge even the simplest plans in a fully objective light—the slightest variation between two possible plans seems to lead to a different emotive content for each. Planning, and the 'rational' art of deliberation that goes with it, does not appear to stray far from emotive content when the weighing of alternative outcomes is considered.

Such emotive weights, however derived, could upon first blush allow plans to be evaluated on a case-by-case basis over states of the world that are not known yet. In this way, emotive weights could be used as a measurement of deliberation, using a subjective measure of 'feel'. This may seem reasonable since plans are usually made over contingencies (which haven't happened yet, or which we don't know are going to happen with any certainty). But note that simply processing several plans under uncertainty, and then ranking them in terms of desirability, is not enough to invoke meaningful emotive content. Everyone appears to have moments of indecision, in which alternative plans appear equally suitable. Moreover, such moments are usually not regarded in a completely objective fashion. Moments of indecision are often accompanied by feelings of frustration, panic, or 'being under pressure' to make a decision. The emotive weight function short-circuits in these cases, and using a degree of emotion as a measurement of deliberation may not be viable.

Thus one may wish to turn elsewhere for a measurement of deliberation, and as plans involve decisions under uncertainty it would seem natural to seek parallels within decision theory. In order to examine this approach in detail, it may be useful at this point to examine one particular area in which decision theory is used throughout the entire discipline: economics (and technically speaking its sister discipline, financial economics or finance). In economics, plans are specified in much the same way as defined above — as mappings between states and actions, which result in a consequence or outcome. In canonical models, uncertainty is usually addressed by specifying all the possible states which might occur, and then the relative likelihood of arriving at any one state (were the initial circumstances to be repeated a great number of times). Indeed, much of economic theory is devoted to taking a small slice of the 'state space', the collection of possible states, and attempting to model individual decision-making as we have defined it here — as a sequence of mutually consistent feasible actions forming a plan which, when compared with any alternative plan, is selected according to some criteria of 'best'.

How are such plans compared in economics and finance? What are the surrogates for the emotional weight functions discussed earlier? Modern quantitative economics has little room for ill-defined characteristics as 'emotional weight functions'. Rather, the primary comparison to be made is that between the benefit that one plan may provide — in the form of a (perhaps subjectively defined) outcome that may be ranked — and the cost of that plan, defined here as the possibility that the plan may go awry. The possibility that a plan may not succeed is defined as its *risk*.

4. Risk, Return and Decision-making: an Extended Example

Consider a world with only two time periods, 'today' and 'tomorrow'. Today there is only a single state: tautologically it is simply 'today'. But tomorrow there may be, say, three possible states that may occur: rain, snow or sun. There is a person in our world, the 'individual', who is allowed (and must chose from) a collection of feasible actions which may be taken tomorrow. In this example, the feasibility constraint is that one, and only one, of the following three objects may be used tomorrow: an umbrella, a snow shovel, or a lawn chair.

Suppose that the individual is able to assign 'happiness' to various collections of states and actions. Specifically, she is *happiest* when 1) it is raining and she is carrying an umbrella, 2) it is snowing and she can use her snow shovel, and 3) it is sunny and she has a lawn chair to sit in. These three outcomes may all have different subjective rankings—for example, the individual might prefer to enjoy the sun in a lawn chair to being dry when it's raining, or to shoveling snow. The other possible combinations, or 'mismatches', e.g. carrying a lawn chair when its snowing, or a snow shovel when it is raining, may be ranked in any order—but the above three options are preferred over any of the mismatches.

Given the above problem, the individual must form a plan—what to carry tomorrow, given that she may only carry one object? That plan should, in an ideal world, be the best plan available—given any other plan, she should prefer this one. And the plan should be consistent—actions should not conflict with each other.[2]

One can well imagine many other examples which are far more realistic or complicated (usually both) to express a decision under uncertainty. But this simple setting should suffice to outline the salient details of risk and how it may relate to deliberation. Note also that this type of example is precisely the form of many simple economic and financial decision problems under uncertainty. For instance, one such model might have several risky assets to invest in, and a limited quantity of funds to invest *before* the assets' returns are known. In our simple example, the carrying capacity assumes the role of the limited quantity of funds, the umbrella, shovel etc. the investment instruments, while the weather is an analogy for the uncertainty of the assets' returns. The ranking of *certainty outcomes* is usually performed in economics with the aid of a "utility function", a tool much maligned both inside and outside the discipline. But this specification is unnecessary as we are dealing with the underlying preferences themselves.

The example so far is incomplete (from the point of view of the probability approaches of Savage and von Neumann-Morgenstern)—although there is a full specification of the states that may happen tomorrow, one has no idea of how *likely* any of the aforementioned states may be. In fact from a behavioral standpoint this is a deep issue: for it is the likelihood of the states, coupled with the preferences over each state (outcome) which dictates the decision that is made. The chance that the decision may be incorrect *ex post* is part of the risk of the decision.

Suppose further that our example takes place in July, in Phoenix, Arizona. One may think that regardless of the likelihood of rain or sun, the chance of snow in Phoenix, Arizona in July is extremely remote. The decision of what article to carry should not be 'weighted' much by the possibility of snow—that is, the relative 'risk' (as colloquially defined) of carrying an umbrella or a lawn chair should not depend upon the likelihood of snow to any large extent. Thus we may restrict the likely states tomorrow to rain or sun. Finally, let us suppose for simplicity that the probability of rain and sun are equal, 50% for each.

It is now possible to construct how the individual might 'feel' when carrying a lawn chair, incorporating all the above information about the states tomorrow. Mathematically such a specification would simply be:

(benefit of a lawn chair in the sun)*0.5 + (benefit of a lawn chair in the rain)*0.5

On the other hand, we can perform exactly the same calculation for the individual's 'feeling' when carrying an umbrella:

(benefit of an umbrella in the sun)*0.5 + (benefit of an umbrella in the rain)*0.5

It is a central tenet of modern economic theory that these two results may be compared. Indeed, they may be ranked. In other words, there is a way to rank preferences over these expected outcomes which will tell the individual whether or not it is the umbrella or the lawn chair which will be carried the following day, regardless of whether or not it rains or shines. (Again, the usual recourse is to specify a utility function which can represent ordinal rankings of alternate outcomes, so that the 'utility maximizing' action is selected.)

One consequence of this approach is that it is able to measure the cost of being wrong. In fact, the approach allows for several such measurements, all of which are used at one point or another in economic analysis. The simplest measurement is just to define the difference in benefit from any two decisions, and pick the action which has the greatest additional benefit over all the others. If there is no one action which is better than all the rest, then one which is better over more of the others than any other action may suffice (the 'least worst' case). The cost of selecting the action, then, is what is 'placed on the line' when the action is actually taken: it is the (usually negative) benefit which may occur if 'the wrong state' occurs. In the above example, it is sitting in a lawn chair in the rain, or carrying an umbrella in the sun.

Another, more sophisticated measurement may be calculated by considering not just the values of the benefits which may accrue to each action in each state, but also the *spread* of benefits, i.e. how closely different benefits over different states resemble each other. In the above example, if the individual does not really care if she were wet or dry, and felt just as happy with an umbrella in the rain as with a lawn chair in the sun, then carrying an umbrella might be just as likely an optimal decision as carrying a lawn chair (such *indifference* in an economic context is discussed below). The benefits are all clustered together in this case, i.e. what is placed 'on the line' as a gamble when selecting an action is not lost (or much reduced) if the wrong state occurs.

If, however, the benefits are spread far apart, then it may matter a great deal which action is chosen conditional upon the state. If the individual absolutely hates getting wet, but does not care much about having a lawn chair in the sun or an umbrella in the sun, then selecting a lawn chair might carry a far greater negative benefit than any potential gains from a lawn chair. This type of asymmetry between positive gains and negative costs was studied extensively in work pioneered by Kahneman and Tversky (1979), who proposed that utility functions be considered asymmetric between positive and negative payoffs. (Kahneman received the 2002 Nobel Prize in Economics for his 'psychological approach' to economic analysis.) The result is that what is placed 'on the line' depends very much upon how 'far away' different benefits are from each other.

Both measurements given above may be summarized in one catch-all category which (in addition to its common usage) has permeated the economics literature, as well as being a key component of financial engineering and economic forecasting. The measurement of the potential cost of an action under alternative states of the world is the *risk* of an action. As defined (heuristically) above, it incorporates the likelihood of a state to occur with the benefits or spread of benefits into a measurement of potential loss (or often, potential gain). For example, the fact that the chance of snow is virtually zero in July meant that it did not figure into the above discussion of potential benefits—we left out both the state of 'snow' and the action of 'carry a snow shovel' because there was no risk of finding oneself in a snowstorm in July.[3] But in situations where there is no unambiguously rare event (rain and sun were both equally likely above), it is the *relative* trade-offs which occur when comparing different benefits that determines which action is more or less risky than another.

The relative comparison of benefit and risk is what influences most economic and financial decision-making (both in theory and in practice) in the world today. In formal mathematical finance benefit is often measured by the (expected or average) return to an investment (or the utility derived from such a return), while risk is usually measured by the variance of the return (a measurement of spread around the average). The goal of most investments is to maximize the return while minimizing the associated risk. Note that risk does not usually solely determine which action is selected—we all know situations in which something is risked, often at a high chance of loss, in order to reap a potentially gigantic reward. Any state or national lottery is an example of such a risk-reward trade-off.

5. Linking Risk to Deliberation

It may seem that we have strayed far afield from the discussion of a vocabulary or lexicon for understanding deliberation, or planning, of the mind (as opposed to the instinctive reactions which may originate in the structure of the brain). But the preceding discussion of risk applies directly the notion of deliberation between alternative options, both directly as a model of individual behavior and indirectly as a proxy for unobservable valuations.

The framework of the preceding example is used in formal models to examine one slice of an immensely complicated economic environment. In those models the decisions that economic agents make are usually instantaneous, i.e. there is little or no consideration given to the amount of time necessary to weigh and evaluate each given alternative, or to the complexity of such a weighing procedure. Paradoxically, most formal models have very complicated solution procedures, leading one to surmise that if the model is a faithful reproduction of real actions taken by real people, then the model's underlying dynamics are somehow implicitly prescribed rather than explicitly calculated by real people. It is in fact folly to presume that individuals really do calculate, for example, differential equations (as is often assumed) to measure the relative returns of two alternative actions, each of which carries a utility value. Rather, the standard assumption is that the solution equations *themselves* carry the dynamics of the decision process, which will be forced to move along the solution path in any real-world situation. The standard physical sciences analogue is that we do not need to know exactly how gravity affects a ball's trajectory in order to play catch — we just 'do' it by coordinating our musculature with optical (and perhaps auditory) feedback.

The debate as to whether or not formal decision theory contains the actual laws of decision-making for real people is not the main focus of this chapter. But one aspect of this debate deserves highlighting: in real circumstances, people usually take time to 'weigh all the options' before forming a plan. Plan formation, as discussed earlier, appears to necessitate deliberation, an explicit pause to decide upon an action, during which time alternative actions are compared. Given the forgoing analysis, then, it would appear natural to measure a 'degree of deliberation' during plan formation with the risk associated with each possible action in the plan.

Of course, all of this may seem self-evident: after all, what are we as individuals doing when deliberating but assessing the 'weight' of each action, with an eye to the possible costs involved? But deliberation is manifested as an amount of *time* taken to make a decision, whereas risk assessment is assumed (in the standard literature) to be instantaneous. Some caution must be used, then, when applying risk measures to deliberation measured as delay.

To illustrate the potential dangers, consider the following example of economic indifference. It was suggested earlier that there are situations in which two alternative actions may have the same benefit associated to them, along with the same risk. That is, it would be difficult to determine which action to prefer, although perhaps both are preferable to all other actions. In this case, a conventional 'economic agent' would be indifferent between the two alternatives—either one will do. To solve this dilemma, most of the extant economics literature simply suggests an *ad hoc* rule to select between the two alternative actions, and the (instantaneous) decision is made.

In reality, alternative actions which give virtually the same benefit are often met with an 'I don't care' attitude—but this does not necessarily resolve itself immediately into one decision or another. There may be a period of indecision in which thoughts vacillate from one alternative action to the other, until either an external source is addressed to help ('what do you think I should do?') or an *ad hoc* suggestion presents itself, or *neither* alternative is chosen ('I don't know what to do!'). There is a delay, the time during which the indecision over indifferent alternatives persists. A low measure of relative risk, then, may lead to a high level of deliberation—risk is once again a natural candidate to help understand why humans deliberate.

At the other extreme, it may be that two alternatives have such different risk profiles that indecision again enters as part of the deliberation process. If one of the alternatives is 'very risky' with respect to the other then the feared loss if 'things go wrong' may lead to worry and indecision about enacting a (so defined) risky plan. The larger the extremes between alternatives, the greater the risk, the larger the indecision until the person is 'really sure'. This has the effect not of changing the risk assessment *per se*, but of allowing the risk assessment to slowly 'sink in' until the individual is convinced that the risk as measured is correct, or is 'worth it'.

Instinctive responses, in contrast, are usually not associated with any meaningful delay in action—the decision as to which action to take and the implementation of that action are regarded as instantaneous. In this case the economic modeling convention fits much better: if humans were truly 'economic animals' from a modeling perspective then all decisions would be instinctive, and thus not deliberated decisions (or plans) at all. The act of planning, and the associated deliberation that comes with it, serves to drive a wedge between the 'economic animal' interpretation of human behavior as instinct, and the 'economic human' who thinks about the alternative actions and then *decides*.

6. Additional Factors I: Knightian Uncertainty

Informally speaking, Knightian uncertainty (coined after Knight's seminal 1921 contribution) may be thought of as 'not knowing what we don't know'. Knightian uncertainty has spawned an enormous literature in the decision-making and economics sciences, and has sparked heated debates on the difference between Knightian uncertainty and risk (as defined earlier). For our purposes a distinction is useful—risk in this setting means that the states of nature which may occur are all known, and the distribution (or likelihood) of these states is known, but we don't know which one will occur. In contrast, Knightian uncertainty is typically taken to mean that either 1) probabilities over known states cannot be given (for whatever reason), or 2) that there are states which are not known to be possible (so that, as in the first case, no probabilities can be assigned).[4]

Knightian uncertainty, so defined, may be demonstrated using our earlier example, where the weather is uncertain and a decision on what to carry must be made. It was said then that the only possible states in July in Phoenix, Arizona are sun and rain—snow is not even considered as an option. However, suppose that once our decision is made (presumably to carry either a lawn chair or an umbrella) we walk outside and find it snowing. The fact that such previously thought impossible states actually occur is an example of an individual's Knightian uncertainty.

Formal economic modeling often has difficulty with Knightian uncertainty. In most models it is imperative that all possible states be known in advance, and that they are each given a probability of occurrence greater than zero, i.e. all states have some (perhaps very small) chance of occurring. In this sense 'surprises' are only defined as rare events coming to pass, and are not the occurrence of events previously thought impossible.

In the real world, accounting for contingencies in the form of plans over states which one doesn't even know are possible is a *planning action* which usually involves deliberation. In this case, the deliberation does not encompass known alternative state-contingent actions and what the proper actions are in such known situations. Rather, the problem is to try and ascertain what states might, while remaining unknown, nonetheless come to pass. In this case it is not possible to assess a risk measurement because an evaluation of the optimal action to take is not possible.

As an example one may consider one of the repercussions of the horrific events that came to pass in the United States in September of 2001. Most of the insurance carriers for the world's air carriers in both Europe and the United States had no actuarial data for the possible state: 'an aircraft is deliberately flown into a building by terrorists'. There was no method of valuing such a possibility, which meant that this outcome had essentially gone unhedged on the part of the airline insurers. Rational weighing of marginal benefits could not take place in this case, leading to incomplete insurance over a state which no one except those responsible had even thought possible prior to September 11th.

Attempting to guess at or understand the frontiers of our own ability to recognize and consider every possible state is another determinant of deliberation during plan formation. If we are reasonably confident that a subset of states is isolated from the states and actions of 'the rest of the world', then we may be reasonably sure that we can condition our actions upon that subset without worrying about what else may 'come in from the outside'. For example, when deciding upon a commuter route from the suburbs to downtown, one does not usually consider the traffic patterns of a city on the other side of the planet, or the density of fish near Antarctica, or any other state whose consequences are thought to be either of limited range or limited duration, or both. Formally speaking, we may partition the set of all states into those states which, when given a particular plan, have an effect on the plan's actions and outcomes, and those states which do not.

If such a partition is not possible, we are faced with a problem. As already discussed, one might need to consider which states may occur that one has no *a priori* knowledge of existing, but which may nonetheless affect the outcome of any plan. So one has to generate a set of actions which are defined as executable only if something one does not know in advance actually occurs! Although this seems rather unrealistic, it happens quite frequently in practice. Most people have generated such action sets for occurrences which are not known, using a 'just in case' principle. If asked 'Just in case what?', many simply shrug and say, 'Just in case anything happens!' The 'just in case' principle is a catch-all for those states which are not known to be possible ahead of time—it is a mental summarization of Knightian uncertainty. And the development of such cases is a form of planning, which requires some method of identifying within the set of feasible actions those which might be implemented if something unknown occurs. We cannot define the states which occur (by definition, they are unknown), but we can nonetheless generate a set of contingent actions which comprise our 'just in case' action set. The act of doing so constitutes a second form of deliberation, and may be measured explicitly by, say, the size of the contingent action set. Many actions in such a set would thus imply a large Knightian uncertainty, as one attempts to be sufficiently 'covered' for any eventuality.

Note that this type of deliberation is again quite different from an instinctive reaction. Instinct is an instantaneous reaction which occurs regardless of the state, even those states which we do not ourselves know may occur. We see examples of such reactions during times of strong emotions: 'I never knew I would get so angry!' or 'Before I knew it I burst into tears!' are examples of statements which imply that the person's response occurred in situations for which the response was generated before the state was even known ('before I knew it'). For those responses we categorize as instinctive, Knightian uncertainty serves no meaningful role.

7. Additional Factors II: Computational Complexity

As a last determinant of deliberation, which was hinted at previously, one may consider the fact that even when all states and actions are known and considered, the optimal action to be chosen may still require time to uncover. The issue of *computational complexity*, that a problem becomes more complicated the more states of the world are added to it, is an old one in theoretical computer science (going back at least into the 1930s with work by Turing, Gödel, and others). More recently it has found some treatment in the economics and finance literature, as it has been realized that the simplest economic models often tax the computational powers of even the theorist to the limit.

As argued earlier, additional deliberation due to complexity may not occur if individuals simply act 'as if' they obey the complicated laws they are supposed to be calculating. But individuals really do try to consider explicitly the cost-benefit analysis presented earlier, especially when the benefits are in terms of wealth. One only needs to consider the filing of an income tax return to see that even simple calculations are time-consuming. To really compare all the possible measures of return vs. risk for e.g. buying a car or a house requires time on the order of weeks or months before a decision is made. The cost of *acquiring* information and *processing* information (note that many authors only consider the latter when speaking of computational complexity) must be entered into any plan which attempts to be based upon existing information.

8. Putting it All Together: A Heuristic Visualization

Using some of the considerations from formal economics and financial economics, three determinants of deliberation in planning, as opposed to instinctive response, have been identified: the weighing of (perhaps return-adjusted) risk, the consideration of *a priori* impossible events (Knightian uncertainty), and computational complexity. The response of deliberation time along the risk spectrum ranges from 1) high deliberation when alternative actions have identical benefits, i.e. low relative risk (indecision due to indifference), to 2) high deliberation when alternative actions have markedly different risk profiles (in particular, when the cost of 'being wrong' is very high), i.e. high relative risk. In between these two the shape of the deliberation-relative risk relationship is indeterminate — but since there are so many instances in which people can and do weigh risk, i.e. make decisions, one may perhaps not go far wrong in assuming that the relationship is u-shaped:

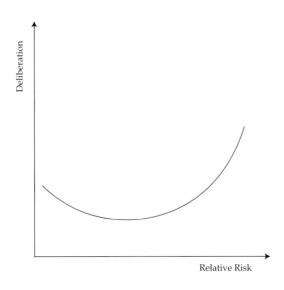

Figure 1

Note that this relationship may only be valid *ceteris paribus*, i.e. holding other determinants equal.

Along the same lines, the degree of computational complexity may be summarized by the number of states and/or actions which must be considered for each plan — one may assume that (again holding other things constant) the deliberation time is simply increasing in the complexity of the problem to be solved:

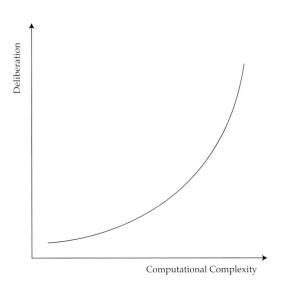

Figure 2

Incorporating Knightian uncertainty, however, poses a problem. It is difficult to measure how many of the states of the world do not influence the decision to be made, and of those, how many such states are impossible to know! It is here that emotive content is possibly a good proxy measurement of Knightian uncertainty over a quantified metric. In decision problems one may feel 'sure' that a decision is the right one, and the deliberation time is low, whereas an 'unsure' feeling may indicate that the 'just in case' possibilities must be given a larger weight.

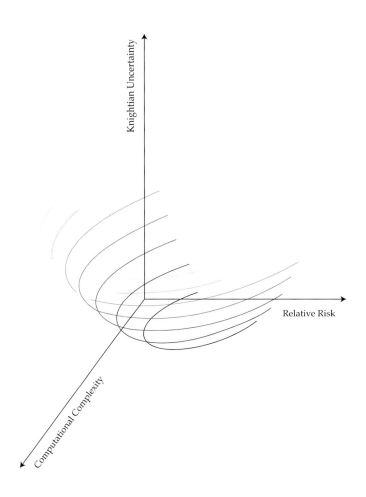

Figure 3

Of course, disentangling the measurement of Knightian uncertainty from other emotive content is difficult. Without recourse to an alternative, however, emotive content may serve as an adequate proxy when restricted to questions designed to provide responses pertaining to such uncertainty. One may then (with some trepidation) assign a feeing of 'sureness' about the possible states as having a low level of deliberation (again, all other things equal), while 'unsureness' means a higher level of deliberation.[5]

The above three-dimensional graph plots 'isoquants of deliberation' given the three determinants of risk, complexity and Knightian uncertainty. Lighter isoquants indicate higher levels of deliberation, while darker isoquants indicate less deliberation.

The determinants of deliberation presented here are an attempt to bring a very simple vocabulary to investigate how plans are formed, and under what circumstances the phenomenon of deliberation may be regarded as a component of plan formation. It is argued that one must incorporate the levels of risk and associated return, the possibility that relevant states may go unforecasted or unknown, and explicit measures of the complexity of a problem in order to help understand the phenomenon of deliberation in plan formation. In particular, this analysis is a preliminary step towards understanding the difference between an instinctive response (considered as a biological imperative, which somehow resides in the structure of the genetic code, and is expressed in the phenotype of brain structure) and a premeditated, considered plan (considered as an implication of consciousness). This does not, of course, shed light on *why* it is that humans with consciousness are able to think and plan — rather, the focus has been on providing a method of discussing and measuring the implications of thought and planning on the deliberative process that such planning requires.

Notes

[1] We exclude from this study the possibility that evolution is such a form of 'introspection' at the macro, or species level. Standard models of evolution state that species which survive through time do so by utilizing successful survival instincts, without any conscious thought on the part of any individual member of the species. It is *mutation* of instinctual strategies over time, and not individual introspection, which allows for a variety of strategies to be tested against the environment — those strategies found wanting die out, while the successful strategies propagate and survive. It is beyond the scope of this monograph to debate whether or not mutation is a form of introspection!

2 In this case there is only one action, which is consistent by default, but in more general examples consistency must be respected.

3 Technically speaking one should not exclude 'carrying a snow shovel' from the feasible action set, as that remains just as possible in July as any other time! But we implicitly assume that a snow shovel in rain or shine is not typically associated with a benefit—or that both such outcomes are ranked so far below any of those with an umbrella or lawn chair that one may safely disregard them.

4 In addition there is an associated notion of *incomplete information*, in which the states of nature which may occur are all known, but the distribution (or likelihood) of which state will actually occur is not known. It is up to the individual to try to learn (or guess) what the possible distribution of future states is, and to select a best action conditional upon that possible distribution. This was addressed in the earlier section on risk.

5 As mentioned earlier, one may also attempt to measure Knightian uncertainty by how many contingent actions are planned for in the 'just in case' scenario. Many contingent actions (a high Knightian uncertainty) would require high deliberation, while a few contingent actions (a low Knightian uncertainty) would result in low deliberation.

References

Arrow, K. (1953; 1964) 'The Role of Securities in the Optimal Allocation of Risk-bearing.' *Review of Economics Studies*, vol. 31, pp. 91-6.

Crawford, C. and D. Krebs, eds. (1998) *Handbook of Evolutionary Psychology: Ideas, Issues and Applications*. New Jersey: Lawrence Erlbaum.

Debreu, G. (1959) *Theory of Value: An Axiomatic Analysis of Economic Equilibrium*. New York: Wiley.

Kahneman, D. and A. Tversky. (1979) 'Prospect Theory: An Analysis of Decision Under Risk.' *Econometrica*, vol. 47, pp. 263-291.

Knight, F. (1921; 1965) *Risk, Uncertainty and Profit*. New York: Harper and Row.

Marshall, A. (1878; 1964) *Principles of Economics: An Introductory Volume*. Eighth edition. London: MacMillan.

von Neumann, J. and O. Morgenstern. (1944) *Theory of Games and Economic Behavior*. Princeton: Princeton University Press.

Savage, L. (1954; 1972) *The Foundations of Statistics. Second edition.* New-York: Dover Publications.

Literary Language and the Scientific Description of Consciousness

Dominic Rainsford

The understanding of consciousness presents modern science with a special difficulty. This is because it is seemingly impossible to describe the object of study in a way that can be shared. As John Searle has argued, 'the ontology of the mental is an irreducibly first-person ontology', and '[t]here is [...] no way for us to picture subjectivity as part of our world view because [...] the subjectivity in question is the picturing' (98). This paper will argue that there are fundamental similarities between ongoing efforts to deal with this problem in cognitive science and the production and study of representations of mental states in literature and critical theory. A number of specific insights from literary studies can usefully be applied to the scientific problem. In fact, it is possible that the scientific problem actually requires some form of 'literary' approach for its solution (or, since it may not be strictly solvable, for its amelioration). The paper will take its starting point from a recent article by the neurophenomenologist Francisco Varela in the *Journal of Consciousness Studies*, in which he calls for 'a re-learning and a mastery of the skill of phenomenological description' as a step towards understanding consciousness—a task that he describes in notably humanistic terms, 'like learning to play an instrument or to speak a new language' and which apparently 'requires us to leave behind a certain image of how science is done' (346-47).

Using language in ways that share many of the characteristics of literature has been an essential resource for philosophers who have sought to characterise consciousness throughout the history of ideas, to the extent that it is hard to argue that such writing is

In Search of a Language for the Mind-Brain, ed. Saleemi, Bohn and Gjedde, *The Dolphin* 33 © 2005 by Aarhus University Press, Denmark. ISBN 87 7934 005 9.

not indeed 'literature' in the sense implied by the disciplines of literary criticism and theory. Here, for example, is George Berkeley using the literary form of a dialogue between two fictional characters, Hylas and Philonous, to advance an argument about the relativity of sense perceptions:

Phil. Besides, it is not only possible but manifest, that there actually are animals, whose eyes are by nature framed to perceive those things, which by reason of their minuteness escape our sight. What think you of those inconceivably small animals perceived by glasses? Must we suppose they are all stark blind? Or, in case they see, can it be imagined their sight hath not the same use in preserving their bodies from injuries, which appears in that of all other animals? And if it hath, is it not evident they must see particles far less than their own bodies, which will present them with a far different view in each object, from that which strikes our senses? Even our own eyes do not always represent objects to us after the same manner. In the *jaundice*, every one knows that all things seem yellow. Is it not therefore highly probable, those animals in whose eyes we discern a very different texture from that of ours, and whose bodies abound with different humours, do not see the same colours in every object that we do? From all of which, should it not seem to follow that all colours are equally apparent, and that none of those which we perceive are really inherent in any outward object?
Hyl. It should.
(166)

Berkeley is functioning as a literary author in a very obvious way here by inventing characters and affecting to transcribe a conversation that never really happened. Moreover, Philonous, within the dialogue, is using aspects of literary art to persuade his interlocutor. In this passage he is persuading Hylas to imagine that he can put himself in the place of a microscopic organism—encouraging him to think that he can move to the boundary of his own mind and achieve some sense of the very different perceptual universe of another, exactly the ambiguous territory between the reader's own experience and the lives of others in which literature seems to come into its own.

Similarly, many well-known texts that would be routinely characterised as works of literature, not philosophy, are notable for their use of distinctive kinds of language that seem designed to give us a more effective or interesting sense of mind than writing that might be characterised as 'unremarkable' or 'everyday', standard in its vocabulary and grammar. The authors who do this necessarily imply certain ideas of what the mind is, and of what constitutes consciousness. In other words, their work has implications for the philosophy and sciences of mind, even if their approach, from a scientific point of view, may have been wholly uninformed. The example I would like to use is from Dickens's *Little Dorrit*, where Flora Finching addresses the serious-minded Arthur Clennam, her suitor of many years previously, who has recently returned from a long period in China and finds Flora much changed from the young woman whom he used to admire:

'Oh good gracious me I hope you never kept yourself a bachelor so long on my account!' tittered Flora; 'but of course you never did why should you, pray don't answer, I don't know where I'm running to, oh do tell me something about the Chinese ladies whether their eyes are really so long and narrow always putting me in mind of mother-of-pearl fish at cards and do they really wear tails down their backs and plaited or is it only the men, and when they pull their hair so very tight off their foreheads don't they hurt themselves, and why do they stick little bells all over their bridges and temples and hats and things or don't they really do it!' Flora gave him another of her old glances. Instantly she went on again, as if he had spoken in reply for some time.

'Then it's all true and they really do! good gracious Arthur! — pray excuse me — old habit — Mr. Clennam far more proper — what a country to live in for so long a time, and with so many lanterns and umbrellas too how very dark and wet the climate ought to be and no doubt actually is, and the sums of money that must be made by those two trades where

everybody carries them and hangs them everywhere, the little
shoes too and the feet screwed back in infancy is quite
surprising, what a traveller you are!'
(144-45)

Dickens, in his amazing, casually brilliant way, is here laying the
groundwork for the so-called 'stream of conscious' styles of High
Modernism. Flora is not just being unintentionally funny; she is
revealing a certain understanding, on the part of her author, of the
way in which ideas might pop up in a specific consciousness, link
to one another, make patterns, go astray, come back, evaporate,
and consequently baffle another consciousness that has the task of
interpreting their verbal carriers. Phenomena of this kind are by
no means restricted to the most exceptional practitioners of
literary writing. In fact, modern and postmodern literature in
general may be said to have certain characteristic, distinctive
implications for the study of mind (which may or may not have
been learned from Dickens): insofar, for example, as it tends to
represent consciousness as a field within which we wander, rather
than a resource that we contain and control. To say that this is a
tendency of relatively *modern* literature is to gesture in the
direction of linking cognitive approaches to the study of literature
as a generalised phenomenon with the currently more entrenched
practices of literary history. This is important since, as Alan
Richardson has recently stated in the journal *Philosophy and
Literature*,

> [T]he appeal of cognitive literary criticism will remain limited
> [...] unless it extends to scholars working within the traditional
> (and newer) literary historical areas. Most of the relevant
> work to date has tended to address in synchronic fashion
> issues like narrative poetics, prosody, literariness, imagery,
> and figurative language. There are as yet scarcely any notable
> attempts to bridge the concerns of literary history with those
> of the cognitive sciences. [...] Literary historians have as yet
> made only scattered attempts to begin gauging the
> significance of the interplay of cognitive universals and
> cultural difference, invariant psychic mechanisms and the

contingent human environments within which they are shaped and which provide much of the material with which they are to work.
(165-66)

Indeed, it seems obvious that literature from various periods reflects different states of knowledge about the mind, and it is also likely to reflect different *states of mind*, insofar as the way individual minds work is determined both by the physical facts of the brain and by cultural factors.

Dickens, with Flora Finching, rather like Berkeley with his microscopic creatures, localizes and externalizes (however ironically, in the case of Berkeley) a type of mental state which he presents as diverging from the human norm. Something like the state that he offers us might nowadays be thought to be more general (if not universal) among humans, and hence pervades many modern and postmodern texts from start to finish (insofar as the concepts of starting and finishing survive in these latter-day mind pictures).

But what does this really tell us about cognition, the mind-brain, or, for that matter, consciousness? Much modern literature may seem to propagate an idea of consciousness, or own or others', as something at least partially opaque, unstable and incommensurable. It might be felt that literature, in this sense, frustrates neuro-philosophical enquiry, that it is even a dead end from a scientific point of view. At the very least, however, it must be possible to use literature constructively in the articulation of a wide (perhaps infinite) range of *concepts* of mind. Literature will only fail, in this respect, if and when human mental capacities fail altogether.

As an example of a specific, up-to-date approach to the understanding of mind that can be illuminated through literature, I shall briefly consider the concept of downward causation. This concept has been said to 'presuppose the assumption that several levels of reality coexist, be it merely as levels of description or as levels of description as well as of ontology. Together with level theories, the concept of emergence is very often used as a designation for the relation between the new or unpredictable property on the higher level and its basis on the lower level. As a kind of immediate extrapolation of this idea, downward causation is used as a designation for an alleged downward effect which emanates from the emergentically [sic] defined higher level onto its constituents in the lower level' (Emmeche, Køppe and Stjernfelt). This can be applied to the discussion of mind, insofar as it provides a theory for consciousness as an emergent phenomenon that modifies itself over time, whose daily fluctuations, more precisely, work downwards (from the momentary and superficial to the underlying and ongoing) so as gradually to make us quite significantly other than what we took ourselves to be. The example that I would like to use in this case is Shakespeare's *Othello*, in which the protagonist's consciousness differs radically at the end of the action from what it was at the beginning, and where, I believe, a sophisticated conception of consciousness's self-transforming power, through a form of downward causation, may be seen to be vividly at work.

Othello, the character, starts out as a resplendent figure, using high-flown language that testifies to a consciousness full of order and beauty and apparent self-understanding. This consciousness has a mystical dimension that causes Othello to idealize his new wife Desdemona and also to attach vast importance to something that Shakespeare seems to have selected for its especially low intrinsic or objective value, the handkerchief that Othello gives to Desdemona. This handkerchief is a higher-level phenomenon in Othello's consciousness, generated by the lower or more fundamental level of that consciousness as it reveals itself in his marvellously self-assured and portentous speech. Iago, who inhabits a very different consciousness, sees Desdemona and the handkerchief differently, and impresses these different constructions upon Othello. Othello disastrously internalises new versions of these higher-level phenomena, Desdemona and the handkerchief, versions that are incompatible with the consciousness that produced his original versions of them. In order to accommodate the new versions, Othello's consciousness changes by a process of downward causation (or, to put it colloquially, by the cart starting to pull the horse, or the tail to wag the dog). This is illustrated by Othello's speech at the beginning of Act V, Scene ii, just before he kills Desdemona:

> It is the cause, it is the cause, my soul,
> Let me not name it to you, you chaste stars:
> It is the cause, yet I'll not shed her blood,
> Nor scar that whiter skin of hers than snow,
> And smooth, as monumental alabaster;
> Yet she must die, else she'll betray more men.

An important dimension of the pathos of this consists in the fact that the cause makes no sense, and that Othello has in fact lost track of the causality that governs the development of his consciousness. He declines to name the cause at first, and then says something about Desdemona betraying more men, a lame excuse that fails to match the grandiloquence that still remains from Othello's previous unspoiled state of consciousness, the man he used to be before downward causation brought about a process of mental growth that has unfortunately proved to be pathological. One could gloss this process with Macbeth's observation, 'I am in blood / Stepp'd in so far, that [...] / Returning were as tedious as go o'er' (III. iv. 135-37). It is not merely tedious; returning for Macbeth, and likewise for Othello, is impossible. They can never be what they were again, and this could be seen as a matter of neurology as much as fate.

If it is a fact that consciousness is an unpredictably evolving phenomenon, in which processes such as downward causation may at any time be active, processes that no-one is necessarily gifted with any more capacity than Othello's to control (indeed 'control' would itself interfere with and alter the mind), then a form of writing that seeks to be ordinary or neutral will tend to deny the reality of consciousness. If consciousness is fundamentally 'emergent' then a writing that reflects consciousness will be distinctive and unpredictable, representing an expansion on the basic, generalisable resources of language that might reasonably be termed 'literary'. The point of this paper is to argue not only that literature usefully reflects advanced ideas about the constitution and operation of mind, but also that a form of 'literariness', or something very like it, is positively necessary when we seek to investigate these fields.

This can be further demonstrated, I believe, if we consider the problem of 'otherness' in postmodern literature and critical theory. Finding a mode of address to the Other may be essentially the same problem as finding a way to describe consciousness. In the first case, one risks denying otherness by giving it an interlocutory form; in the second case, one risks the reduction or betrayal of consciousness by translation into communicable language. The challenge is to go beyond the possibly fruitless relativism of an extreme postmodern or poststructuralist apprehension of otherness to a collaborative project of understanding such as that envisaged by Varela.

One philosopher whose work has had considerable influence in the last few years on literary theorists who wish to take account of the Other is Emmanuel Levinas. Here is a typical Levinasian formulation of the problem of communication between consciousnesses:

It is from subjectivity understood as a self, from the *excidence* [glossed by the editors of this edition as 'extirpation, destruction'] and dispossession of contraction, whereby the Ego does not appear but immolates itself, that the relationship with the other is possible as communication and transcendence. This relation is not simply another quest for certainty, a self-coincidence paradoxically claimed to be the basis of communication. Consequently, all one can say of communication and transcendence is their incertitude. As an adventure of subjectivity which is not governed by the concern to rediscover oneself, an adventure other than the coinciding of consciousness, communication rests on incertitude (here a positive condition) and is possible only as deliberately sacrificed. Communication with the other (*autrui*) can be transcendence only as a dangerous life, as a fine risk to be run. (92)

Here and in much of his work, Levinas indicates that it is impossible to know the other in a way that is compatible with leaving one's own consciousness, or at least self-consciousness, intact. It is quite possible that what he is saying would not quite fit Varela's prescription. Neurologists, as a group, are not well disposed towards poststructuralist philosophers. Levinas could be said to have adopted a mystical and fundamentally unscientific project of avoiding the corruption of another's consciousness and subjectivity through the attempted abdication of one's own: a type of benign, spiritually-motivated suicide. But the problem that he is responding to is a real one for neurologists, philosophers and literary people alike, and in some respects his way of responding to it is at least suggestive of the methodology that Varela recommends. Levinas uses a highly distinctive, highly refined literary language, complete with archaisms or virtual neologisms such as 'excidence', to make himself as egregiously other as he can while still striving with some rigour towards formulating what appear to be laws of consciousness and communication that others may apply in their own manner. He is clearly pushing the boundaries of literary-philosophical language in a principled effort to advance the debate about what it is to have a mind, given the hypothesis that it is not the only mind there is.

I have touched upon two possible responses of literary scholarship and theory to the demands currently being expressed by mind-brain scientists such as Varela. The first response, exemplified in particular by the Dickens and Shakespeare examples, involves the claim that some literary works, through processes of mimesis and analogy, are able to reflect insights into mental processes that may not have been explained any better, so far, by work done within a definition of science that excludes the arts and humanities. This may be because there are aspects of the mind that require a certain literariness for their analysis and expression. This brings me to the second response, exemplified by the Levinas example, which involves the stronger claim that an understanding of mind, and all its ethical consequences, is inextricably linked to the means of expressing it, so that to address fundamental questions of what it is to have a human consciousness is to undertake an adventure of being and saying that is not reducible to the equal understanding of another and which is nevertheless somehow social or collective in its orientation. So that, in other words, in order to make progress with the study of mind, investigators may need to shift their orientation from the traditionally scientific third person towards the traditionally literary first. This may be more or less than Francisco Varela has in mind when he calls for *'disciplined first-person* accounts' based upon an increased 'mastery in phenomenological examination' (344, 347), but he does acknowledge an interest in Buddhist contemplative and descriptive practices (346), and seems quite genuine, therefore, in his stated desire to expand the boundaries of the scientifically admissible.

Levinas, of course, is not everybody's idea of literature, so to conclude I would like to direct your attention to George Herbert's sonnet 'Prayer':

Prayer the Churches banquet, Angels age,
Gods breath in man returning to his birth,
The soul in paraphrase, heart in pilgrimage,
The Christian plummet sounding heav'n and earth;

Engine against th'Almightie, sinners towre,
Reversed thunder, Christ-side-piercing spear,
The six-daies world-transposing in an houre,
A kinde of tune, which all things heare and fear;

Softnesse, and peace, and joy, and love, and blisse,
Exalted Manna, gladnesse of the best,
Heaven in ordinarie, man well drest,
The milkie way, the bird of Paradise,

Church-bels beyond the starres heard, the souls bloud,
The land of spices; something understood.

This is a notoriously enticing and provocative text, hermetic in some respects but lavishly suggestive in others. It has long been taken as a moving attempt to describe the indescribable, to share a notion of the sacred and significant that actually cannot be shared, at least not with other mortals. By whom is this experience supposed to be understood, in the end. By the speaker alone? By

God? By the reader? How can the reader determine the status of what Herbert says. Is his statement precise or rambling? Is it spontaneous free-associating or a disciplined process of focussing upon his inner experience? Can we answer these questions without sharing Herbert's consciousness? In other words, this poem raises issues about consciousness and communication that are still with us. At the very least, it vividly dramatises the problem of making oneself known to another that confronts neurologists and literary theorists alike; at most it responds to that problem by the kind of extravagantly literary description of a state of mind that might serve as analysable data for an expanded science of consciousness, one that will necessarily be multiple and evolutionary, finding room for all the consciousnesses that can either make themselves known or assert their unknowability.

As a final note I would like to express a thought about why I am pursuing the subject of this paper at all—and in doing so respond very briefly to one of the observations made by Ronald Shusterman in his written introduction to the seminar at which the paper was first presented.

Most of my own work up to now has had something to do with questions of literature and ethics. The so-called 'ethical turn' of literary studies in the last years of the twentieth century seems to have developed in parallel with an interest in cognitive approaches to literature. In the main, these two expansions of the field of literary study have been independent of one another, although they seem to share the goal of making literary studies, and the humanities in general, seem more serious and useful. As Professor Shusterman remarks, 'Giving art a cognitive dimension has been one way of certifying its value; giving it a moral dimension has been the other' (par. 5). Perhaps the most interesting way forward would be to link these two dimensions together. Neuroscience may come to provide a factual basis for some assertions and judgements about literature, which may thereby unlock some of literature's ethical potential, which may thereby provide value-based justifications for interfering with literature in a scientific way in the first place (and thus help, incidentally, to justify state support for the humanities).

It occurs to me that there is another way in which the cognitive approach to literature changes the stakes for the ethics of literary study. In involving itself with so-called hard science literature may take on some of the ethical problems which have hitherto seemed peculiar to science. If literature can really help us to understand how the mind works, how long will it be before some literary scholarship contributes, however remotely, to the kind of applied psychology that is of interest to the world of commerce or even the military? Also, in signing up for some sort of 'consilience' model of human knowledge (to use Edward O. Wilson's word), whereby the humanities come together with the sciences to give a complete picture of the universe we live in, are we helping to accelerate the depletion of a vital natural resource— namely, life's supply of interesting questions? Perhaps one function of humanistic study, hitherto, has been to channel at least some of humankind's inventive and intellectual energies into work that does no harm. This may seem both alarmist and fanciful, but there must at least be some degree to which claims that literary study is serious, important and powerful may bring sleepless nights as well as a much-to-be-wished-for accrual of prestige.

References

Berkeley, George. *Three Dialogues between Hylas and Philonous*. 1713. The Principles of Human Knowledge *with Other Writings*. Ed. G. J. Warnock. Glasgow: Fontana-Collins, 1962. 147-259.

Dickens, Charles. *Little Dorrit*. Ed. Harvey Peter Sucksmith. The Clarendon Dickens. Oxford: Clarendon, 1979.

Emmeche, Claus, Simo Køppe and Frederick Stjernfelt. 'Levels, Emergence, and Three Versions of Downward Causation'. *Downward Causation: Minds, Bodies and Matter*. Ed. Peter Bøgh Andersen and others. Århus: Aarhus Universitetsforlag, forthcoming.

Herbert, George. 'Prayer'. *The Temple*. 1633. *Literature Online*. Chadwyck-Healey.   16   Aug.   2000 <http://lion.chadwyck.co.uk>.

Levinas, Emmanuel. 'Substitution'. 1968. Trans. Simon Critchley, Peter Atterton and Graham Noctor. *Basic Philosophical Writings*. Ed. Adriaan T. Peperzak, Simon Critchley and Robert Bernasconi. Bloomington: Indiana UP, 1996. 79-95.

Richardson, Alan. 'Cognitive Science and the Future of Literary Studies'. *Philosophy and Literature* 23.1 (1999): 157-73. *Project Muse*. 16 Aug. 2000 <http://muse.jhu.edu/journals/philosophy_and_literature>.

Searle, John. *The Rediscovery of the Mind*. Cambridge, MA: MIT P, 1992.

Shakespeare, William, *Macbeth*. Ed. Kenneth Muir. The Arden Shakespeare. Rev. ed. London: Methuen, 1962.

--. *Othello*. Ed. M. R. Ridley. The Arden Shakespeare. London: Methuen, 1958.

Shusterman, Ronald. 'The Breath and Finer Spirit ... An Introduction to the Literature and Cognition Seminar'. European Society for the Study of English. 23 Aug. 2000 <http://www.eng.helsinki.fi/doe/ESSE5-2000/index.htm>.

Varela, Francisco J. 'Neurophenomenology: A Methodological Remedy for the Hard Problem'. *Journal of Consciousness Studies* 3.4 (1996): 330-49.

Wilson, Edward O. *Consilience: The Unity of Knowledge*. New York: Knopf, 1998.

On Pain of Irrationality:
Refuting Relativistic Challenges to the
Unifiability of Knowledge

Anjum P. Saleemi

1. The Nature of Rational Inquiry

At the roots of the thesis of unifiability of human knowledge is a belief in the reasonable effectiveness of rationality, a belief that is amply supported by tremendous progress over the centuries in our understanding of real-life facts, but which has been frequently subjected to ridicule by radical skepticism, relativism, and a whole lot of other anti-scientific viewpoints. Rationality is one of the foundations of the mind-brain, perhaps one that is more crucial than others. It should be pointed out that an essential part of the business of being rational is making and recognizing mistakes. In other words, a rational (or scientific) pursuit of knowledge is by definition fallibilistic. Further, rationality is a human faculty or instinct that is extremely complex and little understood; it is very hard to specify what good science is, a lot easier to recognize when it comes along.

In this paper I wish to defend rationality in part (in fact largely) by attacking the cynical view that all knowledge of reality, and by implication the reality itself, is non-objective and necessarily relative to the observer-dependent contingencies. Well aware as one should be of the limits on our knowledge, I do not intend to preach an aggressive, combative and sanctimonious scientism. Far from it, the viewpoint advocated is that rationality is simply an inescapable part of human nature, and what is known as science is simply the limited body of knowledge that just happens to be more reliable in comparison with much of the present-day understanding of ontological phenomena that remain

In Search of a Language for the Mind-Brain, ed. Saleemi, Bohn and Gjedde, *The Dolphin* 33 © 2005 by Aarhus University Press, Denmark. ISBN 87 7934 005 9.

beyond our epistemological grasp. This, however, should not be taken to confer on science a degree of authority that undermines attempts at rational investigation of the less understood phenomena. Science is relatively successful empirical knowledge, which keeps improving and undergoes constant change, whereas to 'non-science' belong the domains wherein we have not achieved great success so far, nor a good grasp of what counts as 'empirical' in them. Given this view, perhaps the distinction between science and non-science isn't philosophically justifiable, being based as it is on the degree of understanding or epistemological reach rather than on any absolute, qualitative factors. I concur with Searle and many others that there is no sharp distinction between science and philosophy; after all not too long go what is called science today was known as natural philosophy! However, there are indeed some differences which are worth being aware of; these are very lucidly discussed by Searle (1999b).

Take the example of the nervous system and its psychological manifestations. A lot is known about the anatomy and physiology of the former, with the brain occupying the centre stage in it. However, the latter are variably understood, especially in respect of how they are grounded in the former. These include perceptual systems (hearing, vision, etc.), memory, emotions, intentionality and consciousness. This last, considered by many to be the hardest problem to resolve, has been the topic of much debate in recent years. We know for a fact that creatures with very complex brains such as ours undergo subjective but nevertheless real experiences, whose explanation remains a mystery. This does not mean, however, that these aren't valid objects of scientific inquiry. Mental facts, such as they are, should be investigated to the extent that they can, though at present their experimental study is not likely to yield any remarkable results in the foreseeable future; rigorous theoretical argumentation, on the other hand, may have a significant contribution to make in leading us towards the refinement and a clearer perception of the problem. In fact it would not be too erroneous to say that we might not yet have much, or any, idea as to what sort of methods will eventually relieve us of the rather heavy explanatory burden involved.

Regardless of this lack of direction, there is nothing that should prohibit rational inquiry of some sort to proceed, be it experimental or philosophical. This broader view of scientific inquiry goes well beyond what is sometimes called *Hume's Fork*, as articulated below.

> Let us ask: Does it [i.e., any kind of inquiry] contain any abstract reasoning concerning quantity and number? No. Does it contain any experimental reasoning, concerning matters of fact and existence? No. Commit it then to flames; for it can contain nothing but sophistry and illusion. (Hume 1748.)

Hume's apparent empiricist bias here will disappear if 'abstract reasoning concerning quantity and number' is construed as 'abstract, rigorous argumentation that in some sense is based upon empirical knowledge' (which perhaps is still not too remote in spirit from Hume's basic idea). One should point out that most interesting philosophy tries to engage exactly in that sort of reasoning, and in this sense, is a precursor of science, as has been historically the case. The following remarks by Tyler Burge are very pertinent in this context:

> Philosophy, both as product and activity, lies in the detailed posing of questions, the clarification of meaning, the development and criticism of argument, the working out of ideas and points of view. (Burge 1992, pp. 3-51.)

Let us return to the issue of human knowledge, which is, there are good reasons to believe, dependent on mental-psychological, and ultimately neurophysiological, phenomena. To assume that, since the nature of much of human knowledge is subjective, one cannot have objective knowledge of any kind would be grossly irresponsible. It's worth reminding oneself that a lot that has been revealed, primarily in the physical sciences, it was possible for scientists to unearth without any explicit knowledge of how it was revealed. Perhaps one of the greatest gift human beings have is that they can understand things without knowing how understanding itself works; such is the nature of either individual or collective reasoning, a spontaneous process that, once set in motion, is virtually unstoppable, though it may have its ups and downs and indeed long periods of stasis. In other words, rationality cannot be just incredibly useful; it is inevitable and inescapable. It can be deployed poorly or well; however, it cannot be bypassed.

An illusion that is prevalent, and that needs to he dispelled, is that there is such a thing as *the* scientific method, such that its persistent application is eventually bound to produce the right results. The truth is that which particular method is effective is determined by the nature of the domain under investigation. What works for physical sciences may not work for the social sciences. There is a battery of techniques available, and undoubtedly many more are going to come into being to meet the challenges of newly discovered or re-demarcated domains. In the end, whether a particular method is effective is proven after the fact, and thus any prescriptive guidelines can at best be transitional pointers in the process of elimination and invention. Needless to say, attempts to abuse quantitative techniques in social sciences have been rampant in modern times, not infrequently providing dubious or trivial insights at the expense of deep understanding that comes only from a broader exercise of reason. In the present context, the study of psychology and cognitive sciences in general are a case in point: versions of the ostensibly scientific method were imported into them wholesale to impart to them a semblance of scientific aura, to the exclusion of a natural use of rational rigour, with results that have been anything but exciting in most cases.

A predictable result of the prevalent scientism in fields much more complex than, let us say, physics has been a total rejection of the idea of objectivity and the adoption of radical relativism of the kind exemplified by the postmodernist movement. Such viewpoints are all too familiar for me to want to describe them except in a cursory manner. As I implied earlier, what follows is a critique that presupposes some knowledge of these approaches on the part of the reader.

Having stated the general context of the discussion to follow, and my overall position, let me first try to provide some background to the critique, so that relativism is located within the broader perspective of contemporary philosophy.

2. Analytic vs. Relativistic Philosophy

The distinction between analytic (Frege, Russell, etc.) and relativistic philosophy (Derrida, Foucault) is implicit in the arguments that follow.[1] Postmodernism (PM) is a popular (some would say vulgar!) version of a radically relativistic, subjectivist, anti-realist, anti-rational, and skeptical viewpoint. Of course its proponents may not quite like this characterization, but I believe it's not unfair. Further, the characterization I assume is also intended to encompasses the more sophisticated versions of the same viewpoint (as, for example, found in Rorty, at times in Quine and Putnam, and on some interpretations in Wittgenstein[2]). Let us, then, have a quick, and inevitably simplified, look at what PM is.

3. Three Facets of Postmodernism

PM is a way of looking at things that encompasses a wide range of things: philosophy, history of science, historical processes, social structures, and so on. In the literary domain, the key notions appear to be multiple interpretability of literary texts and their deconstruction in accordance with particular sociopolitical ethos of a given period. In other words, literary works have a life of their own, independently of the individual intentions of the author. The political discourse of PM is characterized by the conflict between the centre and the periphery of systems of power, and the disempowerment and marginalization of the peripheral or 'the other'. It views science as yet another one of the systems that came into being under the influence and to serve the needs of prevalent sociopolitical factors, with no legitimate claims whatsoever to objectivity, consistency or universality. What is considered to be good science is crucially determined by the societal structures whose officially acceptable truths it spells out in terms which are relative to such structures. The foregoing description is summarized schematically in Figure 1.

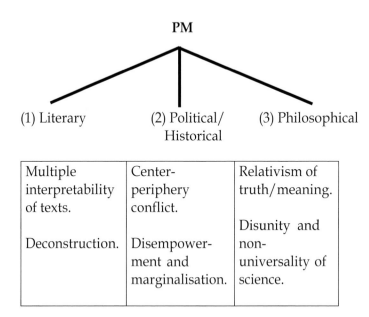

Figure 1: Some Key Facets of Postmodernism

A necessary consequence, and for obvious reasons not a very desirable one, is the negation of the individual potential, creativity and free will – whether in science, literature, or in the sociopolitical context. Admittedly, there is some truth in what is claimed, but the problem seems to be that far too much is claimed at the risk of utter neglect of some very fundamental aspects of human nature, without which the complex collective systems could not exist in the first place. True, societies mould individuals, directly or indirectly, often distorting the decent facets of human nature and highlighting and encouraging the less decent ones, and there is indeed relativism in much of what we do. However, the relative cannot exist without the universal, a point that is particularly reinforced (at least in the present context) in the development of science, which, regardless of any degree of relativism due to this or that set of factors, embodies the essence of a certain type of human endeavour that has no boundaries, cultural or geographical. Of course its applications, namely technological advancements, are necessarily culturally, economically and politically motivated. Although I think complex phenomena, such as the literary and cultural ones, can to some extent benefit from relativism, its extension to scientific inquiry is nothing but disasterous: PM's fatal flaw is that it treats (3) in Figure 1 in the same fashion as (1) and (2). I would like to point out that even in the case of literature, aesthetics, ethics and culture, it is possible to argue that there is a core of features in each case that is universal, and that not everything that matters is subject to the whims of its immediate environment. The parallelism is captured nicely by Frege (1923):

> Just as 'beautiful' points the way for aesthetics and 'good' for ethics, so do words like 'true' for logic. All sciences have truth as their goal; but logic is also concerned with it in quite a different way: logic has much the same relation to truth as physics has to weight and heat. To discover truth is the task of all sciences; it falls to logic to discern the laws of truth.

In the rest of this paper I intend to focus largely on the domain of rationality, and present an array of fallacies, paradoxes, problems and contradictions that radical relativism must confront, and that, in my view, terminally vitiate its credibility as a philosophy (cf. Marwick 2001).

4. Some Fundamental Problems
(a) The Fallacy of Ontological Relativism
A major claim inherent in relativism is that our knowledge of things (i.e., epistemology) is so subjective it cannot possibly provide us access to the absolute nature of reality (i.e., ontology) even in a partial sense. However, it is very easy to show that a relativistic ontology does not follow from a relativistic epistemology (*non sequitur!*); therefore, the latter does not refute ontological realism. What epistemic relativism does refute is the thesis that there is only one privileged conceptual-representational system that corresponds to objective reality, and

that is not a position held to be tenable by anyone except some unrepentant, hopelessly incorrigible empiricists.

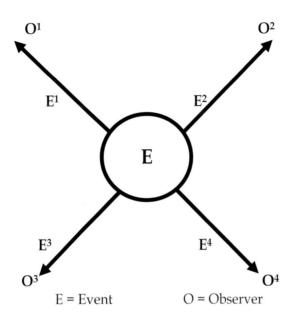

E = Event   O = Observer

Figure 2: **"Rashomon's Problem"**:
Fragmented perception does not entail a fragmented reality.

To illustrate, I will use a metaphor based on Akira Kurosawa's well-known movie *Rashomon*. Suppose an event E takes place, and it is witnessed by four independent observers (denoted as O^1, O^2, O^3, and O^4 in Figure 2) from distinct vantage points, such that each has a different, in many ways conflicting, version of E. These various versions are correspondingly symbolized as E^1, E^2, E^3 and E^4 in the same figure. Evidently, these various versions are going to overlap at least to some extent, as they are accounts of the *same* event. The problem, which may be referred to as *Rashomon's Problem*, in such a case is how to reconstruct the original event, given that the evidence pertaining to it is fragmentary and incomplete. The problem is a very natural one, encountered far too often in ordinary life, in natural sciences and elsewhere to surprise anyone. It also poses a formidable challenge to any investigation of E. None of this, however, even remotely suggests that E did not take place. It would take an enormous leap of logic for one to conclude that the incompleteness of perception implies that there is NO objective real event worth investigating.

Any such conclusion will be based on confusing epistemology with ontology, an example of a genetic fallacy as knowledge of some X is NOT the same as X itself. In fact, multiple epistemic representations of X presuppose the existence of X independently of the observer(s). To put it differently, there could be a world without representations, but there simply couldn't be representations without a world. By the same token, the possibility of a socially constructed nth order reality presupposes the existence of an n-1th order reality that is independent of the social construction, and so on until one reaches 1st order reality: the descent into layers of presuppositions has to bottom out in order to avoid infinite regress. It is worth clarifying that epistemic relativism is the same as conceptual and representational relativism, and ontological realism comprises a combination of subjective (first-person) and objective (third-person) realism, and further that epistemic objectivity is hard, but not impossible, to achieve. Ontological realism does not presuppose epistemic uniqueness, consistency or truth (i.e., the correspondence between knowledge and reality): Our knowledge claims could be multiple, inconsistent, or plainly false, but only relative to some ontology that must be there irrespective of any epistemic claims about it.[3] (See Nagel 1997, and Searle 1999a, and elsewhere, for a thorough discussion of these issues.)

(b) The Reductionist Fallacy
That the rational/scientific worldview is necessarily reductionist is a naïve standpoint; in fact, expansion plays a major role in the development of scientific ideas (Chomsky 2000). I suspect PM's attacks on science often hinge on a reductionist interpretation of how it progresses. (In fact, as Chomsky has often pointed out, science isn't even materialist anymore, as the notion 'matter' lacks

any substance.) As science moves from simple to more and more complex facts, it has to struggle with ever widening circles of interacting cause-and-effect chains, so things become very intricate and sometimes appear to be unmanageable in any given state of knowledge. This, however, does not by any means prove that cause-and-effect relations are merely scientists' fantasies.

(c) The Paradox of Rational Closure

Any attempts to refute rationalism cannot themselves help appealing to rationality of one sort or another (albeit more often than not of a feeble and self-contradictory sort!); in that sense, it can be held to be self-refuting. In its essence, rationality is not an acquired trait merely instilled by culture, but a human instinct, a natural involuntary mental reflex. It's probably part of the 'background' cognitive assumptions, along with the default position pertaining to realism. Partly or largely (or perhaps entirely) due to the contingent biological origins of reason among intelligent, sentient beings, it is not possible to consider it from outside of itself. As to its biological origins, a simple adaptationist evolutionary biology need not be taken to furnish the ultimate and only explanation of the origins of reason or, for that matter, any other mental ability such as language, since evolution seems to contain many sudden turns and shifts whose course might have been driven by accidental factors or by unpredictable secondary consequences of adaptations to environmental changes (as, for example, argued by Gould and Lewontin in several works). On both these accounts, biological reason seems to have privileged access to certain universal laws. In other words, in spite of its various inconsistencies, successes that are only local and partial, and the attendant paradoxes, rationality is the only basic condition of intelligibility and coherence within which any kind of discourse is possible. We are inescapably trapped in reasoning, with no court of appeal other than reason itself. There simply is no vantage point external to it from which it can be attacked, or even critically examined. To conclude, rationality is both ground zero and (to use Thomas Nagel's expression) the last word (Nagel 1997)! No wonder postmodernists are much more inclined to take issue with contemporary rationalists (see Searle

1977, Chomksy and Faucault 1974), and are more sympathetic to the Continental phenemological approaches, which, on their interpretation, do not pose very serious threats to their worldview. (I have a lingering suspicion that their appeal to phenomenology may not be well-founded either, but I do not know enough about the latter to judge the issue.)

(d) The Paradox of (Dis)unity of Knowledge

The relativistic perspective suffers from yet another shortcoming. On the one hand, doubt is cast on the thesis of the unity of science; on the other, disunity (diversity/plurality) is advocated. Herein lies the basis of the endemic ontological underdifferentiation, leading to a disregard for various levels and types of reality: the thesis of the unity of science, not being necessarily reductionist, is perfectly compatible with diversity resulting from various emergent levels of complexity. All that matters is that all laws, basic or emergent, should in principle be relatable via reduction, expansion or just systematic co-occurrence. We do not have perfect knowledge of everything, but judging from the history of science and arguments from plausibility, it appears that great variety of existing phenomena are not entirely unrelated. As Searle (1995) so eloquently points out:

We live in exactly one world, not two or three or seventeen. As far as we currently know, the most fundamental features of that world are as described by physics, chemistry, and the other natural sciences. But the existence of phenomena that are not in any obvious way physical or chemical gives rise to puzzlement. How, for example, can there be states of consciousness or meaningful speech acts as parts of the physical world? — how does it all hang together? — How does a mental reality, a world of consciousness, intentionality, and other mental phenomena fit into a world consisting entirely of physical particles in fields of force?

Searle's view is plausible, but it is undeniably more of an article of faith than a foregone conclusion. It should be acknowledged that it is possible to argue that there could indeed be many worlds, not just one. For example, within our present state of understanding, according to Penrose (1997), at least three distinct worlds can be identified, respectively containing physical (W[1]) , mental (W[2]) and Platonic (W[3]) entities, as shown in Figure 3 (adapted from Penrose), where social (W[4]) facts are ignored (see Searle 1995, and Saleemi 2000 on the latter).

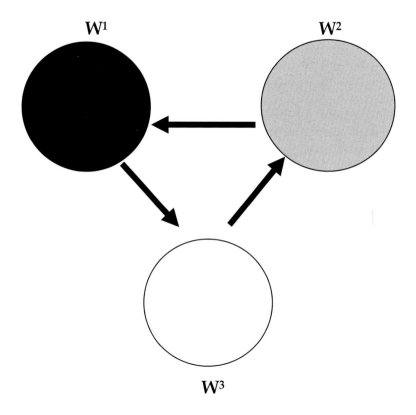

Figure 3: Penrose's Three Worlds

Penrose's arrows obviously imply directionality of influences flowing from one world to another. The interdependence so obtained takes into account three types of kinds, two of them natural (namely, the physical and mental ones) and the remaining one abstract in the traditional Platonic sense, containing, for example, mathematical concepts.

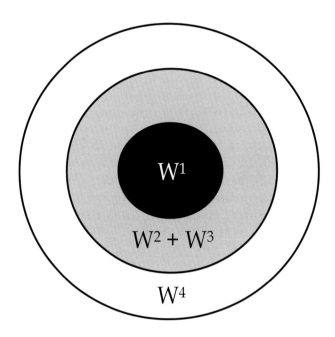

Figure 4: The Unification Hypothesis

Whether or not W^3 is a separate kind is an issue that is not the intention of this paper to resolve, but, on grounds of theoretical economy and empirical soundness, I do not feel like endorsing this picture, especially because it seems quite reasonable to me to collapse W^3 and W^4 so that mental content is understood to subsume so-called Platonic entities, which are derivative, as opposed to the more universally manifested fundamental mental entities such as natural language and common sense: the fundamental mental content comprises primary psychological processes that exist regardless of temporal or cultural background, while derivative mental content emerges from cumulative human effort extending over several generations. This yields a conception of nature that is multi-layered without being disjointed, and which, at the same time, asserts the generality of physics (Fodor 1981). On such a unified view, Figure 3 will have to be recast into something like Figure 4, which depicts an alternative that is more desirable from the present perspective. As mentioned earlier, on the unified view Platonic abstractions are grounded in mental content, as that must be their primary source. The fact that cultural evolution has a role in their emergence and development is not directly reflected in the diagram, but that fact should be taken for granted, as it should be for the rest of the social and cultural phenomena.

Another important aspect of such unification is that the relationships among the sciences involved in the overall investigation can be located within a hierarchy, corresponding to the various levels of reality, that defines the place of each discipline in accordance to the kind of nth order (that is, first-order, second-order or a higher level) hypotheses it is expected to yield (see Figure 5, where H = hypothesis, and T = theory).

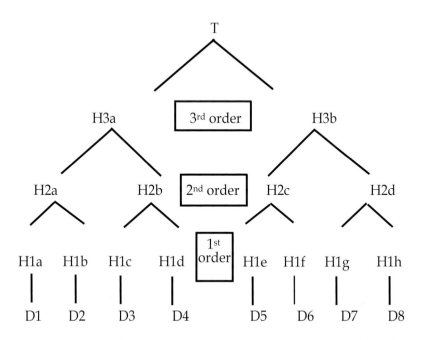

Figure 5: First- and Higher-Order Theories
[Dn = Data Set n]

What Figure 5 depicts is admittedly an idealized and generalized picture, wherein hypotheses (from different disciplines or within the same disciple) accumulate in an orderly progression until they crystallize into a theory. In practice, the development of T might look more like a jigsaw puzzle, so that plausible and verifiable hypotheses may emerge about anywhere in a particularized hierarchy in a somewhat unsystematic fashion.

(e) The Paradox of Universality

Relativism presupposes a common universal core, as the latter has to be there for its relative perceptions to come into being in the first place. However, paradoxically, it denies the existence of anything universal that is true across the board, in all times and at all places, which are counterfactually supporting and exceptionless, as most fundamental causal laws of nature are supposed to be (Fodor 1981). In Hume's words — probably one of the earliest (if not the earliest) statements of counterfactuality (italics added):

> We may define a cause to be an object followed by another, where all the objects, similar to the first, are followed by objects similar to the second. Or, in other words, where, *if the first object had not been, the second never had existed*. (Hume 1748.)

What Hume is stating remains a valid assumption underpinning laws of basic sciences, whose laws of causation are not meant for the here and now, or for any given moment and place; they must be true *simpliciter*, under any circumstances such that the consequent follows only if, and whenever, the antecedent is true. The point is that for any measure of relativism, epistemic or ontological, to be justifiable, some such laws will have to be there in respect of which something is supposed to be relative. In short, a relativism without *any* universal core of truth is simply bad logic.

(f) The Language/Thought Paradox

If it is assumed that language expresses thought, it shouldn't be too hard to see that this seemingly innocuous assumption is an entailment of a strong (and I believe by and large correct) claim that thought, at least in its unmediated form, is prior to language. However, once the linguistic cart is put before the thinking horse, as is common in the most postmodernist 'theory', language becomes an often baffling substitute for thought, in the process undermining the integrity of the latter. Hence the endemic tendency in much postmodernist writing to hide behind words and to use an overly vague and opaque style!

(g) The Problem of Convergence and Communicability

If knowledge were indeed as disjointed as PM claims, it should not be possible for communication to take place across individuals, cultures and time spans, and to converge on similar viewpoints to *any* extent. To the extent that communication works, it demonstrates that:

- different relative conceptual schemes are usually (if not always) mutually convertible in some principled fashion.
- even the putative indeterminacy of meaning and translation (à la Quine), and the variability of linguistic expression, do not succeed in blocking communication hopelessly.

(h) The Problem of Shared Knowledge

Experiences are more often recurrently consistent. They tend to remain substantially the same under diverse conditions, at different times, and for a wide variety of individuals. This would be an inexplicable and bizarre coincidence under radical relativism. Trapped as we all are within the subjectivity of our individual selves, it appears the selves in question as well as the traps in operation cannot be *that* dissimilar.

(i) The Ethical Problem

Despite the liberal, humanistic leanings of most postmodernists, what they say can be taken to mean that there is no universal set of human values, and that morality is merely relative to the needs of a particular individual or culture. In their fervour to negate the values espoused by the powerful, PM and other varieties of relativism might have helped lay the foundations of a deeply immoral world, not a desirable outcome, I should imagine, even by their *own* standards.

A second undesirable ethical consequence of radical relativism has to do with the role of rationality in determining the difference between right and wrong. By itself, rationality is neutral about ethical issues, but when one wants to argue whether a decision or a cause is morally justifiable, the recourse to reasoning is inevitable. It goes without saying that reasoning can, and often is, employed in justifying wrong decisions and causes. That, however, is an example of its abuse, and in order to expose such abuse, once again the only course of action available is to use reason itself.

(j) The Paradox of Power

The claim goes: Established knowledge empowers because it is socially constructed to regulate the distribution of power. However, relativism itself enhances the will to power by reducing objective facts to mere social constructs. This raises the regulatory potential of supposedly opportunistic knowledge to even greater heights. By diminishing the objectivity of knowledge, it turns it into the perfect instrument of manipulation. As what the powerful say is going to be held to be correct, so that all they have to do to support their viewpoints is to put together arguments, *any* arguments that serve their purpose, *subsequent to* the formation of such viewpoints, with reasoning deployed after the fact, as it were. Unfortunately, in our less-than-perfect world this state of affairs is not uncommon. It does not, however, generalize to legitimate reasoning from cause-to-effect, unless one is willing to stretch one's analogical imagination somewhat wildly. What about free will, the possible impact of individual thinking against all odds, and so forth? It is not too wide of the mark to point out how close such a view of disempowerment come to the type of cynical ideology expressed by people like Skinner. As he claims:

A person never becomes truly self-reliant. Even though he deals effectively with things, he is necessarily dependent upon those who have taught him to do so. They have selected the things he is dependent upon and determined the kinds and degrees of dependencies. (Skinner 1971.)

(k) Other Political Fallacies

The recent historical background of contemporary science is admittedly colonial and capitalist. This, however, should not destroy the validity of the genuine scientific endeavour. (Please note I am referring primarily to science, not technology.) This is obviously an example of the political version of the genetic fallacy.

A related fallacy is what may be termed *knowledge-use fallacy*. The validity of a body of knowledge is not to be measured by the uses it is or may be put to. Sound knowledge can be exploited in pursuit of evil intentions or profit- and power-driven motives as much as it may contribute to the common good of mankind. At any rate, neither the social, political, and economic background wherein a particular theory of science originates, nor its negative practical applications, should be taken to be a serious challenge to its validity.

5. Some Reflections on the Ontology of the Literary and Artistic Reality

Straddling the mental and the social facts, and, what is more important, the imagined reality *qua* fact and not as an artificial construct, varieties of literary and artistic reality patently have a life of their own. Yet, they are not divorced from life, which itself may have a good deal of imaginative content. No one except a die-hard empiricist or behaviourist can deny that imagination and creativity are real mental phenomena which build upon both subjective experiences and epistemic access to objective data. In what follows I shall describe some basic features of literary discourse in the first instance, and then, for the sake of concreteness, go on to illustrate these features by discussing a passage from a novel.

(a) Modality of Communication

Artistic reality is not overtly ratiocinative, though rationality is presupposed in it to varying extents. It usually does not rely on explicit argumentation in any direct fashion on the part of the author. Instead, his or her effort aims at embodiment of the subject matter in situations, in evocation of moods and states of mind, demonstration and depiction of events from a certain perspective, and purposeful manipulation of language. This is a partial list of the modes of artistic communication which are not always adopted and executed consciously, as the unconscious forces can often have a very dominant influence on what the writers create.

(b) The Question of Author's Intentions

As implied above, these may be conscious or subconscious. In the latter case even an author her-/himself is not likely to be fully aware of them. Due to the lack of definitive intentional positions ascribable to an author, it should be possible (indeed quite legitimate and desirable), *within certain limits*, to go beyond any standard interpretation, in order to explore the other possibilities inherent in the imaginary universe contained in a work of art.

(c) Possibility of Multiple Interpretations

In light of the foregoing observations, it should be obvious that literary (and many more or less related kinds of) texts are indeed open to many (though not an indefinite number of) interpretations. Successive recontextualization and reinterpretation is justifiable to some extent and may indeed be required due to the very nature of the kind of reality a literary work strives to capture or create. It would be interesting to figure out how the limits on this enterprise, if any, can be defined; these will be necessary to block the possibility of extremely implausible claims, only constrained by the reach of ingenuity of interpretation, that any text (say, Shakespeare's *Hamlet* or *the Bible*) can be construed to be just about anything (for example, about the Second Law of Thermodynamics).

Now let us move on to consider an extract from a novel by Anita Brookner, which appears below.

In the street, as silent as ever, I felt as if I had left home for good. Perhaps leaving home was what it was all about, this new feeling of vulnerability, as if the former protection had been removed. Perhaps all I had ever done, all anyone does, is to leave home, to experiment with life on one's own, without markers. My past experiences now appeared to me as one vast divagation, a series of inevitable mistakes. Too little is known at the outset, when others do one's thinking for one. I had simply failed, as others no doubt fail, when the fledgling judgement proves inadequate to the trials one encounters. Maybe death, when it comes, is another longing for home. (Brookner 1996, p. 165.)

Here the main character's state of mind is being portrayed at a particularly crucial, self-reflective moment of life. The work in question, it should be mentioned, is a modern realistic novel. The character's self-analysis, as expressed by the author, may be considered to be a general thesis about the course of human life, as seen through the character-author's own eyes. Is this indirectly the author's viewpoint or the character's? As far as I can see, there simply is no way of answering this question in a reasonable manner. There's a further question to ponder: Given the sequence of events that led to this analysis, how many alternative analyses are possible? Most probably several are. For instance, if the character was to consult a psychoanalyst, the latter's interpretation most likely would not be the same. Also, another character in the novel could have a different view of things, and so on. In short, the possibility of multiple interpretations in such cases has to be the norm rather than the exception, considering the enormous complexity of human experiences, even more so when these are incorporated in an imaginative reconstruction. Since the domain under investigation is so very intricate, a definitive explanation of the facts will be nearly impossible. Nevertheless, some analyses, as judged by the reader's or the critic's own experiences and insights, are inevitably going to appear more appealing than others, which suggests that, although diverse and not verifiable in any scientific sense, various attempts at understanding the human condition are not likely to be on a par with each other. A work of fiction, in this limited sense and context, may indeed be taken as a sustained 'argument' of a special kind, where events are driven by relatively obscure cause-and-effect relationships.

This is so because literature does not compartmentalize either individual or collective life. It is free to narrowly focus on one aspect of life, let us say, the intricacy and beauty of expression for its own sake, or range over a wide spectrum of its constitutive forces. It probes the depths of the conscious and the unconscious processes in the individual psyche, patterns of social behaviour, the way an individual contributes to, is affected by, or is pitted against, social structures. That, in fact, is exactly what's special about literature. By adopting a fictional or fictive (as opposed to factive) stance, it ratiocinates, connects or interrelates; analyzes emotional struggles, captures extrinsic and intrinsic images, and describes socio-economic and political pressures. It is free to move back and forth in time, or can indeed adopt no fixed timeframe at all. It can deal with the sane and the insane, the inner and the outer, states of the human condition. It can be narrowly rational, almost taking the form of a series of sustained arguments, or go well beyond rationality as it is commonly understood. Literature is able to penetrate every nook and cranny of human existence. More importantly in the present context, the mind is the bridge between one person and others, the individual and societies, among various societies, between past and present, between these last two and the future possibilities, and finally between the fictive and the factive.

Observe that most issues mentioned above are also investigated, albeit differently and with a more or less greater amount of rigour, in various branches of the other types of human intellectual endeavour in a more narrowly focused and compartmentalized way, be they social or physical sciences. Given the limits of concentrated human rationality, breadth is the price to pay for rigour. In literature (and arts in general), rigour is the price for breadth. Much of the talk about the so-called 'two-cutures' of humanities and science, which I strongly suspect is at the bottom of the rejection of scientific rationality, is just a result of the failure to understand this distinction, which in my view merely tells us that science and literature are two ends of a long continuum, not opposing forces.

6. A Few Words about Historical Causation
It is tempting to make a few remarks about history as a kind of rational inquiry. Historians have to establish facts after the fact, and then attempt some explanation of why what happened did happen, unlike a novelist who invents facts and usually punctuates them with explanations and insights from different angles. Historical explanation can never be verified; mankind has no means of experimenting with the past. No historical investigation can fully justifiably assert most of its factual or interpretive claims. Nevertheless, a historian deals with facts, and a good one makes every effort to reach his conclusions as rationally as possible, that is, supported by reliable evidence, based on sound arguments, etc. Because of the amount of uncertainty involved, a certain amount of relativism is unavoidable in history, though to a much lesser degree than in areas like literature. However, this fact should not be exploited to conclude that all history is no better than fiction, written from perspectives merely constructed to serve one ulterior motive or another.

7. Concluding Remarks
In this paper I have tried to put together a cogent case against radical relativism, in many instances using PM as a basket case of rationality gone bad. My view of rationality has been mainly informed by the powerful tradition of analytic philosophy. In the process, some light has been shed as to what rationality is, and it has been asserted that it is a closed system that cannot be criticized from without.

The political, historical, and moral implications of adopting a radically relativistic view are discussed in some detail. In the end, it is outlined how the literary tradition, one of the mainstays of PM, can be located within the broader context of human knowledge which is not necessarily at odds with the scientific, rationalist worldview. To conclude, what I have been calling radical relativism and its various specific manifestations such as PM appear to be in terminal denial of one of the few means of understanding that humans have access to, namely, rationality, which admittedly is not perfect. (Incidentally and ironically, the rationalists in general are more aware of the shortcomings of the methods they pursue than their opponents. To cite an all too familiar example, even most non-mathematicians at least vaguely know what Gödel's Incompleteness Theorem is about. All the same, we all know that there is no tool better than reasoning at our disposal, albeit it may have no proprietary claim to a full understanding of the ultimate nature of things.

Notes

[1] For the sake of economy of exposition, I do not provide the historical documentation from the works of many relativistic and other thinkers other than merely mentioning their names. I assume the works behind the views I am questioning or discussing are well-known. Besides, I have no pretence to, nor the patience, for the kind of scholarship that would consider that sort of exercise to be mandatory. Due to this inadequacy of mine, the amount of documentation provided in the main body of the text and the list of references appearing at the end is rather selective. I would like to make use of this opportunity to quote Jerry Fodor here to reinforce this point: If this work were a work of scholarship, and if I were a scholar, I'd try to make some sort of case for these historical claims; but it's not, and I'm not, so I won't. (Fodor 2000.)

[2] Wittgenstein, probably the most influential philosopher of the last century, was brilliant but at the same time held some views which were profoundly and sometimes erratically problematic. As a result his thinking has led to both the development of 'ordinary language' philosophy — one of the two streams of philosophy within the analytic tradition, most prominently exemplified by Austin and Searle (the other, of course, being the formalist approach represented by Frege, Russell, Putnam, etc.) — and the rampant growth of many nihilistic and extremist forms of subjectivism, relativism, skepticism, and anti-rationalistic views.

[3] An afterthought: It would be interesting to replace the police agent in Kurosawa'a *Rashomon* with an FBI agent, of course with full access to

all sorts of *objective* forensic evidence. The implications of this changed scenario for the issue under discussion should be apparent.

References

Brookner, Anita. 1996. *Altered States*. New York: Random House.

Burge, Tyler. 1992. Philosophy of language and mind: 1950-1990. *The Philosophical Review*, 101.1.

Chomsky, Noam (2000). *New Horizons in the Study of Language and Mind*. Cambridge/New York: Cambridge University Press.

Chomsky, Noam (1997). Language and mind: Current thoughts on ancient problems (Brazil lectures). Reprinted in this volume.

Chomsky, Noam (2000). Linguistics and brain science. In A. Marantz, Y. Miyashita and W. O'Neil (eds), *Image, Language, Brain*. Cambridge, Mass.: MIT Press.

Chomsky, Noam and Michel Foucault (1974). Human nature: Justice versus power (the debate between Chomsky and Foucault). In Fons Elders et al., *Reflexive Waters: The Basic Concerns of Mankind*. London: Souvenir Press: 133-197.

Frege, Gottlob. 1923. Logical investigations. Reprinted in B. McGuiness (ed.), 1984, *Collected Papers on Mathematics, Logic, and Philosophy*. Oxford: Basil Blackwell.

Fodor, Jerry A. 1981. Special sciences. In J. Fodor, *RePresentations*. Cambridge, Mass.: MIT Press.

Fodor, Jerry A. 2000. *The Mind Doesn't Work That Way*. Cambridge, Mass.: MIT Press.

Harré, Rom and Michael Krausz (1996). *Varieties of Relativism*. Oxford: Blackwell.

Harris, James F. (1992). *Against Relativism: A Philosophical Defense of Method*. LaSalle, Illinois: Open Court.

Hume, David. 1748. *An Inquiry Concerning Human Understanding*.

Margolis, Joseph (1991). *The Truth About Relativism*. Oxford & Cambridge, USA: Blackwell.

Marwick, Arthur (2001). All quiet on the postmodern front: The "return to events" in historical study. *Times Literary Supplement*, February 23: 13-14.

Nagel, Thomas (1997). *The Last Word*. N.Y.: Oxford University Press.

Penrose, Roger (1997). *The Large, the Small and the Human Mind*. Cambridge: Cambridge University Press.

Saleemi, Anjum P. 2000. Linguistic, mental and biological laws. In Ib Johansen (ed.), *Fins de Siècle/New Beginnings*. Aarhus: Aarhus University Press.

Searle, John (1977). Reiterating the differences: A reply to Derrida. *Glyph* 2: 198-208.

Searle, John (1995) *The Construction of Social Reality*. N.Y.: The Free Press.

Searle, John (1999a). *Language, Mind and Society*. London: Weidenfeld and Nicolson.

Searle, John (1999b). The future of philosophy. *Philosophical Transactions of the Royal Society of London* (Series B) 354: 2069-2080.

Skinner, B. F. (1971). *Beyond Freedom and Dignity*. New York: Alfred A. Knopf.

CONTRIBUTORS

Martin Atkinson, University of Essex (U.K.)

Ocke-Schwen Bohn, University of Aarhus (Denmark)

Noam Chomsky, Massachusetts Institute of Technology (U.S.A.)

Albert Gjedde, University of Aarhus (Denmark)

Steven Pinker, Harvard University (U.S.A.)

Dominic Rainsford, University of Aarhus (Denmark)

Anjum P. Saleemi, National Chi Nan University (Taiwan)

John Searle, University of California, Berkeley (U.S.A.)

Jamsheed Shorish, Institute of Advanced Studies, Vienna (Austria)

Chris Sinha, University of Portsmouth (U.K.)